The Logic *and* Limits *of* Bankruptcy Law

The Logic *and* Limits *of* Bankruptcy Law

Thomas H. Jackson

BeardBooks
Washington, D.C.

Library of Congress Cataloging-in-Publication Data

Jackson, thomas H., 1950-
    The logic and limits of bankruptcy law / Thomas H. Jackson.
        p. cm.
    Originally published: Cambridge, Mass. : Harvard University Press, 1986.
    Includes indexes.
    ISBN 1-58798-114-9
    1. Bankruptcy--United States. I. Title

KF1524 .J33 2001
346.7307'8--dc21

                                                    2001037982

Printed in the United States of America

For Richard

Preface

THIS BOOK is the culmination of efforts over the past five years to make sense out of bankruptcy law in my teaching and writings. I have become increasingly impressed with the intellectual coherence that underlies bankruptcy law. Its first principles, as I hope to demonstrate, are few and elegant. At the same time, however, I have become convinced that this coherence is frequently obscured by the fact that bankruptcy law affects and requires consideration of virtually every other major substantive area in the legal arena. That fact often causes bankruptcy analysts to ignore its first principles in ad hoc responses to particular interactions. This book will achieve its goal if it prods analysts to think about first principles in analyzing bankruptcy problems.

I am more confident of the usefulness of the principles I will outline in these pages in approaching problems than I am of any particular solution I advocate. One of the advantages of writing this book is that I have returned to my earlier writings in an attempt to integrate them. In doing so, and in responding to the work of others, I sometimes have found my views changing in subtle ways and, indeed, on a few occasions, in rather dramatic ways. I have little doubt that my views will continue to evolve. If a discipline is to remain intellectually alive, that is as it should be. I have also found, however, that my views of the first principles of bankruptcy analysis have strengthened with time.

This book reflects my current thinking on bankruptcy law. Nonetheless, portions draw heavily on some previously published work. Parts of Chapters 1, 3, and 5 reflect "Bankruptcy, Non-Bankruptcy Entitlements, and the Creditors' Bargain," 91 *Yale L.J.* 857 (1982); parts of Chapters 2, 4, and 5 reflect "Translating Assets and Liabilities to the Bankruptcy Forum," 14 *J. Legal Studies* 73 (1985); parts of Chapters 3 and 6 reflect

"Avoiding Powers in Bankruptcy," 36 *Stan. L. Rev.* 725 (1984); parts of Chapter 7 reflect Baird and Jackson, "Corporate Reorganizations and the Treatment of Diverse Ownership Interests: A Comment on Adequate Protection of Secured Creditors in Bankruptcy," 51 *U. Chi. L. Rev.* 97 (1984); finally, parts of Chapters 10 and 11 reflect "The Fresh-Start Policy in Bankruptcy Law," 98 *Harv. L. Rev.* 1393 (1985).

This book owes much to many people, several of them students who have forced me to think through (and modify) the implications of some of my tentative—and not so tentative—views. Useful comments on various portions of the manuscript were provided by John Ayer, Robert Clark, Vern Countryman, Theodore Eisenberg, Ronald Gilson, Louis Kaplow, Anthony Kronman, and Steven Shavell. My greatest intellectual debt, however, goes to a frequent collaborator, Douglas Baird, who has grappled with me in approaching much of bankruptcy law and has fueled countless hours of thought on my part. This book is better in many ways than it would have been without his stimulus. Finally, I owe much to Bonnie, who has sustained and endured with me through the long intense stretches while I was trying to put my thoughts on paper and whose critical eye has made this book easier to read.

T.H.J.

Contents

The Logic and Limits of Bankruptcy Law

The Two Roles of Bankruptcy Law

BANKRUPTCY LAW has been in existence, although intermittently, for almost as long as credit. Its origins can be traced back to the days of Roman law; indeed, its name is derived from statutes of Italian city-states, where it was called *banca rupta* after a medieval custom of breaking the bench of a banker or tradesman who absconded with property of his creditors.[1] After a spotty start in this country, it has been a fixed feature of our legal landscape since 1898.[2] But only with the 1980s has it grown in popular and legal prominence. As it becomes more visible, bankruptcy law has become more controversial and its perceived usefulness more widespread. It is fashionable, for example, to state that keeping firms in operation is a goal of bankruptcy law. It is likewise fashionable to see bankruptcy law as embodying substantive goals of its own that need to be "balanced" with (among others) labor law, with environmental law, or with the rights of secured creditors or other property claimants.[3]

1. Treiman, "Acts of Bankruptcy: A Medieval Concept in Modern Bankruptcy Law," 52 *Harv. L. Rev.* 189 (1938). Bankruptcy was transplanted to England in 1542, when Parliament enacted an "Act Against Such Persons As Do Make Bankrupt," 34 & 35 Henry VIII, ch. 4 (1542). See generally Treiman, "Escaping the Creditors in the Middle Ages," 43 *L.Q. Rev.* 230 (1927).

2. Congress passed the first bankruptcy act in 1800, 2 Stat. 19; it was repealed in 1803. It was next introduced in 1841, 5 Stat. 440, and was repealed eighteen months later. Congress passed another bankruptcy act in 1867, 14 Stat. 517; it was repealed in 1878. The Bankruptcy Act of 1898 was the first "permanent" bankruptcy statute in this country; it survived (with substantial amendments, particularly in 1938) until replaced by the current Bankruptcy Code in 1978. See generally C. Warren, *Bankruptcy Law in United States History* (1935).

3. For an example of a case that sees bankruptcy law's mission as that of keeping firms in operation and sees a corollary need to limit the protections accorded secured creditors,

All of these propositions are derived from an essential truth: bankruptcy law *can* be used to keep firms in operation, and bankruptcy law inevitably touches other bodies of law. But none reflects bankruptcy law's historical function, and insufficient attention has been devoted to how importing these other policies into bankruptcy will affect its long-standing role. Through this book I hope to establish the importance of bankruptcy law in meeting its historical goals—and the limits that notion implies for bankruptcy policy. My view of what bankruptcy law exists to do is, I believe, virtually unquestioned. But I believe that this widely accepted view of what bankruptcy law should be doing also carries with it certain limits, suggests certain things it should *not* be doing. Just as too many spices can spoil the soup, so, too, including too much in bankruptcy law can undermine what everyone agrees it should be doing in the first place.

Bankruptcy law can and should help a firm stay in business when it is worth more to its owners alive than dead. That is a far cry, however, from saying that it is an independent goal of bankruptcy law to keep firms in operation. Not all businesses are worth more to their owners— or to society—alive than dead, and once one recognizes that, one has to identify *which* firms bankruptcy law should assist and why. Saying that bankruptcy law "exists" to help keep firms in operation helps not at all in drawing that line. Instead, a theory of what bankruptcy law can and should do is necessary.

Bankruptcy law, moreover, because it affects all areas of the legal landscape in adjusting rights among creditors and other owners, must deal with labor law, environmental law, and tax law and with the rights of secured creditors and other property claimants. All of these people have contractual or statutory rights to assert claims against a debtor and its assets. As such, they are inevitably affected by bankruptcy law. But it is one thing to say that they are affected by bankruptcy law and quite another to see bankruptcy law as containing a set of substantive legal entitlements against which these other rights must be compromised. Before one jumps to the conclusion that bankruptcy policies need to be balanced with these other policies, one has to be clear what it is that bankruptcy law can and should do—and what it cannot and should not do.

In analyzing bankruptcy law, as with any other body of law, it helps to start by identifying first principles. Those principles can then be de-

---

see *In re* South Village, Inc., 25 Bankr. 987 (Bankr. D. Utah 1982), an opinion written by Ralph Mabey, perhaps the most respected bankruptcy judge on the bench at that time.

veloped by defining their potential operation in the existing social, economic, and legal world to identify precisely what bankruptcy law should encompass, how it can accomplish its goals, and the constraints on its ability to do so.[4] That normative view of bankruptcy law can then be contrasted with the Bankruptcy Code as enacted to see whether and to what extent the existing regime follows the path the principles suggest is the proper one.

The point of this book is to suggest what the underpinnings of bankruptcy law should be and then to apply that learning to a variety of issues while testing the current provisions of the Bankruptcy Code against them. This approach is not unique. In fields as disparate and complex as antitrust, oil and gas, intellectual property, and corporate finance, analysis of discrete legal problems usually begins with a look at the theoretical framework that the law is built upon.[5] But this approach *is* almost unique to bankruptcy law. Much bankruptcy analysis is flawed precisely because it lacks rigor in identifying what is being addressed and why it is a proper concern of bankruptcy law. For that reason, when a new and urgent "problem" is discovered in the context of a bankruptcy proceeding, courts, legislators, and commentators all too often approach its resolution in an ad hoc manner, by viewing bankruptcy law as somehow conflicting with—and perhaps overriding—some other urgent social or economic goal.

I believe that this approach is fundamentally mistaken. Bankruptcy law, at its core, is debt-collection law. This is what we all agree on. When firms or people borrow, things sometimes do not work out as hoped.

4. Bankruptcy law is federal law, not state law. See U.S. Constitution, Art. I, Sec. 8, cl. 4. Its placement there has to do with notions of limits on the territorial power of state courts in our federal system. In a typical credit transaction, for example, a debtor residing in Illinois may borrow money from credit companies located in North Carolina and may own property situated in California. Illinois' power to affect the right of a North Carolina credit company to levy on property located in California may be limited. See, e.g., International Shoe Co. v. Washington, 326 U.S. 310 (1945). This notion applies both to creditor remedies and to discharge. See Ogden v. Saunders, 25 U.S. (12 Wheat.) 212, 358–68 (1827) (discharge under one state's law is no defense to an action brought by citizens of another state in another state's courts). The same problems can be replicated internationally, where, for example, the automatic stay will not affect creditors without "contacts" in the United States from pursuing property outside its borders. Here, comity is necessary. See §304.

5. See, e.g., R. Bork, *The Antitrust Paradox* (1979); R. Posner, *Antitrust Law: An Economic Perspective* (1976); V. Brudney & M. Chirelstein, *Cases and Materials on Corporate Finance* (2d ed. 1979); Libecap & Wiggins, "Contractual Responses to the Common Pool: Prorationing Crude Oil Production," 74 *Am. Econ. Rev.* 87 (1984); S. McDonald, *Petroleum Conservation in the United States* (1970); Friedman, "The Economics of the Common Pool: Property Rights in Exhaustible Resources," 18 *UCLA L. Rev.* 855 (1971).

For any number of reasons—from bad luck, crop failure, unexpected tort liability, dishonesty, or whatever—it is inevitable that some who borrow will not be able to repay what they owe. In a world in which creditors can call on the state to take a debtor's assets from it, it is necessary to establish what to do when debts are greater than assets. Two questions arise: (1) do we place limits on what creditors can take from their debtors; and (2) how do we decide rights among creditors when there are not enough assets to go around?

Much debt-collection law addresses these questions. Bankruptcy law does too, but it does so against the backdrop of other debt-collection law. Indeed, bankruptcy law is an ancillary, parallel system of debt-collection law. That position both defines its usefulness and sets its limits. Bankruptcy law historically has done two things: allowed for some sort of a financial fresh start for individuals and provided creditors with a compulsory and collective forum to sort out their relative entitlements to a debtor's assets. The policy relating to discharge and notions of a fresh start does in fact represent an independent substantive policy that is enacted through bankruptcy law and that must be balanced with other concerns, most notably the notion of open access to the credit markets in the first place. It addresses the question of whether limits should be established on what creditors can get from their debtor.

This substantive policy of a financial fresh start, although important when dealing with debtors who are human beings, is, however, also limited in an important respect. When firms rather than individuals are involved, neither bankruptcy law nor other law places limits on what creditors can get from their "debtor" precisely because the debtor is a fictional legal being. To talk about the need of a corporation or other business entity to use bankruptcy in order to have a fresh start is to conflate a number of issues, none of which have anything to do with giving an honest but unlucky individual a second financial chance. We might care that the assets of a corporation be used effectively, but how assets are used is a question distinct from giving those individuals who "own" them a second chance. There is no need to give a corporate charter a fresh start. When the unit involved is a corporation, the "debtor" is always shorthand terminology for something else—shareholders, managers, workers, or whatever—and we should realize that this something else is what we are talking about. The question of why we give individuals the right to a financial fresh start—and one that they cannot waive by contract (although they can in fact waive it, and a number of other rights, in other ways—such as by commiting murder)—is, to be sure, important, and its answer is somewhat uncertain and controversial. We will return to it in Chapter 10.

For the discussion in the first nine chapters of this book, I set aside the question of a financial fresh start for individuals. The statement that a corporation needs a fresh start reflects something very different—the view that the corporation should continue what it is doing. That issue is one of how assets should be used by those that own them, not one of giving a human being a right to renew his financial life.

The question of how assets are used is the focus of the other principal role of bankruptcy law, and working out its implications will consume our attention for the first nine chapters of this book. This role of bankruptcy law—historically its original function—is that of bankruptcy as a collective debt-collection device, and it deals with the rights of creditors (or owners) inter se. But it is first necessary to be precise what that means. Once one sets aside the question of the need of individuals for a financial fresh start, the remaining principal role of bankruptcy law has been and should be more procedural than substantive. That goal is to permit the owners of assets to use those assets in a way that is most productive to them *as a group* in the face of incentives by individual owners to maximize their own positions. Not all debt-collection rules are created equal. The rules governing debt collection can actually affect the total amount of the assets available to the creditors. When one is dealing with firms, the question is how to convert ownership of the assets from the debtor to its creditors, not how to leave assets with the debtor. But the process of conversion is costly. Bankruptcy law, at its core, is concerned with reducing the costs of conversion. This is the accepted starting point of bankruptcy law—and also the source of the limitations on what bankruptcy law should do. It is that goal, to which the bulk of bankruptcy law and the majority of the provisions of the Bankruptcy Code are devoted, and its associated limitations to which we turn first.[6]

---

6. One working assumption needs to be set forth. The lessons of the normative model I will be using in the first nine chapters are sometimes dismissed by people who believe that they are based on "unrealistic" assumptions and, particularly, that they assume a degree of rationality or calculation that simply is not present. In their present form, however, none of these criticisms is focused enough to justify dismissal of this normative model. Cognitive and volitional shortcomings are more relevant to an analysis of individual behavior—the sort of behavior that discharge deals with—than to an examination of institutional or market behavior. Investments by firms do have market constraints. Firms that systematically act impulsively or underestimate the risks of investments might, to be sure, be weeded out and replaced by firms that calculate risks more carefully. The result seems, however, to be welcome, not undesirable. Remember that the financial failure of

a corporation is distinct from the financial failure of the individuals who own it. When focusing on the latter question, we are in the realm of a financial fresh start for individuals, a topic we put aside for now. As for the former question, there is not much reason to think that the cognitive or volitional biases of individuals will lead to any systematic bias in the market's pricing mechanisms. If, for example, such behavior leads individual investors to react overly enthusiastically to a biotechnology firm's latest public offering, more skilled investors will be able to capitalize on that. Because of the likely presence of such skilled investors, aggregate (that is, marketplace) price levels at the end of the day should show no sign of any systematic underestimation of risks. It is that factor that allows us to defer an examination of individual factors until Chapter 10.

1

The Role of Bankruptcy Law and Collective Action in Debt Collection

BANKRUPTCY LAW and policy have been subject to long-standing debate. This debate is not so much about whether bankruptcy law should exist at all but about how much it should do. All agree that it serves as a collective debt-collection device. Whether, when firms are involved, it should do more is the crux of the dispute. I plan to start by establishing in this chapter what accepted wisdom already acknowledges—that bankruptcy's system of collectivized debt collection is, in principle, beneficial. Most of this book will then be concerned with exploring how that benefit can be realized and, as importantly, how viewing bankruptcy as a collectivized debt-collection device imposes limits on what else bankruptcy can do well. It is in the latter area that the most conflict arises. It exists because bankruptcy analysts have failed to follow through on the first principles of establishing a collectivized debt-collection system. To show why bankruptcy's principal role limits what other functions it can usefully perform is the objective of this book. Toward that end we shall first examine why bankruptcy law *should* be doing what everyone takes as a given.

Bankruptcy law is a response to credit. The essence of credit economies is people and firms—that can be called *debtors*—borrowing money. The reasons for this are varied. In the case of individuals credit may serve as a device to smooth out consumption patterns by means of borrowing against future income. In the case of corporations and other firms it may be a part of a specialization of financing and investment decisions. And just as the reasons for borrowing are varied, so, too, are the methods. The prototype creditor may be a bank or other financial institution that lends money, but that is only one of many ways in which credit is extended. An installment seller extends credit. So does a worker who receives a paycheck on the first of December for work performed in November. The government, in its role as tax collector, also extends credit to the extent that taxes accrue over a year and are due at the end. Similarly, a tort victim who is injured today and must await payment until the end of a lawsuit extends credit of sorts, although involuntarily and (probably) unhappily. Finally, credit is not extended just by "creditors." First-round purchasers of common and preferred stock of a corporation are also lending money to the debtor. Their repayment rights are distinct (they are the residual claimants), but it is proper to view them, too, as having defined rights to call on the assets of the debtor for payment.

Whatever the reasons for lending and whatever its form, the terms on which consensual credit is extended depend to a substantial extent on the likelihood of voluntary repayment and on the means for coercing repayment.[1] We are not concerned here with the means for getting paid when the debtor is solvent—when it has enough assets to satisfy all its obligations in full—but is simply mean-spirited or is genuinely disputing whether it has a duty of payment (as the debtor might be with our putative tort victim or with a supplier who the debtor believes sold it defective goods). The legal remedies for coercing payment when the debtor is solvent concern the rights of a creditor to use the power of the state in pursuit of its claim. This is a question of debtor-creditor law and one to which bankruptcy law historically has had nothing to add, directly at least.

Bankruptcy law can be thought of as growing out of a distinct aspect of debtor-creditor relations: the effect of the debtor's obligation to repay Creditor A on its remaining creditors. This question takes on particular bite only when the debtor does not have enough to repay everyone in full. Even then, however, a developed system exists for paying creditors without bankruptcy.[2] The relevant question is whether that existing system of creditor remedies has any shortcomings that might be ameliorated by an ancillary system known as bankruptcy law.

To explore that question, it is useful to start with the familiar. Creditor

1. The terms of involuntary credit, such as tort claims (and perhaps things such as tax claims, too), are not set by negotiation and thus are less likely to be affected by matters such as the likelihood of voluntary repayment or the means for coercing repayment. Other interests, such as the deterrent effect of tort rules, may, however, be affected. See Schwartz, "Products Liability, Corporate Structure, and Bankruptcy: Toxic Substances and the Remote Risk Relationship," 14 *J. Legal Studies* 689 (1985); Halpern, Trebilcock, & Turnbull, "An Economic Analysis of Limited Liability in Corporation Law," 30 *U. Toronto L. Rev.* 117 (1980); Note, "Tort Creditor Priority in the Secured Credit System: Asbestos Times, the Worst of Times," 36 *Stan. L. Rev.* 1045 (1984).

2. See generally S. Riesenfeld, *Creditors' Remedies and Debtors' Protection* (3d ed. 1979).

remedies outside of bankruptcy (as well as outside other formal, non-bankruptcy collective systems) can be accurately described as a species of "grab law," represented by the key characteristic of first-come, first-served. The creditor first staking a claim to particular assets of the debtor generally is entitled to be paid first out of those assets.[3] It is like buying tickets for a popular rock event or opera: the people first in line get the best seats; those at the end of the line may get nothing at all.

When the issue is credit, the ways that one can stake a place in line are varied. Some involve "voluntary" actions of the debtor: the debtor can simply pay a creditor off or give the creditor a security interest in certain assets that the creditor "perfects" in the prescribed manner (usually by giving the requisite public notice of its claim).[4] In other cases a creditor's place in line is established notwithstanding the lack of the debtor's consent: the creditor can, following involvement of a court, get an "execution lien" or "garnishment" on the assets of the debtor.[5] Or, sometimes, a place in line may simply be given to a particular claimant by governmental fiat, in the form of a "statutory lien" or similar device.[6]

Although the *methods* for establishing a place in line are varied, the fundamental ordering principle is the same. Creditors are paid according to their place in line for particular assets. With a few exceptions, moreover, one's place in line is fixed by the time when one acquires an interest in the assets and takes the appropriate steps to publicize it.[7] A solvent debtor is like a show for which sufficient tickets are available to accom-

---

3. See generally Baird, "Notice Filing and the Problem of Ostensible Ownership," 12 *J. Legal Studies* 53 (1983).

4. In real estate this generally requires the recording of a deed of trust or mortgage with the applicable county recorder. With personal property, governed by Article 9 of the Uniform Commercial Code, it generally requires either the filing of a financing statement in the applicable office or offices or possession of the property by the secured party. See Uniform Commercial Code §§9-302 through 9-305; 9-401 (1978).

5. *Execution lien* generally refers to the lien that arises at or around the time the sheriff, following a judgment and the issuance of a writ of execution, seizes property. With respect to real property, the applicable lien is sometimes called a *judgment lien,* and it arises upon docketing of the judgment in the applicable files. With respect to many kinds of intangible personal property, such as an employer's obligation to pay wages to a debtor or a bank's obligation to pay money the debtor has on deposit with the bank, the applicable lien is called a *garnishment lien,* and it arises upon the serving of a writ of garnishment on the employer or bank, as the case may be. A brief survey of the details of creditor collection may be found in D. Baird & T. Jackson, *Cases, Problems, and Materials on Bankruptcy* ch. 1 (1985).

6. The most common label is *statutory lien,* although other terms (such as *statutory trust*) are commonly used. See Selby v. Ford Motor Co., 590 F.2d 642 (6th Cir. 1979). This point is discussed more fully in Chapter 4.

7. See, for example, the rules for New York, contained in N.Y. CPLR §§5202, 5203, 5232, 5234(b), 5236.

modate all prospective patrons and all seats are considered equally good. In that event one's place in line is largely a matter of indifference. But when there is not enough to go around to satisfy all claimants in full, this method of ordering will define winners and losers based principally on the time when one gets in line.

The question at the core of bankruptcy law is whether a *better* ordering system can be devised that would be worth the inevitable costs associated with implementing a new system. In the case of tickets to a popular rock event or opera, where there must be winners and losers, and putting aside price adjustments,[8] there may be no better way to allocate available seats than on a first-come, first-served basis. In the world of credit, however, there are powerful reasons to think that there *is* a superior way to allocate the assets of an insolvent debtor than first-come, first-served.

The basic problem that bankruptcy law is designed to handle, both as a normative matter and as a positive matter, is that the system of individual creditor remedies may be bad for the creditors *as a group* when there are not enough assets to go around. Because creditors have conflicting rights, there is a tendency in their debt-collection efforts to make a bad situation worse. Bankruptcy law responds to this problem. Debt-collection by means of individual creditor remedies produces a variant of a widespread problem. One way to characterize the problem is as a multiparty game—a type of "prisoner's dilemma."[9] As such, it has elements of what game theorists would describe as an *end period* game, where basic problems of cooperation are generally expected to lead to undesirable outcomes for the group of players as a whole.[10] Another

8. When a show is oversubscribed at a given price, and barring effective scalping laws, people who are first in line can resell the tickets at the market-clearing price. An upward price adjustment by the promoter in the ticket price may simply allow him (rather than those in line) to collect the difference. Although price adjustments arguably are superior to standing in line as a way of allocating tickets to a show, it is a solution that we can safely put aside for our purposes. The ultimate aim of creditor collection devices is collection of money. At the time of collection (as opposed to when the money is loaned, when it may make sense to take a lower interest rate in exchange for security—a place at the front of the line), paying money to improve one's place in line is simply a pointless swap of money for money.

9. A "prisoner's dilemma" rests (as does a common pool problem) on three essential premises. One, that the participants are unable (for one reason or another) to get together and make a collective decision. Two, that the participants are selfish (or cold and calculating) and not altruistic. Three, that the result reached by individual action is worse than a cooperative solution. See A. Rapoport & A. Chammah, *Prisoner's Dilemma* (1965).

10. When one expects that the game will be played an infinite number of times, cooperation may be the best strategy—which contradicts one of the premises necessary to

way of considering it is as a species of what is called a *common pool* problem, which is well known to lawyers in other fields, such as oil and gas.[11]

This role of bankruptcy law is largely unquestioned. But because this role carries limits on what *else* bankruptcy law can do, it is worth considering the basics of the problem so that we understand its essential features before examining whether and why credit may present that problem. The vehicle will be a typical, albeit simple, common pool example. Imagine that you own a lake. There are fish in the lake. You are the only one who has the right to fish in that lake, and no one constrains your decision as to how much fishing to do. You have it in your power to catch all the fish this year and sell them for, say, $100,000.[12] If you did that, however, there would be no fish in the lake next year. It might be better for you—you might maximize your total return from fishing—if you caught and sold some fish this year but left other fish in the lake so that they could multiply and you would have fish in subsequent years. Assume that, by taking this approach, you could earn (adjusting for inflation) $50,000 each year. Having this outcome is like having a perpetual annuity paying $50,000 a year. It has a present value of perhaps $500,000. Since (obviously, I hope) when all other things are equal, $500,000 is better than $100,000, you, as sole owner, would limit your fishing this year unless some other factor influenced you.[13]

---

create a prisoner's dilemma. See R. Axelrod, *The Evolution of Cooperation* (1984); Hirshleifer, "Evolutionary Models in Economics and Law: Cooperation Versus Conflict Strategies," in 4 *Research in Law and Economics* 1 (1982). This is not true, however, when the number of times the game will be played has a known finite horizon. It then takes on the attributes of an end period game, where the dominant strategy is selfish behavior. See R. Axelrod, supra. Although insolvency may signal an end to relationships with one debtor, many creditors will still favor cooperation because of repeat dealings with each other. But not all will expect such repeat dealings, and destructive races to assets can be caused by a few "bad apples." I analyzed bankruptcy as a prisoner's dilemma in Jackson, "Bankruptcy, Non-Bankruptcy Entitlements, and the Creditors' Bargain," 91 *Yale L.J.* 857 (1982).

11. See Hardin, "The Tragedy of the Commons," 162 *Science* 1243 (1968); Libecap & Wiggins, "Contractual Responses to the Common Pool: Prorationing Crude Oil Production," 74 *Am. Econ. Rev.* 87 (1984); Friedman, "The Economics of the Common Pool: Property Rights in Exhaustible Resources," 18 *UCLA L. Rev.* 855 (1971).

12. This discussion assumes no costs—or, more precisely, nets them out; nothing in the example, however, turns on that. It also assumes that you are interested in fish only for the money they bring you; as we will see later, nothing really turns on that assumption either.

13. These other factors are likely to be few in number. If you thought you would die next year, you could still transmit your fishing rights to your children or sell them for $500,000, buying $100,000 of fish from other sources, and giving $400,000 to some other charity. Only if you (and anyone who might buy your rights) were convinced that the

But what if you are not the only one who can fish in this lake? What if a hundred people can do so? The optimal solution has not changed: it would be preferable to leave some fish in the lake to multiply because doing so has a present value of $500,000. But in this case, unlike that where you have to control only yourself, an obstacle exists in achieving that result. If there are a hundred fishermen, you cannot be sure, by limiting *your* fishing, that there will be any more fish next year, unless you can also control the others. You may, then, have an incentive to catch as many fish as you can today because maximizing your take this year (catching, on average, $1,000 worth of fish) is better for you than holding off (catching, say, only $500 worth of fish this year) while others scramble and deplete the stock entirely.[14] If you hold off, your aggregate return is only $500, since nothing will be left for next year or the year after. But that sort of reasoning by each of the hundred fishermen will mean that the stock of fish will be gone by the end of the first season. The fishermen will split $100,000 this year, but there will be no fish— and no money—in future years. Self-interest results in their splitting $100,000, not $500,000.

What is required is some rule that will make all hundred fishermen act as a sole owner would. That is where bankruptcy law enters the picture in a world not of fish but of credit. The grab rules of nonbankruptcy law and their allocation of assets on the basis of first-come, first-served create an incentive on the part of the individual creditors, when they sense that a debtor may have more liabilities than assets, to get in line today (by, for example, getting a sheriff to execute on the debtor's equipment), because if they do not, they run the risk of getting nothing. This decision by numerous individual creditors, however, may be the wrong decision for the creditors as a group. Even though the debtor is insolvent, they might be better off if they held the assets together. Bank-

---

world would end next year or that the government would confiscate your rights next year without compensation might your optimal strategy be to catch all the fish you could this year. In calculating how much fishing to do this year, you would need to weigh numerous factors and would undoubtedly face a number of uncertainties. You would, for example, be estimating reproduction and death rates of the fish, the likelihood of factors such as acid rain affecting future crops of fish, and the like. Thus, in assessing how much to fish, you would face a probability distribution, and one with some degree of uncertainty. You would also face a problem of controlling yourself once you made this decision. None of this, however, undercuts the point in text: you would try to take the course that you thought would bring you the greatest return, in present value terms.

14. Note that this, like the prisoner's dilemma, assumes that you are selfish, not altruistic. Where there are a hundred fishermen, it only takes one selfish one to upset the altruism of the others. Thus, the assumption seems quite reasonable.

ruptcy provides a way to make these diverse individuals act as one, by imposing a *collective* and *compulsory* proceeding on them. Unlike a typical common pool solution, however, the compulsory solution of bankruptcy law does not apply in all places at all times. Instead, it runs parallel with a system of individual debt-collection rules and is available to supplant them when and if needed.

This is the historically recognized purpose of bankruptcy law and perhaps is none too controversial in itself. Because more controversial limits on bankruptcy policy derive from it, however, less allegorical and more precise analysis is necessary. Exactly *how* does bankruptcy law make creditors as a group better off? To find the answer to that question, consider a simple hypothetical example involving credit, not fish. Debtor has a small printing business. Potential creditors estimate that there is a 20 percent chance that Debtor (who is virtuous and will not misbehave) will become insolvent through bad luck, general economic downturn, or whatever. (By insolvency, I mean a condition whereby Debtor will not have enough assets to satisfy his creditors.[15]) At the point of insolvency— I shall make this very simple—the business is expected to be worth $50,000 if sold piecemeal. Creditors also know that each of them will have to spend $1,000 in pursuit of their individual collection efforts should Debtor become insolvent and fail to repay them. Under these circumstances Debtor borrows $25,000 from each of four creditors, Creditors 1 through 4. Because these creditors know that there is this 20 percent chance, they can account for it—and the associated collection costs—in the interest rate they charge Debtor. Assume that each party can watch out for its own interest, and let us see whether, as in the example of fishing, there are reasons to think that these people would favor a set of restrictions on their own behavior (apart from paternalism or other similar considerations).

Given that these creditors can watch out for their own interests, the question to be addressed is *how* these creditors should go about protecting themselves. If the creditors have to protect themselves by means of a costly and inefficient system, Debtor is going to have to pay more to obtain credit.[16] Thus, when we consider them all together—Creditors 1

15. This is, by the way, almost precisely the definition of insolvency in the Bankruptcy Code. Section 101(29) defines insolvent as "with reference to an entity other than a partnership, financial condition such that the sum of such entity's debts is greater than all of such entity's property, at a fair valuation, exclusive of—(i) property tranferred, concealed, or removed with intent to hinder, delay, or defraud such entity's creditors; and (ii) property that may be exempted from property of the estate under section 522 of this title."

16. The extent to which this adjustment will result in the costs being fully transferred

through 4 *and* Debtor—the relevant question is: would the availability of a bankruptcy system reduce the costs of credit?

This requires us to try to identify what bankruptcy's advantages might plausibly be. Identification of abstract advantages is not, however, the end of the issue. One must also compare those possible advantages with the costs of having a bankruptcy system. Determining whether a bankruptcy system would reduce the cost of credit requires a net assessment of charges.

But first the case for bankruptcy's advantages. The common pool example of fish in a lake suggests that one of the advantages to a collective system is a larger aggregate pie. Does that advantage exist in the case of credit? When dealing with businesses, the answer, at least some of the time, would seem to be "yes." The use of individual creditor remedies may lead to a piecemeal dismantling of a debtor's business by the untimely removal of necessary operating assets. To the extent that a non-piecemeal collective process (whether in the form of a liquidation or reorganization) is likely to increase the aggregate value of the pool of assets, its substitution for individual remedies would be advantageous to the creditors as a group. This is derived from a commonplace notion: that a collection of assets is sometimes more valuable together than the same assets would be if spread to the winds. It is often referred to as the surplus of a going-concern value over a liquidation value.

Thus, the most obvious reason for a collective system of creditor collection is to make sure that creditors, in pursuing their individual remedies, do not actually decrease the aggregate value of the assets that will be used to repay them. In our example this situation would occur when a printing press, for example, could be sold to a third party for $20,000, leaving $30,000 of other assets, but the business as a unit could generate sufficient cash so as to have a value of more than $50,000.[17] As such it

---

back to the debtor depends on the elasticities of supply of and demand for credit. See Meckling, "Financial Markets, Default, and Bankruptcy: The Role of the State," 41 *Law & Contemp. Probs.* 13 (Autumn 1977); Weston, "Some Economic Fundamentals for an Analysis of Bankruptcy," 41 *Law & Contemp. Probs.* 47 (Autumn 1977).

17. The reasons for this result are complex. The assumption is that the printing press is worth only $20,000 in the hands of a third party but more in the hands of Debtor. If this is so, however, one might think that the third party could then turn and sell the press to Debtor for more than $20,000 (making its value in the hands of the third party more than $20,000). Indeed, pursuing this path leaves one with the question of why there would have been a default in the first place. See Klein, Crawford, & Alchian, "Vertical Integration, Appropriate Rents, and the Competitive Contracting Process," 21 *J. L. & Econ.* 297, 298–299 (1978). Suffice it to say, for our purposes, that informational and transactional barriers are often sufficient to permit this discrepancy to exist.

is directly analogous to the case of the fish in the lake. Even in cases in which the assets should be sold and the business dismembered, the aggregate value of the assets may be increased by keeping groups of those assets together (the printing press with its custom dies, for example) to be sold as discrete units.

This advantage, however, is not the only one to be derived from a collective system for creditors. Consider what the creditors would get if there were no bankruptcy system (putting aside the ultimate collection costs). Without a collective system all of the creditors in our example know that in the case of Debtor's insolvency the first two creditors to get to (and through) the courthouse (or to Debtor, to persuade Debtor to pay voluntarily), will get $25,000, leaving nothing for the third and fourth. And unless the creditors think that one of them is systematically faster (or friendlier with Debtor), this leaves them with a 50 percent chance of gaining $25,000, and a 50 percent chance of getting nothing.[18] A collective system, however, would ensure that they would each get $12,500.

Would the creditors agree in advance to a system that, in the event of Debtor's insolvency, guaranteed them $12,500, in lieu of a system that gave them a 50 percent chance of $25,000—payment in full—and a 50 percent chance of nothing? Resolution of this question really turns on whether the creditors are better off with the one than the other. There are two reasons to think that they are, even without looking to the question of a going-concern surplus and without considering the costs of an individual collection system. First of all, if these creditors are risk averse, assurance of receiving $12,500 is better than a 50 percent chance of $25,000 and a 50 percent chance of nothing. Even if they can diversify the risk—by lending money to many people—it is probably preferable to eliminate it in the first place.[19] This, then, represents a net advantage to having a collective proceeding.

18. These assumptions may not matter to the actual conclusion. Because of the "race," many of the special advantages one creditor holds may be worthless. Participation in or monitoring against the race will be costly for *all* creditors. In any event there will be residual elements of uncertainty of relative rankings that could be eliminated to the benefit of all creditors. Finally, there would be distinct advantages to a legal rule that presumed equality in the position of all creditors with similar legal entitlements, instead of delving into a case-by-case examination of factors such as "knowledge" or "friendliness." See Chapter 2.

19. Not all creditors, moreover, can achieve the requisite degree of diversification in a cost-effective way. The amount of diversification required to minimize the uncertainty cost may be quite large. See Langbein & Posner, "Market Funds and Trust Investment Law," 1976 *Am. B. Found. Research J.* 1.

One other possible advantage of a collective proceeding should also be noted: there may be costs to the individualized approach to collecting (in addition to the $1,000 collection costs).[20] For example, since each creditor knows that it must "beat out" the others if it wants to be paid in full, it will spend time monitoring Debtor and the other creditors— perhaps frequently checking the courthouse records—to make sure that it will be no worse than second in the race (and therefore still be paid in full). Although some of these activities may be beneficial, many may not be; they will simply be costs of racing against other creditors, and they will cancel each other out. It is like running on a treadmill: you expend a lot of energy but get nowhere. If every creditor is doing this, each one *still* does not know if there is more than a fifty-fifty chance that it will get paid in full. But in one sense, unless the creditors can negotiate a deal with each other, the creditors have no choice. Each creditor has to spend this money just to stay in the race because if it does not, it is a virtual certainty that the others will beat it to the payment punch. Of course, a creditor could decide that it did not want to stay in the race, and just charge Debtor at the time of lending the money for coming in last should Debtor become insolvent. Debtor is not likely, however, to agree to pay a creditor that extra charge for having a lower priority provision, because, once paid that extra amount, the creditor may have an incentive to take steps to remain in the race and make money that way.[21] For that reason it may be hard for a creditor to opt out of the race and get compensated for doing so.

These various costs to using an individual system of creditor remedies suggest that there are, indeed, occasions when a collective system of debt-collection law might be preferable. Bankruptcy provides that system. The single most fruitful way to think about bankruptcy is to see it as ameliorating a common pool problem created by a system of individual

20. The costs of individual creditor remedies, as posited in the example, is $4,000 for the creditors (and presumably some additional costs for the debtor). Bankruptcy costs may (but need not necessarily) be less. The most likely case for cost savings would be where the creditors would attempt to collect their claims at roughly the same time, as one would expect to occur when it was learned that Debtor was insolvent. A single inquiry into recurring collection questions is likely to be less expensive (both for the creditors and for the debtor) than the multiple inquiries necessary in an individualistic remedies system. See Weistart, "The Costs of Bankruptcy," 41 *Law & Contemp. Probs.* 107 (Autumn 1977). Other costs to the bankruptcy process are examined in Chapter 8.

21. The creditor could covenant to subordinate this loan, and the others might be viewed as third-party beneficiaries of that contract, thereby making it enforceable. But the solution has costs of its own, unless the creditor can control Debtor's intake of credit.

creditor remedies. Bankruptcy provides a way to override the creditors' pursuit of their own remedies and to make them work together.[22]

This approach immediately suggests several features of bankruptcy law. First, such a law must usurp individual creditor remedies in order to make the claimants act in an altruistic and cooperative way. Thus, the proceeding is inherently *collective*. Moreover, this system works only if all the creditors are bound to it. To allow a debtor to contract with a creditor to avoid participating in the bankruptcy proceeding would destroy the advantages of a collective system. So the proceeding must be *compulsory* as well. But unlike common pool solutions in oil and gas or fishing, it is not the exclusive system for dividing up assets. It, instead, supplants an existing system of individual creditor remedies, and as we shall see, it is this feature that makes crucial an awareness of its limitations.

Note that the presence of a bankruptcy system does not mandate its use whenever there is a common pool problem. Bankruptcy law stipulates a minimum set of entitlements for claimants. That, in turn, permits them to "bargain in the shadow of the law" and to implement a consensual collective proceeding outside of the bankruptcy process.[23] Because use of the bankruptcy process has costs of its own (as we shall see in Chapter 8), if creditors can consensually gain the sorts of advantages of acting collectively that bankruptcy brings, they could avoid those costs. Accordingly, one would expect that consensual deals among creditors outside the bankruptcy process would often be attempted first. The formal bankruptcy process would presumably be used only when individual advantage-taking in the setting of multiparty negotiations made a consensual deal too costly to strike—which may, however, occur frequently as the number of creditors increases.

These problems with optimal uses of bankruptcy are the subject of Chapter 8. It is possible that the rules specifying when a bankruptcy

22. As such, it reflects the kind of contract that creditors would agree to if they were able to negotiate with each other before extending credit. This is an application of the famous Rawlsian notion of bargaining in the "original position" behind a "veil of ignorance." See J. Rawls, *A Theory of Justice* 136–42 (1971).

23. See Mnookin & Kornhauser, "Bargaining in the Shadow of the Law: The Case of Divorce," 88 *Yale L.J.* 950 (1979). Nonbankruptcy "workouts" are in fact commonly observed. See "The Business in Trouble—A Workout without Bankruptcy," 39 *Bus. Law.* 1041 (1984); Coogan, Broude, & Glatt, "Comments on Some Reorganization Provisions of the Pending Bankruptcy Bills," 30 *Bus. Law.* 1149, 1154–60 (1975); Krause, "Insolvent Debtor Adjustments under Relevant State Court Statutes as against Proceedings under the Bankruptcy Act," 12 *Bus. Law.* 184, 185 (1957).

petition may be filed prevent the commencement of a collective proceeding until it is too late to save the debtor's assets from the self-interested actions of various creditors. Another possibility, however, is that the collective proceeding will begin too soon. Forcing all the creditors to refrain from individual actions (many of which have the effect of monitoring the debtor and preventing it from misbehaving) brings its own costs. Thus, to say that bankruptcy is designed to solve a common pool problem is not to tell us how to design the rules that do that well. These concerns do not, however, undermine the basic insight of what bankruptcy law is all about.

Like all justifications, moreover, this one is subject to a number of qualifications. To say that a common pool problem exists is not to say that individual behavior is entirely self-interested or that legal rules can solve all collective action problems. We often observe people behaving in a cooperative fashion over time even if it appears contrary to their short-run interest.[24] In the credit world, for example, creditors do not always rush to seize a debtor's assets whenever it seems to be in financial trouble. Yet despite this qualification the underlying point remains: sometimes people behave in a self-interested way and would be better off as a group if required to work together. The tragedy of the Texas oil fields in the first half of this century is a notable example of how self-interest led to the depletion of oil that otherwise could have been enjoyed by the group of oil field owners.[25] Creditor relations almost certainly are another area where this essential truth has validity, especially given the fact that creditors may have fewer incentives to cooperate when a debtor is failing than they do when there are greater prospects of repeat dealings with a debtor.

Nor can we be confident that the bankruptcy rules themselves do not create problems. They do, and we will examine later how they should be dealt with. Because these complications play out against a backdrop of basic bankruptcy principles, however, it is preferable for now to make two simplifying assumptions. The first assumption is that insolvency occurs without warning. By this assumption, we eliminate consideration of strategic behavior that is likely to exist when some creditors sense the imminent likelihood of bankruptcy's collective proceeding and attempt to avoid it. This assumption will be relaxed in Chapter 6. The second assumption is that bankruptcy proceedings take no time. By this assumption, we can set aside problems that occur through the passage of

24. Some of the reasons for this are explored in R. Axelrod, supra note 10.

25. See D. Glasner, *Politics, Prices and Petroleum* 32, 143–43 (1985); S. McDonald, *Petroleum Conservation in the United States: an Economic Analysis* 31–42 (1971).

time and the fact that this passage of time affects various claimants in different ways. We can also set aside the complications that result from a debtor's need to encourage people to deal with it while in bankruptcy and the fact that some of these people may wear both prepetition and postpetition hats. This assumption will be relaxed in Chapter 7.

Although imposing these two assumptions is, of course, somewhat unrealistic, doing so clarifies several key features of bankruptcy law. We can later extend our examination by making the inquiry somewhat more realistic. For now, however, it is sufficient to ask whether there is in fact a common pool problem that cannot be solved by creditors contracting among themselves. If the number of creditors is sufficiently small and sufficiently determinate, it may be possible for them to negotiate a solution at the time of insolvency that would avoid many, if not most, of the costs of an individual remedies system,[26] even if they were not bargaining in the shadow of the law. But in cases in which there are large numbers of creditors or the creditors are not immediately known at a particular time (perhaps because they hold contingent or nonmanifested claims), the ability of the creditors to solve the problem of an individual remedies system by an actual agreement may be lost. Bankruptcy provides the desired result by making available a collective system after insolvency has occurred.[27] It is the implications of that view of bankruptcy law that we can now begin to explore.

26. See Hoffman & Spitzer, "Experimental Tests of the Coase Theorem with Large Bargaining Groups," 15 *J. Legal Studies* 149 (1986); Libecap & Wiggins, supra note 11.

27. Bankruptcy is not the only possible legal response. One might imagine a less intrusive one to be a system whereby a debtor could decide whether to agree to allow its assets to be subject to a collective remedies system (such as bankruptcy law) by choice, made public by a nonretractable public filing. If such an election were virtually universal, a legal system such as our current bankruptcy law might be easier to administer.

2

Determining Liabilities and the Basic Role of Nonbankruptcy Law

BANKRUPTCY provides a collective forum for sorting out the rights of "owners" (creditors and others with rights against a debtor's assets) and can be justified because it provides protection against the destructive effects of an individual remedies system when there are not enough assets to go around. This makes the basic process one of determining *who* gets *what*, in *what order*. *Who* is fundamentally a question of claims, or what shall often be referred to as *liabilities*. *What* is fundamentally a question of property of the estate, or what shall often be referred to as *assets*. At one level there is nothing magical about these basic building blocks. A liability is something that makes you less valuable—that you would pay to get rid of. An asset is something that makes you more valuable—that someone would pay you for.

In looking at all of this, it is helpful to think of bankruptcy as follows. What bankruptcy should be doing, in the abstract, is asking how much someone would pay for the assets of a debtor, assuming they could be sold free of liabilities. The resulting money is then taken and distributed to the holders of the liabilities according to their nonbankruptcy entitlements. Essentially, this and the next three chapters simply flesh out this idea against the basic role of bankruptcy law, which we explored in the previous chapter. The question addressed in this chapter and the next is exactly what this means in considering how claimants should be treated in bankruptcy. The basic answer involves seeing the bankruptcy process as protecting, at a minimum, the relative *value* of particular nonbankruptcy entitlements instead of the rights themselves. This is the subject of determining liabilities in bankruptcy and involves the question of how to divide the assets. The question of what the assets are is the subject of the fourth chapter, where we shall see that the question of assets is integrally related to the question of liabilities.

The Destructive Effect of Changes of Relative Entitlements in Bankruptcy

Bankruptcy's basic procedures are designed to ameliorate a common pool problem. The key to effective implementation of this goal is to trigger bankruptcy when, and only when, it is in the interests of the creditors as a group. Consider what this means. Insolvency may be an occasion to collectivize what hitherto had been an individual remedies system. It does not, however, justify the implementation of a different set of relative entitlements, unless doing so is necessary as a part of the move from the individual remedies system. It is not just that the need for a collective proceeding does not go hand in hand with new entitlements. It is that the establishment of new entitlements in bankruptcy conflicts with the collectivization goal. Such changes create incentives for particular holders of rights in assets to resort to bankruptcy in order to gain for themselves the advantages of those changes, even when a bankruptcy proceeding would not be in the collective interest of the investor group. These incentives are predictable and counterproductive because they reintroduce the fundamental problem that bankruptcy law is designed to solve: individual self-interest undermining the interests of the group. These changes are better made *generally* instead of in bankruptcy only.

The problem of changing relative entitlements in bankruptcy not only underlies this book's normative view of bankruptcy law but also forms the basis of the bankruptcy system that has been enacted. The Supreme Court made this point in a case that is as important for recognizing it as the actual issue decided is unimportant. The case, *Butner v. United States*, decided in 1979,[1] involved a secured creditor's claim to rents that accrued on the property serving as collateral after the filing of the bankruptcy petition relative to the claims of the unsecured creditors generally. Under relevant state law, as the Supreme Court described it, the debtor was entitled to the rents as long as it remained in possession or until a state court, on request, ordered the rents to be paid over to the secured creditor. In bankruptcy the unsecured creditors of an insolvent debtor

1. 440 U.S. 48 (1979).

can be viewed as the new equity owners of the debtor and hence entitled to what the debtor was entitled to outside of bankruptcy. This gave rise to the conflict between the secured creditor and the trustee, as representative of the unsecured creditors. The issue that the Supreme Court considered in *Butner* was: What should the source of law be (state or federal) in deciding how the secured creditor may realize on the post-bankruptcy rents? The Court saw the source of law as nonbankruptcy and observed that "the federal bankruptcy court should take whatever steps are necessary to ensure that the [secured creditor] is afforded in federal bankruptcy court the same protections he would have under state law if no bankruptcy had ensued."[2] It justified this result as follows:

> Property interests are created and defined by state law. Unless some federal interest requires a different result, there is no reason why such interests should be analyzed differently simply because an interested party is involved in a bankruptcy proceeding. Uniform treatment of property interests by both state and federal courts within a State serves to reduce uncertainty, to discourage forum shopping, and to prevent a party from receiving "a windfall merely by reason of the happenstance of bankruptcy."[3]

In the notion of forum shopping the Supreme Court expressed the fundamental point.

Yet to say that *Butner* denounced changing relative entitlements only in bankruptcy does not end the matter. It is important to understand *why* such rule changes cut against bankruptcy's recognized goal. This requires the separation of two issues that arise when a debtor is in bankruptcy: first, it is necessary to decide what to do with the debtor's assets, and, second, it is necessary to decide who gets them. The principal proposition I wish to establish here is that only by treating the answer to the second question as a nonbankruptcy issue can it be kept from unfavorably altering the answer to the first. To put this another way, in its role as a collective debt-collection device, bankruptcy law should not create rights. Instead, it should act to ensure that the rights that exist are vindicated to the extent possible. Only in this way can bankruptcy law minimize the conversion costs of transferring an insolvent debtor's assets to its creditors.

This point is easiest to demonstrate by examining a case where there is no occasion to use bankruptcy as a response to a common pool problem—where only one person has rights to the debtor's assets. Such a person, the sole owner of the assets, would have no creditors. Irrespective

2. Id., at 56.
3. Id., at 54–55.

of any thought of bankruptcy, this sole owner would continually re-evaluate his use of the assets. If he were manufacturing buggy whips, at every moment (in theory at least) he would reassess whether this was the best use for those assets. If it was, he would continue; but if it was not, he would stop and either use the assets for some other purpose or sell them, piecemeal or as a unit, to others. This decision would be his alone. And he presumably would make it after determining which action would bring him the most from the assets.[4]

This is, of course, an oversimplification. No person has *full* ownership of assets in the sense that he has absolutely unfettered control over their use. I do not have the right to sell cocaine even if I could make a great deal of money doing so. Similarly, a person making buggy whips may be subject to regulations governing the types of materials he can use, the minimum wages he must pay, or the environmental controls he must observe. These regulations will constrain his decisions and may lead him to choose a different use than he would choose in their absence.

This qualification, however, does not fundamentally undercut the basic point that given an existing array of legal rules, a sole owner would presumably decide to use the assets in the way that would bring him the most. He has, by definition, no need to use bankruptcy to ameliorate a common pool problem because a common pool exists only when there is more than one person with rights. He, accordingly, would be utterly indifferent to bankruptcy policy, unless the debtor's use of it benefited him (by permitting the debtor, for example, to escape an undesirable nonbankruptcy charge). If a charge were placed on assets only in bank-ruptcy law (such as that a debtor could not go out of business without first protecting employees), this owner would remain free to ignore it by going out of business without using bankruptcy. He would only be obligated to take account of such a charge if it were imposed by non-bankruptcy law.

When rights to assets[5] are spread among a number of people, however, as they almost always are, things change. It then becomes necessary to

4. The most what? Generally, I will be speaking as if it is the most money, and for our purposes that will do. Technically, *most* should be defined in terms of what economists would call *utility*, which would allow the person to express his nonmonetary preferences as well. See J. Hirshleifer, *Price Theory and Applications* ch. 2 (2d ed. 1980).

5. I am using *owner* to refer to anyone with rights to the debtor's assets under non-bankruptcy law. I am using *rights* to mean the right to the income stream generated by the firm's assets, the right to receive payment out of the assets, or the right to the assets upon dissolution. Those with rights include not only creditors but also, for example, shareholders, who, like other owners, have a right to a firm's assets (subject to the rights of creditors).

decide not only how best to deploy the assets but also how to split up the returns from those assets.[6] Because of the diversity of the owners, the deployment question creates a common pool problem. Bankruptcy law exists to solve that problem. But the lessons from the common pool show that the answer to the distributional question should not affect the determination of how to deploy the assets.[7] As a group these diverse owners—bondholders, tort victims, trade creditors, shareholders, and others—would want to follow the same course as a sole owner. It is in the interest of the owners as a *group,* in other words, to keep the distributional question from spilling over into the deployment question.

Bankruptcy law is best approached by separating these two questions—the question of how the process can maximize the value of a given pool of assets and the question of how the law should allocate entitlements to whatever pool exists—and limiting bankruptcy law to the first. This distinction makes clear the relationship between bankruptcy rules and nonbankruptcy rules and provides a principle of bankruptcy policy capable of identifying which nonbankruptcy rules may need to be supplanted.

Because there is perhaps no point in bankruptcy policy that is more easily misunderstood, it is worth proceeding carefully. Let us consider one of the most common views of what bankruptcy law should do. This view is that bankruptcy law exists, in part, to help firms stay in business because of an increased social value and/or the jobs that are saved. In one guise this simply restates the common pool problem—that diverse

6. If the assets are sold, these returns may be cash or marketable securities of another company. If the firm is reorganized, the returns will probably be new claims against the firm's assets. Such decisions about the deployment of assets and returns are also made, at least implicitly, each day of a firm's existence, since each day the firm's owners must decide whether to continue the business. For a healthy firm the manner of splitting up the returns from the assets is predetermined by contract or state law.

7. It is similar to another common separation in finance theory: that between investment (i.e., acquisition of an asset) and financing (i.e., paying for the asset). See, e.g., R. Brealey & S. Myers, *Principles of Corporate Finance* 91, 254–56 (1981). The owners may differ in their goals. Many may seek to maximize asset values; some may, however, pursue other goals. This situation, of course, exists outside of bankruptcy as well, where it calls for no particular interventions. See id. (owners of a firm free to maximize asset values); Engel, "An Approach to Corporate Social Responsibility," 32 *Stan. L. Rev.* 1 (1979). No new problems are introduced when dealing with it as a common pool. Those that pursue goals other than money can take the money they receive in bankruptcy, purchase new shares in the assets that are sold (or in other assets), and pursue their goals. Cf. DeAngelo, "Competition and Unanimity," 71 *Am. Econ. Rev.* 18 (1981); Makowski, "Competition and Unanimity Revisited," 73 *Am. Econ. Rev.* 329 (1983).

owners, if unconstrained, will pull apart assets that would be worth more to the group of owners if kept together. Usually, however, the notion of keeping firms in business seems to be meant as an independent policy. For that policy to have independent force, it must mean that, irrespective of the wishes of the owners, a firm's assets should be kept in their current form because somebody—society or workers—is better off.[8]

Incorporating such a policy in a bankruptcy statute, however, would be to mix apples and oranges, if one accepts the view (as everyone seems to) that bankruptcy law also exists as a response to a common pool problem. The question is really one of defining substantive rights. If the group in question—society, or workers, or whatever—deserve such rights, it is counterproductive to locate them only in a bankruptcy statute. Under existing nonbankruptcy law, for example, workers have no substantive entitlements to keep assets in their current form; they are not owners with substantive rights against the assets. For that reason the owners are free to close the business without considering the interests of the workers if doing so brings the owners more money. The fact that those owners have a common pool problem and need to use a collective proceeding to ameliorate it is not a reason to suddenly give a new group—workers—rights that they would not otherwise have and that could be ignored if the bankruptcy process were avoided. The decision whether they should have such rights should not be bankruptcy-specific. It addresses a distributional question as well as a deployment question.[9]

Another way to put this is to note the distinction between saying that something is a problem that Congress should address and saying that something is a problem that Congress should address through bankruptcy law. The first is a federalism question, the second a collective debt-collection question. Whether giving workers substantive rights with regard to how assets are used is desirable, just as whether secured creditors should come ahead of unsecured creditors, is a question of underlying entitlements. Although protecting the victims of economic misfortune who have not been given rights against assets may be an important social and legal question, it is not a question specific to bankruptcy law. How-

8. This may be difficult to show. Although workers in Kalamazoo may lose their jobs when an automobile plant is shut down, the use of those resources in, say, Austin, may provide new jobs to people there. One cannot sensibly address this question by focusing only on the workers who lose jobs in Kalamazoo. Whatever the proper normative outcome to this inquiry, the point remains: it is a policy of nonbankruptcy law, not bankruptcy law, that is (or should be) at issue.

9. This is a point made in Baird, "A World Without Bankruptcy," 48 *Law & Contemp. Probs.* (forthcoming, 1986).

ever the question is answered, a bankruptcy statute would still be necessary, because answering these substantive questions one way instead of the other does not eliminate the common pool problem. Because the issues of who should have entitlements and how to address a common pool problem are distinct, they should be kept separate in the legal response.[10]

Nor is this simply an academic point. Bankruptcy law cannot both give new groups rights and continue effectively to solve a common pool problem. Treating both as bankruptcy questions interferes with bankruptcy's historic function as a superior debt-collection system against insolvent debtors. Fashioning a distinct bankruptcy rule—such as one that gives workers rights they do not hold under nonbankruptcy law— creates incentives for the group advantaged by the distinct bankruptcy rule to use the bankruptcy process even though it is not in the interest of the owners as a group. The consequences can be seen frequently: many cases are begun where the reason for filing for bankruptcy quite clearly is nothing more than the fact that the entity bringing the case is advantaged because of a bankruptcy rule change.[11] Bankruptcy proceedings inevitably carry costs of their own.[12] When bankruptcy is activated for a rule change that benefits one particular class, the net effect may be harmful to the owners as a group. It is this problem that makes such rule changes undesirable as a matter of bankruptcy law.

Even though a nonbankruptcy rule may suffer from infirmities such as unfairness or inefficiency, if the nonbankruptcy rule does not undermine the advantages of a collective proceeding relative to the individual remedies that exist given those entitlements, imposing a different bankruptcy rule is a second-best and perhaps a counterproductive solution. At bottom, bankruptcy is justified in overriding nonbankruptcy rights *because* those rights interfere with the group advantages associated with creditors acting in concert. If the nonbankruptcy rule—for example, a rule permitting owners to close down a business without considering the plight of workers—is thought undesirable for reasons other

10. It follows that it is incorrect to maintain that a federal-state conflict can appropriately be resolved through bankruptcy. It may be that numerous state-created entitlements are counterproductive or the result of special group pressures. It may also be (although it is by no means ineluctably so) that Congress could fashion entitlements that are more resistant to such deficiencies. But it would be a mistake to therefore see bankruptcy law as the appropriate place to resolve such issues. They involve, instead, a general question of federal law. (As for why bankruptcy law is federal law, see Introduction, footnote 4.)

11. We will see illustrations of this when examining rules governing the commencement of cases in Chapter 8.

12. See Chapter 8.

than its interference with a collective proceeding, the proper approach for Congress would be to face that issue squarely and to overturn the rule in general, not just to undermine or reverse it in bankruptcy.[13] The latter course is undesirable because, as *Butner* recognized, it creates incentives for strategic "shopping" between the nonbankruptcy and bankruptcy forums.[14]

Determining Liabilities by Focusing on Relative Values

To this point the discussion has been abstract. But what are these nonbankruptcy entitlements? Exactly how are they to be "respected" in bankruptcy, given that the nature of bankruptcy is to change the situation from an individual to a collective regime? Under what circumstances should these nonbankruptcy entitlements *not* be respected? We can turn

13. This assertion rests on the premise that Congress has such power under the Constitution. Prevailing constitutional doctrine gives Congress extreme latitude under the commerce clause. See, e.g., Katzenbach v. McClung, 379 U.S. 294 (1964); Wickard v. Filburn, 317 U.S. 111 (1942).

14. Butner v. United States, 440 U.S. 48 (1979); see also Shanker, "The Abuse and Use of Federal Bankruptcy Power," 26 *Case Western Res. L. Rev.* 3 (1976). Underlying this argument in text is a desire to see bankruptcy proceedings begin when and only when they are likely to increase net asset values. In Chapter 8 the problem will be explored in the context of incentives for different groups of claimants. See also infra Chapter 7 (incentives for unsecured creditors to choose optimal deployment as reason for paying secured creditors in full during bankruptcy proceedings). The point here is much the same. To the extent that unsecured creditors are the group to be benefited (or not) by a bankruptcy proceeding, one needs to create incentives to have them act in the interests of their group as a whole in making the bankruptcy decision. A class-wide vote as to whether a collective proceeding should be commenced is virtually impossible, see infra Chapter 9. Therefore, to the extent that one needs to have individual creditors act instead in making the bankruptcy decision, one wants them to have, to the extent possible, interests not in conflict with the group vis-à-vis that decision. Avoiding changes in relative values promotes that situation better than any alternative.

Another way to consider this is to envision the likelihood of bargaining breakdowns that would lead to poor uses of the bankruptcy process. If using the bankruptcy process is a poor outcome for the claimants as a group, it is in their interest to consensually avoid it. See infra note 83. Recent economic modeling of the bargaining process suggests that bargaining breakdowns occur with greater frequency as the uncertainty of outcomes increases. A system that provides no strategic advantages for particular claimants in bankruptcy provides little uncertainty in intergroup outcomes and little to bargain over. Conversely, rule changes in bankruptcy give individuals something to bargain over (threatened poor uses of bankruptcy versus payoffs to individuals that would be advantaged by a bankruptcy rule change) as well as uncertainty of outcomes that promote breakdowns. For an application of this kind of bargaining model to a legal problem, see Bebchuk, "Litigation and Settlement Under Imperfect Information," 15 *Rand J. of Econ.* 404 (1984).

now to these more concrete questions and examine how the model of bankruptcy just developed can be used to resolve them. We will first look at how to identify those entitled to participate in the division of assets in bankruptcy and then at the issue of how to rank-order those who are so entitled.

A successful transition from the nonbankruptcy to the bankruptcy forum does not require the preservation of each detail of any given nonbankruptcy right. To be sure, the fewest dislocations are achieved when the bankruptcy system respects the right just as it exists in the nonbankruptcy world, so that the right remains in full force not only against the debtor but also against rival creditors. Dislocations are minimized because bankruptcy law would then not defeat the creditor's right to specific performance of its original entitlement, and its value would accordingly be fixed at exactly what it was in the nonbankruptcy world. Inevitable problems introduced by the valuation process are thereby avoided.

Respecting these rights in full, however, can conflict with the core role of bankruptcy to maximize the value of assets in the face of pressures to ignore the collective weal for individual gain. Thus, it is necessary to weigh the damage that recognizing a particular nonbankruptcy right would cause to collective action against the costs of any incentives that would be potentially created by upsetting that right. Because the collective damage resulting from adhering to a right may sometimes exceed any benefit, a bankruptcy statute sometimes *must* replace nonbankruptcy rights with something else.

Although this might appear to be a difficult principle to apply, in many cases it is not. Consider the simple example of unsecured creditors that we were using in the previous chapter. It is impossible to respect the nonbankruptcy rights of these creditors precisely—if all their rights could be specifically enforced, there would be no cause for a bankruptcy proceeding. To respect all rights specifically is necessarily to overvalue some of them in comparison with the rights held by competing claimants. For example, if all rights were specifically respected, this would mean that creditors' grab remedies would be replicated in bankruptcy. Bankruptcy's collectivization goal, for this reason, requires bankruptcy rules to override individual creditor remedies—a result accomplished by the automatic stay, which we will examine in Chapter 7.

To say that the exercise of a particular right interferes with bankruptcy's collectivizing function does not generally mean, however, that its nonbankruptcy value relative to the value of other creditors' rights cannot be adhered to.[15] Although the question of determining what will be called *relative values* is itself complex and will demand our attention shortly, the basic focus should be clearly kept in mind: we are in a world where one needs to think not in terms of abstract rights but of measuring *relative values*. Where the entitlements themselves should not be fully protected, such as is the case with individual creditor grab remedies, sound bankruptcy policy still calls for the preservation of relative values. Doing so minimizes the strategic gamesmanship that otherwise would hamper the smooth replacement of individual-based remedies with a collective proceeding.

Nonetheless, it is far easier to state than to implement a policy that preserves the relative value among competing rights while abandoning the effort to preserve all entitlements absolutely within the bankruptcy framework. Indeed, this program demands an understanding of large bodies of substantive legal rules—for the purpose of valuing their attributes—as a precondition for implementing bankruptcy law. The substantive analysis is further complicated because the translation from one system to the other may not be precise. Bankruptcy's procedures may not be directly analogous to nonbankruptcy procedures, and creditors' rights outside of bankruptcy may depend on specific contexts that cannot be replicated, but only approximated, within the bankruptcy system.

Notwithstanding these conceptual translation problems, bankruptcy's objective is easy to express, even if hard to implement. The bankruptcy process should duplicate the relative standing among claimants that would exist outside of bankruptcy's collective framework. This is the concept of relative value. The relevant inquiry might be conceived this way: who would be entitled to what under nonbankruptcy law, if (putting aside issues we deal with in Chapter 7 arising out of the fact that bankruptcy proceedings themselves take time) the debtor were to go out of business on the date of the bankruptcy petition and if there were no self-interested grabbing of assets at that point?

Consider this approach as applied to perhaps the most common— and uncontroversial—of bankruptcy's policies, the pro rata treatment

15. If it could be shown that the value of the nonbankruptcy right resulted from some activity that is detrimental to the collectivizing goal of the bankruptcy process itself, then bankruptcy policy would call for disregarding both the right and its relative value. The principal example of this is a prebankruptcy grab by a creditor who intends to opt out of the upcoming collective proceeding. We shall examine this type of opt-out behavior when we relax the assumptions under which we are presently operating, including that bankruptcy occurs without warning. See Chapter 6.

of general unsecured creditors. To the extent that this treatment is justified at all, it is justified by a legal homily such as "bankruptcy courts are courts of equity, and equality is equity."[16] With the benefit of a notion of what bankruptcy law should be doing, however, we can be more precise as to *why* pro rata treatment of unsecured creditors is proper bankruptcy policy.

Imagine that I, together with a professor from Stanford, were each going to lend $10,000 to a common debtor. And imagine that we met with each other and with the debtor before making the loans. The debtor (in a very virtuous moment) asked us: "Assume that you wake up some day and discover that I have only $15,000 in assets, even if they are used in their most productive fashion. We have already agreed that a grab system in this event will function poorly, because the assets might then fetch only $12,000. How do you want to divide the assets that do exist?"

As we saw in Chapter 1, it would be in our joint interest to agree to a collective proceeding (or some other device) that would allow the Stanford professor and me to get a total of $15,000 instead of $12,000. If we were forced, in this preloan meeting, to reach a decision on how we would split the assets in the event of insolvency, what would we decide? Although the agreement we would reach on splitting depends on a number of factors (such as our relative savvy and bargaining skills), I doubt that the two of us could do any better than agree to split them pro rata.[17]

More to the point: what if you were a legal decision maker required to fashion a rule to allocate assets in a collective proceeding because of the realization that the relevant creditors will *not* be able to meet together before the fact and reach a consensual bargain? You need a rule that applies not only to the Stanford professor and me but to innumerable other combinations of creditors, from two to thousands.[18] Assuming that you were concerned only with unsecured creditors, you presumably would devise a pro rata rule that, as applied to our example, would result in splitting the assets fifty-fifty. This represents our odds of getting the money if there were no collective proceeding (50 percent of the time,

---

16. This is a long-standing slogan of bankruptcy law. See Canright v. General Finance Corp., 35 F.Supp. 841, 844 (E.D. Ill. 1940); see also Simonson v. Granquist, 365 U.S. 38 (1962); Kuehner v. Irving Trust Co., 299 U.S. 445 (1937).

17. See Hoffman & Spitzer, "Entitlements, Rights, and Fairness: An Experimental Examination of Subjects' Concepts of Distributive Justice," 14 *J. Legal Studies* 259 (1985).

18. These creditors, moreover, may hold contingent, disputed, unliquidated, or unmatured claims; indeed, as is the case with nonmanifested asbestos victims of Manville, they may not know that they *are* creditors at the date of bankruptcy. It is for these reasons that an *actual* consensual agreement seems unlikely.

I'd get there first and get paid in full; 50 percent of the time, the Stanford professor would get there first and get paid in full).

Nor would anything change if I lent $5,000 and the other professor lent $15,000. The best rule that could be devised for splitting the assets would still reflect our odds of getting the money if there were no collective proceeding, a split in the ratio of one to three. Given that the debtor has $15,000 of assets, this means, in a collective proceeding, that I would collect $3,750 and the Stanford professor would collect $11,250.

This, then, seems to provide our basic apportioning rule, because it mimics the *value* of our expected positions immediately before bankruptcy, at least given that the rule must be fashioned in the absence of information about the creditors involved. No other single apportioning rule works as well across a range of cases. It is also the apportioning rule that the Bankruptcy Code uses and that perhaps fuels the shopworn phrase that "equality is equity." At bottom, it is perhaps best to see this as meaning that those in a similarly situated group—such as general creditors—should split the assets available to their group pro rata, and nothing more.

This point is an offspring of the notion of bankruptcy as a collective debt-collection device. It is, unfortunately, all too easy to lose sight of it. When the creditors are Citibank and Bank of America, we may all be happy to see them treated pro rata. This, however, may not be the case if one of the creditors is a worker who is owed a week's wages or a tort victim whose lungs were destroyed by a product the debtor built, and the other is Bank of America. Bank of America is a creditor with (one presumes) a diversified portfolio. It knows that a certain number of loans are going to be bad, and it can make adjustments in the interest rate it charges if it turns out that a bankruptcy rule gives it less than perfect prorationing. The worker or tort victim, however, is unlikely to be a creditor with a diversified portfolio or with the ability to make adjustments as easily.

Do circumstances such as these affect our basic conclusion about a pro rata division of assets? I would argue that the answer is clearly no, at least when we are speaking of *bankruptcy* policy. The question of whether tort claimants should fare better than general creditors with a diversified portfolio is a general issue about the status of tort claims relative to other kinds of claims. We are no longer simply dealing with a common pool type problem where the objective is to determine how to collectivize debt collection without making things worse than they already are.

The focus, in other words, has shifted from one that is related to bankruptcy to one that is broader. If nonbankruptcy law treats tort victims and the Bank of America as general unsecured creditors with similar rights and collection remedies, bankruptcy law should take that conclusion as a given if it is to implement most effectively *its* unique social and economic role of providing a collective forum to deal with common pool problems in the credit world. Whether the underlying assignment of entitlements is correct is irrelevant when the issue is one of implementing bankruptcy's collectivization policy.

Bankruptcy law's existence can be justified on the ground that often the decision of what to do with assets (subject to baseline legal entitlements) is not the responsibility of a single person but is instead lodged in a number of different entities in a number of different ways. Consider the case of a corporation that has shareholders, unsecured creditors, secured creditors, employees, and managers. Under much modern corporate law it is most useful to view shareholders, unsecured creditors, and secured creditors as the owners of the firm.[19] They have different packages of rights to the assets at different times, but they all have the right to call on the firm's assets under one set of circumstances or another. As commonly referred to, secured creditors have first claim on certain assets; shareholders have residual claims on all the assets; and the unsecured creditors come in between. It may be that the decision as to what to do with the assets is usually lodged in the shareholders, as long as they do not default on their obligations to the creditors. This point, however, only indicates that the rights of the various groups to the assets come in different packages. It is still useful to think of them— secured creditors, unsecured creditors, and shareholders alike—as owners.

It is, at least as a first approximation, less useful to think of the employees or managers as species of owners. Workers may have an entitlement to a certain wage level, but as nonbankruptcy law is currently set up, they have no draw *as workers* on the assets. They have no say as to whether the assets should remain doing what they are doing or not. They may have claims on the assets to secure their wages or the future terms of their collective bargaining agreement, but to the extent that they do, they are creditors, and it is better to think of them as creditors than as workers. Managers, moreover, may have a good deal of day-to-day control and the leverage that comes from controlling the operating machinery, but they have no *legal* rights to use the assets (other than the

---

19. A critical summary of this literature is contained in Brudney, "Corporate Governance, Agency Costs and the Rhetoric of Contract," 85 *Colum. L. Rev.* 1403 (1985).

assets represented by their own services) in opposition to the wishes of the shareholders and creditors. Thus, they have no rights that need to be accounted for in a collective proceeding (again, other than insofar as their future services are needed).

Once one identifies those with rights against the assets, one has identified the pool of owners. These people are determined by rules outside the bankruptcy process. Some of these people have rights superior to (or at least different from) those of others. How the rights of secured creditors, unsecured creditors, and shareholders are identified vis-à-vis one another is a question of their nonbankruptcy entitlements.

A collective insolvency proceeding is directed toward reducing the costs associated with diverse ownership interests. Other problems should be addressed as general problems, not as bankruptcy problems. And just as the filing of a petition in bankruptcy provides little justification for altering the relative rights of owners and nonowners of the firm, so should it have little effect on the rights of owners inter se. Changes in nonbankruptcy rights should be made only if they benefit all those with interests in the firm as a group. A rule change unrelated to the goals of bankruptcy creates incentives for particular holders of rights in assets to resort to bankruptcy in order to gain for themselves the advantages of that rule change, even though a bankruptcy proceeding would not be in the collective interest of the investor group.[20] It is this concept that underlies bankruptcy law's concern with relative values.

Determining Whether a Person Participates in the Bankruptcy Process

From this brief discussion of the valuation of the claims of general creditors in bankruptcy, we can see that the first rule of a collective proceeding designed to serve bankruptcy law's historic role is that it should take the value of entitlements as it finds them. The difficult substantive issue of whether those entitlements are correct is an important question, but it is not a bankruptcy question.

To say that bankruptcy law should take the value of entitlements as it finds them means, in turn, that as a very general approximation bankruptcy should freeze the rights of all the creditors as they were the

20. This phenomenon—often called *misbehavior*—exists whenever rights are fixed by contract and then, after the contract is entered into, circumstances permit one side to profit by not meeting its obligations. See R. Posner, *Economic Analysis of Law* 293–94 (2d ed. 1977); Muris, "Opportunistic Behavior and the Law of Contracts," 65 *Minn. L. Rev.* 521, 532–52 (1981); Jensen & Meckling, "Theory of the Firm: Managerial Behavior, Agency Costs and Ownership Structure," 3 *J. Fin. Econ.* 305, 312–15 (1976).

moment before the collective proceeding started and then value them, so frozen, relative to one another. This requires a determination of what the rights would be worth in the abstract—how much, in other words, a particular claimant would be entitled to were the debtor not insolvent. This may be considered the question of establishing a nominal value. Since the debtor is presumably insolvent, however, all those with claims will not be paid their nominal values in full. Thus, bankruptcy must also concern itself with the question of who gets what, in what order. This is the question of relative value. The important lesson to be derived from thinking of bankruptcy law as a species of debt-collection law is that the source of both nominal and relative values is nonbankruptcy law. Demonstrating why this is so and what it means for bankruptcy law is the focus of the remainder of this chapter.

The relevant time to determine whether someone is a secured creditor or a judgment creditor (or even a creditor at all) is, generally speaking, as of the filing of the petition. That this is so comes from the nature of the common pool. Bankruptcy is a way of implementing a decision as to what to do with assets of a debtor. Its owners are those with rights of some sort or another against the debtor's assets at the moment that implementing decision is made. It is perhaps useful to analogize it to a start-up business. Once capital is acquired and the business is established and running, it has to make its way in the world subject to the legal and economic constraints of our society. So, too, should it be in bankruptcy. Bankruptcy law should determine who are owners of the assets, in the sense of having rights against them, at the moment the bankruptcy petition is filed.[21]

Consider, first, what *types* of rights might be considered to be claims cognizable in bankruptcy—the question addressed in the statute by section 101(4). The principle behind looking to nonbankruptcy law to determine, in the first instance, who the claimants are should be obvious and is directly associated with the notion of preserving relative values. Bankruptcy law would be an odd place to generate new federal causes of action. Each time it does, strategic incentives are created to use the bankruptcy process for individual gain, even if it comes at the expense of the collective weal.[22] Accordingly, nonbankruptcy law should identify

21. This is expressed in the Bankruptcy Code in §101(9). It does not mean that rights arising subsequently against a debtor in bankruptcy are ignored. Quite the contrary. Claims that arise subsequent to the filing of the bankruptcy petition represent costs of running the business and should (at least when they are consensual) be paid before the claims of the group for whom bankruptcy is being run. But exploration of this point involves relaxation of one of our current assumptions—that bankruptcy proceedings take no time.

22. There is, of course, an exception for causes of action that are a *part* of the translation

whether a particular claimant has a right to reach the debtor's assets.

If, for example, a competitor claims that the debtor caused it injury by advertising that the debtor's product was superior, nonbankruptcy law should determine whether there is a right to resort to the debtor's assets to redress that injury—whether there is, in other words, a cognizable cause of action for trade losses. If the debtor is liable because, for example, the relevant state recognizes the tort of commercial disparagement, the competitor should hold a claim cognizable in bankruptcy. If, however, nonbankruptcy law does not provide for a cause of action because, for example, the state does not recognize the tort of commercial disparagement or because such product comparisons are protected by the First Amendment, the competitor should have no higher rights in bankruptcy than outside it and, accordingly, should not participate in the division of the debtor's assets either in or out of bankruptcy.

In all contexts the basic program is the same. The central difficulty lies in identifying the structure of the nonbankruptcy claims to be vindicated in the bankruptcy setting, where the focus is always on the *substance* of the claims and not the *labels* attached to them under state law. A state, for example, may choose (for any number of reasons) not to call something a claim. Whatever its label, however, if the holder has rights against assets of the debtor, it has the attributes of a claim for purposes of bankruptcy.[23]

Determining Nominal Values from Nonbankruptcy Attributes

The kinds of questions concerning the claimants that bankruptcy law must address involve more than deciding who has rights against assets. Assuming that nonbankruptcy law defines the asserted right as a cause of action, how does one place a nominal value on the resulting claim?

---

from an individual to a collective regime and hence that are part of the notion of a system of *bankruptcy* laws. See, e.g., §§544(a); 547, discussed in Chapters 3 and 6. These causes of action, however, sort out relative rights of *existing* claimants; they create no new pool of claimants.

23. This is the error of a case such as *In re* Villarie, 648 F.2d 810 (2d Cir. 1981). In *Villarie* the Second Circuit concluded that a recoupment right by a retirement agency was not a claim in bankruptcy. But like non-recourse secured loans, the attributes of a recoupment right are those of a claim for purposes of bankruptcy law: the right to go against an asset of the debtor. In the case of *Villarie* it was the right to reduce Mr. Villarie's retirement fund benefits. This example is explored in greater detail in Jackson, "Translating Assets and Liabilities to the Bankruptcy Forum," 14 *J. Legal Studies* 73, 78–79 (1985). Other problems created by looking to state labels (such as whether something is a claim) are explored later in this chapter.

Sometimes this inquiry is tied to possible nonbankruptcy procedural defenses that reduce to zero the value of a claim. Such would be the position, for example, of a cause of action barred by an ordinary statute of limitations prior to the date of the filing of the bankruptcy petition. Applying that statutory bar in bankruptcy properly mirrors the zero value of the claim outside bankruptcy.

The Propriety of Loan Acceleration in Bankruptcy. A slightly more difficult issue is raised by an assertion that a cause of action, although it conceivably could be brought later, could not be brought at the time of the commencement of the bankruptcy proceeding. Because these causes of action might be allowed in the future, they often have—as one can see from examining appropriate nonbankruptcy analogies—some existing value under nonbankruptcy law at the time of bankruptcy. In those cases these "unmatured" causes of action, whose existence is not tied to the debtor's future course of operation, should be recognized in bankruptcy as claims. The difficult question is how to give them a nominal value.

This question invites examination of a broader topic: how to treat unmatured claims in bankruptcy. This includes the most common liability of all: an obligation to repay a loan. Consider, for example, an asserted claim based on a thirty-year loan of $10,000 made fifteen years previously at 5 percent interest. This is clearly a claim, because nonbankruptcy law gives the creditor recourse to the debtor's assets in the event that repayment was not forthcoming. The claim arose before the filing of the bankruptcy petition, because even if the debtor were to cease doing business today, it would be obligated to repay the loan or to make provisions for its future repayment. How, then, should the loan be treated in bankruptcy? Should it be treated as due and payable on the occurrence of bankruptcy and, if so, in its face amount (of $10,000) or in some smaller amount reflecting its present value?

This question may best be approached by separating three distinct issues. First, and perhaps most important, how should an unmatured loan be treated when, at the moment of bankruptcy, the debtor is not otherwise in default? Second, if loans are not accelerated by the commencement of bankruptcy itself, can the lender provide, by means of an ipso facto clause, for such acceleration? Third, should the fact of default prior to the time of bankruptcy matter, and, if so, how? We shall examine the first two issues in this chapter. We shall also discuss briefly the third issue, but full analysis of it must await Chapter 6, where we relax our current assumption that bankruptcy's collective proceeding occurs suddenly and no prebankruptcy strategic actions are undertaken.

What should the general rule be for unmatured loans when a bankruptcy proceeding is commenced? As a positive matter the Bankruptcy Code gives one answer and then provides the debtor with an option to give a different answer in a reorganization proceeding. The general answer, announced by the legislative history to section 502, is to treat bankruptcy as an event of default and acceleration.[24] In our example this would mean that the nominal value of the claim is its face amount of $10,000. This automatic acceleration rule also applies in a reorganization under chapter 11, but in that case the debtor is given the opportunity to gain back the original maturity date of the loan by reinstating the terms of the contract—a right that is likely to be exercised principally against secured creditors with below-market loans.[25]

These positive features of bankruptcy law can be analyzed against bankruptcy law's collective debt-collection function. Consider, first, the case of the presumptive rule where a debtor is liquidating in bankruptcy. In that event, even though the present value of the loan, apart from its

---

24. H. Rep. No. 595, 95th Cong., 1st Sess. 352–53 (1977) ("[B]ankruptcy operates as the acceleration of the principal amount of all claims against the debtor"). What if the note in question is one of the zero-interest coupon notes that sprung up (principally because of tax reasons) in the early 1980s? Such a note is one that is purchased from debtor for, say, $60,000 and, on maturity in three years, debtor promises to pay the holder $100,000. Six months after buying it, debtor files for bankruptcy. In bankruptcy, can the holder accelerate the principal and have a claim for $100,000? Here the answer is "no." The legislative history states that in this case the holder gets only what was loaned plus pro rata interest. Id. As a matter of formulating a rule to be used when the loan contract is silent, that conclusion sounds correct. But whether or not it is depends on what normal practice is for defaults of zero-interest coupon notes. Moreover, if a particular zero-interest note was written providing for acceleration of the $100,000 principal in the event of default, there is no particular reason that this contract term should not be respected in bankruptcy. Common practice, however, seems to be that defaults of such notes does not accelerate the entire principal. To that extent the bankruptcy rule mimics the nonbankruptcy entitlement.

25. §1124 The reason that reinstatement will principally be used against secured creditors with below-market loans comes from the fact that reinstatement requires ultimate repayment of the loan in full. Given that, the residual class of claimants (generally the unsecured creditors) will favor reinstatement only when the costs of doing so are smaller than the benefits. A $100,000 secured loan at 5 percent interest due in ten years has a present value substantially less than $100,000 if reinstated (say, $60,000). But an accelerated secured loan of $100,000 will require full payment in bankruptcy. Accordingly, reinstatement would be sensible from the perspective of the residual class, which would thereby take care of the secured creditors with a $60,000 (present value) stream of payments instead of a $100,000 (present value) payment. Unsecured loans are much less likely to share this attribute. If the loan was unsecured, reinstatement would still have a present value cost of approximately $60,000 (or slightly less, because riskier), whereas if unsecured creditors are receiving only twenty cents on the dollar, the matured claim of $100,000 would receive only $20,000. The other unsecured creditors, accordingly, would be better off leaving the claim accelerated.

acceleration feature, is substantially less than $10,000, accelerating the $10,000 principal is almost surely the correct way of mirroring the non-bankruptcy nominal value of that claim. The reason for this, however, is *not* that bankruptcy itself should constitute an event of acceleration. The advent of a collective proceeding itself suggests no nonbankruptcy attribute that should automatically give a right of acceleration. It is, instead, the nonbankruptcy attributes of a *liquidating* debtor that justify the presumptive acceleration rule of section 502.

This rule is consistent with the effort to maintain as closely as possible relevant nonbankruptcy attributes in a bankruptcy proceeding. If an insolvent debtor were being dismembered by creditors outside of bankruptcy, any loan agreement worth its salt would have default and acceleration provisions that would afford the lender its opportunity to share in the spoils without having to wait until the maturing date fifteen years hence, at which time, under a system of individualistic grab remedies, the debtor's assets would be long gone. The decision of a debtor (or its creditors) to liquidate in bankruptcy should change nothing: it represents the kind of event that would trigger such default and acceleration.

This would be true even where the assets are being sold as a unit in a chapter 7 proceeding. In that case the nominal debtor is changing. The buyer of the assets becomes the new debtor on the loan, and the original debtor ultimately disappears, because it is in the process of liquidating. Outside of bankruptcy, the general rule from basic contract law is that repayment obligations on loans can be assigned to a new entity without permission of the lender only if the original entity remains on the hook.[26] In the case of an asset sale in chapter 7, however, the debtor—the original entity—is in the process of *removing* itself from any further responsibility because it is in the process of liquidating and ultimately dissolving. From the perspective of contract law, an attempt to continue a contractual obligation of a debtor beyond a liquidation involving that debtor would almost certainly be viewed as a delegation of that obligation to a new entity, coupled with a divesting of duties by the debtor.[27]

26. "Delegation of performance is a normal and permissible incident of many types of contracts . . . The principal exceptions relate to contracts for personal services and to contracts for the exercise of personal skill or discretion." Restatement (Second) of Contracts, §318, comment c (1981). But the general rule governing delegation of duties, absent explicit agreement, is that "delegation of performance . . . [does not] discharge any duty or liability of the delegating obligor." Id., §318(3). See also id., §316, comment c. These principles apply to loan repayment obligations. See Arkansas Valley Smelting Co. v. Belden Mining Co., 127 U.S. 379 (1888); Texas & N.O.R. Co. v. Phillips, 196 F.2d 692 (5th Cir. 1952); *In re* Adana Mortgage Bankers, 12 Bankr. 977 (Bankr. N.D. Ga. 1980).

27. See, e.g., Western Oil Sales Corp. v. Bliss & Wetherbee, 299 S.W. 637 (Tex. Comm.

In a bankruptcy liquidation, therefore, an automatic acceleration rule may be thought of as an "off the rack" term that duplicates the near-certain contractual outcome in the absence of that rule.[28] Accordingly, the acceleration of a claim in a bankruptcy liquidation accurately mirrors its nonbankruptcy value. This stems, however, not from anything magical about bankruptcy policy but from recognizing the attributes of the situation of a company that decides to liquidate through the bankruptcy forum.[29]

Does this rule, however, create perverse incentives to use the bankruptcy process for individual gain? With a long-term loan at a below-market interest rate, for example, bankruptcy's provision for automatic acceleration might seem to encourage a lender to force a bankruptcy even when it would be wasteful for the creditors as a group. (This incentive structure is, to be sure, common both in and out of bankruptcy. Any lender with a below-market loan outstanding has an incentive to precipitate a default in order to accelerate the principal, collect it, and lend the money again, just as any debtor with an above-market rate has an incentive to cash out of its commitment.)

The answer would seem to be no. The presumptive event of default is *not* the filing of a petition for bankruptcy itself. The justification for acceleration, instead, derives from the fact that the debtor is liquidating and terminating its responsibility for repayment. This matches the bankruptcy proceeding to its closest nonbankruptcy analogue and duplicates the attributes of that nonbankruptcy analogue. But a lender that forces a bankruptcy proceeding to accelerate a below-market loan may not be faced with a debtor who is terminating its existence.

In other words, it is necessary to be careful of the context in which an automatic acceleration rule is being applied. Consider, for example, a debtor that is reorganizing in the bankruptcy forum—continuing, in

---

App. 1927); Boston Ice Co. v. Potter, 123 Mass. 28 (1877); cf. The British Waggon Co. v. Lea & Co., 5 Q.B.D. 149 (1880) (assignment of duties by company in process of winding up permissible "so long as [that company] continues to exist"). But cf. Macke Co. v. Pizza of Gaithersburg, 259 Md. 479, 370 A.2d 645 (1970) (allowing purchaser of obligor to assume contract); Evening News Ass'n v. Peterson, 477 F. Supp. 77 (D.D.C. 1979) (assignment permitted upon merger because assuming corporation was substantially similar to original corporation).

28. See Easterbrook & Fischel, "Corporate Control Transactions," 91 *Yale L.J.* 698 (1982). If nonbankruptcy law implicitly discounted the acceleration of principal when the note contained no explicit interim interest, this presumption would be rebutted.

29. Although a corporation does not receive a discharge in a bankruptcy liquidation, §727(a)(1), the corporation almost certainly will thereupon dissolve under applicable state corporation law.

effect, but with a new set of owners.[30] Is acceleration also proper in such a case? To answer that question, it again seems proper to try to mirror the relevant nonbankruptcy attributes in the bankruptcy proceeding.

Reorganization, as Chapter 9 will develop more fully, can be viewed as a form of a sale, not of the assets but of the debtor itself, in the sense that, as occurs in a merger or a stock takeover, new owners enter the picture. When new owners take over an existing debtor, general non-bankruptcy rules would label this neither a delegation nor a divesting of duties, and hence it would not trigger general contract antiassignment rules.[31] If, outside of bankruptcy, the loan in question would not be accelerated upon a change of ownership of the debtor, then neither should it be automatically accelerated in bankruptcy.

Thus, the general reinstatement rule of section 1124 that is applicable in a bankruptcy reorganization may be viewed as reflecting, in rough fashion, the nonbankruptcy rules underlying the treatment of nondel-egable duties. Since reinstatement under section 1124 is optional, the debtor is, of course, free to have the loan accelerated when it is in its interest to do so (as it would, outside of bankruptcy, generally be able to accelerate repayment by defaulting). Such a rule most accurately mir-rors its nonbankruptcy attributes. But pushing a debtor into bankruptcy provides no greater opportunity for strategic behavior by a lender with a below-market loan than exists outside of bankruptcy.

We have just examined the general rule for treating unmatured loans in bankruptcy. The next question is whether it should be possible to contract around this general rule. Should a lender, through a clause in the loan agreement, be able to specify that the filing of bankruptcy itself occasions a default and acceleration? (This kind of clause is commonly called an *ipso facto clause*.) The current Bankruptcy Code refuses to rec-ognize this kind of ipso facto clause in the case of a reorganizing debtor[32] (and, as we shall see in Chapters 4 and 5, in the case of assets and executory contracts as well). In justifying this, the Senate report explains that this result should cause no consternation: "The holder of a claim or interest who under the plan is restored to his original position, when others receive less or get nothing at all, is fortunate indeed and has no cause to complain."[33] This comment is apparently premised on the un-stated view that bankruptcy is a fortuitous event allowing the lender to

---

30. This view of reorganization is set out more fully in Chapter 9.

31. *In re* Milton L. Ehrlich, Inc., 5 N.Y.2d 275, 157 N.E.2d 495 (1959). See Restatement (Second) of Contracts, §318, illustration 8 (1981).

32. Section 1124(2)(A) permits reinstatement notwithstanding an ipso facto clause.

33. S. Rep. No. 989, 95th Cong., 2d Sess. 120 (1978).

achieve a windfall by accelerating a debt that has a below-market interest rate.[34]

This justification, however, is unsatisfying. It is inaccurate to say that reinstatement of the maturity of a loan is all that a lender is entitled to since it was but a fortuity (for the lender) that its debtor went into bankruptcy. This is a fortuitous event that the lender seems to have bargained for. In essence, one can view the lender as having contracted for an option to call in its respective loan and to reloan the resulting money at the then-market rate.[35] One can also view the lender, moreover, as having already paid for this option (just as a secured lender, for example, has paid for other entitlements that are recognized in bankruptcy). Dismissing the potential rights of a lender by referring to them as "windfalls," then, obscures analysis. The relevant question is whether the presence of an ipso facto clause can be justified, and, if justified, whether such a clause is worth the inevitable strategic costs it creates.

Why might a lender desire an ipso facto clause? The most promising justification seems to be one that views such clauses as serving a role akin to a range of other contractual covenants.[36] The usefulness of such covenants (often called *financial covenant* or *restrictive covenant* clauses) in loans or other contracts is commonly perceived as one of policing.[37] After entering into a loan or a contract at a certain interest rate, a debtor has an incentive to engage in activities that unilaterally increase the riskiness of the loan—by, for example, changing investment decisions to include riskier choices.[38] Financial covenant clauses may be designed to allow a

34. See, e.g., Fogel, "Executory Contracts and Unexpired Leases in the Bankruptcy Code," 64 *Minn. L. Rev.* 341, 349 (1980) (making that argument in the context of executory contracts).

35. For an accessible introduction to options and their uses, see Black, "Fact and Fantasy in the Use of Options," 31 *Fin. Analysts J.* 36 (July–Aug. 1975). For an analysis of corporate liabilities as options, see Black & Scholes, "The Pricing of Options and Corporate Liabilities," 81 *J. Pol. Econ.* 637 (1973).

36. Other explanations seem less promising. One might imagine that such a clause is designed either to provide a creditor with some measure of protection against a debtor's nonsystematic, non-misbehavior-induced risk or to provide a creditor with an opportunity to reevaluate a contract to account for systematic market changes. Neither of these reasons, however, seems convincing in light of other available means for achieving the same goal that would not cause the strategic bankruptcy incentive disadvantages of an ipso facto clause. Nonsystematic risks (other than of the misbehavior sort) can be handled through diversification, and systematic risks can be dealt with equivalently by a shortening of the term of the loan.

37. See, e.g., R. Brealey & S. Myers, *Principles of Corporate Finance* 389–93 (1981); Smith & Warner, "On Financial Contracting: An Analysis of Bond Covenants," 7 *J. Fin. Econ.* 117 (1979).

38. See, e.g., R. Posner, *Economic Analysis of Law* 293–94 (2d ed. 1979); Jensen & Meck-

creditor to police this species of misbehavior by giving the lender the option of calling in the loan if such opportunistic behavior occurs.[39]

An ipso facto clause might be present in a given contract precisely because it serves such a policing role. To be sure, it does not allow a creditor to say "because you have misbehaved, I am terminating the loan," because it identifies no misbehavior. The contract or loan may be terminated only *after* the debtor has gone into bankruptcy. As such, it may serve as a broad-brush *in terrorem* clause designed to deter misbehavior in general by imposing a cost on the debtor who resorts to bankruptcy and hence imposing a cost on engaging in activities that increase the likelihood of bankruptcy.

The problem with this analysis is that it assumes that the debtor bears the costs of this clause. An aspect of the problem of diverse ownership, however, exists here. These clauses would have an effect on a reorganization (where acceleration is not the order of the day) and might harm the remaining unsecured creditors by requiring them to pay for a (secured) claim at its face amount instead of its unaccelerated present value worth. The group that is likely to bear the costs of this clause in bankruptcy, accordingly, is not the debtor (or its shareholders) but the other creditors. Thus, the debtor may have no particular incentive in negotiating loans to exclude such clauses,[40] and other creditors may have no effective way of forcing the debtor to exclude them.[41] It may be

---

ling, "Theory of the Firm: Managerial Behavior, Agency Costs and Ownership Structure," 3 *J. Fin. Econ.* 305, 334–37 (1976).

39. Miller, "The Wealth Transfers of Bankruptcy: Some Illustrative Examples," 41 *Law & Contemp. Probs.* 39, 43 (Autumn 1977). This is not to say that such financial covenant clauses necessarily reduce the *costs* of policing. Rather, they have an *in terrorem* effect by saying that *if* a debtor is caught misbehaving, there will be certain costly consequences.

40. This is a species of opportunism. See generally O. Williamson, *Markets and Hierarchies* (1975); Levmore, "Monitors and Freeriders in Commercial and Corporate Settings," 92 *Yale L.J.* 49 (1982); Jensen & Meckling, "Theory of the Firm: Managerial Behavior, Agency Costs and Ownership Structure," 3 *J. Fin. Econ.* 305, 334–37 (1976). Both parties (and particularly the debtor), of course, may be deterred from doing this because of reputational concerns, See Leff, "Injury, Ignorance and Spite—The Dynamics of Coercive Collection," 80 *Yale L.J.* 1, 25–36 (1970).

41. This latter point is tricky. If their inclusion harms other creditors, one might think that the other creditors would require the debtor not to agree to ipso facto clauses. See Jackson, "Bankruptcy, Non-Bankruptcy Entitlements, and the Creditors' Bargain," 91 *Yale L.J.* 857, 889 n.147 (1982). But no one creditor might think it worth its while to negotiate such an exclusion, if the costs of monitoring would be borne by it but the benefits of exclusion would inure to the class of unsecured creditors. Moreover, such a clause, if included, might be hard to enforce (in bankruptcy, it would have little value). Thus, it is possible to believe that banning ipso facto clauses would be in the interests of the creditors as a group, and that they would not be consensually banned. Creditors would, then,

preferable, therefore, to refuse to recognize clauses negotiated by the debtor whose impact will be felt almost exclusively by other creditors, notwithstanding their possible prophylactic role, because they have effect only upon insolvency (or similar occurrence). In that case other monitoring clauses, the effects of which might be felt by the debtor, could be used instead.[42]

Ipso facto clauses, in other words, may reflect the type of rights that bankruptcy law is justified in ignoring because they may be destructive of the collective weal in bankruptcy. That rationale, however, extends only to a ban on ipso facto clauses. In addition to the general rule for unmatured loans and the problem of contracting around the general rule, we still have to consider a third aspect of acceleration. If the debtor has defaulted on the loan prior to bankruptcy, is reinstatement of that loan proper? Again, the inquiry is fueled, as a positive matter, by section 1124, which provides that reinstatement is permissible if the defaults are cured. The normative question, however, is whether this outcome is proper.

Viewed from the perspective of nonbankruptcy attributes, the answer would appear at first to be no. Absent some grace period in the loan contract or applicable law itself, a lender, following a material breach, usually has the power of acceleration and is free to ignore "cure" offers by the debtor. Mirroring this nonbankruptcy attribute in bankruptcy, accordingly, would seem to call for loss of the power of reinstatement under section 1124 if there was a prebankruptcy default, unless the contract or applicable law provided for a cure period that had not yet expired on the date of bankruptcy.

We are not ready to complete the analysis of the question of the effect of prebankruptcy defaults, however. In a world in which neither the debtor nor its creditors saw bankruptcy (or insolvency) coming—our current operating assumption—we could rely on the nonbankruptcy attributes just identified. But relaxing that assumption, we will see that a debtor might default for two (related) reasons that bankruptcy law may properly be concerned with: a default occasioned so as to favor the creditor (by permitting it to accelerate a loan before the occurrence of bankruptcy) or a default occasioned by a debtor's realization that it was insolvent and did not care who received its carcass. For this reason a full

---

presumably simply *charge* for this risk (like innumerable other risks). But that increases the debtor's cost of credit. A debtor might be better off if it could precommit to not entering into ipso facto clauses. A legal ban on them provides that result.

42. There are alternatives, although perhaps not perfect substitutes. See previous discussion.

examination of the question of what effect a prebankruptcy default should have on the power of reinstatement in section 1124 must be deferred until Chapter 6, where planning in the immediate prebankruptcy period is examined.

Special Aspects of Claims That Are Not Fixed at the Time of Bankruptcy. Another important aspect of the translation problem surrounding liabilities concerns the question of fixing nominal values where the values of claims are not already fixed in the nonbankruptcy forum. Setting the value of these unliquidated claims may be both costly and time-consuming.[43] To determine whether someone has a successful antitrust claim against the debtor, for example, may take several years as a matter of nonbankruptcy law, and even more time may then be needed to place a nominal value on that claim. The whole procedure, moreover, may cost hundreds of thousands of dollars.

Does the principle that bankruptcy law derives valuations from nonbankruptcy law require adherence to these nonbankruptcy valuation procedures? Consider the case of a debtor that is liquidating in bankruptcy. It would, of course, be possible to follow nonbankruptcy procedures by deferring disposition of the debtor's assets (or their proceeds) to any group that would share at or below the level of priority accorded the entity with the unliquidated claim. The claim could then be liquidated in ordinary ways. Such a procedure would be workable, although cumbersome, as some mechanism must be introduced to keep track of the various other claimants so that they, finally, could be paid whenever all prior or equal claims had been liquidated.[44]

This process could even be formalized to make it easier for liquidated claimants to cash out at any time. All liquidated claimants (other than those, such as secured creditors, who could safely be cashed out today) could, for example, be given shares against the pool of assets (or their proceeds). These shares, together with those issued to other claimants as their claims became liquidated, would be cashed out after all unliquidated claims had been determined. How much each claimant would ultimately get would depend on (1) the nominal size of its claim (as determined by the number of shares) versus the other claims in the pool, and (2) the relative priority of those shares vis-à-vis the shares held by other claimants. If any claimant wished to cash out before that ultimate

43. For the sake of brevity I will refer to the various types of claims identified by §101(4) as *unliquidated claims.*

44. There would also be a question of whether anyone representing the debtor would have the proper incentives to resist the assertion of a claim.

distribution, it could sell its shares in a secondary market for a price that reflected the expected payout in the ultimate distribution.

This solution, however, may give undue deference to nonbankruptcy valuation procedures. These procedures, even if they make sense when claims will be paid in full, may make little sense when the resulting claim will receive only ten cents on the dollar, as will often be the case in bankruptcy. The relatively fixed costs (such as attorneys' fees) associated with nonbankruptcy claim liquidation procedures may loom unduly large when translated into the bankruptcy forum. It may be in the interests of all the claimants to expedite the process and thereby scale down its costs. For that reason a bankruptcy system might legitimately adopt its own procedures for estimating the expected value of a claim if successful and the probability of its success. Although the normal nonbankruptcy trial procedures may be watered down or eliminated, as long as there is no bias in the direction of estimation, then there is no particular reason to think that the *value* of those nonbankruptcy procedural rights has been interfered with.[45]

This point is perhaps clearest in the case of unmatured claims, where the only needed adjustment (if any) is discounting to present value. In principle, however, the process is no different, or normatively less desirable, with respect to claims that are contingent, unliquidated, or disputed. As such, these estimation procedures would be another instance where a nonbankruptcy right was supplanted in bankruptcy but where the value of that right would be protected. Aside from problems relating to commencement of a bankruptcy case simply to gain access to these

45. Since this *does* involve a rule change, it might create incentives to use bankruptcy for reasons other than a common pool problem (although it will often simply lower the costs to the group, adding to the size of the pie). For example, it may be in the interest of a litigant to use bankruptcy to lower the cost of litigation, although predicting *when* is difficult. See R. Posner, *Economic Analysis of Law* 445–54 (2d ed. 1977). This is an application of the inevitable: because *some* of bankruptcy's rules (substantive or procedural) will be different from nonbankruptcy rules, the bankruptcy system inevitably is going to create incentives to use it for the wrong reasons. When they occur, they can be ameliorated by other features of bankruptcy law, such as restrictions on commencement of a case (see Chapter 8). But the basic point is that one should be sensitive to rule changes in bankruptcy because of this tendency. Some changes (such as the one discussed in text) may still be worth making, but others will not be. There is one further consideration: the debtor that would be insolvent only if nonbankruptcy litigation costs are borne but would be solvent if it could take advantage of bankruptcy's streamlined procedures. (It is conceivable that this was the status of Manville Corp. in 1982.) Is resort to bankruptcy in this case proper? Although it would seem to require a rule change in bankruptcy, the answer nevertheless seems to be "yes": without the use of bankruptcy, there is insolvency and a resulting common pool problem.

valuation procedures, which will be discussed in Chapter 8, the problems with this procedure stem less from the theoretical nature of the valuation process than from the practical (and perhaps constitutional) problems that arise from having such determinations made by a judge in the absence of full-blown trial procedures. Estimating values does not improperly extend bankruptcy law to nonbankruptcy areas as long as there is no reason to think that the estimation process is systematically skewed in one direction or another.[46]

What is improper, however, is what was done in *Bittner v. Borne Chemical Co.*[47] In *Bittner* the shareholders of The Roflite Company had brought a tortious interference counterclaim against the debtor, Borne Chemical Co. Borne Chemical then filed for bankruptcy. The bankruptcy judge valued the claim at zero for purposes of the bankruptcy proceeding. In part the consequences of this decision were ameliorated by his requirement that the claim be reconsidered if a state court ever decided in favor of the Roflite shareholders on the counterclaim. In this way their ultimate payment probably would not be seriously jeopardized.[48] There are other consequences to valuing claims, however, such as voting on a plan of reorganization, and the decision clearly affected them. The Third Circuit affirmed, noting that, according to the bankruptcy judge's finding of fact, the Roflite shareholders' "chances of ultimately succeeding in the state court action are uncertain at best." The Third Circuit went on to say:

> Yet, if the court had valued the Roflite stockholders' claims according to the present probability of success, the Roflite stockholders might well have acquired a significant, if not controlling, voice in the reorganization proceedings . . . By valuing the ultimate merits of the Roflite stockholders'

46. There are reasons, however, to think that bankruptcy judges may be biased in favor of assisting those who are identified and whose claims are established. See Blum, "The Law and Language of Corporate Reorganizations," 17 *U. Chi. L. Rev.* 565 (1950); see also R. Nisbett & L. Ross, *Human Inference: Strategies and Shortcomings of Social Judgment* 43–62 (1980) (cognitive processes tend to lead us to overemphasize what is most "vivid"). We will see this bias in another context in Chapter 9. This tension may not be one that is unique to bankruptcy. Dissolution under state law requires that assets be set aside for claims that are not liquidated—see, e.g., Calif. Corp. Code, §1905(2)—and the same problem of estimating unliquidated claims is likely to arise there as well.

47. 691 F.2d 134 (3d Cir. 1982).

48. The bankruptcy judge also required Borne Chemical, a debtor in a corporate reorganization (where claims *are* discharged following the reorganization, §1141), to waive discharge of the Roflite shareholders' claim. Presumably this meant that, if the Roflite shareholders subsequently won on their counterclaim, they would be treated along with the other unsecured creditors—probably by having stock issued to them, thereby diluting the postbankruptcy ownership of the remaining prebankruptcy unsecured creditors.

claims at zero, and temporarily disallowing them until the final resolution of the state action, the bankruptcy court avoided the possibility of a protracted and inequitable reorganization proceeding while ensuring that Borne will be responsible to pay a dividend on the claims in the event that the state court decides in the Roflite stockholders' favor.[49]

This reasoning, however, does skew nonbankruptcy values. It is based on valuing a disputed and unliquidated claim below the "present probability of success" to make sure that too much voice is not given to a claimant who indeed might be found later not to have a claim at all. The present probability of success, however, already discounts that voice. After all, there is another side to the story. If the claim *is* later established, a claim estimated today at its present probability of success is undervalued.[50] The only solution that ensures that, on average, the vote of such claimants is neither too large nor too small is estimating the nominal value of the claim, taking into account the chance of success. If it is not desirable to wait until all events have run their natural course (and there are costs to doing so), bankruptcy law must establish estimation procedures. But nothing in bankruptcy law justifies a deliberate attempt to ignore proper valuations in these procedures.

The point can be extended in considering the bankruptcy petitions of asbestos manufacturers like Manville Corp. and UNR Industries, whose

---

49. 691 F.2d, at 137.

50. This valuation fallacy was reflected in the proposal of the Commission on Bankruptcy Laws of the United States to allow excluded classes to participate in a reorganization if, at the time of a "second look," the enterprise had done better than expected. See Report of the Commission on the Bankruptcy Laws of the United States (pt. 2), H.R. Doc. No. 137, 93d Cong., 1st Sess. 241 (1973) (setting forth §7-303[3] of the proposed Bankruptcy Act of 1973); see also Rochelle & Balzersen, "Recommendations for Amendments to Chapter X," 46 *Am. Bankr. L.J.* 93, 99–102 (1972) (proposing a similar "second look" rule). Such proposals are sharply and cogently criticized, generally on the same grounds as developed in text, in Spitzer v. Stichman (*In re* Hudson & M.R.R.), 278 F.2d 109, 410 (2d Cir. 1960); Brudney, "The Bankruptcy Commission's Proposed 'Modifications' of the Absolute Priority Rule," 48 *Am. Bankr. L.J.* 305, 331–35 (1974); Note "The Proposed Bankruptcy Act: Changes in the Absolute Priority Rule for Corporate Reorganizations," 87 *Harv. L. Rev.* 1786, 1811–16 (1974). The decision in *Bittner* might possibly be justified on another ground by a focus on nonbankruptcy attributes. It may be that the claim is entitled to no say in the deployment question until it "ripens"—i.e., upon judgment. In a dissolution of a corporation, for example, no provision may need be made for a claim unless and until it would have to be accounted for on the firm's financials. See Cal. Corp. Code §§114, 1807(d), 1808(a)(1). If so, it may be proper in a reorganization to provide for the possible claim in terms of payment but not give its holder a voice in the reorganization. This provision may most accurately mirror nonbankruptcy entitlements. But the justification is not then one of "too much voice" in the abstract but an attempt to mirror nonbankruptcy attributes.

legal position has been the source of much academic and public interest since the early 1980s.[51] At the core of the debate is the status of "future" asbestos victims. These are people who have had contact with asbestos in the past, but who, as of the date of the relevant bankruptcy petition, had not yet manifested any injury. From the perspective of nominal values, these "nonmanifested" victims are best understood as "creditors" holding existing "claims" because their future causes of action under state law have a present value today under the applicable nonbankruptcy law.[52] These tort claims, moreover, "arose" before the filing of the bankruptcy petition because they are based on past completed actions of the debtor. If the debtor were to cease doing business on the filing of the bankruptcy petition, that fact would not influence the likelihood that the claimants would eventually exhibit the signs of an asbestos-related disease attributable to the debtor's product. The company's future survival is irrelevant to whether or not the disease or injury manifests itself; it is relevant only to the issue of payment

That there has been a debate, however, is largely due to a confusion of the role of nonbankruptcy law. Although it properly gives content to words in the Bankruptcy Code such as *claim* or *arose* that delimit those entitled to participate in bankruptcy's collective proceeding, there is no particular reason to think that one should resort to nonbankruptcy law

51. See generally Roe, "Bankruptcy and Tort," 84 *Colum. L. Rev.* 846 (1984); Note, "Mass Tort Claims and the Corporate Tortfeasor: Bankruptcy Reorganization and Legislative Compensation Versus the Common-Law Tort System," 61 *Tex. L. Rev.* 1297 (1983); Note, "The Manville Bankruptcy: Treating Mass Tort Claims in Chapter 11 Proceedings," 96 *Harv. L. Rev.* 1121 (1983).

52. To say that, as a matter of normative theory, these claims should be dealt with in bankruptcy is not to suggest that the practical problems are not themselves tremendously difficult. See *In re* UNR Industries, Inc., 725 F.2d 1111 (7th Cir. 1984) (Posner, J.); sources cited supra note 51. In examining the issue of what claims should be dealt with in bankruptcy, moreover, one must focus on the question of value under the appropriate nonbankruptcy analogy. For example, another group of tort claimants would appear to be prepetition under the analysis in text: those who, after the date the debtor filed for bankruptcy, first came into contact with asbestos products manufactured and sold prior to the debtor's bankruptcy filing (such as contact with asbestos ceiling tiles in schools). For the reasons that will be explored in text, however, if these victims would receive nothing in a state-law dissolution—because, for example, reserves would not have to be set aside for them, cf. Cal. Corp. Code §§114, 1807(d), 1808(a)(1)—mimicking the nearest nonbankruptcy analogy may call for their exclusion as prepetition claims in bankruptcy. Their status would then be that of postpetition claims, if the debtor has a postpetition existence. This treatment may skew the optimal decision between continuation and piecemeal liquidation (for the reasons explored in text), but, if so, the skew comes from nonbankruptcy law, where it also exists. This general subject is explored in greater detail in Chapter 7 in conjunction with Reading Co. v. Brown, 391 U.S. 471 (1968).

to define those words.[53] To be sure, courts must resort to nonbankruptcy law to determine who is entitled to participate in the distribution of assets, but nothing in this process suggests that one also must look at what state law *calls* some asserted claim. Doing so would confuse attributes (where nonbankruptcy rules play a crucial role) with labels (where nonbankruptcy rules should play no role). In the contested issue in the bankruptcies of Manville and UNR, for example, the attributes are (1) whether the right being asserted, based on an asbestos-related tort, is cognizable under state law (it is); (2) whether such a cause of action has some value at the time of the bankruptcy proceeding (it does, if it is not barred by the statute of limitations)[54]; and (3) whether such a cause of action arises out of the past of the debtor (it does). If those attributes are present, then the person is—and should be—a creditor holding a claim within the meaning of the Bankruptcy Code. How state law chooses to label those attributes (for any number of a variety of nonbankruptcy reasons) is of no moment.[55]

This is not, however, simply a semantic matter. The failure to include the nonmanifested tort victims as creditors holding claims would almost certainly disrupt the nonbankruptcy relative values of those with rights against a debtor's assets. This, in turn, may result in the wrong decision as to what to do with the assets. Consider the following scenario. You are the president and major shareholder of a company that, according to a recent report you have just received, has claims (used in the broadest sense) outstanding (i.e., based on the company's past activities) against it with a present value of $4 billion. Included in this figure are future tort claims with a present value of approximately $2 billion; although you do not know who will bring them, an actuarial estimate has been

53. Most courts to date have looked to state-law labels. See *In re* UNR Industries, 29 Bankr. 741 (N.D. Ill. 1983); *In re* Amatex Corp., 30 Bankr. 309 (Bankr. E.D. Pa.), *aff'd,* 27 Bankr. 613 (E.D. Pa. 1983), *rev.,* 755 F.2d 1034 (3d Cir. 1985); *In re* Gladding Corp., 20 Bankr. 566 (Bankr. D. Mass. 1982).

54. In some states the statute of limitations may begin running upon inhalation and not be tolled. See, e.g., Steinhardt v. Johns-Manville Corp., 54 N.Y.2d 1008, 430 N.E.2d 1297, 446 N.Y.S.2d 244 (1981).

55. The Seventh Circuit noted that in some states these unascertained asbestos victims have claims as defined by state law, while in other states they do not, *In re* UNR Industries, Inc., 725 F.2d 1111 (7th Cir. 1984). It is unlikely that there are any differences, however, in the way these victims would be treated for purposes of state law, since these labels almost certainly derive from different ways of framing a statute of limitations postponement issue. If so, it would be inappropriate to have different bankruptcy treatment simply because of divergent state labels. Differences in substantive treatment upon a state-law dissolution would, however, matter. See supra note 52.

made as to the number of suits that will be brought along with an estimate as to the average recovery per suit. Also included are present tort claimants—those who already filed suit—and trade creditors, banks, and so forth. For present purposes, to keep it simple (and because it ultimately does not make any difference), assume that your company has no secured debt.

You also have a report that the company has assets that are worth about $1.5 billion if sold off piece by piece and about $2 billion if kept together in the current business. The figure of $1.5 billion reflects what buyers would pay for individual assets of your company and represents their valuation of what those individual assets would bring to them over time. The $2 billion figure is calculated the same way; the only difference is that it is generated by determining what it is worth to keep those assets together, doing what they are now doing.[56] It represents, for example, the buyer's (or the market's) prediction that the assets can generate $250 million of income (adjusted for inflation) in perpetuity. The $250 million is net after future operating expenses like wages, supplies, and taxes. It is like an annuity, except that it is, of course, riskier, which means that it will be valued for less than a riskless annuity that generated $250 million a year. This $2 billion figure, then, means that people would not pay more than $2 billion for the right to capture your company's future income stream—this $250 million a year—even if there were *no* claims against the assets at the time they were bought.

There *are* claims against your company, however. In fact, there are so many claims that the company is insolvent in the following sense. It might be able to generate the cash to pay off claims as they arise for the present, but ultimately the company's assets are not expected to generate more than $2 billion in present-day cash. Its liabilities, moreover, have a present-day value of $4 billion. However its assets are used, then, your company is expected to eventually run out of money (and out of business).

Today you have received the report showing $2 billion in nonmanifested but statistically likely tort claims. Tomorrow your accountants will require you to disclose that fact on your company's financial reports.[57] Even though you, as a principal shareholder, might prefer to postpone dealing with the situation,[58] the result of this disclosure is likely to ac-

---

56. See, e.g., 1 A. Dewing, *The Financial Policy of Corporations* 295–96 (5th ed. 1953).

57. Statement of Financial Accounting Standards ¶5; FASB C59.105; FASB Interpretation No. 14; see generally J. Burton, R. Palmer, & R. Kay, *Handbook of Accounting and Auditing* ch. 29 (1981).

58. See Baird & Jackson, "Corporate Reorganizations and the Treatment of Diverse

celerate the actions of others. The consequences of a system of individual grab remedies is likely to undermine any attempt to continue business as usual. Creditors such as banks that have the option to call in their money are likely to do so now, while they still can be paid in full. To finance this withdrawal of capital, assets will eventually have to be sold. The release of the information, in other words, may make your company a prime candidate for a bankruptcy proceeding (although who is going to file the petition that starts the case is a problem).

What are your options? You can try to dissolve the company under state law and sell off its assets piece by piece. This will bring $1.5 billion. Your company's claimants will satisfy themselves against this, and they will have no one else to go after (as the tort doctrine of successor liability almost certainly will not apply to the person who buys one drill press from your company). Your company will, in essence, dispose of $4 billion of claims with $1.5 billion in assets. That is a fundamental attribute of the concept of corporations as entities with liabilities limited by their assets. As for who gets the money, it is a question of nonbankruptcy law (as no bankruptcy proceeding has been commenced). Often, as a matter of state law, a dissolving corporation must establish reserves for non-accrued claims—at least if they must be shown on its balance sheet.[59] These claims probably would, and therefore the $4 billion in claimants presumably share the $1.5 billion in assets.

There is, however, a better outcome for the group. If some way can be found to keep the company's assets together, to maintain the business as a going concern freed of these existing liabilities, the creditors will then receive $2 billion in cash. This could be accomplished by a sale of the company to a conglomerate like Allied Chemical or to Carl Icahn or to the public for $2 billion, *if* it could be sold free of claims arising out of its past. (The company could also be reorganized—which, as Chapter 9 will explore, means, in essence, to sell the company to the claimants.)

This, however, assumes that your company can dispense with the tort claims arising out of its past but that have not yet manifested themselves. If it cannot, and given that such "future" claims have a present value of $2 billion, no one will pay anything for your company's assets, except to the extent that they can milk them first (using the ubiquitous grab law) or to the extent that they can establish priority over the tort claimants

Ownership Interests: A Comment on Adequate Protection of Secured Creditors in Bankruptcy," 51 *U. Chi. L. Rev.* 97 (1984).

59. These dissolution rules seem to assume solvent corporations.

by imposing a capital structure with senior debt in it. Prospective buyers might calculate that through devices such as these they can preserve $1 billion (present value) of the assets for themselves. Aside from losses in value owing to the milking, this means that they calculate that $1 billion will go to the "future" tort claimants.[60]

Under this scenario the situation looks fairly good for the group of creditors: we have garnered for them $2 billion—$1 billion from the sale and $1 billion that they will be expected to get from the company that has been sold.[61] But here the question of whether nonmanifested tort victims have claims cognizable in bankruptcy cuts in. If one cannot eliminate these nonmanifested claims either by dissolving under state law (because other creditors must share with them in the assets) or by a going-concern sale outside of bankruptcy (because of successor liability), a holding that says such tort victims do not hold prepetition claims in bankruptcy gives the other creditors a golden opportunity: the other creditors can run the company through bankruptcy before dissolving it under state law. Under section 726, only holders of claims are entitled to participate in the bankruptcy distribution.[62] Thus, when the company is sold for scrap in bankruptcy, the "existing" creditors get $1.5 billion to split among their $2 billion in claims. The company then leaves bankruptcy. Nothing is discharged (because liquidating corporations do not receive discharges in bankruptcy).[63] The nonmanifested tort claimants are still around and, as their claims mature, they can still sue your company. But it has no assets, having been stripped of them in bankruptcy. The company *now* dissolves under state law, and the tort claimants are finished. There is no one to sue. They, in essence, have been sold down the river with zero.

This is not simply a distributional problem. For our purposes the problem is that of a common pool. Such an outcome is bad for the creditors taken as a group because they get $1.5 billion instead of $2 billion. But the present creditors have an incentive to fight for it because they would get the entire $1.5 billion themselves.[64] In this way individual

60. The figure may be somewhat less than $1 billion if there is a subsequent piecemeal breakup of the company at a time when it continues to be worth more held together. The numbers in text ignore this complication, which would not affect the ultimate point.

61. Who gets the $1 billion from the sale is, of course, a matter of nonbankruptcy law.

62. Section 726(a)(1) through (4) all make reference to the *payment of claims*. Subsection (a)(5) covers interest on claims, and (a)(6) covers return of the residual to the debtor.

63. §727(a)(1).

64. *Wall Street Journal,* January 31, 1984, p. 1 (attorney for existing tort victims suggests liquidation, as his group would be paid in full).

greed can subvert the common welfare, precisely the problem that bankruptcy law is designed to ameliorate.

Can the "existing" creditors in this hypothetical do even better and capture the entire $2 billion for themselves by selling the company as a going concern for $2 billion *and* excluding the nonmanifested tort claimants from distribution? If so, it would be a distributional problem, not a common pool problem. But it is hard to see how the existing creditors could do this. They cannot as a matter of tort law, because of the doctrine of successor liability.[65] As for using bankruptcy, if the nonmanifested tort claimants are not included in the bankruptcy process because it is determined that they are not creditors holding claims, their rights will not be discharged in bankruptcy either. Any buyer will take the assets subject to their claims (either in a reorganization or through the tort doctrine of successor liability).

This means that the buyer will not pay $2 billion for the assets, but (under our assumed facts) only $1 billion. And having excluded the nonmanifested claimants from bankruptcy, other creditors will not want to divide the $1 billion they can get by selling the company as a unit. They, after all, can get $1.5 billion by selling the company in bankruptcy, piecemeal. This means that the best the "existing" creditors can do is to sell the company for scrap. As we have seen, however, that is the wrong solution. By excluding nonmanifested tort victims from the category of creditors holding prepetition claims, we have created an incentive for the known group to reach for the wrong-size pie. It is the group, moreover, that presumably decides what to do with the assets.[66]

The preferable solution here is to *include* the nonmanifested tort victims in the bankruptcy process as holders of claims, so they get to share in the assets, but then to sell the assets free of all such claims for $2 billion.[67] We want, again, to make the asset "pie" as large as possible and

---

65. For a brief look at this doctrine, see Jackson, supra note 23.

66. One could judicially take away this power and require the assets to be sold as a unit. In that case the right deployment question could be reached without holding that nonmanifested tort victims held claims. This solution, however, seems alien to the current structure of the Bankruptcy Code.

67. To sell the assets free of the claims might seem to ignore the nonbankruptcy doctrine of successor liability. For an argument why ignoring that doctrine might be proper in a context where the tort victims are being provided for, see Jackson, supra note 23, at 94–97. Cf. §363(f)(4), (5). Alternatively, one could respect the successor liability doctrine by including the nonmanifested tort claimants in the bankruptcy proceeding but limit them to pursuit of the assets that are sold. See §1141(a), (c), (d). The proceeds from the sale of those assets would go to the remaining claimants. For a discussion of what to do with the

avoid wrong-size outcomes that result from fights about how to divide it. This is done by respecting the nonbankruptcy valuations, not changing them because of a nonbankruptcy label of "no claim."[68]

Analytically, exactly the same type of problem arose in *Ohio v. Kovacs*[69] where the issue was whether a toxic waste clean-up order was dischargeable in bankruptcy. The issue had bite because the debtor was an individual, and a finding of nondischargeability would mean that the state could pursue the debtor's future income following bankruptcy. But the State of Ohio argued for that result by asserting that the clean-up order was not a claim (as only liabilities on claims are discharged in bankruptcy). Its technical argument was that this was an "equitable right of performance" and not within the definition of *claim* in section 101(4).[70]

Focusing on labels, not attributes, is not the way to get a bankruptcy issue decided correctly. The Supreme Court, in holding that under the particular facts of *Kovacs* the clean-up order was a claim,[71] saved Ohio from itself. As Justice O'Connor sketched in her concurrence,[72] Ohio's argument was perverse. If Ohio were right, when it faced enforcing a clean-up order against a corporate polluter in bankruptcy, it might have talked itself out of any share of the assets at all. In a chapter 7 liquidation proceeding, after the assets are sold the proceeds are distributed first to recognized property claimants and then as specified in section 726 of

---

pool of money for nonmanifested tort claimants, see Roe, supra note 51; Rosenberg, "The Causal Connection in Mass Exposure Cases: A 'Public Law' Vision of the Tort System," 97 *Harv. L. Rev.* 849 (1984).

68. This example also illustrates why it is important to separate the asset deploymet question from the distribution question. In mid-1985 Manville announced a plan whereby it would set aside a pool of assets for asbestosis victims, including approximately 50 percent of the common stock in the company. It was reported that the unanimous opinion was that this meant Manville's filing was a "landmark blunder," because its shareholders had to give up more than half their stock (*N.Y. Times*, Aug. 3, 1985, p. 1). But viewed from the perspective of the owners as a group (creditors as well as shareholders), the fact that the shareholders must give up their stock is simply a result of a nonbankruptcy distributional decision (creditors come ahead of shareholders). If Manville was insolvent, its filing was not a blunder from the perspective of the owners as a group. It was a mistake, perhaps, from the perspective of the shareholders, but only if they could have continued to pay themselves dividends or otherwise delay. That, however, even if true, seems to be an incomplete focus.

69. 105 S.Ct. 705 (1985).

70. The relevant portion of §101(4) reads: "right to an equitable remedy for breach of performance if such breach gives rise to a right to payment, whether or not such right to an equitable remedy is reduced to judgment, fixed, contingent, matured, unmatured, disputed, undisputed, secured, or unsecured."

71. 105 S.Ct., at 710–11.

72. Id., at 712. See also Baird & Jackson, "*Kovacs* and Toxic Wastes in Bankruptcy," 36 *Stan. L. Rev.* 1199 (1984).

the Bankruptcy Code. Section 726, however, speaks only of payments on claims and makes no distinction based on whether the debtor is an individual or a corporation. If the assertion were correct that Kovacs' obligation to Ohio was not a claim, the general creditors of a corporate polluter would share in the proceeds in a bankruptcy liquidation. Ohio would receive nothing, as under its own argument it did not hold a claim. Corporations receive no discharge in chapter 7, but it makes no difference whether they do or not. After the bankruptcy distribution the obligation of a corporate debtor to clean up a toxic waste site would not be enforceable as a practical matter because the debtor would have no assets. In any event the obligation would disappear when the corporation dissolved under state law, after the bankruptcy proceeding.

This clearly upsets the relative nonbankruptcy entitlements of the various parties in interest. Had the corporate debtor dissolved under state law without resorting to bankruptcy, Ohio would have received its share of the debtor's assets on account of the debtor's obligation to clean up the toxic waste site. Bankruptcy law should not be interpreted to upset such state entitlements. But lacking a firm focus of the normative implications of bankruptcy theory, Ohio lost sight of the fact that what was in question was the relative entitlements of the various parties and painted itself into a legal corner from which the Supreme Court had to extricate it.

What, then, does one do with the argument that an obligation to clean up toxic wastes is neither "a right to payment" nor "an equitable remedy for breach of performance," breach of which gives rise to a right to payment? In the interpretation of these phrases there is a distinction that makes sense and that can be used to infuse the meaning of the somewhat inartful definition of *claim*. Excluding some forms of equitable relief from the definition of claim makes sense if one considers its role, together with section 101(9), as one of distinguishing two kinds of obligations: those obligations of a debtor that result from activities engaged in before the filing of the petition and whose consequences *continue* to exist even if the debtor were to go out of business or die the moment that the bankruptcy petition is filed, and those obligations that arise because of the debtor's continued existence and that would not arise if the debtor were to cease operations or die.

So viewed, an order to clean up toxic wastes that already have been deposited would be a claim because the remedy arises out of a prepetition action by the debtor the consequences of which do not depend on the debtor's continued existence. By contrast, an injunction to cease polluting would not be a prepetition claim within the meaning of the Bankruptcy

Code because it is directed at future operations. If the debtor ceases to exist, the injunction has no force because there will be no further pollution. Measured as of the date of bankruptcy, its value depends on something entirely within the debtor's control: having future operations. Thus it should have a zero value as of the date of bankruptcy. Concluding that it is not a prepetition claim accomplishes that.

The Bankruptcy Code, to be sure, does not always adhere to the collectivization norm. Indeed, the failure of an articulated normative theory of bankruptcy law perhaps makes remarkable the extent to which the "is" corresponds to the "ought" in the field of liabilities in bankruptcy. But the collectivization norm also provides a basis to criticize the statute that exists. The Bankruptcy Code's treatment of claims for damages arising out of long-term leases of real property or long-term employment contracts provides a fruitful example. Here the crux of the problem is in determining how to set the nominal value of the claim. In both these cases the Bankruptcy Code places a maximum on the claim's nominal value.[73] The rationales for such limitations, however, not only are unsatisfying on their own terms but, more important, they have nothing to do with the role of bankruptcy as a collective debt-collection device. Consider the claim of a landlord. Bankruptcy law limits a claim for damages resulting from breach of a lease. In cases where nominal damages, as calculated according to nonbankruptcy rules, exceed one year's reserved rent, the Bankruptcy Code sets a maximum on the landlord's nominal claim to 15 percent of the rent reserved for the remainder of the term or three years' reserved rent, whichever is less.[74] The justifications for this limitation appear to be twofold. First, it is asserted that otherwise the claim of a landlord might be "too large," with the consequence that full recognition would "prevent other general unsecured creditors from recovering a dividend."[75] Second, it is argued that permitting a landlord to assert its full claim would make the landlord the undeserving beneficiary of a speculative guess about the future course of real estate.[76]

73. §§502(b)(6), (b)(7).

74. §502(b)(6).

75. See H. Rep. No. 595, supra note 24, at 353 ("It is designed to compensate the landlord for his loss while not permitting a claim so large [based on a long-term lease] as to prevent other general unsecured creditors from recovering a dividend from the estate"). Increasing the nominal amount of one claim at the same level of other claims cannot, of course, prevent the remaining claimants from recovering anything; it can only affect the relative size of their recovery.

76. See Kuehner v. Irving Trust Co., 299 U.S. 445 (1937) (justifying result); Oldden v. Tonto Realty Co., 143 F.2d 916 (2d Cir. 1944) (same).

Neither justification is satisfactory on its own terms. The claims of landlords are determined according to standard contract expectancy formulas. If the nominal claim is large, it is only because the damages, calculated in ordinary ways, are large. Uncertainty about the future, moreover, does not necessarily favor a landlord. The nature of uncertainty is that things may end up better or worse than today's best guess.[77]

Thinking about claims determination in the light of the role of bankruptcy, moreover, reveals a second flaw in the reasoning that resulted in a limitation on a landlord's recovery. Even if either justification for limiting such claims *were* correct as a matter of abstract inquiry, bankruptcy is not the correct place to implement it. Claimants that are treated better outside of bankruptcy (because they are accorded larger nominal claims) are simply not equals in bankruptcy. They are like the holders of property rights that bankruptcy law generally recognizes without independently reexamining their abstract worthiness. For that reason, even though a state law (assuming it existed) that generally treated landlords relatively better than other claimants might be an inappropriate non-bankruptcy policy, recognition of that differential treatment nonetheless remains appropriate bankruptcy policy. Bankruptcy moves from the individual to the collective. If landlords do better in the nonbankruptcy regime, then they should do better in bankruptcy as well. Casting the issue as one of bankruptcy policy misstates what is at issue and creates incentives to use bankruptcy for reasons that may not be collectively optimal.

Determining How a Claimant Participates in Bankruptcy:
The Question of Relative Values

We have already looked at how the principle of taking entitlements from nonbankruptcy law accounts for the pro rata treatment in bankruptcy of those in a similar class. The principle also applies with regard to respecting the relative values of those in different nonbankruptcy classes. Consider the example of fish in the lake. With one hundred fishermen the optimal rule to deal with the common pool problem would be one that specified a maximum catch of $50,000 of fish a year, and that, assuming no relevant differences in the fishermen, divided up that catch into one hundred equal piles of $500 each this year and every subsequent

---

77. An argument based on temporal uncertainty is particularly unsatisfactory in light of other long-term contracts (such as installment sales or personal property leases) that are not covered by this restriction.

year. (This would be enforced, for example, by assigning to each fisherman a license to catch only a certain number of fish.)

Suppose that, in assigning entitlements initially to the one hundred fishermen, one fisherman was permitted to catch two times as many fish as any other fisherman—or the initial entitlement was allocated in a way that one fisherman was entitled to catch $20,000 of fish before the others were entitled to catch anything.[78] One may question whether such an initial assignment of entitlements would be wise, but that question is irrelevant to a common pool problem. Whatever the initial assignment of entitlements, there is still likely to be a common pool problem.

That this is so derives from the fact that the optimal solution for the group has not changed. The deployment question is distinct from the distributional question. The fishermen are still better off as a group if they catch $50,000 of fish this year, leaving fish to reproduce, so that there will be $50,000 of fish every year in the future. The fact that some fishermen do better than others as a matter of initial entitlements is irrelevant to this deployment outcome. (Indeed, if one fisherman came absolutely ahead of the others with respect to the entire catch, we would have our prototype of a sole owner, where we started.) If one fisherman is given an initial entitlement of catching twice as many fish as others, a person given the responsibility of solving the common pool problem could do so by issuing a permit to that fisherman to catch $1,000 of fish, while all others would be limited to $500. Similarly, if the initial entitlement to one fisherman was the ability to catch $20,000 of fish in priority to the others, the common pool problem could still be solved without upsetting the relative value of the initial entitlement by giving that fisherman the right to catch $20,000 of fish each year first and splitting the remaining $30,000 of permitted catch each year pro rata among the other ninety-nine fishermen.

Thus, the common pool problem—a deployment problem—can be solved without upsetting the relative values of the initial entitlements—a distributional problem. When considering credit, moreover, a collective rule that respects the relative values of the initial entitlements is preferable to any other rule. No other rule in bankruptcy could solve the resulting common pool problem without inviting the use of bankruptcy simply for purposes of effecting rule changes.[79]

---

78. The examples are inspired by a correspondence I had with Vern Countryman regarding the fishing common pool example set forth in Chapter 1. A fisherman (which I am not), he responded: "I don't believe you could get all fishermen to agree to a limit if they understood that some of them would be able to sink their hooks in advance." Letter of April 22, 1985.

79. This is perhaps not true in the fish example. In that example one sets the limit on

Consider the question of security interests in bankruptcy. Assume for purposes of this discussion that the holder of a security interest has taken the applicable steps required by nonbankruptcy law and, accordingly, has the right to use assets to satisfy the debtor's duty to repay it ahead not only of subsequent secured creditors but also of subsequent lien creditors or general unsecured creditors. (This secured creditor is like our fisherman with a right to catch the first $20,000 of fish.) Assuming that we have made a societal decision to permit creditors to take security interests, the question before us is how to treat this interest in bankruptcy.

On the one hand, reaching the right deployment outcome may require that the specific nonbankruptcy rights of the secured creditor—specifically, the right to remove the assets and sell them on default—should not be respected in full. As we have seen, unsecured creditors have several reasons for desiring a collective proceeding. One of the most important is that the assets might be worth more together as a group. If the right of a secured creditor to remove collateral from the debtor's estate and remain outside of any collective proceeding were respected in kind, this advantage would be diminished or lost. To say this, however, is not to say that the value of the secured creditor's entitlement cannot be respected.[80] The benefit from collectivization exists by restraining the

---

catch and divides it as directed. In the case of credit, however, the common pool solution is an *alternative* to another existing system. When there are two parallel debt-collection systems, rule changes between them introduce problems that a single system—such as fishing—does not face.

80. Perhaps it is worth imagining this in terms of a hypothetical deal among creditors, assuming that they could negotiate. Through collectivization, as we have seen, there are opportunities to increase the value of the pool of assets over what would exist in an individual remedies system. The introduction of secured creditors, accordingly, should not make a difference. It remains in the joint interest of the unsecured creditors (and hence in the debtor's interest as well) to have a secured creditor included in the collective proceeding. A secured creditor, on the other hand, would have no reason to object to such an inclusion *if* left as well off as before.

The premise of Kaldor-Hicks efficiency—that a move is desirable if the winners *could* compensate the losers, even if no such compensation occurs—suggests, in the abstract, that the advantages of a collective proceeding might warrant its implementation even if the entitlements of secured creditors were not recognized. See Coleman, "Efficiency, Utility and Wealth Maximization," 8 *Hofstra L. Rev.* 509 (1980) (a reasonably accessible discussion of Kaldor-Hicks efficiency in legal context). But in practice such a solution would create other problems, such as strategic behavior and nonoptimal bankruptcy decisions, making it less desirable than a solution that respected the value of nonbankruptcy entitlements.

A collective proceeding that allocates all of the gains to the unsecured creditors is not, of course, the only system possible. Indeed, in an actual consensual bargain it is unlikely that secured creditors would agree to the bargain unless they received *some* of the gains resulting from that bargain. The analogy here goes no further than to show that the secured creditor would be *indifferent* between the two systems. But a legal rule whereby the gains are allocated entirely to the unsecured creditors has certain advantages. Such a

right; reallocating values is simply a distributional matter. Deciding on entitlements is independent of the need to solve a common pool problem. In a world in which secured creditors come first, there is going to be a common pool problem that bankruptcy law can address. And in a world in which all creditors share pro rata, there is still going to be a common pool problem that bankruptcy law can address. Resolving the entitlement question one way or the other is, therefore, irrelevant to addressing a common pool concern. They are not independent, however, in the sense that it is counterproductive for the common pool system to use different entitlements from the individual grab remedies system. Like all distributional matters, changing the rules in bankruptcy may reintroduce the grab problem that bankruptcy law is supposed to be avoiding.

This point can be sharpened by considering the hypothetical examined earlier, except now assume that Creditor 1 is a creditor with a security interest in Debtor's printing press, the principal piece of Debtor's business equipment. The press could be sold for $50,000 on the open market. By virtue of this security interest, Creditor 1, outside of bankruptcy, is assured of receiving $50,000, the amount of its loan. If Creditor 1 is able to proceed independently of the other creditors when Debtor is insolvent, Creditor 1 might force a piecemeal liquidation when it removes the printing press. If the business, however, is worth $80,000 as a going concern and only $60,000 if sold piecemeal, the removal of the printing press by Creditor 1 would mean that the remaining creditors would receive only $10,000 on account of their claims. If, however, the collective proceeding allowed the assets to be sold as a unit for $80,000, it would be possible to pay Creditor 1 its $50,000 and still have $30,000 left over for the remaining creditors. This is an application of the fact that, as with fish, the optimal group outcome is independent of the way the assets are split.

This issue will be further discussed in Chapter 7, when we examine the question of how a secured creditor should be compensated for loss of its specific right to repossess and sell collateral. For now it is important to understand the distinction between respecting the right and respecting the relative value of that right, and how bankruptcy law should be concerned primarily with the latter. It is, moreover, important to see the other side of this coin: the consequences of respecting neither the right nor the value of the right.

---

system is easy to operate. Moreover, who should pay for the costs of bankruptcy can be more precisely determined when its benefits *and* costs are all allocated to a single class. See Chapter 7.

What would happen? Assume that the rule in bankruptcy was that all creditors shared alike, whether or not they had a security interest enforceable outside of bankruptcy. One consequence is obvious: a secured creditor with knowledge of this rule at the time of making a loan will be expected to charge the debtor for this increase in its risk. This will lead to an increase in the cost of secured credit (because it is more risky) and to a decrease in the cost of unsecured credit (because it is less risky). Whether or not this result is desirable depends on whether the decision to allow secured credit was a good thing.[81] If one thinks that secured creditors get too much (i.e., that secured credit is not fundamentally a good thing), one can always change the nonbankruptcy rule and do away with secured credit.

The relevant question is whether there is anything wrong with expressing this dislike for secured credit by leaving the nonbankruptcy entitlement (secured creditors come first) but refusing to respect the value of it in bankruptcy. And the answer is "yes," because of the second consequence. When there are two parallel systems of debt collection, different substantive entitlements in the two systems invite wrong deployment decisions for the group as a whole because of individual incentives regarding distributional outcomes. Making a rule change such as this in bankruptcy will lead the unsecured creditors to opt for a bankruptcy proceeding in order to gain access to this distributional rule change (which is favorable to them and unfavorable to the secured creditor), even when bankruptcy is a poor forum from the perspective of the creditors as a group. Bankruptcy proceedings have costs of their own. It may be the case that permitting the nonbankruptcy world to run its course is the best available option. This might occur, for example, if Debtor's business was worth $60,000 broken up piecemeal and less than that as a going concern. It might cost the creditors as a group less to allow Creditor 1 to repossess the printing press and to sell it for $50,000 and to have Debtor sell the remaining assets for $10,000 than it would be to invoke bankruptcy, where the costs of the bankruptcy proceeding might reduce the net value of the assets from $60,000 to, say, $50,000.[82]

---

81. This is not an easy question to answer. See Jackson & Schwartz, "Vacuum of Fact or Vacuous Theory: A Reply to Professor Kripke," 133 *U. Pa. L. Rev.* 987 (1985), and sources cited therein.

82. This reduction in value might come from a number of sources. Perhaps the most frequent one relates to the informational content of bankruptcy about the firm's chances for success. Had Chrysler Corporation filed for bankruptcy in the late 1970s, for example, most expected that it would have exacerbated its problem of selling cars, even though its chances of success might otherwise be as great or greater in bankruptcy, because of the message that inevitably would be read into Chrysler's filing. See Chapter 8.

In that event Creditors 2 through 4 do much better, as each gets $12,500 instead of $2,500. But it is not just Creditor 1 who is worse off (getting $12,500 instead of $50,000); it is the group as a whole, for they have split $50,000 among themselves instead of $60,000.[83]

For this reason the relative ranking of entitlements—that is, the ordering of claims—is also an integral part of their bankruptcy valuation. A secured creditor with a nominal claim of $10,000 may actually receive $10,000, whereas an unsecured creditor with a nominal claim of $10,000 may actually receive only $1,000. As their nominal claims are the same, the highter priority rights of the secured creditor account for the different amount that each receives in the bankruptcy process.

The concept of relative value is not exhausted by considering creditors alone. Shareholders of a corporation, for example, have a right under nonbankruptcy law to the assets of that corporation; the unique nonbankruptcy attribute of that right, however, is its residual nature. That attribute (as well as the right to any upside potential) is reflected in valuing the shareholders' claims against those of competing claimants in the bankruptcy setting.[84] Shareholders get paid if, but only if, the claims of all others have been paid in full first. This is the way the world operates outside of bankruptcy, and it therefore is the way it should operate in bankruptcy.

More generally, whether the issue is one of ordering secured creditors vis-à-vis unsecured creditors, unsecured creditors vis-à-vis shareholders, or even unsecured creditors inter se, bankruptcy law has—or should have—little to say about the relative ordering of claims. That issue is a quintessential nonbankruptcy one of attributes. Bankruptcy law can do

---

83. The creditors, to be sure, might try to contract around this poor bankruptcy result by negotiating among themselves outside of bankruptcy (with Creditor 1 ultimately ending up with some sum between $12,500 and $50,000). This scenario involves complex, costly, and potentially intractable negotiations, especially if one considers the more realistic case of hundreds of creditors, not just four. Avoidance of these eve-of-bankruptcy negotiations would, therefore, appear preferable. It is in the interest of the creditors as a group to have bankruptcy triggered when, and only when, doing so increases the payout to them as a group. The best way for them to do this would be to agree, initially, to respect the value of Creditor 1's nonbankruptcy entitlements in bankruptcy. Given the fact that reaching such an actual agreement is likely to be intractable and a legal rule is needed as a substitute, the best bankruptcy rule would accordingly be one that respects the relative value of the secured creditor's nonbankruptcy entitlements. Only such a rule can solve the common pool problem without reintroducing the problem in the guise of forum shopping by self-interested creditors seeking a rule change beneficial to them alone.

84. If the company is insolvent, the shareholders may have lost any right to the upside potential as a matter of nonbankruptcy law. See Black & Scholes, supra note 35 (viewing common stock in terms of option contract).

no better in fulfilling its accepted role than to adhere to the valuations that derive from that external ordering scheme.

However simple this point seems in the abstract, bankruptcy law occasionally loses sight of it. Secured credit is sometimes a notable example, although here the statutory response has been largely in line with the normative theory.[85] In other cases the point has simply been missed entirely. Consider, for example, the question of the subordination of securities law claims in bankruptcy.[86] Section 510(b) requires the subordination of any claim either for rescission of the purchase or sale of a security of the debtor or for a damage claim arising from the purchase or sale of such a security. Such claims are to be subordinated "to all claims or interests that are senior to or equal the claim or interest represented by such security." The intellectual basis for this section is a 1973 article by John Slain and Homer Kripke.[87] The crux of their argument was that allowing a person to assert a claim in bankruptcy as an unsecured creditor based on the purchase of an equity interest impermissibly permitted the buyer of a risky security to bootstrap himself into a less risky class. They viewed the problem as one of risk allocation and saw the relevant risks as two: "(1) the risk of business insolvency from whatever cause; and (2) the risk of illegality in securities issuance."[88] The first risk they saw as a basic part of accepting equity instead of debt; the second risk they characterized as a risk that the enterprise was making an illegal

85. See *In re* Martin, 761 F.2d 472 (8th Cir. 1985); Grundy Nat'l Bank v. Tandem Mining Corp., 754 F.2d 1436 (3d Cir. 1985); *In re* American Mariner Industries, Inc., 734 F.2d 426 (9th cir. 1984); Baird & Jackson, supra note 58; Note, "Compensation for Time Value as Part of Adequate Protection during the Automatic Stay in Bankruptcy," 50 *U. Chi. L. Rev.* 305, 309–22 (1983). This is explored in Chapter 7.

86. The issue is not limited to securities claims. Bankruptcy has a doctrine of "equitable subordination." See §510(c); Taylor v. Standard Gas & Electric Co., 306 U.S. 307(1939); Clark, "The Duties of the Corporate Debtor to Its Creditors," 90 *Harv. L. Rev.* 505 (1977). The Supreme Court has made it clear that equitable subordination is not dependent on nonbankruptcy law, Prudence Realization Corp. v. Geist, 316 U.S. 89, 95 (1942): "The court of bankruptcy is a court of equity to which the judicial administration of the bankrupt's estates is committed . . . and it is for that court—not without appropriate regard for rights acquired under rules of state law—to define and apply federal law in determining the extent to which the inequitable conduct of a claimant is acquired or asserting his claim in bankruptcy requires its subordination to other claims which, in other respects, are of the same class." If bankruptcy law is viewed as a collective debt-collection device, however, such a disregard of nonbankruptcy law is incorrect. See also §726(a)(4).

87. Slain & Kripke, "The Interface between Securities Regulation and Bankruptcy—Allocating the Risk of Illegal Securities Issuance between Securityholders and the Issuer's Creditors," 48 *N.Y.U. L. Rev.* 261 (1973); see Proposed Bankruptcy Act of 1973 §4–406(a)(1), contained in Report of the Commission on the Bankruptcy Laws of the United States, Part II 115 (1973), H. Doc. No. 137, 93rd Cong., 1st Sess. (1973).

88. Slain & Kripke, supra note 87, at 286–88.

stock offering to the equity shareholder. In either case Slain and Kripke argued that there was no basis to reallocate that risk in a bankruptcy proceeding to the general creditors, which treating any resulting damage claims as general unsecured claims would do.

In a 1983 article Kenneth Davis challenged this rationale and its implementation in section 510(b), arguing that it is difficult to distinguish the risk to unsecured creditors caused by fraud in the issuance of securities from other risks (such as antitrust violations by the debtor) that they also bear.[89] Davis's solution is to separate the loss in value of the security caused by business risks (where the purchaser of equity securities, in his view, bears greater risk in return for the possibility of greater return) and the loss in value of the security caused by fraud (or the like) in the issuance (where the purchaser of equity securities, in Davis's view, does not agree to bear that risk).[90]

Whatever the merits of any particular resolution of this debate, it is odd to see it discussed as a matter of bankruptcy policy. If state law treats the holders of security law claims as general creditors, these people enjoy attributes—such as rights of levy—that ordinary shareholders do not enjoy. The issue of what the status of securities law claims should be vis-à-vis other claims against a debtor ultimately comes down to whether certain shareholders (those holding fraud claims) should be allowed to assume the attributes of creditors. That issue is inherently one of nonbankruptcy law. Once nonbankruptcy law has decided on the ordering, it is improper to insist on a different result in bankruptcy based on whether a particular party agreed or did not agree to bear a particular risk. In all cases the risks that any party bears have been set by nonbankruptcy law. There is no reason to reorder priorities—to reallocate the relative value of such claims—simply because the process of disbursement has been collectivized. For that reason, whether or not section 510(b) is good policy, it is not good bankruptcy policy.

To be sure, the issue of resolving relative attributes is not always easy, particularly when the focus is on rights among creditors as opposed to the more common (contract-based) focus of rights of a creditor against a debtor. Nonbankruptcy law sometimes provides a particular claimant with a prior right to some or all of the assets of the debtor. These claimants may be holders of consensual security interests, execution liens, statutory liens, or any one of a number of other interests that have the effect of permitting the holder to assert a prior claim to some or all of

89. Davis, "The Status of Defrauded Securityholders in Corporate Bankruptcy," 1983 *Duke L.J.* 1, 22–23.
90. Id., at 41.

the debtor's assets. Because nonbankruptcy law raising this issue comes in myriad forms, however, determining how to characterize the priority of a particular claim in bankruptcy may require sensitive understanding of the nature of the nonbankruptcy right and how it should be recognized in bankruptcy.

How, for example, should a contract that gives the nonbankrupt party a right of specific performance be treated in bankruptcy? Suppose that a debtor has contracted to sell his Chagall painting to Creditor A for $10,000 and his computer to Creditor B for $10,000. Under applicable state law Creditor A has a right of specific performance in conjunction with its contract, but Creditor B's rights on breach are limited, as with ordinary contract creditors, to monetary damages only. Creditor A and Creditor B have both paid the entire sums called for in the contract, and the debtor then files for bankruptcy. Creditor B's claim is that of an unsecured creditor, either in restitution (for his $10,000) or in expectancy, for breach of contract (which, for purposes of simplicity, will be presumed to be zero, apart from the claim to recover the $10,000). If in the debtor's bankruptcy the unsecured creditors are getting paid ten cents on the dollar, Creditor B will receive $1,000.

How should Creditor A's claim be treated, given its state-law right of specific performance? In recent contract scholarship the right of specific performance has been illuminatingly analyzed as a property right.[91] If one were to attempt to apply that analysis to bankruptcy, it might seem at first glance that Creditor A should receive the painting, effectively satisfying Creditor A's claim at one hundred cents on the dollar, a far cry from the ten cents on the dollar payable to general unsecured claimants, such as Creditor B. This is the result that seems to be reached in bankruptcy when the issue is raised.[92] But it focuses on the wrong attribute. To award specific performance is to respect Creditor A's right in full when it is unlikely that a decision to award specific performance is intended, as a matter of nonbankruptcy law, to alter the relative ordering of claims between Creditor A and Creditor B (not to mention the other creditors) dramatically. In discussing rights among creditors, Douglas Baird and I have noted the importance of distinguishing be-

91. Schwartz, "The Case for Specific Performance," 89 *Yale L.J.* 271 (1979); Kronman, "Specific Performance," 45 *U. Chi. L. Rev.* 351 (1978).

92. See Proyector Electronics, S.A. v. Alper, 37 Bankr. 931 (Bankr. E.D. Pa. 1983) (specific performance doctrine followed in bankruptcy); cf. Nimmer, "Executory Contracts in Bankruptcy: Protecting the Fundamental Terms of the Bargain," 54 *U. Colo. L. Rev.* 507, 524–31 (1983) (apparently reaching this conclusion in the context of executory contracts).

tween what we call a "property" right and a "priority" right[93]—a distinction that is central to the present context because it is necessary to focus not on the state-law label but on the attributes of that label and, most importantly here, on the value of those attributes vis-à-vis other claimants of the debtor.

The right of specific performance of certain contracts is most often justified on the ground that it secures the party enjoying that right against the undercompensation that would otherwise result from treating the claim as one that could be satisfied by monetary damages. That rationale, however, essentially describes a two-party relationship between the contracting parties. It does not mandate giving Creditor A $10,000 (in cash or in kind) while leaving Creditor B only $1,000. Instead, the relevant focus in bankruptcy (and one that makes the issue sometimes hard) is the question of attributes considered from the perspective of creditor versus creditor, not the attributes of a right a creditor has against the debtor. It is a question of priority, not property.

With that focus a further examination of state law is likely to reveal that, considered vis-à-vis the claims of other creditors, the value of a right of specific performance in a contract for a unique good on the eve of bankruptcy was nothing close to one hundred cents on the dollar. In our example the relevant question for fixing relative values is how state law would treat Creditor A versus an execution creditor on the Chagall at the time of the bankruptcy proceeding, not how state law would treat Creditor A against the debtor. The nonbankruptcy solution is almost surely to favor the execution creditor because of the ostensible ownership created when the buyer (Creditor A) left the Chagall in the debtor's hands following the sale.[94] So for that reason, allowing specific performance to justify payment in full to Creditor A in bankruptcy erroneously promotes a property right against the debtor—specific performance—into a priority right against other creditors. Specific performance in its normal contractual context, accordingly, should not be respected at its nominal value, because at bottom the relevant questions are nonbank-

93. D. Baird & T. Jackson, *Cases, Problems, and Materials on Security Interests in Personal Property* 1–3 (1984).

94. Although Uniform Commercial Code §2–402(1) (1978) provides that unsecured creditors' rights to goods identified to a contract are subject to a buyer's right of specific performance under §2–716, that provision is expressly made subject to §2–402(2). Under §2–402(2), "[a] creditor of the seller may treat a sale or an identification of goods to a contract for sale as void if as against him a retention of possession by a seller is fraudulent under any rule of law of the state where the goods were situated." Many states deem such retention as possession to be conclusively fraudulent. See, e.g., Cal. Civ. Code §3440 (West 1970).

ruptcy ones that are not answerable by looking at labels (such as calling a specific performance right a property right). Instead, the focus must be on examining the *value* of that right under nonbankruptcy law vis-à-vis the debtor's other claimants at the moment of bankruptcy. It is this focus that needs to be kept in mind in translating liabilities to the bankruptcy forum.

3

Refining Liabilities: The Basic Trustee Avoiding Powers of Section 544

BANKRUPTCY LAW, as we have seen, should focus primarily on values, not rights. This point facilitates an examination of the trustee's basic avoiding powers (setting aside, until Chapter 6, the power to avoid preferential transfers, a power that arises out of distinct concerns). To one familiar with bankruptcy law, discussing avoiding powers at this point might seem odd. Avoiding powers seem to relate to the gathering of the estate. Section 541 allows the trustee to step into the shoes of the debtor in gathering property of the estate, and the avoiding powers (suggestively located in nearby sections) augment that activity by giving the trustee certain other powers to bring assets into the estate.

There is an undeniable validity to this way of viewing the situation. Substantial and inevitable overlap exists between the question of what are the assets that bankruptcy is concerned with and the question of how liabilities are ordered in bankruptcy. Even so, I think it is fruitful to consider the trustee's basic avoiding powers as part of determining the relative ordering of liabilities. Thus, its location here—between a basic discussion of liabilities and a discussion of property of the estate—of assets.

Two kinds of what are commonly considered avoiding powers can be distinguished. The first group, comprised of those powers that can be used to preserve the advantages associated with the collective nature of the bankruptcy proceeding, may best be thought of those that arrange rights among the creditors inter se. These avoiding powers, most notably the "strong arm" power of the trustee under section 544(a), are the subject of this chapter and Chapter 6.

A second group of powers generally considered to be avoiding powers have nothing to do with implementing the move from an individual to a collective regime. The prototype of such powers is fraudulent conveyance laws. Laws that strike down actions designed to hinder, delay, or defraud creditors, or transfers made by insolvent debtors for less than fair consideration, are not an offspring of nor particularly related to the bankruptcy process itself. Whereas the avoiding powers in the first group adjust the rights of creditors vis-à-vis other creditors, fraudulent conveyance law adjusts the rights of creditors vis-à-vis the debtor. That the second group of avoiding powers does not spring from a need to implement bankruptcy's collective proceeding becomes evident when one observes that the fraudulent conveyance principle not only resides in section 548 of the Bankruptcy Code but also operates outside of bankruptcy, as it has done for more than four hundred years.[1] It retains its force in bankruptcy, as do other nonbankruptcy rights, through section 544(b). Although no particular harm results from calling fraudulent conveyance law an avoiding power of the trustee in bankruptcy, one must recognize its distinct and less collectivist justification. Fraudulent conveyance law will be set aside for now, to be examined briefly after considering the trustee's preference power in Chapter 6. We will see there that whereas the preference power is integral to implementing bankruptcy in a world of strategic behavior, bankruptcy's tinkering with fraudulent conveyance law is more questionable.

We shall concentrate our examination here on the avoiding powers embodied in section 544, although we shall look, at the end of this chapter, at a related power directed at state-created priorities and bankruptcy statutory liens and embodied in part in section 545. Viewing bankruptcy as a collective device designed to solve a common pool problem facilitates examination of the contours of these avoiding powers as well as their inherent limitations. A number of long-standing problems associated with the use of the avoiding powers now embodied in sections 544 and 545 stem from the failure to identify the underlying purpose of each particular avoiding power in the context of bankruptcy's collectivization norm. Because of that failure, judges, legislators, and commentators have not focused on the types of behavior that a particular avoiding power was designed to affect and, accordingly, have not appreciated the limits of the reach of each particular power. To remedy this situation, it is necessary to understand the basic role of the avoiding powers described in section 544.

1. See Uniform Fraudulent Conveyance Act (1919); 13 Eliz., ch. 5 (1570).

The Trustee as Hypothetical Lien Creditor or Purchaser

As with all bankruptcy rules, the basis of avoiding powers should be to protect the advantages of bankruptcy's collectivization of the debt-collection process. Consider the trustee's power to assert the rights of a hypothetical lien creditor—the so-called strong-arm power of section 544(a).[2] The trustee is able to "avoid" interests that creditors hold in property of the estate if such interests would be subordinate to an execution lien creditor's interest outside of bankruptcy. Its relationship to the collectivization norm is that it presumptively enables the trustee to preserve the equality in value that existed among these creditors' rights at the moment before bankruptcy. Instead of changing relative entitlements, the lien creditor power does just the opposite. It is, therefore, proper to view the use of this avoiding power as implementing the notion of relative values explored in the previous chapter.

The best illustration of this is the ability of the trustee to avoid unperfected security interests, surely the property right most frequently avoided under the strong-arm power.[3] The assertion that the trustee strikes down these interests to preserve nonbankruptcy relative values might seem odd at first to anyone with a basic familiarity of the nonbankruptcy rights of unperfected secured creditors.[4] Outside of bank-

2. That section provides: "The trustee shall have, as of the commencement of the case, and without regard to any knowledge of the trustee or any creditor, the rights and powers of, or may avoid any transfer of property of the debtor or any obligation incurred by the debtor that is voidable by—(1) a creditor that extends credit to the debtor at the time of the commencement of the case, and that obtains, at such time and with respect to such credit, a judicial lien on all property on which a creditor on a simple contract could have obtained a judicial lien, whether or not such a creditor exists; (2) a creditor that extends credit to the debtor at the time of the commencement of the case, and obtains, at such time and with respect to such credit, an execution against the debtor that is returned unsatisfied at such time, whether or not such a creditor exists; and (3) a bona fide purchaser of real property from the debtor, against whom applicable law permits such transfer to be perfected, that obtains the status of a bona fide purchaser and has perfected such transfer at the time of the commencement of the case, whether or not such a purchaser exists."

3. Under Uniform Commercial Code §9–301(1)(b)(1978), an unperfected security interest is subordinate to "a person who becomes a lien creditor before the security interest is perfected," and under Uniform Commercial Code §9–301(3), a lien creditor means not only "a creditor who has acquired a lien on the property involved by attachment, levy or the like" but also "a trustee in bankruptcy from the date of the filing of the petition." This latter provision is strangely located in a state statute. Although bankruptcy law takes attributes from state law, state law should not itself dictate bankruptcy's outcome. Whether the trustee should have the powers of a lien creditor is (or should be) a bankruptcy question; what those powers of a lien creditor are is (or should be) a nonbankruptcy question.

4. Perfection requires attachment, Uniform Commercial Code §9–203(1), (2) (1978),

ruptcy, in order for an unsecured creditor to prevail over an unperfected security interest, the unsecured creditor must perfect a property right (such as a security interest or an execution lien) in its own right, and it must do so before the competing security interest is perfected.

Consequently, if one were to take a conceptual snapshot at the moment before bankruptcy, the picture may not appear to reflect presumptive equality of values at all. An unperfected secured creditor would prevail over the unsecured creditor if the "race" were to end then and there. Because it would prevail, the relative value of the unperfected secured creditor may seem to be greater than that of its unsecured counterpart. If so, then it would seem to follow that bankruptcy policy does not justify striking down, on behalf of the unsecured creditors, an unperfected security interest that none of them could defeat at the time bankruptcy was filed. This argument has been more forcefully developed by John McCoid, one of the most perceptive bankruptcy analysts. He asserts:

> When bankruptcy stops the race, these parties are not equals because the secured party is ahead. Hypothetical lien creditor status does not just preserve the status quo; it reverses the order of priority and thus does more than substitute the trustee for the unsecured creditors.
>
> Perhaps that made a kind of sense in the Nineteenth Century and even in 1910. Then commencement of bankruptcy did not end the race of both parties as it does today . . . With the secured party still "running," something was required if the trustee was to have meaningful representative status. Under the present structure which stops the race for both parties, however, hypothetical lien creditor status provides more than mere representation. It gives unsecured creditors what they did not have outside of bankruptcy, and, perhaps, something they could not quickly have obtained. Indeed, it may provide, as does hypothetical bona fide purchaser status in connection with real estate, an incentive to initiate bankruptcy to obtain an otherwise unavailable advantage.[5]

McCoid correctly focuses on relative values. Although justified on the ground of preserving relative values, however, his rule may not mirror values across a range of cases as well as does a rule that permits a trustee to avoid interests a lien creditor could have avoided on the date of bankruptcy. Consider the following argument. The relative position of

---

plus "the applicable steps required for perfection," Uniform Commercial Code §9–303(1). These steps, set forth in Uniform Commercial Code §§9–302 through 9–306, generally consist of the secured creditor's filing a financing statement in the appropriate public files or taking possession of the collateral.

5. McCoid, "Bankruptcy, the Avoiding Powers, and Unperfected Security Interests," 59 *Am. Bankr. L.J.* 175 (1985).

the two classes of creditors—unperfected secured and unsecured—is only partially—and misleadingly—depicted by a snapshot of their respective positions at the moment before bankruptcy. The unperfected secured party is, to be sure, entitled to prevail over the unsecured party *if* no further action is taken. The more relevant point in determining values, however, may be that neither party has in fact taken the step that assures ultimate victory—that actually fixes one's place in line. Which party would have taken that final step first is unknown the moment before bankruptcy. Had it acted first, the secured creditor could have prevailed by taking possession of the collateral or by filing a notice of its interest. The unsecured creditor, conversely, could have assured itself of priority by acting first, either by taking and perfecting a consensual security interest in the property or by obtaining a nonconsensual attachment or execution lien on the property.

This analysis suggests that neither party has any significant advantage the moment before bankruptcy. Common wisdom, to be sure, has the unperfected secured creditor on the threshold of victory, but that view may in fact be quite misleading.[6] An unperfected secured creditor needs either the debtor's active cooperation to file a financing statement (which requires the debtor's signature) or to get paid, or its passive cooperation, to repossess the assets.[7] Apart from that, the unperfected secured creditor, like its unsecured counterpart, needs to invoke the judicial process. The remaining steps of an unperfected secured creditor are not likely to be easier than those of an unsecured creditor who, with the debtor's active cooperation, can either get paid, get a security interest of its own, or take possession of assets. Thus, as a matter of nonbankruptcy law, relative values may in fact be virtually equal.

Even if they are not, however, section 544(a) may still be justified in giving the trustee the powers of a lien creditor because of the nature of relative values and of bankruptcy rules. Assume for now that in a one-on-one race with any particular unsecured creditor, it is possible to posit with a fair degree of confidence ultimate victory for the secured creditor. In such a world McCoid's view of relative values might be correct. But we need a rule that applies to a range of cases, including one where there are tens or even thousands of unsecured creditors. Consider the position of an unperfected secured creditor who is facing a *pool* of un-

6. I make this point in Baird & Jackson, "Corporate Reorganizations and the Treatment of Diverse Ownership Interests: A Comment on Adequate Protection of Secured Creditors in Bankruptcy," 51 *U. Chi. L. Rev.* 97, 112–13 (1984).

7. Repossession without court involvement is possible only if it can be done without "breach of the peace." Uniform Commercial Code §9–503 (1978).

secured creditors as its competitors. There, the relevant race generally would not be one-on-one but would pit the unperfected secured creditor against numerous unsecured creditors (and perhaps against other unperfected secured creditors). If any one of the unsecured creditors were to be paid or were to obtain a lien or perfected securing interest first, the unperfected secured creditor pro tanto would lose its priority.

Across the pool of unsecured creditors, some of whom may be close to judgments or attachments, an unperfected secured creditor accordingly faces a substantial danger of being trumped. Evaluating the outcome of the unfinished race thus becomes problematic. Because prior to the debtor's bankruptcy neither the unperfected secured creditor nor any of its unsecured counterparts have taken the ultimate step that assures priority outside of bankruptcy, it may be preferable to consider them as standing, at that moment, in relative positions of equality, at least for purposes of fashioning a valuation rule instead of a costly case-by-case standard. In "avoiding" the secured party's unperfected interest, the trustee does not confer victory upon the unsecured creditors; rather, he assures a tie, which may be the best one can do.

For example, assume that an unperfected secured creditor would win nine out of ten races with any particular unsecured creditor. Assume, further (for simplicity's sake) that every creditor has a $1,000 claim and that the debtor's assets are worth $1,000. If the debtor has only two creditors, Unperfected Creditor and General Creditor, their relative values the moment before bankruptcy are, respectively, $900 and $100. But what if the debtor has, along with Unperfected Creditor, not one but one hundred General Creditors? The relative values the moment before bankruptcy of Unperfected Creditor's claim is now only $100, because nine out of ten times a General Creditor would win the race. If there were a thousand General Creditors, the relative value of Unperfected Creditor's claim would fall to $10. Although the relative value of Unperfected Creditor's claim always remains greater than that of any particular General Creditor's claim (and by the same percentage), if the choice is between treating Unperfected Creditor as having won the race (and thus giving it $1,000 on account of its claim), or sharing pari passu with the General Creditors, the latter course seems sounder when the relative value of Unperfected Creditor's claim is nowhere near $1,000.

McCoid is correct to note that the consequence of treating all as equals will create "an incentive to initiate bankruptcy to obtain an otherwise unavailable advantage." This problem springs, however, from the fact that the rule is not an exact mirror of underlying values—under our current assumption it undervalues the unperfected secured creditor's prebankruptcy status. But his favored rule suffers from the same kind of infirmity, and indeed the mismatch may be greater. As McCoid astutely observes, however, the question of relative mismatch may not be decisive. He focuses (correctly) as well on the incentives to misuse bankruptcy created by one rule or the other. So viewed, his rule arguably might create less of such an incentive. Unperfected Creditor, upon discovering its lack of perfection, might simply perfect (if debtor lets it), rather than file for bankruptcy. But this point can be overstated. Just as Unperfected Creditor might (or might not) perfect instead of file for bankruptcy, so, too, might any General Creditor simply prefer to take the steps that would lead to its getting priority (and $1,000), rather than file a petition (where it must share pro rata with numerous other creditors). The incentives to use bankruptcy for selfish reasons of one rule as opposed to another, accordingly, are not particularly clear, even if we assume that the relative value of Unperfected Creditor's claim is greater than that of any General Creditor's claim. We are still left with a choice between two presumptive rules, and generally the one that mirrors relative values most accurately seems preferable.

From this discussion we may conclude that neither rule is appropriate and that we should try to preserve the relative values of the claims of Unperfected Creditor and General Creditors more exactly by, for example, giving Unperfected Creditor nine times as much on account of its claim, in bankruptcy, as any General Creditor gets. This, however, assumes that the relative value *is* greater, whereas we have seen that it may not be. But even assuming that such an approach may be theoretically more pristine, it is unlikely to be preferable in practice. It requires the calculation not only of matters such as the actual ratio of assets to liabilities but also of imponderables (such as the actual chances of victory). Such calculations quickly become even more complex where there are numerous unperfected secured creditors, each of which may win (or lose) the race not only against the General Creditors but also against the other unperfected secured creditors. For this reason, the "lien creditor" rule of section 544(a) may be justified as the best and easiest off-the-rack rule that can be devised, and preferable to a more costly case-by-case standard.[8]

8. In addition, such analysis suggests that perhaps the trustee should also be given the power of general creditors who, on account of their existing debts, take and perfect a consensual security interest at the time of bankruptcy. If under nonbankruptcy law such consensual creditors take priority over unperfected secured creditors, the fact that lien creditors do not under state law may make no difference. The rationale for such an additional avoiding power, however, is vastly different from that underlying §544(a)(3).

The rationale, however, also indicates the limits on the trustee's hypothetical-based avoiding power—and here McCoid and I are in full agreement. The justification for the trustee's power as a hypothetical lien creditor ultimately rests on nonbankruptcy entitlements. It measures (albeit with some imprecision) the values of the relative rights of competing claimants to the debtor's property by the yardstick of the value of nonbankruptcy rights existing the moment before bankruptcy.[9] Once those rights are fixed outside bankruptcy, nothing in the collectivizing nature of bankruptcy calls for the reallocation of their value inside bankruptcy.

This point, although simple, has a number of implications for the shape and direction of section 544(a).[10] Consider first section 544(a)(3),

---

See following text. For a discussion of the ability of claimants with unmatured claims (such as unmanifested tort claimants) to gain the protection of §544(a), see Jackson, "Avoiding Powers in Bankruptcy," 36 *Stan. L. Rev.* 725, 750–56 (1984).

9. See *In re* Harms, 7 Bankr. 398 (Bankr. D. Colo. 1980) (noting that the answer to the question of the trustee's rights "is a matter of state law"). This principle was expressed by a House Report accompanying a 1910 amendment to the Bankruptcy Act of 1898 that gave the trustee, for the first time, "better" title to property than the bankrupt had: "In this way, in effect, proceedings in bankruptcy will give to creditors all the rights that creditors under the state law might have had had there been no bankruptcy and from which they are debarred by the bankruptcy—certainly a very desirable and eminently fair position to be granted to the trustee." H. Rep. No. 511, 61st Cong., 2d Sess. 7 (1910); but cf. Countryman, "Justice Douglas: Expositor of the Bankruptcy Code," 16 *UCLA L. Rev.* 773, 782–87 (1969) (suggesting that was a rationalization of the power, not a definition or limitation thereof).

10. In addition to the problem discussed in text, another problem remains. In §544(a) the strong-arm power was rewritten to give the trustee the enumerated powers "without regard to any knowledge of the trustee or of any creditor." This change followed a recommendation of Professor Countryman. Countryman, "The Use of State Law in Bankruptcy Cases (pt. 1)," 47 *N.Y.U. L. Rev.* 631, 652–56 (1972).

Although a knowledge requirement in sorting out priorities is perhaps unwise as a matter of nonbankruptcy law—see Baird & Jackson, "Information, Uncertainty, and the Transfer of Property," 13 *J. Legal Studies* 299 (1984) (criticizing use of knowledge as a factor in determining priorities)—this again simply restates the inquiry of nonbankruptcy law, which is where the focus should be. Nothing related to the *bankruptcy* process suggests that a different rule needs to be adopted to fulfill the purposes of bankruptcy. Even an assertion that, because knowledge is fact-specific and likely to vary from creditor to creditor, it will be difficult to prove across the board, does not *necessarily* justify ignoring that nonbankruptcy requirement in bankruptcy, for the same is true outside of bankruptcy.

The change in bankruptcy may be justified only if knowledge were being applied to a percentage of the nonbankruptcy recovery. For example, if proving knowledge were a fixed cost (say $100 per claimant), even if the rule made sense outside of bankruptcy, where the general recovery averaged, say, $1,000, it may not be worth that fixed cost where the general recovery, on an individual creditor basis, was substantially less. This type of justification for doing away with knowledge requirements in bankruptcy, however, is substantially different. Knowledge of the *trustee*, of course, is irrelevant to this collective-

which permits the trustee to avoid any transfer of property of the debtor that is "voidable by . . . a bona fide purchaser of real property from the debtor, against whom applicable law permits such transfer to be perfected, that obtains the status of a bona fide purchaser and has perfected such transfer at the time of the commencement of the case, whether or not such a purchaser exists."[11] The syllogism that presumably resulted in the promulgation of this section is understandable but unrelated to the collectivization norm.

Although legislative history on this point is nonexistent,[12] the drafters of the Bankruptcy Code appear to have concluded that the trustee's strong-arm power principally addressed the evil of property interests with ostensible ownership problems that remained despite available curative measures under nonbankruptcy law.[13] The problem was—or

---

creditor-based inquiry and is properly ignored. See Commercial Credit Co. v. Davidson, 112 F.2d 54 (5th Cir. 1940); *In re* Lindsey, 131 F. Supp. 11 (D. N.J. 1955).

11. §544(a)(3). Use of the bona fide purchaser test with respect to the trustee's strong-arm power is new with the Bankruptcy Code. See H. Rep. No. 595, 95th Cong., 1st Sess. 370 (1977). It has existed for a longer time under the trustee's preference power. See §60a(2) of the Bankruptcy Act of 1898, 11 U.S.C. §96a(2) (repealed prospectively Oct. 1, 1979). Its use there is no less troublesome. See Chapter 6.

12. The legislative history notes only that §544(a)(3) does not require the impossible, namely, a filing or recording when state law does not provide for it at all, 124 Cong. Rec. H. 11097 (daily ed. Sept. 28, 1978); see *In re* Elin, 20 Bankr. 1012 (D.N.J. 1982) (legislative history to §544(a)(3) is "scant and sheds little light" on the provision).

13. Kennedy, "Secured Creditors under the Bankruptcy Reform Act," 15 *Ind. L. Rev.* 477, 483 (1982) (strong-arm power grew out of "a recognition that secret liens offend bankruptcy policy"); see also Report of the Commission on the Bankruptcy Laws of the United States, H. Doc. No. 137, 93rd Cong., 1st Sess., Part I, at 18 (1977) ("One of the essential features of any bankruptcy law is the inclusion of provisions designed to invalidate secret transfers made by the bankrupt"); H. Rep. No. 551, 61st Cong., 2d Sess. 8–9 (1910) (notoriety problem is "the bottom principle of the right to legislate against secret liens"). A bona fide purchaser test was added (along with a lien creditor test) to the preference section's definition of transfer at the time of the amendments made by the Chandler Act of 1938. That addition was a reaction against "equitable lien" cases such as Sexton v. Kessler, 225 U.S. 90 (1912). It was added explicitly on the ground that secret liens were evil. See, e.g., Analysis of H.R. 12889, 74th Cong., 2d Sess. 188 (1936) ("The purpose of this test is to strike down secret transfers, and thus the transfer is to be deemed made when it becomes known and not when it was actually made"). After Congress discovered that the bona fide purchaser test jeopardized all non-notification accounts receivable financing—see Corn Exchange Nat'l Bank & Trust Co. v. Klauder, 318 U.S. 434 (1943)— Congress limited the bona fide purchaser test in the preference section to transfers of real estate. See generally 2 G. Gilmore, *Security Interests in Personal Property* 1300–05 (1965). One can safely assume that the same animus against secret transfers motivated the draftsmen in 1978 in promulgating §544(a)(3). See Morris, "Bankruptcy Law Reform: Preferences, Secret Liens and Floating Liens," 54 *Minn. L. Rev.* 737, 759–60 and n. 61 (1970) (suggesting need to revise strong-arm power to include bona fide purchaser test).

seemed—obvious: having a lien creditor's power alone would not enable the trustee to trump all interests with uncured ostensible ownership problems. A number of states permitted various interests in real property that could be but had not yet been recorded to be effective against nonconsensual claimants, such as holders of judgment liens. These unrecorded interests, however, were not effective against most consensual claimants, such as subsequent purchasers of interests in the property who had neither actual nor constructive notice of the earlier unrecorded interest at the time of purchase.

This limitation appeared susceptible to a simple correction. Where applicable law prescribed a form of notoriety as a condition for "full" protection against competing claims, and where such notoriety of a particular interest had not been given prior to bankruptcy, that interest should be invalid against the trustee. To accomplish that, the drafters found that they had to give the trustee the powers of a bona fide purchaser against interests in realty.

That syllogism, as simple as it may seem, fundamentally misconceives the reason that bankruptcy policy calls for a strong-arm avoiding power. Ostensible ownership may—and often does—create problems, but it does not do so in a way that harms a collective proceeding relative to a system of individual remedies. Accordingly, no bankruptcy-related reason requires an "anti-secret-lien" principle in bankruptcy where nonbankruptcy law says that general unsecured creditors can do nothing about it.

Deciding the issue of whether section 544(a)(3) correctly furthers bankruptcy's collectivizing goal requires an examination of the values of various creditors' rights the moment before bankruptcy instead of an incantation about the generalized evils of secret liens. In short, to the extent that they based the enactment of section 544(a)(3) on an anti-secret-lien principle, the drafters misperceived the inquiry, because they ignored the vitally important fact that real property law often *is* different from personal property law. It is the value of those differences *among creditors* that should be the focus of bankruptcy law.[14] At first glance this

14. But see Morris, supra note 13, at 759 (bona fide purchaser test is necessary because "both transferees are equally blameworthy; there is no reason to treat them differently"; dismisses notion that "this anomaly is one of state law, not bankruptcy law" on ground that "there has been a policy of preventing this difference from spilling over into bankruptcy"). Bankruptcy law does not override state-created ostensible ownership problems where state law allows those problems to exist without any public notoriety at all. For example, leases or bailments of goods are effective against people claiming through a debtor despite the ostensible ownership problems those interests create. Similarly, trust rights are permitted to exist notwithstanding notoriety problems. As long as these interests

comparison is unfavorable to the existence of section 544(a)(3). In states that have a bona fide purchaser rule, unsecured creditors are unable, outside of bankruptcy, to defeat the holder of an unrecorded real estate interest directly.[15]

It is possible, however, that this first glance undervalues the rights of general creditors. At a sale pursuant to a judgment creditor's execution, a third party may purchase the real property in question. If that purchaser is without knowledge of the unrecorded interest, and if the notice given in connection with the sale has not caught the attention of the holder of that unrecorded interest, many states may permit the lien creditor to keep the proceeds and in that fashion defeat (albeit indirectly) the claim of the holder of the unrecorded interest.[16] As a matter of state law it may be difficult to value the comparative rights of the judgment creditor and the holder of the unrecorded interest under such a scheme because the comparative values depend on the likelihood that the holder of the unrecorded interest would come forward before disbursement of the sale proceeds. In such a case section 544(a)(3) might be justified as a presumptive valuation rule. The value being presumed, however, still springs from state law, not bankruptcy policy.

Whether or not section 544(a)(3) is desirable, in short, depends on the relative attributes of unrecorded real estate mortgagees and unsecured creditors under state law. Focusing on ostensible ownership itself is, as a matter of bankruptcy law, a red herring; the issue derives instead from state law and requires, in the first instance, a comparison of the relative value of entitlements under state law. In fact, Congress left untouched many nonbankruptcy ostensible ownership problems that

---

are not vulnerable to attack from anyone—other than perhaps a buyer in ordinary course—claiming through the debtor, bankruptcy law respects them. The fact that state law permits certain unrecorded interests to be defeated by other purchasers changes nothing with respect to unsecured creditors. As a result it is disingenuous to suggest that bankruptcy law embodies a disclosure requirement; it does not, at least where state law has no procedure for giving notoriety.

15. The unsecured creditor could trump the holder of the unrecorded real estate interest by becoming a bona fide purchaser. To do this, however, the unsecured creditor would have to give *new* value and would prevail only to the extent of that value. This limitation decisively distinguishes this possibility from the proposal advanced, supra note 8, for an avoiding power based on an ability of general creditors to take consensual security interests under nonbankruptcy law that trump unperfected interests.

16. This requires finding that the bona fide purchaser takes free of the unrecorded interest—see, e.g., Hugh v. Williams, 218 Mass. 448, 105 N.E. 1056 (1914); S. Riesenfeld, *Cases and Materials on Creditors' Remedies and Debtors' Protection* 137 (3d ed. 1979)—and that the judgment creditor has priority as to the proceeds.

constitute more of a practical problem than unrecorded realty interests.[17]

This point is related to a more fundamental insight about the relationship between the avoiding powers of the trustee and the rights of creditors under nonbankruptcy law. In viewing bankruptcy as a species of debt-collection law, the trustee acts simply as a collection agent charged with implementing a collective proceeding for the benefit of all. If none of the unsecured creditors could have upset a transfer outside bankruptcy, the trustee as their collection agent should not be able to upset that transfer inside bankruptcy. Enabling him to do so would shift the expected distribution of assets among creditors upon the commencement of bankruptcy. The concern here, however, is not simply distributional—that some creditors would win and some would lose—but that the creditors as a group would suffer a net loss because the incentives for strategic use of bankruptcy by individual creditors would increase. Curing nonbankruptcy problems in bankruptcy may be preferable to not curing them at all, but curing these problems across the board is unquestionably the best approach. Implementing such reform through bankruptcy law simply obscures the underlying issues.

Section 544(b) and the Legacy of *Moore v. Bay*

For the same reasons the ability of a trustee in bankruptcy to upset a property interest created under nonbankruptcy law should be measured by the creditors who had the power to do so outside of bankruptcy and should be exercised solely for their benefit. It remains a question of determining relative values. This point can be examined by looking at section 544(b),[18] which gives the trustee the rights of an existing unsecured creditor. If the trustee can find such a creditor, the trustee may succeed to its rights and may avoid interests that the creditor could have avoided. Moreover, under the doctrine supposedly enunciated by *Moore v. Bay*,[19] which Congress states that it codified in section 544(b), the trustee may avoid such interests in their entirety, even if the creditor whose rights the trustee succeeds to could only have avoided them in

17. See supra note 14.

18. Section 544(b) provides that "[t]he trustee may avoid any transfer of an interest of the debtor in property or any obligation incurred by the debtor that is voidable under applicable law by a creditor holding an unsecured claim that is allowable under section 502 of this title or that is not allowable only under section 502(e) of this title."

19. 284 U.S. 4 (1931).

part (because the individual creditor's rights would have been limited to the amount of its claim). Finally, under section 551 the trustee takes over such avoided interest for the benefit of the unsecured creditors generally.[20]

The notion that the trustee may assert the rights of an existing unsecured creditor is itself unobjectionable. In a collective proceeding the trustee, in the name of order and economy, may act as agent for creditors in asserting the various rights different creditors have, many of which may overlap. Bankruptcy's debt-collection role takes us no further than seeing the trustee as collection agent. Section 544(b), however, goes considerably further. The reasons for this stem, in large part at least, from a one-page opinion authored by Justice Holmes in 1931.

That opinion, *Moore v. Bay*, has been widely criticized[21]—and occasionally defended[22]—for deciding (as it is commonly read) that a trustee's power to avoid property interests, although derived from the rights held by an existing creditor, can transcend those rights and avoid the interests totally. In the rush to criticize that quantitative expansion of the avoiding power, the other, clearer, holding of *Moore v. Bay*—that the "rights of the trustee by subrogation are to be enforced for the benefit of the estate"[23]—has generally been treated as if it were innocuous.[24] That holding, however, because it represents a shift in the relative value of

20. Section 551 provides that any transfer avoided "is preserved for the benefit of the estate but only with respect to property of the estate." Pursuant to the analysis in this book, who should get the benefit of the avoiding of a property interest should turn, in the first instance, on the resolution of that question under nonbankruptcy law. See Jackson, supra note 8, at 743 n. 50 (analysis of this point).

21. See, e.g., J. MacLachlan, *Bankruptcy* 330–31 (1956) ("one of the most glaring misconstructions to be encountered in the history of Anglo-American law"). The Proposed Bankruptcy Act of 1973 favored overruling Moore v. Bay, see §4–604, in Report of the Commission on the Bankruptcy Laws of the United States, H. Doc. No. 137, 93rd Cong., 1st Sess., Part II, at 160 (1973); see also id., Part I, at 18 (rule of Moore v. Bay "is unfair and unjustified").

22. Countryman, in particular, has been a strong supporter of the rule, and it apparently was largely through his efforts that Moore v. Bay survives in §544(b). See Letter of Countryman of February 25, 1976, to Senate Committee on the Judiciary, in Hearings before the Subcommittee on Improvements in Judicial Machinery of the Committee on the Judiciary of the United States Senate on S. 235 and S. 236, 94th Cong., 2d Sess., Part III, 1 at 7 (1976); Letter of Countryman of December 19, 1975, id., Part II, at 1040.

23. 234 U.S., at 4–5.

24. Kennedy, "The Trustee in Bankruptcy as a Secured Creditor Under the Uniform Commercial Code," 65 *Mich. L. Rev.* 1419, 1421 (1967) ("No question has ever been raised as to the correctness of the disposition of this latter issue"); see also MacLachlan, "The Impact of Bankruptcy on Secured Transactions," 60 *Colum. L. Rev.* 593 (1960).

rights among unsecured creditors, is no less troublesome, and for the same reasons.

Assume that Secured Party had a security interest securing a $10,000 claim on property worth at least that amount. Apart from that debt, Debtor, at the time it filed for bankruptcy, had unsecured claims against it totaling $100,000. Unsecured claims worth $5,000, because they arose during the gap between the time the security interest was taken and the time it was recorded, were superior to that interest under applicable state law.[25] The remaining $95,000 arose after the recording of the security interest and under state law were subordinate to it.

Since nonbankruptcy law is the basis for determining rights in bankruptcy, the trustee, accordingly should be able to act as collection agent, avoid $5,000 of Secured Party's interest, and preserve that avoided interest for the benefit of the gap unsecured creditors but not for the benefit of the subsequent creditors.[26] Under this reading relative value of nonbankruptcy rights are preserved among the unsecured creditors.

Virtually no one argues for that result, however. The virtually universal reading of *Moore v. Bay* is that the Supreme Court held that the security interest could be avoided entirely, and the $10,000 so recovered was an asset of the estate to be shared by all unsecured creditors. It is that outcome that section 544(b) embodies. Many have disagreed with this solution, believing instead that the trustee's recovery should be measured by the $5,000 of gap claims, but that the $5,000 recovered should be taken "for the benefit of the estate."

Both outcomes, however, upset the relative value of rights that had already been fixed outside of bankruptcy. Neither outcome is necessary to assure the advantages of substituting collective for individual remedies. The only difference in the two outcomes is the group that is being harmed. If section 544(b) were recast so that $5,000 were preserved and distributed among the unsecured creditors as a group (the outcome

25. These facts are based on *In re* Sassard & Kimball Co., 45 F.2d 449 (9th Cir. 1930), *rev'd*, 284 U.S. 4 (1931). Such a system was common before enactment of the Uniform Commercial Code. A substantially different result would exist under the Uniform Commercial Code. See infra note 28.

26. This is probably the outcome in *In re* Sassard & Kimball Co., 45 F.2d 449 (9th Cir. 1930), *rev'd* 284 U.S. 4 (1931). See Jackson, supra note 8, at 746 n. 64. Prior case law had focused, and split, on the issue of who gained the benefit of the trustee's recovery. Compare Mullen v. Warner (*In re* Moore), 11 F.2d 62 (4th Cir. 1926) (recovery of the trustee becomes a general asset of the estate) with American Trust & Savings Bank v. Duncan, 254 Fed. 780 (5th Cir. 1918) (when the trustee succeeds to a right possessed by only some of a bankrupt's creditors, "other creditors have no right to share in the amount so recovered").

seemingly favored by most commentators), the costs it would be imposing, compared with nonbankruptcy values, would be on the gap unsecured creditors, not on the holder of the security interest. The group of creditors thereby harmed seem entirely blameless under any theory of entitlements. The holder of the security interest, who created the ostensible ownership problem in the first place, ironically might be slightly better off than it would have been outside of bankruptcy, because it would participate, pro rata, in the $5,000 so avoided.[27]

Viewing section 544(b) from the perspective of bankruptcy as a set of procedures governing debt collection, then, suggests that the perpetuation of *Moore v. Bay* (as commonly read) in the new statute is unfortunate because it upsets instead of implements the notion of relative values.[28]

27. To see that this is so, consider an extension of the hypothetical developed in text. Debtor has, in addition to the asset worth $10,000 that is subject to the $10,000 security interest, assets worth $50,000. Outside of bankruptcy, holders of the $5,000 of claims that can defeat Secured Party's interest will get paid in full. Secured Party will get the $5,000 that remains of the $10,000 asset. Its remaining $5,000 claim will be unsecured and added to the $95,000 of remaining unsecured claims. Since there are $50,000 of assets remaining, these unsecured creditors will receive, on average (assuming no collective proceeding) fifty cents on the dollar. Secured Party, accordingly, will expect to receive $7,500—$5,000 from its "unavoided" chattel mortgage and $2,500 from a distribution made on its unsecured claim.

Under what appears to be the favored outcome, the $5,000 that is avoided would not go, in bankruptcy, to the $5,000 of claims that could avoid it outside of bankruptcy. Instead, the $5,000 would become an asset of the estate, available to the unsecured creditors generally—the $95,000 of other unsecured creditors plus the $5,000 of unsecured creditors whose rights measured the avoiding rights of the trustee plus the $5,000 avoided interest of Secured Party. This would make the pool of unsecured claims grow to $105,000. The pool of assets has also grown, however, by the same amount, as it is now $55,000, not $50,000. Each unsecured claimant, therefore, will get slightly more than fifty cents on the dollar (52.38 cents); Secured Party will end up with slightly more ($7,619) than its nonbankruptcy expectancy of $7,500.

Section 4–604(b)(1) of the Proposed Bankruptcy Act of 1973 not only would have reversed Moore v. Bay on the issue of the amount that could be avoided in bankruptcy but also would have limited the beneficiaries of that recovery to those whose interests the trustee succeeded to. See Report of the Commission on the Bankruptcy Laws of the United States, H. Doc. No. 137, 93rd Cong., 1st Sess., Part I, at 20 (1973); see also J. MacLachlan, supra note 21, at 322 (such a result "would not be stultifying"). But see Hearings Before the Subcommittee on Improvements in Judicial Machinery of the Committee on the Judiciary, United States Senate, on S. 235 and S. 236, 94th Cong., 1st Sess., Part II, at 984 (1975) (position of National Bankruptcy Conference that the trustee should not be cast "in the role of a private attorney" and that "all of the other avoiding powers of the trustee . . . are exercised for the benefit of the entire estate, which is to say for all of the creditors").

28. The impact of the doctrine of Moore v. Bay is substantially less today than it was earlier, because of a change in state law and a clarification of the avoiding power. The Uniform Commercial Code provides that tardily perfected security interests are subor-

It also suggests the less obvious point that the general thrust of section 544(b) is also unprincipled, to the extent that it forces a particular unsecured creditor to share the valuable right to avoid a property interest with the entire class of unsecured creditors.[29] The harm is imposed on different parties and may differ in amount, but the nature of the harm—the upsetting of relative values—is no different in principle. It leads, moreover, to the same result: the creation of incentives to resort to bankruptcy, not for collective reasons, but for reasons of individual advantage.

State-created Priorities and Statutory Liens

The range of property interests that are not recognized in bankruptcy does not end with those that the trustee can reach using section 544. Over the course of this century some rules created by nonbankruptcy law have emerged that have the effect of giving some claimants priority over others in bankruptcy. These laws—putting aside those allowing the creation and priority of consensual interests—are of two types. Some are rules that fix the rights of these claimants relative to others in all places and at all times. A mechanic's lien is a good example of this. A mechanic acquires a property right in property that it repairs that is good against competing claimants, at least if the mechanic remains in possession of the repaired property. No principle of bankruptcy law would call for ignoring the relative value of such an entitlement in bankruptcy. This will be called a *true statutory lien*, meaning that it is a priority right that is effective outside of bankruptcy and accordingly should be respected inside bankruptcy as well.

---

dinated only to those creditors that acquire a property interest—an execution lien or a perfected security interest—during the gap. Uniform Commercial Code §§9–301(1)(b), 9–312(5) (1978). The trustee may not succeed to the rights of such a creditor because §544(b) only allows him to do so in the case of unsecured creditors. The impact of *Moore v. Bay,* however, is not entirely gone: it may still have an effect on transactions that, although avoidable by *some* unsecured creditors under state law, are not avoidable by *all* unsecured creditors on the date of bankruptcy. See, e.g., Uniform Fraudulent Conveyance Act §§4–6 (1919) (actions fraudulent as to *existing* creditors, unlike §7 fraudulent conveyances, which are fraudulent "as to both present and future creditors"); Uniform Commercial Code §6–109 (1978) (noncomplying bulk transfers are avoidable by those creditors "holding claims based on transactions or events occurring before the bulk transfer"). Cf. *In re* Verco Industries, 704 F.2d 1134 (9th Cir. 1983). See generally McLaughlin, "Application of the Uniform Fraudulent Conveyance Act," 46 *Harv. L. Rev.* 404, 430 (1933).

29. If the cost of distinguishing between the two classes of unsecured creditors is high, the analysis is more complex. See supra note 10.

A state, however, may create another kind of priority right—one that applies only when the debtor is in bankruptcy or in another collective proceeding or perhaps when the debtor is insolvent. This could either be cast as a state-created priority—a "statutory advantage to be given effect on distribution"[30]—or as a lien that becomes effective upon bankruptcy (or similar nonbankruptcy occurrence).[31] These will be called *state-created priorities* and *bankruptcy statutory liens.*[32]

Beginning in the 1930s bankruptcy law has moved to refuse to recognize attempts by a state to elevate the relative position of the claims of any one type of claimant in bankruptcy through the device of either a state-created priority or a bankruptcy statutory lien.[33] The purpose of this interdiction should be clear against the backdrop we have been exploring. The reason is not that it is bad to allow states to prefer some creditors to others. To be sure, state-created priorities and bankruptcy statutory liens attempt to direct relative positions in bankruptcy. In their effect in bankruptcy, however, they are indistinguishable from other types of nonbankruptcy entitlements routinely recognized in bankruptcy.[34]

30. J. MacLachlan, supra note 21, at 145 (distinguishing a priority from a property right). A brief history of the demise of state-created priorities is contained in Analysis of H.R. 12889, 74th Cong., 2d Sess. 201 (1936).

31. The 1938 legislation, which eliminated the bankruptcy priority for state-created priorities, also expressly validated state-created statutory liens but declared that they would be paid after administrative expenses and wages priorities. Chandler Act, ch. 575, §67c, 52 Stat. 877 (1938). In 1952 an amendment struck down all statutory liens that attached to personal property and were not accompanied by "possession, levy, sequestration or distraint," Act of July 7, 1952, ch. 579, 66 Stat. 420. See generally Kennedy, "Statutory Liens in Bankruptcy," 39 *Minn. L. Rev.* 697, 703–22 (1955). When this test proved unsatisfactory, Congress amended §67c of the Bankruptcy Act of 1898 to strike down statutory liens that became "effective upon the insolvency of the debtor, or upon distribution or liquidation of his property, or upon execution against his property levied at the instance of one other than the lienor" or were not "perfected or enforceable at the date of bankruptcy against one acquiring the rights of a bona fide purchaser from the debtor on that date." Bankruptcy Act of 1898 §67(c). This is the test that is now embodied in §545.

32. These three categories are set out and described in *In re* Telemart Enterprises, Inc., 524 F.2d 761 (9th Cir. 1975). Generally, *Telemart* noted, true statutory liens are "valid" in bankruptcy (i.e., the holder's property right will be respected in bankruptcy, and that holder may exercise it in full), whereas the other two categories—what it called "spurious" statutory liens and state priorities—were not to be recognized in bankruptcy.

33. Chandler Act, ch. 575, 52 Stat. 840–940 (1938). See S. Rep. No. 1159, 89th Cong., 2d Sess. (1966); *In re* Federal's, 553 F.2d 509 (6th Cir. 1977).

34. Occasionally, a state-created priority will be distinguished from a lien on the ground that its holder is paid only after all "true" lienholders have been paid and therefore is somewhat suspicious. See Comment, "Statutory Liens Under Section 67c of the Bankruptcy Act: Some Problems of Definition," 43 *Tul. L. Rev.* 305 (1969). From the perspective of

The difficulty with state-created priorities and bankruptcy statutory liens is that they suffer from the same problem examined in the first chapter: self-interest leading to uses of the bankruptcy process that run contrary to the interests of the creditors as a group. A creditor enjoying a state-created priority will demand to be treated similarly outside of bankruptcy as well. A creditor with such a priority right, moreover, may try to initiate a bankruptcy proceeding because bankruptcy serves it well, even though a collective proceeding would not be beneficial to the group of creditors. Either the bankruptcy proceeding will be commenced, or the creditors will try to negotiate around that result—a negotiation process that, because of the number of creditors involved and associated free-rider and hold-out problems, may be largely intractable. State-created priorities and bankruptcy statutory liens are, in that respect, like ipso facto clauses examined in Chapter 2. Bankruptcy's refusal to recognize them solves this problem and requires that a state that wishes to give someone a priority should do so by means of an entitlement that is good both in and out of bankruptcy's collective forum.[35]

This distinction is easy to formulate and apply: the sorting between good and bad statutory entitlements is done according to whether they apply across the board or are bankruptcy-specific. But a failure to keep in mind the limited role of bankruptcy as a collective debt-collection device has led to substantial confusion in the application of the prohibition on state-created entitlements good only in bankruptcy.[36] If an

---

general creditors, however, the effect is the same: the person with the entitlement must be paid in full first. See *Strom v. Peikes*, 123 F.2d 1003, 1006 (2d Cir. 1941).

35. The puzzle with respect to state-created priorities and bankruptcy statutory liens is why a state would enact an entitlement that is good only in bankruptcy. Part of the answer is that, at least based on reported cases from the past three decades or so, few such statutes have been passed. See sources cited, next note. Once such state-created priorities and bankruptcy statutory liens survive the "bankruptcy only" interdiction of §545, however, there is no reason to analyze them differently from consensual liens. Thus, the tests of §544(a)—limited as discussed earlier in the chapter—should then apply. Section 545(2), however, uses instead a bona fide purchaser test, which is too broad for the reasons discussed previously. Compare S. Rep. No. 989, 95th Cong., 2d Sess. 86 (1978) (making similar point with respect to applicability of bona fide purchaser test to tax liens) with 124 Cong. Rec. H. 11,097 (Sept. 28, 1978) (explicitly noting that tax liens are subject to bona fide purchaser test).

36. Since the date of these enactments few statutes involving a true state-created priority or bankruptcy statutory lien have been tested. A possible example of such a statute was Mass. Gen. Laws Ann. ch. 254, §31 (West 1961). The statute "causes a lien to arise in favor of materialmen upon the adjudication in bankruptcy of certain contractors." N.W. Day Supply Co. v. Valenti, 343 F.2d 756 (1st Cir. 1965) (declaring the statute invalid in bankruptcy); see also Strom v. Peikes, 123 F.2d 1003 (2d Cir. 1941). Even a statute such as Uniform Commercial Code §9–306(4) (1978) does not seem to give an incentive to a

entitlement is enforceable outside of bankruptcy, there is no reason, stemming from the justifications underlying condemnation of state-created priorities or bankruptcy statutory liens, to refuse recognition of the value of the entitlement in bankruptcy.[37] For example, consider a state statute that refuses to permit transfer of a liquor license until particular debts are paid—perhaps taxes to the state or debts arising from the supply of liquor. Or perhaps the statute says that upon the sale of a liquor business the state (or liquor suppliers) have priority in *all* the assets of the business. These statutes effectively give priority, by one means or another, to the state or to liquor suppliers. It may be hard to justify these statutes, but justification of nonbankruptcy entitlements is not the point when examining bankruptcy law. Bankruptcy law takes relative values as it finds them in order to effectively implement its policies unless recognition of those relative values actually interferes with bankruptcy's attempt to ameliorate a common pool problem through collectivization.

So viewed, these kinds of statutes (or at least their relative values) should be respected in bankruptcy. Analysis of these issues is straightforward, as a bankruptcy matter, once one sees that the question is simply one of relative rights among claimants outside of bankruptcy. Consider, for example, the effect of a statute that refused to permit a transfer of a liquor license unless the transferor had paid (or otherwise made satisfactory arrangements to pay) all debts or taxes arising from the conduct of the liquor business. In analyzing such a statute, in *Anchorage International Inn,* the Ninth Circuit saw clearly the relevant bankruptcy issue and brushed aside arguments that this statute was invalid as a state-created priority:

> The mechanic's lien and the security interest under the Uniform Commercial Code are but two examples of interests in particular property, created pursuant to state statutes, that are fully respected by the general bankruptcy law. The trustee's contention that states cannot allow some creditors to receive more of the proceeds of the sale of a bankrupt's assets than others receive is thus incorrect . . .

---

secured creditor to file for bankruptcy, as it generally gives it less than the secured creditor would receive outside of bankruptcy. See 2 G. Gilmore, supra note 13, at 1337–38. The section, for that reason, ironically may give a strategic advantage to *unsecured* creditors. As such, it may be thought of as equally undesirable; but §9–306(4) has never been challenged on that ground.

37. The failure to recognize this simple point has led to a variety of confusing and ill-considered decisions of appellate courts. Indeed, the pre-1938 explicit recognition of state-created priorities by the Bankruptcy Act of 1898 may itself be the root of the evil.

[T]he Alaska statute does not conflict with the federal distribution scheme because there is no general federal policy against state-created liens that favor one class of creditors over another. [The statute] does not, as the bankruptcy court concluded, "frustrate the [Bankruptcy] Act's purpose of providing an equitable distribution of a bankrupt's non-exempt property to all creditors of the same class." Creditors who hold prior rights under the Alaska statue are simply not in the "same class" as other creditors.

Since federal bankruptcy law does override state-created priorities that apply only in the event of bankruptcy, we must examine the statute to determine whether it in fact has force and effect independent of the bankruptcy proceeding . . . We conclude that the creditors' rights created by the Alaska statute exist independent of the debtor's insolvency and accordingly should be recognized by the trustee.

Regardless of when a license holder seeks to transfer an Alaska liquor license, all liquor-related claims must be paid first . . . The transfer caused by the trustee's need to liquidate the assets of the estate is no different from any other transfer in or outside of bankruptcy.[38]

This opinion is a straightforward application of bankruptcy as a response to a common pool problem in interpreting the mandates of the statute.[39]

---

38. 718 F.2d 1446, 1451–52 (9th Cir. 1983).

39. Analysis has not always been that easy, however, for the Ninth Circuit. For a long time it was seduced by a different notion of state-created priorities. *Anchorage International Inn* was preceded by substantial embarrassments caused by the court's inability to sort out what was wrong with state-created priorities or bankruptcy statutory liens. Eight years earlier, in *In re* Leslie, 520 F.2d 761 (9th Cir. 1975), for example, the Ninth Circuit struck down a statute giving priority, as a condition of transfer of a liquor license, in the proceeds of the liquor license and other business assets, to liquor suppliers (over the claims of other general creditors). It struck down the statute on two grounds. For one, the Ninth Circuit reasoned, the statute "creates statutory priorities, not statutory liens. See Grover Escrow Corp. v. Gole, 1969, 71 Cal.2d 61, 65, 77 Cal. Rptr. 21, 23, 453 P.2d 461, 463 (characterizing [the state statute] as establishing a mandatory and exclusive system of priorities)" (id. at 762). As for the second ground, the Ninth Circuit found that the state had attempted to direct the priorities to more than the liquor license, an asset the state had created, and "while a state, as the creator of a liquor license, may validly impose conditions on its transferability for the state's own benefit, it may not, consistently with paramount federal law, impose conditions which discriminate in favor of a particular class of creditors" (id. at 763). But these reasons do not withstand analysis. As for the first, the Ninth Circuit pointed to an opinion of the California Supreme Court that, to be sure, *called* the interest created by the statutory scheme a *priority*, not a *lien*. But one of the principal observations derived from the collectivization norm is that bankruptcy takes attributes, not labels, from nonbankruptcy law. The opinion in question clearly was using a common word to describe a result: victory for the holder of the interest. See Grover Escrow Corp. v. Gole, 71 Cal.2d 61, 62, 453 P.2d 461, 461, 77 Cal. Rptr. 21, 21 (1969) (statute gives "priority" to those listed over those who levy). The relevant attribute—fully met in any reading of the California opinion—was whether the interest was effective outside of bankruptcy. The state's label for that attribute is of no relevance whatsoever. As for the second reason, it is hard to fathom why the court thought that the issue of who was benefited was important, except

It, moreover, provides a clue for examining property of the estate questions, the subject we turn to next.

---

in the unprincipled sense of helping the court distinguish an earlier case, *In re* Leslie, 520 F.2d, at 762 (distinguishing United States v. State of California, 281 F.2d 726 [9th Cir. 1960]).

4

Determining the Assets Available for Distribution

THE DETERMINATION of liabilities is only half of what the basic bankruptcy process needs to concern itself with. The assets of the debtor as well as its liabilities must be fixed in order to determine the estate of a debtor available for distribution to particular claimants. The liabilities of the estate reduce what is available to the remaining residual claimants, while the assets increase it. In deciding what counts as an asset, we can start by answering a simple question: is the estate more valuable with the item under consideration than without it?

For the most part, the task of determining assets is fairly straightforward. The assembled assets of the debtor form an "estate." Under section 541 this estate is comprised of all "legal or equitable interests of the debtor in property as of the commencement of the case." Thus, if Debtor is a retail store and has no secured creditors, its inventory, its equipment, and the store itself (assuming that Debtor owns it) are property of the estate. This is proper because Debtor is more valuable with these things than without them. If Debtor leases property, the bankruptcy estate consists only of Debtor's interest in the property, namely, its right to use the property during the duration of the leasehold. Again, including this is proper because (putting aside for the moment the question of the associated liabilities[1]) Debtor is more valuable with this leased property than without it. The estate also includes intangible property, such as accounts receivable and the patents, trade secrets, and copyrights that Debtor holds. As a first approximation, in the case of a corporate debtor, property of the estate is simply any right the debtor enjoys that enhances its value.

1. I examine the question of executory contracts in Chapter 5.

This definition of property of the estate needs several qualifications when dealing with debtors who are individuals. A bankruptcy proceeding gives individuals a discharge right. To give substance to the individual's entitlement to a fresh start free of past indebtedness, one must draw a distinction between certain kinds of assets. The most valuable asset individuals have is usually their future income stream from labor, and this asset is not part of the bankruptcy estate, at least to the extent that it can be traced to labor and not to capital.[2] It is unnecessary to make this distinction in the case of a corporation. A corporation's present value turns on its ability to earn money in the future using its existing assets. Accordingly, it is proper to consider rents, profits, and proceeds of existing assets as a part of the bankruptcy estate, a result codified in section 541(a)(6).

A related but distinct issue concerns property that an individual debtor owns at the time of the petition but is nevertheless thought necessary for the fresh start. For example, one might allow an individual to keep, in addition to his future income stream, the clothes on his back and the tools of his trade. As the Bankruptcy Code is structured, however, such property, unlike future income, is deemed property of the estate under section 541. Another Code section distinguishes between property of the estate that creditors may enjoy and property that the individual debtor is allowed to keep.[3] These distinctions relate more to the question of the individual's right to a financial fresh start than to any process whereby assets are gathered for distribution among creditors, our current focus. In this chapter we examine the general problem of identifying assets of the debtor that creditors in bankruptcy can look to for the purpose of satisfying obligations owed them.

Identifying Assets and Identifying to Whom They Have Value

At first glance the questions of assets and liabilities appear to be at opposite poles. Nonetheless there is a close, indeed symbiotic, relationship between the two issues. One must focus on *who* benefits from having something declared an asset. From the perspective of the class of residual claimants, it is possible to determine what is an asset only after the priority interests of the various claimants are set out. This point is obviously true when one contemplates the rights of a bailor to have goods returned to

2. §541(a)(6); see *In re* Fitzsimmons, 725 F.2d 1208 (9th Cir. 1984).
3. §522.

it: its property interest is respected in full and the residual claimants get nothing.[4] Goods on lease or on bailment to a debtor are, as a matter of nonbankruptcy law, considered to be owned by the lessor or bailor, notwithstanding the fact that the debtor is in possession of the assets. In these cases nonbankruptcy law is clear in its determination: all claimants derive their rights to assert claims against assets through the debtor and accordingly must take the assets as they come into the hands of the debtor. Creditors of a dry cleaner, for example, cannot lay claim to all the clothes being cleaned at the time the dry cleaner files a bankruptcy petition. One way of expressing this conclusion is to say that the owners of the clothes "win" relative to the creditors of the dry cleaners.

That point is equally true where the estate can claim for the benefit of unsecured creditors only the equity interest in land or chattels that are subject to either statutory liens or security interests. General creditors have only residual rights to property that is subject to a properly perfected security interest. The security interest is itself a property right giving a particular creditor rights superior to the debtor and the other creditors in certain assets. In contrast to the case of clothes at the dry cleaner, we tend to think of this situation as one of ordering claimants against property owned by the debtor, because nonbankruptcy law would locate title in the debtor. But location of title is a label, and bankruptcy law should be concerned with attributes. Thus, similar conclusions can be reached whether the focus is one of determining relative orderings of liabilities—the nominal topic of the previous two chapters—or one of determining the extent of the debtor's rights in property—the nominal topic of this chapter.

For example, at the conclusion of the previous chapter the focus was on certain statutory priorities or liens. They were examined in that context because nonbankruptcy law had framed the issue as one of determining rankings against an asset that nonbankruptcy law said the debtor owned. But *reversing* the way nonbankruptcy law frames the issue can and often does lead to the same outcome. Consider the case of statutory trusts. A statutory trust is a device that locates nominal ownership other than in the hands of the debtor. A typical statutory trust was dealt with in *Selby v. Ford Motor Co.*[5] A Michigan statute provided for a "trust fund" for the benefit of subcontractors of funds paid by the owner to the contractor, and the contractor "shall be considered a trustee of all such

---

4. This is expressed in §541(a) by the concept that what comes into the estate is not "property" but the debtor's "interests" in property. See H. Rep. No. 595, 95th Cong., 1st Sess. 352–53 (1977).

5. 590 F.2d 642 (6th Cir. 1979).

funds."[6] Analytically, this way of characterizing the situation is no different, from the perspective of relevant attributes (i.e., rights among claimants), from what would result if a state statute that gave the subcontractor a true statutory lien on the funds. In the one case (the trust) nominal ownership of the funds is lodged in the subcontractor, and hence the asset is not viewed as "belonging" to the contractor in the first instance; in the other case (the lien) nominal ownership of the funds is lodged in the contractor, and the asset is viewed as the contractor's, subject, however, to the rights of subcontractors to get paid first from it. From the perspective of bankruptcy law, there is no relevant difference. As long as the statutory trust is effective against creditors outside of bankruptcy, its relative value should be respected in bankruptcy as well. *Selby*, noting "the traditional role of the state in creating and defining the underlying property interests," agreed.

In its discussion the court noted that commentators had argued for invalidity, asserting that "statutory trusts should be treated as statutory liens because statutory trusts function as a security device, and 'the application of a national bankruptcy statute to legal interests diversely defined' by the states requires classification 'on the basis of function rather than nomenclature.' " [7] Although the assimilation of statutory trusts and statutory liens is sensible, the result would be opposite to that sought by the commentators. Whether classified as a statutory trust or a statutory lien, the subcontractors' interest in *Selby* warranted recognition in bankruptcy precisely *because* one cares about function, not nomenclature. The important issue is to focus on the relevant function for purposes of bankruptcy, which surely is the question of relative entitlements.

The point, moreover, also applies to many other types of rights. Someone may, for example, have the right to refuse to transfer a certain chattel to a debtor or to decline to renew an existing lease unless and until certain debts are paid. Yet no matter how the rights are described as a matter of state law, the substantive consequences among claimants are the same: the holder of the right gets to satisfy his claim first; other claimants get only what is left over. The analytical structure is the same no matter whether the doctrinal question is posed as one of identifying the property of the estate or as one of determining the relative value of a particular claim.

6. Mich. Comp. Laws Ann. §570.151 (1967).

7. 590 F.2d, at 646 (quoting Note, "The Statutory Trust Fund in Bankruptcy," 50 *Yale L.J.* 1268, 1271 [1941]).

The current tests under bankruptcy law for determining the property of the estate, then, have been needlessly complicated by a failure to observe the close linkages between assets and liabilities outside bankruptcy law. Certain assets that appear to an outside observer to be the debtor's[8] and hence available to the debtor's claimants, for example, may be assets that nonbankruptcy law says belong to someone else. This can be rephrased to say that the person who claims to own the property in question is entitled to prevail over the other claimants of the debtor. However the inquiry is phrased, the outcome should be the same.

The proper approach, therefore, is to examine any concrete situation from the vantage point of an unsecured creditor attempting to execute on a particular asset or to assert a security interest in it. This is the vantage point of section 544(a), examined in the last chapter. In deciding how to pay claimants in the bankruptcy process, it is first necessary to determine how much there is. Moreover, it is necessary to ask how much there is from the perspective of someone. Generally, this issue is addressed from the perspective of the unsecured creditors. This approach demonstrates the relationship between determining assets and determining liabilities because deciding how much there is from the perspective of the unsecured creditors often requires one to resolve the *ordering* of claimants against what is there. If unsecured creditors cannot execute against an asset as a matter of nonbankruptcy law, then that property has no value to them and should not be considered to be (to that extent, at least) property of the estate. And if execution by an unsecured creditor must take a back seat to some other entity's rights, then only the residual value would be an asset from the perspective of the unsecured creditors.

Using the proper approach shows the analytical error of cases such as *In re Gunder*.[9] In that case a father bought an automobile for his child. The automobile was titled in the name of the father, apparently for the purpose of permitting the father to get a discount on insurance. The bankruptcy judge, sensing that such was the motivation behind leaving the title in the name of the father, viewed the automobile as "really" belonging to the child and hence as property of the estate of the child within the meaning of section 541. Because the attributes of ownership of the automobile are fixed by state law, however, the conclusion does not necessarily follow from the premise. The father may have put the

---

8. Because, for example, of ostensible ownership.
9. 8 Bankr. 390 (Bankr. S.D. Ohio 1980).

title in his name solely for purposes of insurance, but the state-law *consequences* of doing that may not have been limited by the father's motivation.

According to the bankruptcy judge, the relevant state statute made ownership of the automobile as listed on the certificate of title "conclusive" as to who owned the automobile.[10] Notwithstanding this, the judge announced that state law cannot interfere with bankruptcy policy.[11] But he focused on the wrong issue if the effect of the state statute was to make the automobile unavailable to creditors of the child outside of bankruptcy. The relevant inquiry in *Gunder,* in other words, should have been on the *attributes* of the state statute. Did it mean that creditors of the child could not execute on the automobile? Did it mean that the child could not grant a security interest in the automobile to one of his creditors? If the answers to those questions were "yes," then the automobile should not have been considered to be property of the estate. It is then, as far as state law is concerned, like property on lease or bailment: having value to the debtor and his creditors only net of the rights of the lessor or bailor. There is no reason to upset that determination in bankruptcy.

This error, however, is not unique to the judge in *Gunder.* We have seen, for example, how nonbankruptcy attributes, not labels, suggest that state-created rights, whether labeled statutory liens or statutory trusts, should be respected in bankruptcy, as long as they are not limited in effectiveness to bankruptcy. But notwithstanding this point and its general acceptance in cases such as *Selby* and *Anchorage International Inn,* bankruptcy policy is commonly viewed as limiting the extent of statutory liens or statutory trusts. Consider, for example, *Elliott v. Bumb.*[12] In that case by California statute an issuer of money orders (called, in the statute, the *agent*) held the proceeds of money orders "in trust" for the benefit of the person in whose name the money order was issued (called the *licensee*). The statute further provided that if the agent commingled the proceeds with its own assets, "all assets of such agent shall be impressed with a trust in favor of . . . the licensee in the amount equal to the aggregate funds received or which should have been received by the agent

10. Id.

11. Id.: "The policy of the Bankruptcy Code, as reflected in . . . §541, is to provide for an estate consisting of all legal and equitable property interests of the debtor. [The state statute] cannot be applied in this proceeding to the extent that it purports to deny to the bankruptcy court the right to hear evidence pertaining to any interest which the debtors may have in the [automobile]."

12. 356 F.2d 749 (9th Cir.), cert. denied, 385 U.S. 829 (1966).

from such sale." The trust would remain until the amount due to the licensee was paid in full. The court held that this was a valid statutory trust that would be respected in bankruptcy because "[a]lthough one may become bankrupt, property which is held by him in trust belongs to the beneficiaries of the trust," but that it was valid only to the extent that the proceeds of the sale could be traced. To the extent that the impressed trust extended further, it would not be recognized in bankruptcy, because, according to the court, such an outcome relieves the seller of its normal obligation to trace the proceeds of the sale and thus effectively gives those sellers a priority over other general creditors in the unsecured portion of the debtor's estate. It held that this violated the principles of bankruptcy law: "Giving effect to the provisions of [the statute] . . . would open the door to state creation of priorities in favor of various classes of creditors by labeling such priorities as 'trusts.' This would tend to thwart or obstruct the scheme of federal bankruptcy law."[13]

This outcome, along with its reasoning, is widely accepted.[14] Yet it reflects a misconception of bankruptcy law. Although the sellers may have been relieved of the "normal" trust duty of tracing, that is just an attribute of this particular statutory trust. There is no reason to think that bankruptcy law has—or should have—a tracing rule that invalidates nonbankruptcy rules to the contrary. The relevant question[15] is the one

13. Id., at 754–55.

14. *In re* Telemart Enterprises, Inc., 624 F.2d 761 (9th Cir. 1975), for example, had this to say about the *Elliott* distinction: "Under state law, the issuer of the money order accepted payment only in the capacity of a trustee; he never held absolute ownership of the funds. We respected the state's definition of the issuer's relationship to those paid-in funds. On the other hand, we disregarded the state's attempt to impose a 'trust' on funds whose ownership had vested previously in the issuer. Regardless of the state's terminology, the effect of the statute was to give one class of creditors—purchasers of money orders—priority in the distribution of the bankrupt issuer's general assets." See also *In re* Independence Land Title Co. of Illinois, 18 Bankr. 673 (Bankr. N.D. Ill. 1982) ("Numerous cases have held that when a trustee possesses funds which the debtor once held as trustee or agent, the person claiming such funds is a general unsecured creditor to the extent he cannot identify or trace the funds in the trustee's hands back to the original trust or escrow account"); *In re* Casio Electric Corp., 28 Bankr. 191 (Bankr. E.D.N.Y. 1983). This view apparently derives from United States v. Randall, 401 U.S. 513 (1971) and Cunningham v. Brown, 265 U.S. 1, 11 (1924). But cf. *In re* Hurrican Elkhorn Coal Corp. II, 32 Bankr. 737, 740–41 (W.D. Ky. 1983) (deeming Elliott v. Bumb "implicitly repudiated" in Selby v. Ford Motor Co., 590 F.2d 646 [6th Cir. 1979]).

15. The discussion in text puts aside a question in the case that involved the particulars of the Bankruptcy Act of 1898. At that time §67(c)(2) of that Act invalidated, as against the trustee, statutory liens "on personal property not accompanied by possession of, or by levy upon or by sequestration or distraint of, such property." Arguably, this statutory provision justified the result in *Elliott*, although not its reasoning. This statutory provision, moreover, is subject to the same normative criticisms.

that the court never addressed in *Elliott:* the effect of this impressed trust vis-à-vis lien creditors and subsequent secured parties outside of bankruptcy. If it was valid against them outside of bankruptcy, there is no reason stemming from the collectivization of the process to refuse recognition of the value of that right in bankruptcy.[16] The general acceptance of *Elliott,* however, stems from the widespread failure to recognize this simple point about the relationship between nonbankruptcy rights and bankruptcy values.[17]

The above analysis can be extended further. Many assets are of value to a debtor and his general creditors but only net of some payment to someone else. This was the situation, for example, in the classic Supreme Court case, *Chicago Board of Trade v. Johnson.*[18] In that case William Henderson, the debtor, acting on behalf of his several companies, had a seat on the Chicago Board of Trade. These companies had accrued debts to other members of the Board of Trade. When Henderson was put into bankruptcy, his trustee wanted to sell the membership for cash. A rule of the Board of Trade, however, provided that, although members were entitled to transfer their seats to others meeting the membership requirements, this right of transfer could occur only after the debts of the transferor's companies to other members of the Board of Trade had been paid in full.

The trustee argued, and the District Court agreed, that he should be able to transfer the property in spite of the restrictions on transfer. He argued that unless he was able to do so, some of Henderson's creditors—those with seats on the Board of Trade—would do better than his other creditors, because those with seats would have to be paid in full before the membership could be sold. The Board of Trade, however, argued that the seat was not even property of the estate, pointing to an opinion

16. The statute appeared to validate the trust outside of bankruptcy by stating that an amount equal to the trust funds "shall not be subject to attachment, levy of execution or sequestration, by order of court."

17. See 124 Cong. Rec. H. 11,114 (Sept. 28, 1979) (floor statement of Rep. Edwards) (courts should permit the Internal Revenue Service to use reasonable assumptions to demonstrate that amounts of withheld taxes are still in the possession of the debtor). The Ninth Circuit, however, apparently continues to adhere to the view that tracing into commingled funds violates bankruptcy policy. See *In re* North American Coin & Currency, Ltd., 767 F.2d 1573, 1575 (9th Cir. 1985) ("we cannot accept the proposition that the bankruptcy estate is automatically deprived of any funds that state law might find subject to a constructive trust . . . [B]ecause of countervailing policies behind the Bankruptcy Act, [we held in *Elliott v. Bumb* that] state law could not be permitted to impose a trust on commingled property of a bankrupt's estate").

18. 264 U.S. 1 (1924).

of the highest court of the state *saying* that such a membership was not "property."[19]

It should be easy to see, from the vantage point of our theory, that neither side had it right. Bankruptcy law cares about attributes, not labels; hence, the state court label of "no property" is irrelevant. And the relevant attribute is: does this have value? Moreover, the question of value must be asked in context: value to whom? It is clear that, at least assuming that Henderson was not going to use it, the membership had value, in the first instance, to the other members, because it could not be sold without first paying them off in full. It is in that respect akin to the statutory scheme governing liquor licenses that we saw in the previous chapter in the discussion of *Anchorage International Inn.*

For that reason the trustee was wrong as well. The membership is property because it has value to the *class* of Henderson's creditors considered as a group. But—and this is why the trustee was wrong—it is treated in bankruptcy as it existed outside of bankruptcy, with its value to general creditors sharply restricted because of the relative priority of the claims of other members.

The Supreme Court saw this and correctly identified the inquiry as one of attributes under state law (and not the state law label of "no property"); so examined, the membership had value to the general unsecured creditors of the debtor only after the debts to the members of the Board of Trade were paid in full.[20] The Court, by respecting the value of the rights of the members, was determining both the ordering of claims and the value of the assets to the residual claimants.[21]

This analysis can now be extended by considering a modified version of the *Chicago Board of Trade* case. Assume that transfer of membership was not permitted by the rules of the Board of Trade. In such a case, we are dealing with a peculiar—but by no means fictional—kind of asset: a debtor is better off if it has this membership than if it does not, but its value is confined.[22] Outside of bankruptcy the debtor cannot sell this

---

19. Barclay v. Smith, 107 Ill. 349 (1883).

20. 264 U.S., at 14–15. The most relevant attribute for this purpose was the inability of lien creditors to trump the rights of the members. The Court noted that the right of transfer or sale was "subject to a right of his creditors to prevent his transfer or sale till he settled with them, a right in some respects similar to the typical lien of the common law."

21. See Countryman, "The Use of State Law in Bankruptcy Cases (pt. 1)," 47 *N.Y.U. L. Rev.* 407, 438 (1972) (discussing *Chicago Board of Trade* and noting "while what is 'property' was a question of federal bankruptcy law, the attributes of that property were still determined by state law and . . . the trustee won a Pyrrhic victory").

22. This is an attribute, for example, of FAA landing rights. In *In re* Braniff, 700 F.2d 935 (5th Cir. 1983), the Fifth Circuit appropriately held that they could not be sold by an

membership to raise cash. Nor can it use the membership as collateral for a loan (because the lender could never foreclose on it). Nor, for the same reason, can the debtor's creditors ever levy on it. The value of the membership, then, is reflected only in the fact that the debtor is able to make more money with it than without it.

Is the membership property of the estate? The answer would seem to be "yes" but subject to the caveat that the peculiar attributes of this asset limit its value. If debtor's business is being liquidated, the asset has no value outside of bankruptcy, so it has no value, in those circumstances, *in* bankruptcy either. Similarly, the asset has no value if the debtor does not need it any more, even if it is staying in business, because the asset cannot be sold. (Its value, in that instance, reverts to the Board of Trade.) But if the business is being reorganized, it is possible that the membership may have value to the creditors. Whether it does depends on analyzing the *nature* of that reorganization by assimilating its attributes to the relevant nonbankruptcy ones, which permit the debtor to keep the membership but which prohibit others from using it.

To explore this last point more fully, it is useful to analyze several kinds of rights against this backdrop. One case that illustrates the problem concerns the right to draw on funds under a letter of credit. Consider the facts of *In re Swift Aire Lines, Inc.*[23] Swift Aire was a commercial air service. One of its largest creditors was Wells Fargo Bank. One of the arrangements that Swift Aire and Wells Fargo had reached was a deal that Colin, the principal shareholder of Swift Aire, would agree to contribute, by loan or purchase of stock, $775,000 to Swift Aire, should it be determined that the business needed the money to continue operations. As is common in such deals, Wells Fargo insisted that Colin obtain a standby letter of credit from a bank in favor of Swift Aire that could be drawn on if Swift Aire needed cash. In this sense the letter of credit, an independent obligation of the bank that issues it, stands as assurance that the money will be forthcoming irrespective of the desires or solvency of Colin at the time the money is due. The key attribute of a letter of credit is that it is a binding obligation of a bank to honor drafts drawn on it when a complying draft is presented with the exact documents called for in the letter of credit.[24] In this case the letter of credit, which was issued by Crocker Bank, called for no documents. Instead, the letter

---

airline in bankruptcy to another airline. It, however, incorrectly concluded that FAA landing rights were not "property." Id., at 942. They were, but they were restricted in value by applicable nonbankruptcy rules.

23. 30 Bankr. 490 (9th Cir. Bankr. App. 1983).

24. See Baird, "Standby Letters of Credit in Bankruptcy," 49 *U. Chi. L. Rev.* 130 (1982).

of credit specified that the draft used to draw on the credit must state that the funds were necessary for the continued operations of Swift Aire and that it be signed by the corporate secretary of Swift Aire.

Swift Aire filed for bankruptcy, and its trustee attempted to draw on the letter of credit by presenting a draft requesting the funds signed by the trustee. Crocker refused to honor the letter of credit. Aside from the question of whether the trustee correctly stated that the money was necessary for the continued operations of Swift Aire (which was liquidating),[25] the basic question presented by the case was whether the trustee in bankruptcy could draw on a letter of credit that had named the debtor as the beneficiary.

In addressing that issue, one begins with an examination of underlying attributes. If the letter of credit had stated that Crocker would honor drafts on it drawn either by Swift Aire or by its trustee in bankruptcy, there would be no problem.[26] When Swift Aire filed for bankruptcy and the trustee attempted to draw on the letter of credit, he would have been capable of presenting a complying draft—one that complied *exactly* with the requirements of the letter of credit.[27]

Does the problem change if the letter of credit does not mention the ability of the trustee to draw on the letter of credit but simply says that it can be drawn on by Swift Aire? Analysis still depends on the non-bankruptcy attributes of a letter of credit, but now we must also try to analogize the status of the trustee *to* those nonbankruptcy attributes. It may, for example, be one thing to say that the trustee can draw on the letter of credit but quite another to say that the trustee can assign that right to, say, Pan Am. The first question one needs to ask is what a draw by the trustee represents: is it effectively, according to the best non-bankruptcy analogy, a draw by Swift Aire, or is it effectively a draw by Pan Am? In *Swift Aire* the letter of credit called for a statement signed by the corporate secretary of Swift Aire. That requirement—unlike, say, one calling for the signature of "John Smith, as corporate secretary"— would be satisfied by the signature of whoever happened to be the corporate secretary of Swift Aire at the time of the draw. The letter of credit, for example, presumably could have been drawn on by the cor-

25. It is conceivable that the draw could have been enjoined on the ground of fraud, but that is a nonbankruptcy issue concerning letter of credit law. See Uniform Commercial Code §5–114(2) (1978); Sztejn v. Schroder Banking Corp., 177 Misc. 719, 722, 31 N.Y.S.2d 631, 634–35 (Sup. Ct. 1941).

26. In the actual case Colin had agreed with Wells Fargo that the letter of credit could be drawn on in bankruptcy. This statement, however, was not included in the letter of credit issued by Crocker.

27. Uniform Commercial Code §5–114 (1978).

porate secretary following a change of its owners or managers or in a state-law dissolution of Swift Aire. The question then becomes one of how best to mirror those attributes by meshing what occurs in bankruptcy with the relevant nonbankruptcy attributes. Here, the trustee in bankruptcy looks like a surrogate for the officers of Swift Aire. The best way to allow bankruptcy law to mirror state law, accordingly, would be to allow the bankruptcy trustee to draw on the letter of credit.[28]

This tie between nonbankruptcy attributes and what occurs in bankruptcy was recognized by the Supreme Court in considering another unusual form of property. In *Commodity Futures Exchange Commission v. Weintraub*[29] the question was whether the trustee of a debtor in a chapter 7 liquidation could waive the corporate attorney-client privilege. That privilege, which permits a corporation to protect communications between its management and its attorneys,[30] had been invoked by Weintraub, who had represented Chicago Discount Commodity Brokers, the debtor, as an attorney in the past. The trustee attempted to waive it on behalf of the debtor. Weintraub resisted, asserting in essence that the right was a right personal to the company and did not pass to its trustee and that, moreover, permitting the trustee to waive the privilege so as to investigate management would "chill" the privilege.[31]

In light of our analysis of letters of credit, what is wrong with Weintraub's argument should be clear. One needs to start analyzing a question of assets (or liabilities) in bankruptcy by focusing on its relevant nonbankruptcy attributes. The attorney-client privilege of a corporation is a privilege that resides in its current management. Outside of bankruptcy, existing management of the corporation can waive the privilege in order to investigate the actions of its predecessors.[32] Thus, management of the company always runs the risk that communications it holds

---

28. The actual case addressed the correct question (one focuses on nonbankruptcy attributes) but then seemed to confuse the analysis of the status of the trustee. It held, *In re* Swift Aire Lines, Inc., 30 Bankr. 490 (9th Cir. Bankr. App. 1983): "Swift's officers and directors have no power or authority to deal with the estate, its assets or its affairs. The trustee, only, is empowered to dispose of business assets, and when appropriate authority is obtained, to operate the business. By filing bankruptcy, Swift has made it impossible for Wells Fargo or Swift to draw against the letter of credit. Since there is no longer a corporate secretary able to act for the debtor, the statement required by the letter of credit cannot be signed by the designated individual." The last sentence of this statement elevates meaningless form over substance.

29. 105 S.Ct. 1986 (1985).

30. 8 J. Wigmore, *Evidence* §2292, at 554 (J. McNaughton rev. ed. 1961).

31. See Commodity Futures Exchange Comm. v. Weintraub, 722 F.2d 338, 342–43 (7th Cir. 1984), *rev'd*, 105 S.Ct. 1986 (1985).

32. See, e.g., *In re* O.P.M. Leasing Servs., Inc., 670 F.2d 383, 386 (2d Cir. 1982); *In re* Grand Jury Investigation, 599 F.2d 1224, 1236 (3d Cir. 1979).

with the corporation's attorneys will be disclosed should management of the corporation change, as might occur, for example, following a change in stock ownership in the company.

The ability of a bankruptcy trustee to waive the privilege should be clear. Bankruptcy is properly viewed as an occasion where the ownership of the corporation does in fact fundamentally change. Whereas before bankruptcy the shareholders are the ones with the decision-making powers, they forfeit that right to creditors upon default, and bankruptcy presumptively indicates a default through insolvency. Thus, it is proper to view the creditors as the owners of a firm in bankruptcy and the trustee as their manager. Just as a letter of credit that requires the signature of the corporate secretary can be drawn by the trustee, so, too, can the trustee step into the shoes of management and exercise a right that resides in current management of the company.[33] This point was clearly expressed by the Supreme Court in *Weintraub:* "[W]e conclude that vesting in the trustee control of the corporation's attorney-client privilege most closely comports with the allocation of the waiver power to management outside of bankruptcy without in any way obstructing the careful design of the Bankruptcy Code."[34] Thus, the issue is not one of "chilling" the privilege because of an independent bankruptcy policy. To the extent that the privilege is chilled, it is a result of the nonbankruptcy attributes of that privilege.[35] Bankruptcy law simply mirrors those attributes when it permits the trustee to waive the privilege.

Restrictions on Assets and the Role of Section 541(c)

As we have seen, the basic rule for liabilities in bankruptcy is that they are accelerated, at least when the debtor is liquidating. The basic rule

33. See Comment, "Waiver of the Attorney-Client Privilege by the Trustee in Bankruptcy," 51 *U. Chi. L. Rev.* 1230, 1245 (1984) ("Under this framework, the role of the trustee in bankruptcy is most closely analogous, in the case of a corporate debtor, to that of new management, and thus the trustee should possess the same power to waive the attorney-client privilege that new management would have outside of bankruptcy").

34. 105 S.Ct., at 1994. The court noted, as well, that if the debtor is insolvent, "the trustee's exercise of the corporation's attorney-client privilege will benefit only creditors, but there is nothing anomalous in this result; rather, it is in keeping with the hierarchy of interests . . ." Id.

35. The Supreme Court noted that the risk of chilling the attorney-client privilege "is no greater here than in the case of a solvent corporation, where individual officers and directors always run the risk that successor management might waive the . . . privilege with respect to prior management's communication with counsel." Id., at 1995. Judged by the standards discussed here, *Weintraub* gets high marks indeed.

for assets, however, seems to be to the contrary. Section 541(c)(1) provides that

> an interest of the debtor in property becomes property of the estate . . . notwithstanding any provision in an agreement, transfer instrument, or applicable nonbankruptcy law—
>
> (A) that restricts or conditions transfer of such interest by the debtor; or
>
> (B) that is conditioned on the insolvency or financial condition of the debtor, on the commencement of a case under this title, or on the appointment of or taking possession by a trustee in a case under this title or a custodian before such commencement, and that effects or gives an option to effect a forfeiture, modification, or termination of the debtor's interest in property.

In many cases, such as where an asset is owned outright by a debtor, the possibility of its losing its value in bankruptcy is not a problem. Like a matured loan, there is no issue of acceleration because there is nothing to accelerate. But sometimes the concept of acceleration is a consideration. Consider the case of an asset that is being used by the debtor subject to the power of another to remove it upon the occasion of certain events. If one of the events that occasions loss of the use of the asset is bankruptcy or a similar financial event, section 541(c)(1)(B) states that the asset becomes property of the estate notwithstanding that provision.

The symbiotic relationship between assets and liabilities in bankruptcy may suggest, at first glance, a tension between this doctrine and the general rule of liabilities, which, as we saw in Chapter 2, provides for automatic acceleration, at least in a liquidation proceeding. For a below-market loan—a liability—also has attributes of an asset. The value of a below-market loan is that assets can be sold for more if they can be sold with that loan in place than without it, a fact learned by many home sellers (and buyers) during the past decade, when having an "assumable" mortgage at a low interest rate often added greatly to the value of a house.

But at least in connection with the pure assets of a debtor—those that the debtor has the use of but has no corresponding obligation other than to return them upon the occurrence of specified events—the rule of section 541(c)(1)(B) seems proper. Recall that the justification for the acceleration of liabilities was not so much that a bankruptcy case had been commenced as that a liquidating debtor could not meet the nonbankruptcy attributes for delegation. Similarly, assets should become property of the estate without treating bankruptcy *itself* as working a forfeiture. Once in bankruptcy, an asset (such as FAA landing rights) may have no value if the debtor liquidates, because the restrictions on assignment are a nonbankruptcy attribute that should be respected in bankruptcy, but this is a far cry from saying that the asset is not property of the estate. If the debtor reorganized, for example, the asset would continue to have value.

Thus, in the analysis of clauses that attempt to terminate property interests upon the filing of bankruptcy, it is possible to borrow from an analogous discussion of liabilities. Like state-created priorities and bankruptcy statutory liens and like ipso facto clauses in connection with loans, provisions that remove assets from the debtor upon the occurrence of bankruptcy may create an improper incentive to start a bankruptcy proceeding when it is not in response to a common pool problem. The loss of the asset to the debtor generally creates a winner as well as losers. The losers are the claimants of the debtor, who now must share a smaller asset pool. The winner is the reversionary owner of the asset upon termination of the debtor's interest in it. That person may have an interest in seeing the debtor placed in bankruptcy, in order to return to it the asset that otherwise brings it no return (since it is coupled with no corresponding liability of the debtor).

To say that there is a cost to allowing such provisions, however, is only half the story. It must be determined whether there is an offsetting benefit that suggests that such clauses should be permitted notwithstanding that cost. The issue is the same as the one we examined in connection with ipso facto clauses in loan agreements. When the debtor's use of the asset is connected with no corresponding obligation of the debtor (other than to avoid bankruptcy), moreover, it is even hard to see the provision as serving some monitoring role against misbehavior of the debtor. In the event of terminating an asset, there is nothing for the debtor to misbehave against: no corresponding obligation to the reversionary owner of the asset. The most plausible beneficial justification for the existence of such a provision is that the advent of bankruptcy itself works harm to the reversionary owner, such as a loss of reputation. To the extent, however, that that is the justifiction for such a provision, it would be proper to respect the value of the provision in bankruptcy without respecting the provision itself. For, so characterized, the clause is designed to prevent damages occurring on the loss of reputation. This can then be viewed as a possible liability secured by the asset. The reversionary owner then takes on the characteristics of a secured creditor in bankruptcy, and the value of the right, if not the right itself, should be protected.

The reputational damages, to be sure, might be hard to prove, which is why the clause was written in the first place as a specific performance clause instead of a damages clause. But as we have already seen, the fact that a clause is cast as a specific performance clause is not itself sufficient to justify respecting it in full, because the issue is not one of the rights of the debtor versus the reversionary owner, but, now, the rights of third parties of the debtor versus the reversionary owner. And there the conversion of a specific performance right into a secured damages claim may be entirely proper.

To this point the discussion has been aimed at the anti–ipso facto clause directive of section 541(c)(1)(B). What of section 541(c)(1)(A), which provides that assets become property of the estate notwithstanding restrictions on transfer? As we have seen in discussing unusual rights such as letter of credit draws or waivers of a corporate attorney-client privilege, this provision has a logical reading—one that is fully consistent with the debt-collection role of bankruptcy: that assets become property of the estate but are fully subject to their nonbankruptcy attributes.

Consider a provision banning assignment of an asset. As we have seen, that is the essense of an asset such as a letter of credit, where the right to draw is not assignable as a matter of law. Notwithstanding that, however, the letter of credit becomes property of the estate, and the trustee succeeds to the right to draw if new management of the debtor could have succeeded to the draw outside of bankruptcy. To say this, however, is not to say much—only that a draw by the trustee has no more the attributes of an assignment than does a draw by new management outside of bankruptcy. The letter of credit remains subject to its terms. Thus, in *Swift Aire* the right to draw may have had no value to Swift Aire, which was liquidating, because of a requirement that it could be drawn on only for the continuing operations of the airline.

Moreover, section 541(c)(1)(A) speaks not at all to the question of whether it is possible to assign the asset to another party. That is a nonbankruptcy attribute that may restrict its value, because it may permit the asset to be used as long as the debtor remains in operation but will not permit the asset to be sold to another if it has no further use for it. This result, which applies to things from FAA landing rights to tax-loss carryforwards, simply follows again from the basic notion of bankruptcy as one implementing, in a collective forum, a series of rights (or their values) in existence outside of bankruptcy. Thus, when nonbankruptcy law draws a distinction between the use of an asset by the debtor, albeit with new owners or managers, and the use of an asset by a different entity, bankruptcy law can and should respect that distinction. Section 541(c)(1)(A) implements that distinction and, properly characterized, has no further role.

5

Executory Contracts in Bankruptcy: The Combination of Assets and Liabilities

HAVING EXAMINED liabilities and then assets, we are now ready to turn to the subject of executory contracts in bankruptcy. An executory contract, although not defined by the Bankruptcy Code, is generally considered for purposes of bankruptcy to be a contract on which performance remains due, to some material extent, on the part of *both* contracting parties, so that failure of either side to fulfill its remaining performance obligations would constitute a breach, justifying the failure of the other party to complete *its* unperformed obligations under the contract. The classic definition of executory contracts for purposes of bankruptcy was that given by Vern Countryman: "a contract under which the obligation of both the bankrupt and the other party to the contract are so far unperformed that the failure of either to complete performance would constitute a material breach excusing the performance of the other."[1] This seems to be the definition generally, although by no means exclusively, used in bankruptcy law.[2] However defined, executory contracts are the subject of a special section in the Bankruptcy Code, section 365, and a series of special rules.

Executory contracts, however, have few unique elements for purposes of bankruptcy analysis. Indeed, much of the difficulty caused by executory contracts arises out of the failure to perceive the relationship between assets and the liabilities in bankruptcy and how they interact in

---

1. Countryman, "Executory Contracts in Bankruptcy (pt. 1)," 57 *Minn. L. Rev.* 439, 460 (1973).

2. See H. Rep. No. 595, 95th Cong., 1st Sess. 347 (1977); Jensen v. Continental Finance Corp., 591 F.2d 477, 481 (8th Cir. 1979). For other definitions, see concluding pages of this chapter. Section 365 deals also with "unexpired leases." I shall include them in the term *executory contract*.

the case of executory contracts. Fundamentally, executory contracts, as Countryman has defined them and as the Bankruptcy Code seems to intend, are nothing more than mixed assets and liabilities arising out of the same transaction.[3] This can be seen by considering a simple example. Say Debtor, on December 1, entered into a contract with Supplier for Supplier to ship 1,000 pairs of pants on February 1, with payment by Debtor of $10,000 on April 1. From December 1 until February 1 the contract is executory because either side could breach its yet unperformed obligation, giving rise to a power of termination by the other side. Supplier could fail to deliver the pants, for example, in which case Debtor would be relieved of its obligation to pay $10,000. Conversely, Debtor could announce that it would not pay for the pants when delivered, and this "anticipatory repudiation" would relieve Supplier of its obligation to deliver the pants. Thus, up until February 1 this contract is both an asset of Debtor's (the right to receive 1,000 pairs of pants) and a liability (the obligation to pay $10,000).

This mixture of an unperformed asset and a liability in the same contract is the special attribute of an executory contract. But after February 1, if Supplier meets its obligation to deliver conforming pants, the contract is no longer executory. This is so, because once the nonbankrupt party has fully performed, the issue is only one of a liability of the debtor—a claim. In our example, following delivery of 1,000 pairs of conforming pants on February 1, Debtor becomes owner of the pants, and Supplier (unless it took a security interest or can rely on the limited protections of section 2-702 of the Uniform Commercial Code[4]) becomes an unsecured creditor of Debtor. Supplier's claim is, at that time, analytically no different from claims arising out of simple loan transactions where Debtor has not repaid borrowed money. Since it is nothing more than a claim, there is no point in talking about "assumption" or "rejection" of the contract in terms different from those we analyzed in Chapter 2.

3. Countryman recognized at least half this truth. See Bordewieck & Countryman, "The Rejection of Collective Bargaining Agreements by Chapter 11 Debtors," 57 *Am. Bankr. L. Rev.* 293, 303 (1983) ("Were it not for §365, all contracts and leases in which the debtor had a legal or equitable prepetition interest would become property of the estate under §541(a)(1). Perhaps §365 should be viewed as a limitation on §541(a)(1) giving the debtor . . . an option to decide whether executory contracts and unexpired leases should become property of the estate").

4. Uniform Commercial Code §2-702(2) (1978), provides: "Where the seller discovers that the buyer has received goods on credit while insolvent he may reclaim the goods upon demand made within ten days after the receipt, but if mispresentation of solvency has been made to the particular seller in writing within three months before delivery the ten day limitation does not apply." With some changes (which, under the analysis of this book, are questionable) the Bankruptcy Code respects this right, §546.

If, however, the debtor has performed fully, then the contract is not executory for precisely the opposite reason. Since the debtor only has to await a return performance by the other party, the contract is an asset of the estate. In our example, if Debtor prepaid for the pants on February 1, with delivery scheduled for April 1, then once payment was made, Debtor has a right to receive the pants that is no longer contingent on performance by Debtor. That right is property of the estate. It makes no more sense to talk about the Debtor's choice between "assumption" and "rejection" of this contract right than it does about such a choice with respect to other assets. Accordingly, the framework for analyzing this issue would be that of assets as discussed in Chapter 4.

Contracts, however, that remain to be performed to a substantial extent by both parties—such as our hypothetical contract prior to February 1—bear attributes both of assets and of liabilities. The debtor's unperformed obligations are liabilities from the perspective of the debtor's other claimants, while the nonbankrupt party's unperformed obligations are an asset from their perspective. The question of how to treat these mixed contracts in bankruptcy would have been aided if bankruptcy law had traced out the consequences of recognizing any such contract as *both* an asset and a liability. Such an analysis would take the form of that used to resolve cases such as *Chicago Board of Trade*[5] where an asset was coupled to a particular liability. In such cases one determines relative values and the residual value of the asset concurrently. This is accomplished by netting out the difference between the asset and the liability, and the holder of the liability is given a superior claim to the extent of the value of the asset. There is conceptually no reason to treat executory contracts any differently.

In *Chicago Board of Trade,* for example, the debtor held an asset (membership in the Board of Trade) that could be sold for, say, $10,000. But because of the rules of the Board of Trade, it could not be sold without first paying off membership debts. If there were $6,000 of such debts, the net value of the asset would have been $4,000 to the debtor's other claimants. If, however, there were $15,000 of such debts, the membership liabilities would exceed the value of the asset, and there would be no residual value to the other claimants. There is no reason to reach a different result simply because one characterizes the membership as an executory contract.

This principle, of course, may be extended. For example, a lease that has one year to run at a rental of $10,000 may or may not be valuable to the other claimants, depending on the value of the leased space to

5. 264 U.S. 1 (1924). See supra Chapter 4.

the debtor. If, however, the lessor has the right to terminate the lease under nonbankruptcy law, then *Chicago Board of Trade* would suggest that the value of the lease to the debtor's other claimants would be net of the liability to the landlord—which, in this case, may be a residual of zero.

Rejection and the Nonbankruptcy Attributes of Breach

Understanding this simple relation between assets and liabilities would remove much of the current obscurity in bankruptcy law surrounding executory contracts. Much case law and existing analysis relating to whether a contract is executory create unnecessary work when the question is one of rejection.[6] Apart from contracts that effectively give the holder a right of specific performance, rejection is simply tantamount to a breach of the contract permitted under nonbankruptcy law. Under applicable nonbankruptcy law a breach generally gives rise to a monetary claim for damages. Thus, if Debtor had a contract with Creditor to buy 1,000 bushels of wheat for $4 a bushel and the price of wheat falls to $3 a bushel, Debtor, whether or not it is in bankruptcy, can "reject" the contract and purchase wheat elsewhere for $3 a bushel. If Debtor is solvent, this path does not sound particularly promising, for Debtor's gain from this breach ($1,000) would seem to be matched by Creditor's $1,000 damage claim.[7] But if Debtor is insolvent, a breach in bankruptcy is sensible from the perspective of the creditors as a group, at least as long as Creditor does not have an effective security interest in $1,000 or more of Debtor's assets. By not performing the contract, Debtor saves $1,000. Creditor, to be sure, holds a $1,000 claim, but assuming that claim is unsecured, it will not be paid in full. Thus, some portion of the $1,000 saved by rejection is available for Debtor's other unsecured creditors.

This appears at first glance to be simply a wealth transfer from Creditor to Debtor's other general creditors, with no effect on the group as a whole. Permitting the rejection nonetheless is proper in bankruptcy, because of the notion of relative values. Creditor is just like the other unsecured creditors: a party with a nominal claim that, because Debtor is insolvent, will not have its expectancies met in full. There is no reason

---

6. See, e.g., *In re* Chicago, R.I. & P. RR Co., 604 F.2d 1002 (7th Cir. 1979); *In re* Oxford Royal Mushroom Products, Inc., 45 Bankr. 792 (Bankr. E.D. Pa. 1985); cf. Nimmer, "Executory Contracts in Bankruptcy: Protecting the Fundamental Terms of the Bargain," 54 *U. Colo. L. Rev.* 507, 513 (1983).

7. See, e.g., A. Farnsworth, *Contracts* 838–48 (1982).

Creditor should have its claim paid in full (by required adherence to the contract) when all other unsecured creditors are getting only a few cents on the dollar. Rejection, then, provides a way of *equalizing* things among creditors when the liability represented by the contract exceeds the value of the asset represented by a contract.

The same situation would result in the absence of a special executory contract section with an explicit power to reject. As we saw in Chapter 2, when a debtor borrows money, its obligation to repay is (or can be) breached when the debtor goes into bankruptcy. Nothing more is at stake in the rejection of most contracts in bankruptcy. For that reason, when the issue is one of rejection of an ordinary contract, it makes no difference whether the contract is executory (in which case rejection gives rise to a claim for damages) or nonexecutory (in which case the debtor's obligations—such as loan payment—are breached either because the debtor is liquidating or because the debtor decides to place the lender in the pool of creditors by anticipatorily declaring nonrepayment in full, in which case it also gives rise to a claim for damages).

Here, as before, however, the ability to reject should depend on nonbankruptcy attributes. It was earlier noted that normal rules of contractual specific performance—such as arise when Debtor contracts to sell its Chagall to Buyer for $10,000—when analyzed as a question of rights among creditors, do not require that the specific performance right should be respected in kind. In those cases, because lien creditors outside of bankruptcy could trump the holder of the specific performance right who left the property with the debtor, neither the specific performance right nor its value should be respected in full in bankruptcy. There is no reason a different conclusion would follow simply because the contract is executory.[8]

Sometimes, however, analysis of the applicable nonbankruptcy attributes suggests that specific performance would apply even when analyzing the issue as one of relative rankings among creditors. Consider the following. Debtor owns Blackacre and has leased it to Lessee.[9] Under applicable nonbankruptcy law, even when Debtor breaches its obligations

---

8. For example, Buyer may have prepaid $9,000 of the $10,000 contract price for the Chagall, instead of (as assumed supra Chapter 2) the entire $10,000.

9. This example is loosely based on *In re* Minges, 602 F.2d 38 (2d Cir. 1979). In *Minges* there was a secured lender with a security interest in Blackacre. The court saw rejection as proper only if it would benefit the general creditors instead of simply constituting a wealth transfer between the secured lender and the lessee. But since the secured lender has agreed to be subordinate to the rights of the lessee, the proper normative justification would have been that, since the lessee took precedence over the secured lender outside of bankruptcy, their relative positions should not be reversed in bankruptcy.

under the lease, Lessee (because it has a possessory property interest in Blackacre) cannot be deprived of its possession without its consent.[10] This right, moreover, because it is possessory, is effective against creditors of Debtor.[11] To the extent that this is so, Debtor should not be able to regain possession of Blackacre, over Lessee's objection, by rejecting the lease in bankruptcy. Section 365(h) provides for this result, but it should not depend on finding a special safe-harbor in the Bankruptcy Code. For example, if Debtor leases not Blackacre, but Green Machine—an item of personal property—to Lessee, as long as nonbankruptcy law provides for the same result in the case of an attempted breach of the lease by Debtor (that Lessee has the right to continue in possession), and if this result is also effective against creditors of Debtor (as is probably the case when Lessee is in possession), section 365 should not be construed to provide a different result on rejection in bankruptcy.

The point of this discussion is twofold. First, in most cases the power to reject in section 365 should be viewed as no more than stating the obvious: that contracts can be breached, converting the other party into the holder of a damage claim (which may or may not be secured). Second, the nonbankruptcy limitations of the power to reject must also be recognized. Many nonbankruptcy rights, although created pursuant to a contract, take on a life of their own once created and become effective not only against the debtor but also against others (such as creditors) claiming through the debtor. Nothing in bankruptcy's collectivization principle calls for a different allocative outcome in bankruptcy.

Many of the most troublesome problems created by automatic application of the ability to reject contracts in bankruptcy could have been avoided had this simple relation between bankruptcy law and nonbankruptcy attributes been kept in mind. For example, consider a license agreement where Debtor is the licensor, having licensed Manufacturer with the exclusive right to use a computer chip technology upon payment of an initial license fee of $100,000, and thereafter at the rate of ten cents per chip used. This is probably an executory contract, because both Debtor and Manufacturer have continuing duties to the other.[12] But

10. "A lease is partly the conveyance of an estate, which is deemed fully executed once the tenant takes possession. Therefore the weight of authority is that the conveyance aspect of a lease may not ordinarily be unilaterally disturbed by a debtor landlord or his trustee." *In re* Minges, 602 F.2d 38, 41 (2d Cir. 1979).

11. Cf. McCannon v. Marston, 679 F.2d 13 (3d Cir. 1982).

12. Manufacturer has the obligation to pay ten cents a chip; Debtor has (at least) the obligation not to license the technology to anyone else. See, e.g., Lubrizol Enterprises v. Richmond Metal Finishers, 756 F.2d 1043 (4th Cir. 1985), cert. denied, 106 S.Ct. 1285 (1986); *In re* Petur U.S.A. Instrument Co., 35 Bankr. 561 (Bankr. W.D. Wash. 1983); cf.

irrespective of its characterization, there is no reason to think that Debtor, in bankruptcy, should be able to reject the license agreement (as it would do if it wanted to license the technology to someone else or take advantage of a successful implementation of the technology by relicensing Manufacturer at a higher rate). No such outcome could occur outside of bankruptcy, as Manufacturer would have the right to enjoin Debtor from breaching the license agreement. Declaring the contract to be executory (instead of, say, an outright sale of the technology) should not create a different bankruptcy result because of the unthinking application of a right of rejection written into section 365. This is the kind of nonbankruptcy specific performance right that seems effective not only against Debtor but also against those that claim through Debtor, be they creditors, lien creditors, or purchasers. Accordingly, an examination of relative values suggests that rejection should not be permitted in bankruptcy.

Application of this point would have suggested a different outcome in the Supreme Court's decision in *National Labor Relations Board v. Bildisco & Bildisco,*[13] a case that dealt with whether collective bargaining agreements could be rejected in bankruptcy. At least as a normative matter[14] collective bargaining agreements may call for substantially different treatment in bankruptcy than do ordinary executory contracts because, on analysis, the value of the right provided employees by the National Labor Relations Act vis-à-vis other claimants may be much closer to that of an entity holding a full-fledged property (and priority) right. If so, there may be little point to an attempt to disregard the right, because the relative value of the right, properly understood, is far greater than that of an unsecured creditor. Rejection of the labor contract and treating the resulting claim as unsecured may respect neither the right nor its relative value.

Federal labor law determines when a new employer is bound by the terms of a collective bargaining agreement of the old employer.[15] Under

---

In re Rovine Corp., 6 Bankr. 661 (Bankr. W.D. Tenn. 1980) (franchise agreement with covenant not to compete).

13. 465 U.S. 513 (1984).

14. Section 365 may have carried with it so much baggage at that time that perhaps the fault was Congress's for not specifying distinctions. (This is more likely the case following Congress's enactment of §1113 in 1984. Although it conceivably could be construed as a rule designed to simplify, but mirror, nonbankruptcy NLRB rules, it is unlikely that such a rationale motivated the section.) The normative point is the same: there is no reason to grant a debtor a new substantive power over executory contracts.

15. National Labor Relations Act §§8(a)(5), 8(d), 29 U.S.C. §158(a)(5), (d) (1975); see N.L.R.B. v. Bildisco & Bildisco, 465 U.S. 513 (1984) ("the practical effect of the enforce-

the policies of the National Labor Relations Board, if a company that purchases the assets of another company bears few of the ownership or managerial attributes of the company whose assets were purchased, it is freed of the collective bargaining agreements of the purchased company.[16] Apart from this, however, the labor union has a right of specific performance with respect to the collective bargaining agreement. There is good reason to believe that the reasons for holding collective bargaining agreements enforceable against successor corporations so long as their assets are not splintered up or sold to a new entity are quite different from those at work in the context of an ordinary contract. The function of the labor law rule seems directed at *preferring* the protected group of union members by giving them a set of nonwaivable precedural rights effective both against the debtor and its other claimants.[17] In this context the workers' right to enforce a collective bargaining agreement except in cases of either a piecemeal liquidation or the sale of the business to a substantially new group of owners appears to take the form of a non-bankruptcy property (and priority) right.

If the analysis rightly captures the relevant considerations of non-bankruptcy law and policy, then bankruptcy law should mirror the rights established by labor law by enforcing them as they exist or by respecting their relative value. This would mean that the collective bargaining agreement could be rejected in a liquidation of the debtor, because permitting rejection in that context mirrors the nonbankruptcy attributes of labor law policy. But in a reorganization of the debtor the best non-bankruptcy analogue seems to be the continuation of the debtor, with new owners. To the extent that federal labor law does not permit disaffirmance of collective bargaining agreements in that context, there is

---

ment action would be to require adherence to the terms of the collective bargaining agreement"); N.L.R.B. v. Lion Oil Co., 352 U.S. 282, 285 (1956).

16. See Howard Johnson Co. v. Detroit Local Joint Executive Board, 417 U.S. 249 (1974); N.L.R.B. v. Burns International Services, Inc., 406 U.S. 272, 281–91 (1972); Note, "The Bargaining Obligations of Successor Employers," 88 *Harv. L. Rev.* 759 (1975).

17. See, e.g., Allied Chemical Workers v. Pittsburgh Plate Glass Co., 404 U.S. 157 (1971); John Wiley & Sons, Inc. v. Livingston, 376 U.S. 543, 550 (1964); United Steelworkers v. Warrier & Gulf Navigation Co., 363 U.S. 574, 578–80 (1960); N.L.R.B. v. American Nat'l Insurance Co., 343 U.S. 395 (1951). This may be in contrast to damage claims (such as back pay awards) as distinct from bargaining rights, cf. Nathanson v. N.L.R.B., 344 U.S. 25, 28–29 (1952) ("The policy of the National Labor Relations Act is fully served by recognizing the claim for back pay as one to be paid from the estate"). Thus, the issue is one of recognizing applicable nonbankruptcy analogies, not, as is commonly perceived, one of "balancing" labor law policy with bankruptcy law. The balancing approach continues, however, to dominate analysis. See, e.g., George, "Collective Bargaining in Chapter 11 and Beyond," 95 *Yale L.J.* 300 (1985).

no reason to think that creditors (the new owners) should have that right in bankruptcy.

Other creditors consequently have an incentive to force the bankrupt entity into a piecemeal liquidation.[18] This risk, however, does not justify disregarding the relative value of the right because recognizing it does not make the situation *worse* in bankruptcy. Labor law is part of the warp and woof of the fabric that exists independently of bankruptcy. Its existence may make things worse for creditors as a group by requiring the actual consent of one particular group in order to override the right,[19] but its existence does not make things worse for creditors in a collective proceeding than outside it. There is, accordingly, no bankruptcy law policy to "balance" with labor law policy.

In all case there is no normative reason to apply the concept of rejection beyond its nonbankruptcy channels, where it is used to equalize the status of those claimants who outside of bankruptcy were equals. When it is used to substantively rearrange entitlements by equalizing those who are not nonbankruptcy equals, it is used improperly.

The General Rule and a Critique of Section 365(c) and (f)

The importance of understanding the nature of executory contracts is broader than the topic of rejection. Recognizing that all executory con-

18. Included in this attempt to mirror attributes is a determination whether the entity emerging out of bankruptcy satisfies the "new entity" tests of labor law described previously. That question demands that one assess the quantum of managerial and ownership changes that occurred in the bankruptcy process. See Blazer Industries, Inc., 236 N.L.R.B. 103, 109–10 (1978). This translation problem raises factual problems in the reorganization context (e.g., is the change in ownership substantial enough?), and it may engender some uncertainty in application if the issue arises before confirmation of a plan of reorganization. The relevant point, however, is that this is a factual question, not one of independent bankruptcy policy, where the distributional question is tied to the deployment question. Unlike with most cases, where the two inquiries should be kept distinct, here the skewing in the choice of deployment is a result of a nonbankruptcy tie between the two questions.

19. In theory, labor can be bought off by reallocating some of the going-concern value from the other creditors. Cf. Coase, "The Problem of Social Costs," 3 *J. Law & Econ.* 1 (1960); Brief for the National Labor Relations Board in N.L.R.B. v. Bildisco & Bildisco, at 23 ("if collective bargaining agreements are not set aside in bankruptcy, unions have an interest in agreeing to the modification of burdensome contract terms to prevent employers from going out of business, thereby preserving jobs for their members"). Realistically, the bargain may be unobtainable because of the number of parties involved or because the costs to the union of agreeing to a "lesser" bargaining agreement (e.g., the effect any such agreement may have on other collective bargaining agreements with other employers) may be greater than any associated benefit to this particular employer.

tracts raise the same type of inquiries as other claims or property cases—having mixed attributes of both assets and liabilities, subject to the special feature that the asset is coupled to the liability—has a number of implications for the proper shape and direction of the Bankruptcy Code. Some of these implications can be clarified by looking at executory contracts in the three contexts in which we examined liabilities in Chapter 2 and assets in Chapter 4. First, what should be the presumptive rule in bankruptcy for executory contracts not yet in default? Second, what should occur in bankruptcy in the case of a prebankruptcy default? Third, what effect should be given to contractual ipso facto clauses? Not surprisingly, answers to these questions spring naturally from the answers associated with assets and liabilities and provide a basis for a critical inquiry into section 365's special rules.

We have already seen that the general rules for treating assets and liabilities in bankruptcy are derived from a recognition of the attributes of the closest nonbankruptcy analogue. In the case of a liquidating corporate debtor, for example, the best analogy was that of a dissolving corporation under state law. Since a dissolving debtor ceases to exist, there are several nonbankruptcy consequences. In the case of liabilities, where the general contract rule is that there can be no delegation of performance if there is also a divesting of duties, the dissolution accordingly would presumptively constitute a default and acceleration of the liability. The discussion of assets followed the same approach: in the case of an asset that could be used by the debtor but not assigned (such as FAA landing rights),[20] the debtor's dissolution would mean that the asset had no value to the debtor's general creditors. Accordingly, although such an asset would properly be characterized as property of the estate, its nonbankruptcy attributes would give it a zero value in a bankruptcy liquidation.

The same analysis should be used to examine executory contracts. Because, definitionally, the debtor had an unperfomed obligation, the contractual bar on divestment of duties would preclude delegation of performance coupled with a divestment of duties. Accordingly, for a debtor liquidating in bankruptcy, unless the nonbankrupt party consented to an assignment, or unless the debtor could perform its obligation before liquidating, its executory contracts should be viewed as breached (anticipatorily) by the debtor, giving rise to a loss of the associated asset *and* the obligation to pay for it. What remains, of course, may be a claim

20. See *In re* Braniff, 700 F.2d 935 (5th Cir. 1983) for a discussion of the attributes of FAA landing rights.

for damages by the nonbankrupt party, if it has suffered damages. Like other liabilities, this damage claim would be unsecured, unless the non-bankrupt party had protected itself with a security interest or the state had protected it with a form of statutory lien (or the like).

This result flows from the structure of assets and liabilities in bankruptcy. As a result of the failure to understand the asset and liability in each executory contract, however, the current Bankruptcy Code has moved in a substantially different direction. A liquidating debtor can assume most executory contracts. Any contract it can assume, moreover, can be assigned pursuant to section 365(f). A debtor would do this, presumably, when its executory contract was favorable from its perspective. For example, Debtor might have a lease of office space from Lessor with five years to run at $20,000 (present value) a year. If the market rate for such leases is now $25,000 (present value) a year, Debtor's lease is a net asset (netting out the present value of the asset—$125,000— and the $100,000 liability) of $25,000. If Debtor breaches this lease, it gets nothing (no asset, but no damage claim either); Lessor gets the opportunity to re-let the space and thereby make $25,000 more. If Debtor, however, could assign this lease, it could obtain $25,000 for its unsecured creditors.

Apparently on the view that unsecured creditors get more if executory contracts can be assigned,[21] section 365 permits their assignment. This approach, however, ignores the principle of reflecting nonbankruptcy attributes in a collective regime. To use our example as an illustration, the fact that Debtor cannot use its lease (because it is liquidating) and cannot assign it under applicable nonbankruptcy law means, to be sure, that Lessor and not Debtor's general creditors gets the "extra" $25,000.[22] The question of relative ordering of claimants, however, because it is a distributional question and not a deployment question, is not a bankruptcy issue. Nothing in the collectivization norm calls for reallocating values in bankruptcy or giving any special breaks (other than those that

21. See, e.g., Silverstein, "Rejection of Executory Contracts in Bankruptcy and Reorganization," 31 *U. Chi. L. Rev.* 467, 468 (1964) (executory contract section designed to free the "estate to pay a larger dividend to general creditors"); Fogel, "Executory Contracts and Unexpired Leases in the Bankruptcy Code," 64 *Minn. L. Rev.* 341, 349 (1980).

22. Sometimes, as with the contract with Supplier for pairs of pants, even a liquidating Debtor could gain the advantages of a favorable contract by remaining in operation long enough to pay for the pants and then reselling them to a third party. In such a case assumption should be possible, even though Debtor is liquidating, because Debtor is able to complete the contract. Again, the ability vel non to assume comes from an examination of nonbankruptcy attributes, not per se from the use of bankruptcy or a decision to liquidate in bankruptcy.

follow from collectivization itself) to general creditors in bankruptcy.

Section 365(f) is not only incompatible with normal bankruptcy principles but also inconsistent with the treatment of liabilities in bankruptcy. To see why, recall that an unaccelerated below-market loan is also an asset from the debtor's perspective. If a debtor could sell an asset with such a loan, the asset could fetch more than if the asset were being sold without the below-market financing. Yet loans *are* accelerated in a bankruptcy liquidation (although not necessarily in a reorganization), precluding this option. Recognizing an executory contract as nothing more than an associated asset and liability reveals the inconsistency of permitting a liquidating debtor to assign below-market executory contracts.[23]

The rule of section 365(f) suffers from one more defect. It strikes down antiassignment clauses, instead requiring the assignee to give adequate assurance of future performance. These provisions require one to determine whether something is effectively an antiassignment clause (in which case it is ignored) or is effectively a term of the contract (in which case it must be adhered to). The problem is that no such line can be drawn with precision.[24] An antiassignment clause—such as "*A* cannot assign his obligation to deliver wheat to me"—can be redrafted, with considerable accuracy, to become a term of the contract—"*A* personally must deliver to me wheat *A* has grown on *A*'s farm, located in Blackacre, Kansas." These issues could be largely avoided, if section 365 recognized that the source of attributes should be nonbankruptcy law, not special bankruptcy policy.

To this point the focus has been on the proper treatment of executory contracts in the case of a liquidating debtor. What, however, of the case of a debtor that is reorganizing? Again, the previous discussion of assets and liabilities in bankruptcy can be drawn on. It seems presumptively proper to treat a reorganizing debtor as undergoing a transformation equivalent to a change of ownership of the debtor outside of bankruptcy.

---

23. For a numerical example showing the similarity of the loan and the executory contract, see Jackson, "Bankruptcy, Non-Bankruptcy Entitlements, and the Creditors' Bargain," 91 *Yale L.J.* 857, 883–85 (1982). In this respect the proposal of the Commission on Bankruptcy Laws was more consistent with bankruptcy principles. See Report of the Commission on Bankruptcy Laws of the United States, H.R. Doc. 137, 93rd Cong., 1st Sess., pt. 1 at 198 (1973) ("In a liquidation situation . . . the right of the nondebtor party to choose to deal only with the debtor, as provided by an anti-assignment or similar contractual clause, should be preserved").

24. See, e.g., *In re* U.L. Radio Corp., 19 Bankr. 537 (Bankr. S.D.N.Y. 1982) (clause restricting use to an "electronics store" is disregarded so lease could be assigned to a restaurant).

If a contract to deliver 1,000 pairs of pants to Debtor would survive a nonbankruptcy change of ownership of Debtor, it should be a contract that Debtor—or more precisely, its creditors—can use (or breach) in bankruptcy as well. It is in this context that the power of assumption makes the most sense.

This, however, is a right of a reorganizing debtor to use executory contracts whose net value is positive, and it derives from nonbankruptcy attributes. Similarly, our previous discussion of *assignments* of executory contracts can be reanalyzed in the case of a reorganizing debtor against relevant nonbankruptcy attributes, because if the reorganizing debtor has no use for the executory contract, nonbankruptcy attributes still govern assignment of it to a third party. Since the debtor, in a reorganization, remains in existence, it is possible to delegate duties without the debtor divesting itself of responsibilities. In these cases assumption and assignment *are* proper, but only to the extent permitted by nonbankruptcy law: if the contract contains an antiassignment clause that is effective under nonbankruptcy law, it is wrong to ignore it in bankruptcy, as section 365(f) does. Analysis of antiassignment clauses should spring from nonbankruptcy attributes.

The failure of the drafters of section 365 to appreciate the limited normative role of bankruptcy policy has led to a curious failure to differentiate between assumption and assignment. Section 365(c) and (f) prohibit the assumption or assignment of executory contracts where "applicable law excuses a party, other than the debtor . . . from accepting performance from or rendering performance to an entity other than the debtor or the debtor in possession or an assignee of such contract or lease," including explicitly contracts to make loans or to extend financial accommodations. This (once one resolves some linguistic ambiguities created by the 1984 amendments[25]) precludes assumption where "applicable law" prohibits assignment. This line is drawn at the wrong place. In the case of personal service contracts and the like—where applicable law prohibits assignment without consent—the point of the restriction is to ensure that the nonbankrupt party gets performance

---

25. The addition of the language "or an assignee," if read literally, may render the entire section superfluous; it apparently should be read to mean a *consensual* assignee. The addition of "or the debtor in possession" does not seem to cure the problem addressed in text. This section still would seem to prohibit assumption *by* the trustee or debtor in possession when applicable law refuses nonconsensual assignment to an entity *other than* the debtor or debtor in possession. Whether this garbled drafting will be used to reach the result that assumption is proper but assignment is not is an open question.

from precisely who it contracted with.[26] If Placido Domingo contracts to sing the role of Don Jose in "Carmen" at the Met, he cannot assign the contract to (say) me.

This, however, should not prevent a reorganizing debtor from *assuming* a contract, if applicable nonbankruptcy law does not treat a change in the ownership of the debtor as an assignment. Consider the case of FAA landing rights (as if they were executory contracts). In this case "applicable law" prohibits assignment. Yet if an airline is reorganizing in bankruptcy, the relevant nonbankruptcy question should be whether the FAA landing rights survive a change of ownership. Section 365(c), however, operates as a bar because that nonbankruptcy question is ignored. With personal service contracts (and the like) the line should be drawn at assignment, not necessarily at assumption.

Assumption Following Default and Ipso Facto Clauses

An examination of executory contracts in light of the remaining two questions—should executory contracts be assumable irrespective of default and should ipso facto clauses be respected—can now proceed quickly. No new twists are introduced by executory contracts in these contexts; the same analysis used in discussing assets and liabilities can be undertaken.

Consider the case of a prebankruptcy default. Section 365(b) permits assumption notwithstanding defaults as long as the defaults are cured or promptly will be cured. As we have seen, however, such a cure power sweeps too broadly because it is unrelated to the reasons for bankruptcy itself. A debtor who loses a valuable executory contract outside of bankruptcy because of a default presumptively should fare no better in bankruptcy either. The two exceptions to this occur when the debtor defaults either to favor the nonbankrupt party (by returning a valuable asset to it and allowing the party to remove itself from an impending collective proceeding) or because the debtor knows it is insolvent and simply no longer cares what happens to its assets. The first problem is properly analyzed (as the current Bankruptcy Code does not) as a species of preference law. The case of debtor passivity raises the same sorts of questions. These issues will be discussed in the next chapter. In these instances a limited reach-back rule may be proper. Even then section 365(b), which is unlimited in time, sweeps too broadly.

26. See, e.g., Restatement (Second) of Contracts §318, comment c (1981).

As for ipso facto clauses, we have seen that a presumptive rule barring their effectiveness may be justified for both assets and liabilities. Since an executory contract is best thought of as a mixed asset and liability, nothing, accordingly, should change. But it is important to note that, in the context of bankruptcy as a device to ameliorate a common pool problem, the effect of refusing to recognize ipso facto clauses would be far smaller than in the world of section 365. Substantial nonbankruptcy restrictions, which section 365 tosses aside in an unprincipled manner, should continue to operate. Under such a regime a liquidating debtor, for example, could not effectively assume many executory contracts nor (unless permitted by the contract) could it assign them because of application of the nonbankruptcy norm of no divestment of duties. A reorganizing debtor, moreover, could assume executory contracts, but antiassignment clauses, either in the contract itself or in applicable law, would continue to be recognized. Thus, nonrecognition of ipso facto clauses in bankruptcy would have a substantially smaller effect than currently is the case.

A Concluding Note on Section 365

Section 365, as we have seen, is substantially flawed when examined from the perspective of bankruptcy law as a debt-collection device. Its flaws stem from a failure to perceive the derivative nature of executory contracts from ordinary assets and liabilities, and consequently it disregards nonbankruptcy rights so as to benefit general creditors (and, correspondingly, harm some other claimant, usually the party on the other side of the contract). These changes are unfortunate in themselves, but equally unfortunate is the invitation such an inappropriate substantive rule extends for the manipulation of other concepts so as to similarly favor general creditors.

Consider, for example, *In re Booth*.[27] In *Booth* the court was faced with the question of whether a debtor, who was a vendee under a contract for deed, had an executory contract. The essential feature of a contract for deed is that the vendor retains title until the time the vendee has fully paid for the land. It sounds executory, under Countryman's test: vendee still has to pay and vendor still has to deliver title.[28] Whether executory or not, when the issue is rejection, the characterization should

27. 19 Bankr. 53 (Bankr. D. Utah 1982).
28. See *In re* Alexander, 670 F.2d 885 (9th Cir. 1982).

not matter. Outside of bankruptcy, if vendee defaults, the characterization of title retention by the vendor suggest that the vendor gets the property back, and that would be true even if the land was worth more than the contract price of (say) $100,000. Rejection in bankruptcy, even under section 365, carries the same consequences.

In many states land is sold through a somewhat different mechanism: title passes at the time of possession by the vendee, but the vendor retains a security interest in the land to secure payment of the purchase price. This kind of transaction is not executory under Countryman's test, because the vendor has no further obligations. Again, when the issue is one of rejection, it does not matter whether section 365 applies. Outside of bankruptcy, if the vendee defaults, the vendor can foreclose on the land. But if the land is worth more than the purchase price of $100,000, the vendee (in theory at least) gets to keep the excess.

Thus, when the issue is one of rejection, whether the bankruptcy characterization of the deal is as an executory contract or not should not matter because here section 365 acts in conformity with the general treatment of assets and liabilities in bankruptcy. Because of their different nonbankruptcy characteristics, however, the bankruptcy treatment of the two cases should be different upon rejection. In the case of a contract for deed, the vendor gets the property back. If it is worth $150,000 instead of $100,000, vendor, not vendee's creditors, gets that extra value.[29] In the case of the secured sale, however, the vendor has a secured claim for the purchase price of $100,000. Although the value of that is recognized in bankruptcy, vendee's creditors, not vendor, get the "extra" $50,000.

Who gets the $50,000, in other words, seems to be a quintessential nonbankruptcy distributional issue that bankruptcy law should respect and that use of section 365 itself would not affect. The court in *Booth*, however, decided that it would be "better" for the debtor's unsecured creditors to recharacterize the contract for deed as a secured sale, because the excess would then flow to the unsecured creditors, not to the vendor. It reached that conclusion by seeing section 365 as "an index to when assumption or rejection of a contract will 'benefit the estate' and therefore of when a contract is executory."[30] Since the general creditors would receive a greater amount of money if the contract were "viewed as a lien than as an executory contract," *Booth* recharacterized it, reasoning that "[t]he bankruptcy court, as a court of equity, regards substance over

29. Rejection might nonetheless occur, because, for example, the purchase contract carries with it an extremely high interest rate.

30. 19 Bankr., at 55. See also id., at 58 (citing Silverstein, supra note 21).

form, demands equality of treatment among creditors, and loathes a forfeiture."[31]

Although this recharacterization is popular,[32] it has nothing to do with the *effect* of using section 365 when the issue is one of rejection. *Booth* was not simply applying a different bankruptcy label and then using special powers of section 365, but rather it was substantively recharacterizing the underlying property right from a contract for deed to a secured sale. It was this change in the underlying substantive attributes of the transaction, not the use of section 365, that gained the surplus for the debtor's general creditors. That the *Booth* court viewed section 365 as the justification for a property recharacterization and that many other judges concur suggest how far that section has strayed from bankruptcy's normative underpinnings as a collective debt-collection device and how it invites others to stray with it.

31. 19 Bankr., at 58.
32. See, e.g., *In re* Adolphsen, 38 Bankr. 780 (D. Minn. 1983); *In re* Gladding Corp., 22 Bankr. 632 (Bankr. D. Mass. 1982). Not all courts agree: see, e.g., Shaw v. Dawson, 48 Bankr. 857 (D.N.M. 1985); *In re* Britton, 43 Bankr. 605 (Bankr. E.D. Mich. 1984).

6

Prebankruptcy Opt-Out Activity and the Role of Preference Law

To THIS POINT bankruptcy proceedings were assumed to occur without warning. With this assumption it was possible to examine the essential features of the bankruptcy process without worrying about strategic responses of creditors that might undermine what bankruptcy was trying to do. We now relax that assumption. The descent of a healthy firm into insolvency and then bankruptcy is often a slow one. Claimants can sometimes see what is happening, and they may learn about the impending trouble and the likelihood of a collective proceeding at different times.

This creates a new problem. If a debtor's liabilities exceed its assets, even the best-run collective proceeding cannot give general creditors a hundred cents on the dollar. The creditors that are the first to learn about the debtor's difficulties may try to collect what they are owed before the collective proceeding starts, instead of beginning the proceeding themselves. The irony is that this kind of action replicates the problem bankruptcy law was designed to solve: pursuit of individual interest may leave the group of creditors worse off. Because bankruptcy's solution to the common pool problem involves a change in the rules of the collection game, it may reintroduce the original problem.

In addition, a somewhat related problem may exist: when a firm appears insolvent and the likelihood is great that the firm will have to be turned over to its creditors, the shareholders no longer have much of an incentive to watch out for the interests of the creditors. This problem exists even in the healthiest of companies,[1] but it is heightened as insolvency looms on the horizon.

---

1. This problem involves a species of diverse ownership. See R. Brealey & S. Myers, *Principles of Corporate Finance* 657 (1981).

These problems of individual incentives (whether by creditors or shareholders) in the prebankruptcy period may make things worse for the group. They are the subject of this chapter, although their focus is somewhat distinct. When focusing on the action of creditors to "opt out" of an impending collective proceeding, we are examining a response caused by the change from an individualistic remedies system to a collective system. It is the focus of preference law, and it is integral to the collectivization process itself. In focusing on the actions of shareholders, however, we are examining an aspect of a problem that would exist whether or not a collective proceeding was commenced and hence one that is not itself integral to the bankruptcy process. The problem is generally considered through the lens of fraudulent conveyance law, although it is somewhat broader than that. Although both problems will be addressed in this chapter, greater attention will be given to the preference problem, as it is one related to bankruptcy itself.

Preference Law: The Transitional Avoiding Power

The basic role of preference law is widely accepted.[2] In their simplest form preferences are transfers that favor one existing creditor over another. Debtor prefers Creditor A to Creditor B if Debtor pays Creditor A before it pays Creditor B. Such behavior is conventionally not thought to be a fraudulent conveyance—assuming Debtor is not motivated by an actual desire to delay, hinder, or defraud Creditor B—because Debtor's antecedent debt to Creditor A is considered to be fair consideration for the transfer (of cash presumably) that Debtor makes.[3]

This can be stated another and more illuminating way. Preference law, unlike fraudulent conveyance law,[4] is not a part of the arsenal of

2. See, e.g., Seligson, "The Code and the Bankruptcy Act," 42 *N.Y.U. L. Rev.* 292 (1967): "A cornerstone of the bankruptcy structure is the principle that equal treatment for those similarly situated must be achieved. It would be highly inequitable to disregard what transpires prior to the filing of the bankruptcy petition; to do so would encourage a race among creditors, engender favoritism by the debtor, and result in inequality of distribution. At bankruptcy, the bankrupt would be left with only tag ends and remnants of unencumbered assets." See also, Eisenberg, "Bankruptcy Law in Perspective," 28 *UCLA L. Rev.* 953, 963 (1982); Morris, "Bankruptcy Law Reform: Preferences, Secret Liens and Floating Liens," 54 *Minn. L. Rev.* 737, 738 (1970). For an exhaustive discussion of preference law, see Countryman, "The Concept of a Voidable Preference in Bankruptcy," 38 *Vand. L. Rev.* 713 (1985).

3. See Uniform Fraudulent Conveyance Act §3(a) (1919).

4. At bottom, fraudulent conveyance law relates to actions taken by a debtor that its creditors would want to prohibit irrespective of the advent of a collective proceeding. The

rights and remedies between a debtor and its creditors. Rather, preference law focuses on relationships *among* creditors in light of the advantages of a collective proceeding. Preferences generally are permitted
outside of bankruptcy, because the subject of rights of creditors among
themselves is generally controlled by the rule of first-come, first-served.
Rules that require creditors to respect the interests of other creditors
are of concern only when the creditors perceive that there may not be
enough to go around. Absent that worry, there can be, by definition, no
conflict among creditors.

A corollary of the idea that every creditor is left to its own devices to
ensure repayment is that a debtor could prefer one creditor to another.[5]
Any system that prevented preferences, therefore, would necessarily be
a collective system in which creditors could not recover from their debtor
without accounting for the interests of other creditors. For this reason
preferences are not inherently objectionable outside of bankruptcy (or
other collective proceedings); the idea of preference law is part and
parcel of the substitution of collective remedies for individual remedies.

In the implementation of the notion of bankruptcy as a collective debt-
collection device, we have seen that relative values should generally be
respected. To this point relative values have been discussed at a point
in time identified by the start of the bankruptcy process. But we now
have to move backward in time because of the problem of strategic
planning in the prebankruptcy period. We return to the essence of the
problem we examined in Chapter 1: creditors, like others, have incentives to advance their own interests, even if it is at the expense of a
greater collective benefit. Once a debtor becomes insolvent (or is thought
likely to become insolvent), each creditor has an incentive to engage in
a race for assets, not just to assure itself that it will get paid in full, but
also because the creditor knows that, if it does not race, and its fellow
creditors do, it will be left with nothing.

We would face no distinct problem if a debtor's insolvency were an
easily determined, widely known single point in time. In that case a
collective proceeding could be instituted immediately with the advent of
that insolvency (and the creditors' knowledge thereof). The status of
insolvency, however, rarely has these attributes. Creditors usually are

---

line is not always easy to draw in practice, but, as this book will suggest, the theoretical
line is clear.

5. See, e.g., Smith v. Whitman, 39 N.J. 397, 402, 189 A.2d 15, 18 (1963) ("True, a
creditor who collects from an insolvent debtor fares better than other claimants. Yet, if
the transfer were set aside in favor of another creditor, there would be a substitution of
one preference for another").

aware of the likelihood of a debtor's insolvency—or, more accurately, a resulting, collective proceeding—and some may recognize it before others. Some of the creditors may know that the collective proceeding is imminent and take advantage of this knowledge to have their own claims satisfied and thereby to opt out of the collective proceeding altogether. Sometimes debtors, moreover, knowing that bankruptcy is imminent, may pay first the creditors that they like or that they think they will need in the future. By the time a bankruptcy petition is actually filed, those creditors that remain would have to share in "tag ends and remnants" of assets.[6]

This behavior would not be in the collective interest of the creditors because it reintroduces the common pool problem. Preference law is best viewed as a solution to this replication of the common pool problem that results from strategic planning in the prebankruptcy period. Preference law, therefore, is essentially a transitional rule designed to prevent individual creditors from opting out of the collective proceeding once that event becomes likely.[7] It is part of the attempt to ameliorate the effects of a common pool problem that justifies a collective proceeding in the first place.

When considering preference law, one should keep in mind the evil that it is concerned with. Approached from the perspective of the common pool, preference law exists to prevent creditors from trying to change their existing position vis-à-vis other creditors in anticipation of bankruptcy's collective proceeding (or having the debtor do it for them). It is not designed to prevent creditors from being preferred, so to speak, at the time of the original loan (such as by taking a security interest). Such a contemporaneous "preference" is part of establishing the non-bankruptcy entitlements and does not undermine the move from an individual to a collective regime of debt collection. It is, accordingly, outside preference law's normative reach. Nor should preference law be designed to strike down *all* postloan activity that gains payment for one creditor ahead of another, because such behavior is a part of the idea of individual creditor remedies and its principle of first-come, first-served. Preference law should, instead, be concerned with postloan behavior directed at attempts to improve one's relative status in an impending

6. 3 *Collier's on Bankruptcy* ¶60.01 at 744 (14th ed. 1977).

7. See Note, "Preferential Transfers and the Value of the Insolvent Firm," 87 *Yale L.J.* 1449 (1978); see also McCoid, "Bankruptcy, Preferences and Efficiency: An Expression of Doubt," 67 *Va. L. Rev.* 249 (1981). To the extent that preference law is successful, it also will deter expenditures made solely for the purpose of discovering and racing against an incipient insolvency and related collective proceeding.

collective proceeding such as bankruptcy—attempts to opt out of the class of unsecured creditors into a class of paid (or secured) creditors. It is, in short, designed to deter individual opt-out behavior that would undermine the advantages to be gained from a collective proceeding.[8]

This opt-out behavior comes in two ostensibly different forms, and modern preference law captures both. The first kind of behavior is proscribed by what may be described as the "anti-last-minute-grab" policy. Imagine that Debtor has assets worth $100 and owes two creditors, Bank and Finance Company, $100 each. If bankruptcy was commenced, under the collective rule, each creditor would receive $50. If Debtor, in light of the impending bankruptcy, "prefers" Bank by paying Bank's debt in full or by granting Bank a security interest in all of its property, or if Bank acts to prefer itself by acquiring a judicial lien, the trustee may well be able to set aside any of these transactions as a preference.[9] If the trustee does set aside the preference and recover the $100, both Finance Company and Bank will receive $50 in the bankruptcy proceeding.[10]

8. Because preference law is a *creditor* misbehavior rule directed at actions creditors take among themselves, activities that represent *debtor* misbehavior against creditors and not, even inferentially, intercreditor misbehavior (see infra note 58) are not preferential, although they may be subject to fraudulent conveyance attack. A gift by a debtor to a relative while insolvent, for example, is not preferential, see §547(b)(1), even though the harm imposed on creditors will be greater than a comparable-sized payment to a creditor on account of an antecedent debt. It is a wrong against creditors unrelated to the advent of a collective proceeding. Likewise, dividends to shareholders of an insolvent company may be fraudulent conveyances (and may violate state corporation laws), but they are not voidable as preferences. See, e.g., Model Business Corporation Act §§2(n), 6, 45, 46(a), 66 (1969); Clark, "The Duties of the Corporate Debtor to Its Creditors," 90 *Harv. L. Rev.* 505, 554–60 (1977).

9. §547(b). This example is obviously unrealistic. If Debtor paid Bank $100, there would be no more assets, although it would still be in Finance Company's interest to start a bankruptcy proceeding to undo the preference. Nothing would change, however, if the number of creditors (and the quantity of assets) were greater.

10. The anti-last-minute-grab goal of the preference section also informs the question of valuation and its timing. Section 547(b)(5) requires that the transfer must enable the creditor to do better than it would have done had the transfer not been made and the creditor received a distribution under chapter 7. The thrust of the section is clear, but its literal timing seems misdirected. For example, consider a case where a creditor is owed $10,000. On January 1 the creditor receives from the debtor a payment of $6,000 in full satisfaction of its claim. If the debtor were to file for bankruptcy on that date, its unsecured creditors would expect to receive payments of 60 percent. As it turns out, the debtor does not file for bankruptcy until March 1, at which time its unsecured creditors can expect to receive payments of 50 percent of their claims. After the bankruptcy proceeding is finished and the actual distribution is made, on November 1, the debtor's creditors actually receive 40 percent of their claims. On which date is it proper to base the comparison? Section 547(b)(5) suggests that it is November 1, the date of the actual distribution, but the policies

Another category of behavior proscribed by modern preference law is addressed by what may be described at the "anti-tardy-perfection" policy. Suppose that Finance Company, a year or two prior to bankruptcy, entered into an agreement with Debtor to secure Finance Company's loan with a security interest in all of Debtor's personal property. Finance Company, however, neither took possession of Debtor's property nor filed a financing statement until ten days prior to Debtor's bankruptcy petition. Since Finance Company filed its financing statement before Bank got an execution lien, Finance Company would be entitled, under Article 9, to be paid ahead of Bank, even though Finance Company was exceedingly slow at perfecting its security interest.[11] Section 547(e) of the Bankruptcy Code, however, ignores that outcome by manipulating the time of the transfer of the security interest: by delaying its filing, Finance Company is said to have received a transfer at the moment of the filing which, because it is on account of an antecedent debt, is subject to avoidance by the trustee in bankruptcy.[12]

---

underlying the preference section suggest that the relevant comparison should be made using expected values as of the date of the transfer, January 1. This suggests that the resolution in Palmer Clay Products v. Brown, 297 U.S. 227, 229 (1936) is, as a normative matter, wrong. In that case the Supreme Court stated that whether there was a preference was determined "not by what the situation would have been if the debtor's assets had been liquidated and distributed among his creditors at the time the alleged preferential payment was made, but by the actual effect of the payment as determined when bankruptcy results." More recently cases have recognized that it is appropriate to determine the value of the asset that is transferred as of the time of the transfer, see, e.g., *In re* Abramson, 715 F.2d 934, 939 (5th Cir. 1983), notwithstanding that the asset later actually increases or decreases in value. Putting aside cases where the payment was in full (or nearly so)—where there would be no upside by waiting—since expected values include both upside and downside potential, if the expected value of the transfer and the expected value of the claim are equal on the date of the transfer, opt-out behavior has presumably not taken place.

In theory the proper values are those subjective values of a creditor. But, as discussed in text, the difficulties of proof justify using marketplace expected values as a rule in place of a standard. Of course, because valuations—even market valuations—at the date of the transfer may be difficult to ascertain after the fact, it may be appropriate to presume that the values determined in bankruptcy are the appropriate ones. But in that case it is important to remember that such values are being used as easily ascertained surrogates for something else, not because they are appropriate in their own right.

11. Uniform Commercial Code §9–301(1)(b) (1978).

12. Section 547(e)(1)(B) provides, in the case of personal property, that a transfer "is perfected when a creditor on a simple contract cannot acquire a judicial lien that is superior to the interest of the transferee." Section 547(e)(2) provides that a transfer is "made" "at the time such transfer is perfected," unless the transfer is perfected within ten days of when it "takes effect." The definition of when a transfer is perfected in the case of real property (other than fixtures) is, under §547(e)(1)(A), "when a bona fide purchaser of such property from the debtor against whom applicable law permits such transfer to be perfected cannot acquire an interest that is superior to the interest of the transferee." For

Are both of these policies appropriately related to the goals of a preference section? The common wisdom is that the first is. Most recognize that the preference section, by striking down last-minute grabs designed to benefit existing individual creditors, enables the creditors as a group to gain the advantages of a collective proceeding. Even here, however, one must be careful to distinguish grabs that involve payment or the taking of other tangible property, on the one hand, and grabs that involve taking security interests or liens, on the other hand.

Since bankruptcy is, at bottom, designed to deter individual actions that undermine an ability to maximize a pool of assets, individual actions directed toward removing assets from that pool lie at the core of what bankruptcy exists to prevent. But the taking of liens or security interests (although they, too, are property rights) do not physically remove assets from the pool. Rather, such actions seem, in the first instance, simply to redistribute the assets in any given pool among the claimants. Nonetheless, such actions, if engaged in on account of existing debts with an eye toward an impending bankruptcy, also undermine the goals of bankruptcy and fail to offer any affirmative value that might nonetheless justify them. Permitting creditors to take security interests or liens on account of existing debts on the eve of bankruptcy encourages a wasteful race either to take property from the debtor or to obtain security interests in or liens on assets of the debtor. The result is additional costs to the creditors, both in the race itself and in the dispersion of outcomes, that reduce the *net* collective value of the pool of assets. Nor is it likely that such costs are justified on any theory of offsetting benefits. Whether or not secured credit can be explained on efficiency grounds,[13] it is unlikely that any such explanations will cover postloan security interests obtained on the eve of bankruptcy. Therefore, although somewhat different in focus, both tangible property grabs and grabs involving the taking of security interests or liens on the eve of bankruptcy on account of existing debts seem ultimately to undermine, in much the same way, the basic reasons for having a bankruptcy process. They all amount to individual actions designed to avoid a collective proceeding that would upset its advantages.

Few people have questioned the basic thrust of the anti-last-minute-grab policy. The anti-tardy-perfection policy, however, is commonly viewed

---

the reasons outlined in the discussion of §544(a)(3), use of a bona fide purchaser test is not justified by bankruptcy policy (see Chapter 3). The bona fide purchaser test was added in the Chandler Amendments in 1938 and was limited, in 1950, to transfers of real property. See generally J. MacLachlan, *Bankruptcy* 295–301 (1956).

13. See supra Chapter 2, note 81.

as unrelated to preference law. In the case of a delayed perfection of a security interest, the property right (i.e., the security interest) itself was granted well before the preference period, and the problem with the transaction from the perspective of third party creditors was that of ostensible ownership. And, as earlier noted, ostensible ownership itself is not a problem related only to bankruptcy. Robert Jordan and William Warren, for example, have called these *false preferences,* a "superficially similar but entirely distinct problem." The distinct problem they see "is the evil of the secret lien," and although "[i]t is understandable that there should be a policy against secret liens," they question whether it should be done by the "technique of turning secret liens into false preferences."[14]

This bifurcation of the two policies, however, is unwarranted, at least when the anti-tardy-perfection policy is narrowed to refer to delayed notoriety problems that could have been attacked during the delay by unsecured creditors by obtaining a lien or otherwise. In Chapter 3 we examined the wisdom of giving the trustee the powers of a lien creditor on the date of bankruptcy. Assuming that power is justified, the opt-out nature of delayed perfection follows axiomatically. It has nothing to do with an anti-secret-lien policy in bankruptcy law, however. Bankruptcy law, as we have seen, starts with relative values of nonbankruptcy entitlements. If nonbankruptcy law expresses a policy against secret liens and if that policy is implemented in a way that permits unsecured creditors to attack them (such as by getting a lien), bankruptcy law presumptively respects the resulting relative values by giving the trustee the powers of a lien creditor.

Once that policy is in place, an unperfected secured creditor will be treated as an unsecured creditor in bankruptcy. One of its opt-out strategies, however, would be to become a perfected secured creditor. Because preference law should appropriately be concerned with that substantive fact and not with labels (does state law consider late perfection a transfer of the debtor's property), delayed perfection, like other opt-out activities, is properly within the scope of preference law and not a "false" preference at all.

The correctness of this can be seen another way. During the time that the anti-last-minute-grab policy prevents the general creditors from upping their status to that of a lien creditor, the anti-tardy-perfection policy restricts existing *secured* creditors from improving their position vis-à-vis general creditors by imposing a similar limitation on them. Without the

14. See R. Jordan & W. Warren, *Bankruptcy* 355–56 (1985). See also Morris, supra note 2, at 759–61 ("Such a transaction is not factually a preference and the law of preferences is not the appropriate vehicle for handling secret liens in bankruptcy").

latter policy, the hands of unsecured creditors would be tied with respect to opting out and avoiding the trustee's section 544(a) power, but the hands of the unperfected secured creditor, who similarly wants to avoid the impact of section 544(a), would not be. The core goal of preserving relative values would be undermined by permitting one group of otherwise presumptive equals in bankruptcy to continue to race while tying the other group down.

The anti-tardy-perfection idea, in short, is a *part* of preference law's anti-grab function, and it is wrong to view it as embodying a distinct policy. At bottom, they are reaching similar behavior that simply comes in two distinct manifestations. Together they provide a transitional rule that preserves the benefits of a collective proceeding notwithstanding the fact that such proceedings rarely commence instantaneously with the discovery of information about the pending need for them. Given this underlying role, what should an optimal preference section look like? To what extent does the current preference provision in section 547 of the Bankruptcy Code achieve the goals it is intended to serve?

In principle, a bankruptcy statute's section on voidable preferences should basically read as follows: "If a creditor tries to change his position after the extension of credit in order to improve his lot in an anticipated bankruptcy (or other collective) proceeding, or if the debtor at the behest of such creditor so tries to change the position for such creditor in order to improve such creditor's lot in an anticipated bankruptcy (or other collective) proceeding, the creditor must return any advantage so obtained." Such wording would most accurately reflect the policies that shape a preference section.

Having a perfect fit with underlying objectives is not the only goal of statutes, however. Sometimes it may be better to have a clear rule that handles the problem in an administratively easy fashion.[15] Such a rule may be better because the costs of such a rule (in striking down transactions that the policies do not reach and in letting through transactions that the policies suggest should be struck down) are less than the costs of a better fitting but fuzzier standard. Preference law has never felt comfortable with any balance between a rule and a standard.[16] During

15. For a discussion of the role of rules and standards, see Baird & Weisberg, "Rules, Standards, and the Battle of the Forms: A Reassessment of §2-207," 68 *Va. L. Rev.* 1217 (1982); Kennedy, "Form and Substance in Private Law Adjudication," 89 *Harv. L. Rev.* 1685, 1687–1713 (1976); Ehrlich & Posner, "An Economic Analysis of Legal Rulemaking," 3 *J. Legal Studies* 257 (1974).

16. Weisberg, "Commercial Morality, the Merchant Character, and the History of the Voidable Preference," 39 *Stan. L. Rev.* 1 (1986).

this century the basic thrust of preference law has been in the direction of a rule. The basic preference section of the Bankruptcy Code leans toward per se rules rather than loose standards in deciding what is a preference. The idea of these rules is to prohibit most of the transfers that are objectionable (creditors taking special action with respect to an insolvent debtor's property in anticipation of a collective proceeding) and to leave untouched transactions that are unobjectionable. This objectivization of preference law remains largely intact in examining involuntary creditor remedies as well as the granting of security interests or their late perfection. But it is substantially weakened in the case of actual payments to a creditor by a 1984 amendment to the safe-harbor in section 547(c)(2), which invites case-by-case inquiry into the bona fides of the creditor's (and debtor's) payment motives.[17] Once one accepts that a preference rule is inevitably going to be both overbroad and under-broad, however, it would seem to be preferable to establish a payment rule (such as payments made within 45 days of when the debt was first due) than to return to a standard. As the result of a poor rule promulgated in 1978 (a safe-harbor for payments within 45 days of when a debt was *incurred*), however, Congress, probably unfortunately, simply returned to a standard.

Whatever the exact balance struck between rules and standards, bearing in mind the role that preference law should play in preserving the advantages of a collective proceeding provides a focus within which preference law's various details may be examined and its limits explored. For example, the need to define *transfer* in such a way so as to cover the late recording of a property interest that would have been vulnerable to creditor attack[18] is explained by the role of the anti-tardy-perfection policy. Yet limits are also inherent in preference law's role. When the definition of *transfer* avoids transactions that the creditors individually could not have struck down, such as is done when the trustee uses the bona fide purchaser standard of section 547(e)(1)(A) against real property transfers, it is used for reasons that have nothing to do with collectivization and should properly be left to general law.

---

17. Section 547(c)(2), as amended in 1984, provides that the trustee may not avoid a transfer under section 547(b) "to the extent that such a transfer was—(A) in payment of a debt incurred by the debtor in the ordinary course of business or financial affairs of the debtor and the transferee; (B) made in the ordinary course of business or financial affairs of the debtor and the transferee; and (C) made according to ordinary business terms." See Dunham & Price, "The End of Preference Liability for Unsecured Creditors: New Section 547(c)(2) of the Bankruptcy Code," 60 *Ind. L. J.* 487 (1985).

18. §547(e).

Sometimes the tension between rules and standards requires one to decide whether to use an easy-to-apply rule, notwithstanding that it is overbroad and underbroad in various ways, or to engage in a more fact-specific inquiry. Consider, for example, the question of whether the return of goods within the preference period to a true consignor who never took any of the notoriety steps required by section 2-326(3) of the Uniform Commercial Code should be viewed as a preferential transfer.[19] Since under nonbankruptcy law the consigned goods are considered to be "owned" at all times by the consignor, it is possible to conclude that there is no transfer of "an interest of the *debtor* in property." But before deciding whether that is the correct response, one should determine whether this conclusion results from a literal application of the term *an interest of the debtor in property* or from a limitation on what bankruptcy law should be doing. As for the latter view, the focus should be on rights among creditors (a priority issue), not on nominal title location between a claimant and the debtor (a property issue). Section 2-326(2) of the Uniform Commercial Code subjects the rights of the true consignor[20] with an uncured ostensible ownership problem to the consignee's "creditors." That provision is sufficient to bring the return of consigned goods within the rationale of the preference section. If the goods were not returned, the trustee (and hence the general creditors) would win over the consignor using section 544(a). Their return can therefore be viewed as opt-out activity on the part of a consignor.

Thus, the question is not the normative one of whether this is preferential (it is), but the question of whether one should treat the term *an interest of the debtor in property* as enunciating a rule that is inevitably going to be overbroad or underbroad. The ninety-day requirement, for example, functions as a quintessential rule. No one denies that it is likely to be overbroad and underbroad in application. But the point of that timetable is to allow preference issues to be decided without fact-specific inquiries into intent by the creditor.

19. See *In re* A. J. Nichols, Ltd, 21 Bankr. 612 (Bankr. N.D. Ga. 1982). Case law prior to the enactment of the Uniform Commercial Code, which imposed a notoriety requirement on consignors as a condition of priority over creditors of the consignee, had held that the return of consigned goods was not preferential. See Kemp-Booth Co. v. Calvin, 84 F.2d 377 (9th Cir. 1936); Dwight v. Horn, 215 Iowa 31, 244 N.W. 702 (1932).

20. Under some courts' reading of Uniform Commercial Code §2-326 (1978), true consignments are made subject to the rule of §2-326(2) only if they fall within the scope of §2-326(3). See, e.g., American Nat'l Bank of Denver v. First Nat'l Bank of Glenwood Springs, 28 Colo. App. 486, 476 P.2d 304 (1970). Under that reading some true consignments may not be reached by §2-326(2). Cf. *In re* Mincow Bag Co., 29 A.D.2d 400, 288 N.Y.S.2d 364 (1968), *aff'd mem.*, 24 N.Y.2d 776, 300 N.Y.S.2d 115, 248 N.E.2d 26 (1969).

No similar defense seems to apply to the term *an interest of the debtor in property,* however. It is not hard to determine whether a consignor would lose to general creditors or to a lien creditor; indeed, it is an answer that must be given, because of section 544(a), in any case where the consignor had not reacquired the goods before the consignee's bankruptcy. Thus, it seems far preferable to read *an interest of the debtor in property* as a statutory phrase asking not for labels but whether the general creditors of a debtor would have been able to claim, but for the activity in question, the property as theirs in bankruptcy.

Conversely, a transfer of property that is indisputably the debtor's (in the sense that title is located in the debtor) should not presumptively be preferential, where the transfer of that property does not diminish the property that the remaining creditors have to enjoy. The transfer of exempt property, contrary to the view expressed by the Commission on the Bankruptcy Laws of the United States,[21] would be such an example. Exempt property is not available for general creditors in bankruptcy. Thus, when someone takes the asset from the debtor, the assets available to the creditors as a group have not changed at all. That aspect of exempt property informs how preference law should treat it. The benefited creditor has, to be sure, opted out of bankruptcy's collective proceeding but not—absent further activity by the debtor (such as repurchasing exempt property with nonexempt property)—at the expense of other creditors.[22] Indeed, the other creditors have one less competitor for the nonexempt assets of the debtor and presumably are *better* off as a result

21. The Commission on the Bankruptcy Laws of the United States thought that decisions under the Bankruptcy Act of 1898 that deemed the transfer of exempt property non-preferential were not supportable. The Report of the Commission on the Bankruptcy Laws of the United States, H. Doc. No. 137, 93rd Cong., 1st Sess. Part I, at 204 (1973) states: "There is no valid reason supporting the case law that is being overruled; the mere fact that the property used to prefer a creditor may be claimed as exempt does not establish a reason why preference attack is not appropriate. The goals of equality and avoidance of unwise extension of credit would be furthered by allowing preference attack. The only rationale for the cases is that other creditors are not hurt since they are not entitled to expect payment or security from exempt property." The "only rationale" supporting the rule that transfers of exempt property are not preferential, however, is *the* one rationale offered by a consideration of the normative role of preference law in bankruptcy. It is odd to see it dismissed so lightly. Cf. *In re* Hale, 15 Bankr. 565 (Bankr. S.D. Ohio 1981).

22. The repurchase, moreover, might constitute debtor misbehavior against creditors reachable under a fraudulent conveyance rationale. See *In re* Reed, 700 F.2d 986 (5th Cir. 1983) (discussed in Chapter 11). If other property were to become exempt automatically— for example, if the debtor had two automobiles and could only exempt one—the transfer of one of the automobiles might have detrimental consequences for the other creditors. But in that case it is possible to say that the debtor did not transfer exempt property in the first place.

of the transfer than they would have been had the transfer not been made. From the perspective of other creditors, this transaction is similar to the voluntary payment of the creditor's claim by a friend of the debtor.[23] Whatever problems may be thought to exist in the transaction vis-à-vis the debtor,[24] the transfer of exempt property to a creditor is not within the scope of the preference rationale, which is based on intracreditor concerns.

Another question of scope can be informed by examining the relationship of preference law to bankruptcy's debt-collection role. In Chapter 5 we explored the rationale for allowing a debtor in bankruptcy to assume executory contracts when its estate would be benefited by doing do. One of the standard requirements for assumption is that the executory contract or unexpired lease still be in force, in the sense that it had not been terminated before the filing of the bankruptcy proceeding. How should bankruptcy laws treat an eve-of-bankruptcy termination of an executory contract? Remember that executory contracts have attributes of mixed assets and liabilities. An executory contract that the debtor would want to assume would be one in which the asset portion exceeded the liability portion. But eve-of-bankruptcy terminations of executory contracts under those circumstances can be seen to reflect the sort of

23. See generally National Bank of Newport v. National Herkimer County Bank, 225 U.S. 178 (1912); I-T-E Circuit Breaker Co. v. Holtzman, 354 F.2d 102 (9th Cir. 1965). Conceivably, a friend's willingness to pay could be viewed as an asset that otherwise would have been available to the creditors generally, but the nexus is uncertain enough that a flat rule leaving such transfers outside the scope of the preference section seems justified.

24. The action may be thought to be undesirable vis-à-vis the debtor because, for example, allowing it might be thought to give creditors an incentive to place pressure on individuals to pay them with exempt property, or because a minimum of exempt property to which every individual debtor is entitled is considered necessary and such transfers interfere with that fresh-start policy. See generally Harris, "A Reply to Theodore Eisenberg's Bankruptcy Law in Perspective," 30 *UCLA L. Rev.* 327, 340–45 (1982). For these reasons Congress may decide that some of these transfers should be avoidable by the debtor, and §522(f)-(h) permits some such interests to be avoided. The reason for allowing such avoidance, however, is fundamentally different from the justification for avoidance by the trustee under §§544–547: it is related to the individual debtor's exemption rights, not to intercreditor equality. See, e.g., Deel Rent-a-Car, Inc. v. Levine, 721 F.2d 750, 758 (11th Cir. 1983) ("The availability of assets to the creditors cannot be relevant to an action by the debtor to avoid a preference pursuant to sections 522(h) and 547. Section 522(h) is designed to protect the debtor alone); *In re* Riddervold, 647 F.2d 342 (2d Cir. 1981) ("In view of the accepted learning that '[a] preference is not an act evil in itself but one prohibited by the Bankruptcy Act in the interest of equality of division' . . . it is not clear why the 1978 Code extended the power to avoid preferences to bankrupts"). The rationale for the debtor's ability to avoid interests that impair exemptions, as it is related to the social policy concerning the fresh start for debtors who are individuals, is examined in Chapter 11.

opt-out activity that occurs when general creditors attempt to improve their status on the eve of bankruptcy through payment, a lien, or otherwise.

Consider the case of an executory contract whereby Debtor promises to pay Supplier $10,000 for 1,000 pairs of pants. After entering into the contract, the market price of pants rises, and thirty days before bankruptcy the pants have a market value of $15,000. If this contract were to be assumed in bankruptcy, and assuming no further changes in value, Supplier would receive $10,000, and the general creditors would net $5,000 from the transaction (by paying out $10,000 and getting pants worth $15,000). But if Supplier can get out of this contract—other than by breach—before bankruptcy, Supplier can improve its lot. For example, if Supplier can get Debtor to agree to cancel the contract, Supplier would then be able to resell the pants to another buyer for $15,000. By that action Supplier would have $5,000 more and the general creditors $5,000 less than if no cancellation occurred and the contract was assumed in bankruptcy. Similarly, if Debtor materially breached the contract, Supplier could terminate it and improve its position by $5,000.

Such a transaction would seem to have hallmarks of opt-out activity in the sense that by the termination Supplier would do better than it would have in bankruptcy and the general creditors would do worse.[25] Does it matter, however, that Supplier cannot opt out without the cooperation of Debtor? That is to say, any unilateral attempt to terminate the contract on Supplier's behalf would constitute a breach, which would not improve Supplier's lot at all. Supplier would gain a benefit only if *Debtor* breached (giving Supplier a power of termination) or if Supplier and Debtor agreed to cancel the contract.

This feature should not make a difference. Standard preference law reaches not only unilateral actions by creditors (such as by acquiring a lien), but also actions, such as getting paid or obtaining a security interest, that require the cooperation of the debtor. One might question why Debtor would default against Supplier when the contract is so favorable or would agree to cancel a contract that is favorable, but one need not search long for the answer. It is a problem of diverse ownership. When Debtor is insolvent, the beneficiaries of the contract with Supplier will be the unsecured creditors. In the prebankruptcy period, before the creditors have taken over the show, Debtor (or more accurately, the shareholders or their representatives) may simply not care who gets

---

25. This discussion is subject to a caveat we explore in the next chapter. If Supplier had the right to insist on payment in full *in* bankruptcy (because its future supplies were needed), this cancellation may not reflect opt-out activity.

the assets. Just as a debtor may pay an unsecured creditor on the eve of bankruptcy when the unsecured creditor seeks to opt out of a bankruptcy proceeding, so, too, is it possible to see Debtor's eve-of-bankruptcy cancellation or default as either an attempt to aid Supplier or simply a consequence of Debtor's unconcern about who shares in its spoils.

Thus, there is no particular reason why preference law should not reach eve-of-bankruptcy cancellations of executory contracts. This rationale also suggests the answer to an issue we left unresolved both in Chapter 2 and in Chapter 5. In Chapter 2 the question was whether it was proper for loan agreements to be reinstated under section 1124 notwithstanding defaults. In Chapter 5 the question was whether the ability of a debtor under section 365 to assume executory contracts in bankruptcy notwithstanding a default implemented bankruptcy's collectivization norm or not. We can now see the answer to both questions, and it is the same.[26] Because of the problem of debtor passivity when faced with insolvency, permitting defaults to be cured in bankruptcy is justified, but only with respect to defaults that occur within the preference period. Permitting the debtor to assume notwithstanding a default, whether or not termination of the contract actually occurs before bankruptcy, can be seen as a part of undoing the harm strategic planning on the eve of bankruptcy can do to the collective proceeding.

This suggests two consequences, neither of which current bankruptcy law seems to implement. First, terminations of executory contracts or below-market loans prior to bankruptcy, whether or not following a default, should be reached by the preference section. Second, permitting the cure of defaults when there has not been a prebankruptcy termination should be limited to defaults that occurred within the preference period.

The current preference section could be read to reach prebankruptcy terminations or cancellations of executory contracts, a consequence that is none too surprising once one starts viewing executory

26. There is a caveat to this discussion. The premise is that the debtor has defaulted on (or let lapse) a *favorable* contract or lease because of passivity. Sometimes this is not the reason at all—the contract may have looked unfavorable in March and only favorable with the hindsight wisdom of August. But, again, we may need to rely on a rule instead of a fact-specific standard. It is also for this reason that I think other eve-of-bankruptcy transactions—such as contemporaneous loans and security interests—should not be reachable by preference law, even though they *may* be due to debtor passivity. In such cases the likelihood of passivity is not high enough to warrant application of a rule. Cf. Baird & Jackson, "Fraudulent Conveyance Law and Its Proper Domain," 38 *Vand. L. Rev.* 829 (1985).

contracts as both assets and liabilities. To continue with our example, the executory right of Debtor to receive performance from Supplier is an asset, in the sense that Debtor is more valuable with it than without it. It is the right to receive $15,000 of pants. Upon a cancellation or a termination, this asset goes to Supplier, who then takes over the right to receive $15,000 from the sale of pants. Thus, it would seem to fit comfortably in the notion of a transfer of "an interest of the debtor in property"; it also would seem to be a transfer "on account of an antecedent debt."[27] The executory contract also represents a liability of Debtor to Supplier, the obligation to pay $10,000. It is a debt that, although contingent on performance by Supplier, is created at the time the executory contract is entered into. When the contract is cancelled or terminated, Supplier gets the pants in lieu of its right to receive $10,000 from Debtor. Thus, the transfer can be seen as satisfying an antecedent debt owed to Supplier. The failure of courts and commentators to use section 547 in analyzing prebankruptcy terminations of executory contracts,[28] therefore, is not a result of a statutory limitation in section 547. It, rather, appears to result from the failure to appreciate the fact that an executory contract should be analyzed as a mixed asset and liability.

One other basic question about the role of preference law deserves some attention. McCoid has questioned whether preference law in its current form can fulfill its role of deterring opt-out behavior: "The only sanction for unsuccessful preference behavior is recapture plus payment of interest from the time of the demand for the return or from the commencement of proceedings to recover the property. At worst, return of the property simply restores the status quo. Use of the property during the period before demand or during the proceedings to recover may even yield a net advantage to the creditor. If a creditor may be able to keep the payment and at worst only has to return it, he has every incentive to accept it."[29]

In one respect McCoid is surely right: there is no reason to start interest running on recaptured preferences only from the commencement of the case. As such, the problem has a simple solution. But the deeper issue is whether recapture is a sufficient deterrent to accomplish preference law's goal. If a creditor only has to give back what it took, the creditor may well decide to try to opt out; the collective proceeding may never start, or it may start only after the preference period has run.

27. These phrases are from §547(b).
28. See *In re* Jermoo's, Inc., 38 Bankr. 197 (Bankr. W.D. Wisc. 1984).
29. McCoid, supra note 7, at 264.

There is no perfect answer to this point. To be sure, as McCoid himself recognizes, the "every incentive" point is overstated.[30] The actions to obtain the preference and perhaps the actions later to resist its recapture cost the creditor money. These dead-weight costs will deter (as does recapture itself) some preferential activity. But even accounting for this fact, it is probably the case that "a creditor frequently will conclude that the sensible course is to accept the preference and to hope for success."[31] Nonetheless, the important question is whether there is a better alternative. McCoid suggests that perhaps preference law should be abolished. But showing that it underdeters is not to say that it provides no deterrence at all. Any solution that reduces the benefits of a course of action will reduce its incidence. Between a choice of no preference law and a preference law that recaptures only, the latter seems preferable.

Deterrence could, of course, be increased by increasing the penalty. Such an approach is used in antitrust law, where violations carry treble damage awards.[32] This solution, however, seems unpromising for preference law. In the case of antitrust law, the actions being prohibited are those that one wants generally to prohibit. Preferences, however, are bad only in light of a collective proceeding. If it were possible to identify with precision those actions that involved intentional opt-out behavior, perhaps a penalty would be appropriate. But once a decision has been made to use a rule that enables preference questions to be decided with relative ease, there are obvious costs to penalizing transfers reached by section 547. The current preference rule may not be optimal in balancing the costs and benefits of its use, but there is no clear advantage to a different rule either.

Preference Law and Secured Creditors

Focusing on the role of preference law in aiding the transition to bankruptcy's collective forum illuminates the relationship between preference law and secured credit. Payments to fully secured creditors have never been considered preferential.[33] In light of the underlying role of pref-

30. Id., at 265–66.
31. Id., at 264.
32. Clayton Act §4.
33. See, e.g., *In re* Conn, 9 Bankr. 431 (Bankr. N.D. Ohio 1981). As a matter of the statutory provision this is commonly thought to be the result of the requirement of §547(b)(5) that a transfer is preferential only if, *inter alia*, it enables the "creditor to receive more than such creditor would receive if (A) the case were a case under chapter 7 of this title;

erence law in preventing behavior designed to benefit an individual creditor by avoiding bankruptcy's collective forum, such an exclusion is entirely proper. As we have seen, bankruptcy law should respect the relative value of entitlements fixed before the transition to bankruptcy because the common pool problem is unrelated to the allocation of the original entitlements. And to the extent that the *value* of a secured creditor's entitlements are respected fully in bankruptcy, there is no reason to believe that avoidance of bankruptcy's collective proceeding underlies a fully secured creditor's receipt of payment on the eve of bankruptcy.[34]

When a secured creditor repossesses collateral—other than cash or cash substitutes—before the commencement of the bankruptcy proceeding, the issue is somewhat distinct. Noncash assets may be worth more to the debtor (as part of an ongoing enterprise) than they are to a third party. In this instance the creditors as a group can be made better off (without harm to the secured creditor) if the assets are returned to the debtor. In *Whiting Pools*[35] the Supreme Court analyzed this issue in terms of section 542 of the Bankruptcy Code[36] and determined that a secured creditor must return repossessed collateral to the debtor. In return, the debtor must provide "adequate protection."[37] Assuming that adequate protection fully compensates the creditor for its nonbankruptcy rights, this provides the proper incentive: the debtor requests the return of the property if but only if its value to the debtor exceeds its value to a third party, on which adequate protection is (or should be) based.

Although analyzed in terms of section 542, the issue in *Whiting Pools* in fact has several facets, at least one of which involves a nascent preference-type issue. Until these different facets are understood, the *Whiting*

(B) the transfer had not been made; and (C) such creditor received payment of such debt to the extent provided by the provisions of this title."

34. Bankruptcy law has, in fact, reflected an odd practical tension. It has long been widely suspected that, as a result of inflated asset valuations, secured creditors are systematically undercompensated in bankruptcy reorganizations, notwithstanding that lip service is paid to the notion that secured creditors are entitled to be paid in full first. See Chapter 7. Moreover, *during* bankruptcy proceedings some judges have explicitly advocated undercompensating secured creditors by denying them compensation for the "time value" of money. For present purposes the point is that as long as such undercompensation exists in bankruptcy, it is not true that secured creditors are wholly outside the rationale of the preference section.

35. United States v. Whiting Pools, Inc., 462 U.S. 198 (1983).

36. Section 542(a) requires turnover to the estate "of property that the trustee may use, sell or lease under section 363 of this title."

37. §§361, 362, 363; see United States v. Whiting Pools, Inc., 462 U.S. 198, 207 (1983). We examine more fully the proper meaning of "adequate protection" in Chapter 7.

Pools issue has potential for mischief. Consider, first, a fully secured creditor who, following default, repossesses the collateral. After repossession but before final dispostion one of the state-law rights enjoyed by the debtor is the right to redeem the collateral "by tendering fulfillment of all obligations secured by the collateral."[38] If the collateral is worth more in the hands of the debtor than in the hands of a third party, and if the third-party value of the collateral is greater than the debt to the creditor, it follows that it is in the interest of the debtor (and its creditors) to redeem.

In these circumstances it may appear odd that the debtor defaulted in the first place. At least a part of the reason may be that the debtor, when insolvent, simply did not have a sufficient incentive to keep the assets together, as the beneficiaries had become, effectively, the other creditors. And the other creditors, acting individually, were most likely too dispersed to achieve an effective consensual solution that did not involve free-riders and holdouts. Bankruptcy proceedings are designed to solve that problem by providing a mechanism to ensure a proper decision as to what to do with the assets—including keeping assets that are worth more in the hands of the debtor than in the hands of a third party. As with similar preference responses elsewhere in bankruptcy law, repossession by a secured creditor on the eve of bankruptcy should not bind the creditors in bankruptcy, who should be able to return to the status quo and have the collateral returned. Seen another way, requiring turnover upon the receipt of adequate compensation is, in effect, redeeming the collateral. What changes, however, is that the *value* of the redemption right is preserved, in place of the actual *right* itself. As such, it is just a variant of the automatic stay cases we shall examine in the next chapter, where the secured creditor's *right* to repossess and sell the collateral is taken away, as a matter of bankruptcy policy, but where the *value* of that right is adequately protected.

Another facet to *Whiting Pools* can be analyzed by focusing on repossession by the *under*secured creditor. An undersecured creditor who repossesses collateral may be attempting to "skim" off a portion of the difference in value of the collateral in the hands of the debtor as opposed to the value of the collateral in the hands of a third party. If a creditor who acquires a security interest only legitimately obtains the right to sell the collateral to a third party,[39] an attempt to gain more, by virtue of

38. Uniform Commercial Code §9-506 (1978).

39. This is a crucial assumption, but it seems to comport with the thrust of Uniform Commercial Code §9-504 (1978). One could argue that the secured creditor's nonbankruptcy entitlement *includes* the extra leverage he acquires, by repossession, over the debtor,

the collateral's "extra" value to the debtor, may be viewed as a species of misbehavior by the undersecured creditor against the debtor (and, in bankruptcy, against the debtor's other creditors). Alternatively, an undersecured creditor may be trying to improve its position in bankruptcy through redemption. After repossession the only way a debtor can reacquire the collateral directly is through redemption. Under article 9, however, redemption requires paying the *entire* debt.[40] To the extent that the debt is undercollateralized, any such payment before bankruptcy would be preferential. Requiring redemption in bankruptcy as a prerequisite to the return of the collateral would, likewise, reward such behavior (by allowing the undersecured creditor to receive indirectly what it could not receive directly), to the detriment of the bankruptcy proceeding itself.

When the debtor is solvent, this kind of activity normally is not a worry, both because the debtor can prevent it by avoiding default (and it is in its interest to do so) and because the payment itself of the whole debt is not wrongful to the interests of any other group. But when the debtor is insolvent, the debtor may not care sufficiently to stop the repossession, in which case the resulting harm is imposed on the other creditors.

Because secured creditors are properly constrained in their efforts to repossess once a bankruptcy proceeding has commenced (as we will see in the next chapter), it is therefore possible to view such an eve-of-bankruptcy repossession as within preference law's grasp. Because this ability to obtain more lasts only as long as the creditor holds the property,[41] *Whiting Pools* may accurately reflect the contours of the problem.

in the ability to extract a portion of the excess value to the debtor over that of a third party. Cf. Reivman v. Burlington Northern Railroad Co., No. 85 Civ. 3694 (S.D.N.Y. June 21, 1985). The difficulty with this analysis, however, is that if a debtor is solvent, it is unlikely that repossession would occur; the debtor could block the secured creditor's acquisition of that leverage in the first place. But when a debtor is insolvent, its indifference as to what happens to its assets may allow such repossession, notwithstanding that it is not in the interests of the creditors as a group.

Another subtle question also arises in this analysis: if the asset is more valuable in the hands of the debtor than in the hands of a third party, why does not the price at which the asset can be sold simply reflect an ability of the third party to sell the asset, at the enhanced price, to the debtor? Without delving deeply into it, the answer seems to be tied to informational and transactional costs. As for the ability of the debtor to buy the asset at the repossession sale, the answer to that tracks the discussion in text: the substitution (via adequate protection) of the value of the right for the right itself.

40. Uniform Commercial Code §9-506 (1978).

41. If the secured creditor has already sold the property pursuant to §9-504 of the Uniform Commercial Code, the secured creditor cannot be trying to use the property as a lever to exact more than the price a third party would be willing to pay for the property.

But *Whiting Pools* may then more appropriately be viewed as a resolution of two separate problems—a redemption problem for fully secured creditors and an opt-out problem for undersecured creditors—than as a "property of the estate" problem, a line of analysis that seems formalistic and troublesome.[42]

Considering preference law as a response to the problems caused by moving from an individual remedies system to a collective regime also allows us to focus on one of the most warmly debated issues of the past generation in commercial law: the extent to which Article 9's floating lien should be recognized in bankruptcy.[43] When a secured party takes a security interest in collateral (usually inventory or accounts) that "floats" over after-acquired collateral,[44] should the fact that new collateral is acquired by the debtor during the preference period be deemed a voidable preference?

When the issue was first raised in the 1960s, the answer was "no." This answer was normative as much as it was positive. In *DuBay v. Williams*,[45] for example, Judge Hufstedler identified section 60, the old Bankruptcy Act's preference section, as embodying two policies: the anti-last-minute-grab policy and the anti-tardy-perfection policy.[46] She then obvserved that the floating lien itself violated neither of those policies. The security interest in question was properly noted by a public filing long before the advent of bankruptcy, and other creditors were therefore not misled about the situation. And because the acquisition to the security agreement of new collateral took place automatically, no readily available presumption could be made from the fact that the lien "floated" that

42. See, e.g., Cross Electric Co. v. United States, 664 F.2d 1218 (4th Cir. 1981) (debtor's "rights" after repossession are those of surplus, redemption, and required disposition; these are not sufficient to constitute property of a type that the debtor can sell or use to support a turnover under §542). The Supreme Court avoided the troubling language of §542 by making the meaningless comment that §542 was a "definition," not a "limitation." United States v. Whiting Pools, Inc., 462 U.S. 198, 203 (1983).

43. The course of this debate is recounted in Kronman, "The Treatment of Security Interests in After-Acquired Property Under the Proposed Bankruptcy Act," 124 *U. Pa. L. Rev.* 110 (1975).

44. See Uniform Commercial Code §§9-203(3), 9-204(1), 9-204(3), 9-205, 9-206, 9-306(2) (1978).

45. 417 F.2d 1277 (9th Cir. 1969); see also Grain Merchants v. Union Bank & Savings Co., 408 F.2d 209 (7th Cir.), *cert. denied,* 396 U.S. 827 (1969); *In re* King-Porter Co., 446 F.2d 722 (5th Cir. 1971).

46. 417 F.2d, at 1288 ("Congress intended to achieve two aims: (1) to prevent an insistent creditor from harvesting more than his fair share of the insolvent's assets by obtaining tranfers from the debtor on the eve of bankruptcy, and (2) to discourage extension of credit to debtors under circumstances which concealed from general creditors the precarious financial condition of the debtor").

receipt of new items of collateral during the preference period was due to any last-minute preferential activity either on the part of the creditor or on the part of the debtor.[47]

This is not to say, however, that no such preferential activity could exist within the framework; as Judge Hufstedler recognized, it could. Rather the point is that the policy reasoning of *DuBay* was fundamentally correct. There was no reason to *presume,* from the fact that a lien "floats," that opt-out activity was taking place to benefit one creditor at the expense of others.

The ultimate statutory response to *DuBay* is a "two-point net improvement" test in section 547(c)(5) of the Bankruptcy Code. Under that test a security interest in inventory or receivables otherwise falling prey to the requirements of the preference section (which has been modified to reach the attachment of security interests to after-acquired collateral)[48] is protected against avoidance by the trustee in bankruptcy to the extent that the secured party either does not improve its position during the preference period or can show that its improvement in position was not "to the prejudice of other creditors holding unsecured claims."[49]

This provision is generally considered a compromise between the two sides of the floating lien battles that took place in the 1960s and early 1970s,[50] and, like many compromises, it expresses no clear principle of its own. But there is another, more satisfying, way to view section 547(c)(5). It may be seen as implementing the preference section's anti-last-minute-grab policy by way of a presumptive rule. So viewed, the two-point net improvement test announces a presumption: improvements in position by a secured creditor holding a security interest in inventory or accounts within the preference period are unusual and therefore will be presumed to result from a last-minute grab by the secured creditor.[51]

47. Id., at 1289.

48. §547(e)(3).

49. §547(c)(5). The requirement that the improvement in position is avoidable only if it is "to the prejudice of other creditors holding unsecured claims" comes from a suggestion made by Homer Kripke, based on an allocation formula in Meinhard, Greeff and Co. v. Edens, 189 F.2d 792 (4th Cir. 1951), that was incorporated into §4-607 of the Proposed Bankruptcy Act of 1973. See Report of the Commission on the Bankruptcy Laws of the United States, H. Doc. No. 137, 93rd Cong., 1st Sess., Part I, at 209–10 (1973).

50. See, e.g., Kronman, supra note 43.

51. See National Bankruptcy Conference, Report of the Committee on Coordination of the Bankruptcy Act and the Uniform Commercial Code (1970), reprinted in H. Rep. No. 595, 95th Cong., 1st Sess. 216 (1977). That report, from the so-called Gilmore Committee, stated that the two-point test "seeks to catch in the preference net particularly those situations in which the transferee (as by crash sales of inventory below cost to feed the receivables) has sought to manipulate the prebankruptcy situation to his own advantage.

That creditor, however, may defeat that presumption by showing that the increase was not the result of a last-minute grab—by showing, in the language of the statute, that it was not to the prejudice of other creditors holding unsecured claims. So viewed, a general rule has been substituted for a case-by-case analysis, but the general rule implements an established policy.[52]

Because the process that led to section 547(c)(5) was not informed by a consensus as to the role of preference law—or even by any clear theory of how preference law should relate to a nonbankruptcy rule such as the floating lien—this description may be more a fortuitous recharacterization of the two-point net improvement test than an elaboration of the drafting motivations that produced it.[53] The two-point net improvement test does not, for example, tailor the presumption to the policy in a fully lucid way. Unless the presumption is to be conclusive (for ease of proof), the ability to rebut it should presumably go the other way as well: the trustee should be able to show that deliberate preferential behavior occurred during that ninety-day period, even though the result of that behavior did not result in an improvement in position as measured by the two-point test.[54]

A more troublesome product of the changes that resulted in the two-point net improvement test also suggests that they were implemented without an awareness of the justification for a preference rule in the first place. However well the changes fit general preference policy in dealing with the transactions the drafters had in mind, they stray from that policy when applied to other problems.

For example, to avoid the statutory reasoning of *DuBay,* section 547(e) redefines the date of a transfer.[55] This redefinition may, however, strike

---

(In the normal course of a business declining into bankruptcy the position of an inventory or receivables lender, far from improving, will almost certainly deteriorate)."

52. Cf. Harris, supra note 24, at 336 ("This choice is consistent with the Code's policy of reducing litigation over difficult questions of fact at the risk of catching unobjectionable transactions in the preference net").

53. See, e.g., Eisenberg, "Bankruptcy Law in Perspective: A Rejoinder," 30 *UCLA L. Rev.* 617, 631 (1983) ("A more natural reading . . . seems to be that the writers were concerned that secured parties, whether or not they had engaged in manipulative behavior, were simply able to get too large a share of the debtor's assets.").

54. This is essentially the result §553(a)(3) permits the trustee to reach with respect to the incurrence of debts by a creditor "for the purpose of obtaining a right of set-off against the debtor," notwithstanding a comparable two-point net improvement test in §553(b).

55. Section 547(e), in particular, provides that, for purposes of preference attack, "a transfer is not made until the debtor has acquired rights in the property transferred." The House Report notes that this subsection, "more than any other," overrules *DuBay,* H. Rep. No. 595, 95th Cong., 1st Sess. 374 (1977).

down unrelated activity. Consider the case of garnishments of wages by or assignments of rents to creditors that are put in place outside of the preference period. Are wages or rents paid to such creditors inside the preference period, pursuant to such assignments or garnishments, preferential? The newly fashioned definition of *transfer* states that no transfer can be made for purposes of the preference section until the debtor has "rights in the property transferred." This statutory definition of transfer may mean that there is no transfer of rents or of wages until they are earned or paid and, read literally, would render the payment of such rents or wages to the assignee or garnishee preferential.[56]

Yet the accrual of wages or rents within the preference period based on a garnishment or assignment outside the preference period does not violate preference law's underlying policies. The activity is not manipulative as among creditors: it represents neither a tardy perfection (as it was fully publicized) nor a last-minute grab (as the grab, if any, took place *ab initio*).[57] Moreover, in contrast to the case of a security interest in a type of collateral whose components are constantly changing such as inventory or accounts, it does not seem that there *ever* is much opportunity here for deliberate preferential behavior.[58] Where the security interest is in a mass of inventory or accounts, the issue that gives rise to a preference question at all—and hence the need for the two-point net improvement test—relates to the reasons for the acquisition, within the preference period, of *new* items of inventory or accounts that are added to that mass. Where the interest involved is the assignment of rents off

56. See *In re Diversified World Investments, Inc*, 12 Bankr. 517 (Bankr. S.D. Tenn. 1981). The preference problems of an assignment of rents arising out of a lease of personal property can probably be avoided by taking a security interest in the right to rents, which is an Article 9 "account," Uniform Commercial Code §9-106 (1978), in which case the payment of the rents themselves would be "proceeds," protected by §547(c)(5), if not by §547(b)(5). Similarly, a security interest in real estate rentals, if properly perfected, should be protected because of the definition of *receivables* in §547(a)(3). The garnishment of wages, however, would not seem to fit in the safe-harbor of §547(c)(5), even if the transaction were restructured.

57. Cf. *In re* Riddervold, 647 F.2d 342 (2nd Cir. 1981) (case involved garnishment; held, under New York law, "after the sheriff has taken the steps described in [the garnishment statute], the debtor has no property or interest in property subject to the levy which can be transferred"). Most other courts have disagreed with *Riddervold*. See, e.g., *In re* Tabita, 38 Bankr. 511 (Bankr. E.D. Pa. 1984); *In re* Mayo, 19 Bankr. 630 (E.D. Va. 1981); *In re* Larson, 21 Bankr. 264 (Bankr. D. Utah 1982); *In re* Eggleston, 19 Bankr. 280 (Bankr. M.D. Tenn. 1982); but see *In re* Coppie, 728 F.2d 951 (7th Cir. 1984).

58. Deliberate manipulative conduct in such cases is conceivable—for example, a creditor with a wage garnishment might persuade the debtor not to switch jobs to a new, higher-paying one—but it does not appear likely enough to be appropriately handled by means of a flat rule striking down all such assignments or garnishments.

of a single contract or the garnishment of wages, however, the room for manipulation seems much narrower, simply because there is no substitution the quantity of which can be easily affected by deliberate behavior.

Although section 547(c)(5) may continue the objectification of preference law into presumptive categories—a trend that is not objectionable in itself even if it sometimes results in overbreadth or underbreadth—it would be unfortunate to find that the policies that animate the preference section itself have been obscured. The result may well be a preference section that, by serving goals other than preserving the advantages of a collective proceeding, undermines that proceeding. A firm notion of the reasons for bankruptcy and hence for a preference section can help focus application of that power.

Fraudulent Conveyance Law and Debtor Passivity

At several points in this chapter the discussion of eve-of-bankruptcy transactions has focused on debtor indifference. I suggested that the problems created by such indifference for a collective proceeding were much the same as those caused by intentional creditor opt-out activity. In both cases the results undermined the collective proceeding, and therefore it was proper that bankruptcy law itself interdict such activity. Absent a collective proceeding, transactions resulting from creditor pressure or debtor indifference seem a part of the warp and woof of individual creditor remedies; they are not clearly enough wrongs to justify their prohibition in that context.

This situation is different from that of a series of creditor powers generally analyzed under the rubric of fraudulent conveyance law. Fraudulent conveyance law applies both inside and outside a collective proceeding such as bankruptcy. This nonbankruptcy application expresses a great deal about the conceptual difference between the roles of preference law and of fraudulent conveyance law in sorting out legal rights. Preference law sorts out rights among the creditors themselves; fraudulent conveyance law polices the relationship between the debtor and its creditors. That is to say, preference law, like most other trustee avoiding powers, is designed to preserve the advantages to creditors as a group of resorting to a collective proceeding. Conversely, fraudulent conveyance law protects creditors as a group against misbehavior by their debtor whether or not a collective proceeding is needed. It, accordingly, is not related to solving common pool problems.

Many of the difficulties associated with fraudulent conveyance law arise from the failure to distinguish the general role of fraudulent conveyance law from the bankruptcy-oriented role of preference law. The presence of two fraudulent conveyance sections in the Bankruptcy Code has exacerbated these difficulties. The Bankruptcy Code applies fraudulent conveyance law not only through section 544(b), which incorporates state fraudulent conveyance law,[59] but also through section 548, which establishes a related but ultimately distinct bankruptcy law of fraudulent conveyances. Bankruptcy-tailored fraudulent conveyance rules, such as those in section 548, would be justified if fraudulent conveyance law, like the trustee's other avoiding powers, was related to the reasons for a collective proceeding. But since fraudulent conveyance law springs from an entirely different source, its separate existence in a bankruptcy statute is more problematic. It would then need to be justified on the ground of administrative convenience: that, like claims estimation procedures, it unified and simplified the rules of fifty discrete states. Yet this justification still depends on bankruptcy law's implementing state policy in a rule-oriented fashion, not deliberately changing it. It is doubtful that it has ever been justified on such grounds.

Fraudulent conveyance law generally comes into play only if a debtor becomes insolvent and is unable to pay all its creditors. This is true even when the law serves a prophylactic function, such as deterring actions by a debtor to gamble at the expense of its creditors—to risk insolvency for the prospect of a large upside gain from which it alone will benefit.[60] Although fraudulent conveyance law is generally necessary only if a debtor becomes insolvent, that does not mean that it is essentially related to the justifications for a bankruptcy process. Of course, activities covered by fraudulent conveyance law are not entirely unrelated to bankruptcy. For example, a debtor's dissipation or concealment of assets may frustrate the realization of the assets' higher going-concern value as much as grabs by creditors. But such transactions are undesirable when the debtor is insolvent even in the absence of any common pool problem—such as when the debtor has only one creditor—and are thought sufficiently undesirable that a flat ban is appropriate. Hence, the justification for fraudulent conveyance law is fundamentally broader than are the reasons for a bankruptcy proceeding.

Fraudulent conveyance law, then, is distinctly less collectivist in its

59. Such incorporation, subject to the qualification about Moore v. Bay discussed in Chapter 3, is proper, as this implements nonbankruptcy rights in bankruptcy.

60. The proper normative reach of fraudulent conveyance law is explored in Baird & Jackson, supra note 26; Clark, supra note 8.

justification. It is, instead, a part of the warp and woof of debtor-creditor relations; in terms of bankruptcy law it should be seen as part of the initial establishment of entitlements, not as something that bankruptcy policy should itself have anything to say about. The essence of fraudulent conveyance law is to prevent manipulative activities by the debtor. If the activity in question is a manipulation by a creditor vis-à-vis other creditors, then it should succumb, if at all, to a preference-type rationale rather than to a fraudulent-conveyance-type rationale.[61] Sometimes, to be sure, sorting out different actions is none too easy. Is it an opt-out action by a creditor? Does it result from debtor passivity that harms a collective proceeding? Or is it simply a wrong by a debtor against the creditors unrelated to a collective proceeding?

These distinctions are important in certain transactions. One of the more perplexing recent additions to fraudulent conveyance case law that has arisen in the context of a bankruptcy proceeding, using section 548 of the Bankruptcy Code, is the trustee's attack on mortgage foreclosure sales.[62] These cases typically involve fact situations such as the following. Bank lends $60,000 to Debtor and secures this loan by taking and recording a mortgage on Blackacre, which is owned by Debtor. Later, Debtor defaults on the loan, and Bank forecloses on the property. Following state procedures, Bank holds a foreclosure sale of the property at which it or a third party buys the property for $60,000. Within a year of that foreclosure sale Debtor files for bankruptcy, whereupon the trustee asserts that the foreclosure sale was a fraudulent conveyance because Blackacre was not sold for a fair consideration (being worth, the trustee asserts, more than $75,000 at the time of the sale) and because it was sold at a time when Debtor was insolvent.

---

61. Clark, supra note 8; McLaughlin, "Application of the Uniform Fraudulent Conveyance Act," 46 *Harv. L. Rev.* 404 (1933). The classic work on fraudulent conveyance law remains G. Glenn, *Fraudulent Conveyances and Preferences* (rev. ed. 1940). Glenn started that work by noting (id., at 1) that "[t]he preference materially differs from the fraudulent conveyance, because it sins, not against the single creditor's right of realization, but only against the collective right, of the creditors as a class, that arises when their debtor becomes insolvent." See Michel v. J's Foods, Inc., 661 P.2d 474 (N.M. 1983) ("The purpose of [the Uniform Fraudulent Conveyance] Act is to protect creditors when a *debtor* has made a conveyance of his property which diminishes the creditor's assets to the detriment of the rights of the creditor") (emphasis in original).

62. Compare *In re* Hulm, 738 F.2d 323 (8th Cir. 1984); Abramson v. Lakewood Nat'l Bank and Trust Co., 647 F.2d 547 (5th Cir. 1981); Durrett v. Washington Nat'l Ins. Co., 621 F.2d 201 (5th Cir. 1980); *In re* Richardson, 23 Bankr. 434 (Bankr. D. Utah 1982), with *In re* Madrid, 725 F.2d 1197 (9th Cir. 1984); *In re* Alsop, 14 Bankr. 982 (Bankr. D. Alaska 1981), aff'd, 22 Bankr. 1017 (D. Alaska 1982).

The facts of these cases do not support a presumption of debtor-induced misbehavior. Indeed, to the extent that misbehavior appears, the cases suggest the possibility of misbehavior by the creditor against the debtor. Unlike preference-type behavior, however, where the misbehavior involves the creditor seeking his just due at the expense of other creditors in an impending collective proceeding, the misbehavior in these cases involves the creditor trying to get *more* than his just due.[63] As such, the creditor wrongs the debtor generally, not just other creditors in cases when there are not enough assets to go around.

This account, however, may oversimplify the setting in which foreclosure sales take place. Any debtor that permits a foreclosure to proceed is likely to be insolvent. Accordingly, the debtor may have an insufficient incentive to resist a foreclosing creditor's efforts to purchase an asset at a foreclosure sale for less than fair value. The debtor will lose its assets anyway and may not particularly care who gets them. For that reason the transaction may suggest a transfer by a debtor, made while insolvent, for less than fair consideration, which would be prey to fraudulent conveyance law's rule-oriented branch. But whether that is right or not is not a question of bankruptcy law. The problem that is created here, whether by creditor insistence, debtor passivity, or a mixture of both, is one of a wrong against other creditors that would exist whether or not a collective proceeding were commenced. When a creditor gets paid more than is its due at a time when the debtor is insolvent, that should be actionable by other creditors irrespective of whether a collective proceeding is commenced. Indeed, the various state rules regulating foreclosure sales can be seen as a response to this type of problem, designed to allow other creditors to protect themselves.

However analyzed, it is not a problem related to bankruptcy law because it does not involve opt-out behavior that is destructive of the collective proceeding. When the issue does not seem to be inherently misbehavior-induced activity by a debtor against its creditors or debtor-passivity harmful to creditor interests apart from collectivization, fraudulent conveyance law appears to be the wrong vehicle.[64] To the extent

63. A secured party has few incentives to allow an item of collateral to be sold to third parties for less than the amount of the indebtedness, because that leaves it with an unsecured deficiency. See Schwartz, "The Enforceability of Security Interests in Consumer Goods," 26 *J. Law & Econ.* 117 (1983). A secured creditor may purchase collateral itself for less than fair value, even if that sale is for less than the indebtedness, because the deficiency claim plus the capture of the excess value may exceed the value to it of attributing the fair market value of the property against the indebtedness.

64. Section 101 (48) defines *transfer* as including involuntary transfers, and a corre-

that section 548 is used to reach these transactions when state fraudulent conveyance law would not be used, the result seems normatively unprincipled.[65]

---

sponding change was made (perhaps inadvertently) to §548 in 1984. In the context of fraudulent conveyance law true involuntary transfers contradict the notion of debtor-based wrongdoing. Involuntary transfers may well be preferential, but they are not fraudulent conveyances. See *In re* Madrid, 725 F.2d 1197, 1203–04 (9th Cir. 1984) (Farris, J., concurring) ("One cannot presume fraud by the debtor in a transaction where the debtor was not a party . . . I would therefore hold that only transfers where the bankrupt was a participant can be set aside for absence of 'reasonably equivalent value' "); Abramson v. Lakewood Bank and Trust Co., 647 F.2d 547 (5th Cir. 1981) (Clark, J., dissenting); Sheffield Progressive v. Kingston Tool Co., 405 N.E.2d 985 (Mass. App. 1980). Also, transfers of exempt property may not be fraudulent (unless other property thereupon becomes exempt); see *In re* Tredwell, 699 F.2d 1050 (11th Cir. 1983); see also supra notes 21–24 (discussion of preferences and transfers of exempt property).

65. See also Kindom Uranium Corp. v. Vance, 269 F.2d 104 (10th Cir. 1959), which involved classic preferential activity—a creditor's late recording of a deed—but was analyzed as a fraudulent conveyance. The case is criticized in Jackson, "Avoiding Powers in Bankruptcy," 36 *Stan. L. Rev.* 725, 783–86 (1984). Similarly, an insider preference was inappropriately analyzed as a fraudulent conveyance in Bullard v. Aluminum Co. of America, 468 F.2d 11 (7th Cir. 1972). See W. Warren & W. Hogan, *Cases and Materials on Debtor-Creditor Law* 407 (2d ed. 1981).

7

Running Bankruptcy's Collective Proceeding

IN THIS CHAPTER we explore the consequences of bankruptcy's collectivization goal in a world in which a bankruptcy proceeding takes time. Because that is the case, opportunities for strategic behavior exist in the postbankruptcy period, just as they do in the prebankruptcy period. We shall examine how rules designed to cope with that situation should be shaped against the backdrop of bankruptcy's collective debt-collection function.

The move to a collective regime where assets are held together often means that the concept of relative values is the relevant consideration rather than recognition of actual rights. Thus, for example, responding to a common pool problem requires that individual creditor remedies such as execution and the like stop upon the commencement of a bankruptcy proceeding. Exercise of the default rights of secured creditors, moreover, also must stop and be replaced by value protection instead. This outcome is achieved by the automatic stay, currently embodied in section 362 of the Bankruptcy Code

The core role of that section is clear: its goal is to stop actions by creditors in pursuit of individual self-interest that presumptively could undermine the common good. But the reasons for imposing the automatic stay and for continuing it vary enormously depending on the type of creditor and the type of action. When a debtor is insolvent, the automatic stay as applied to the actions of general unsecured creditors should usually remain in effect for the duration of the bankruptcy proceeding, because the concept of relative values demands that this class of creditors wait for pro rata distribution at the conclusion of the case.

The justification for continuing the automatic stay against a secured party is different. In that case, because of the concept of relative values, distributional concerns do not justify waiting until the conclusion of the bankruptcy process. Instead, the justification for the stay must be that the creditors as a group are sometimes better off if the secured creditor's collateral remains in place, with the value of the secured creditor's rights respected instead of the rights themselves. This justification is, however, more limited than that for leaving the stay in place against unsecured creditors. The debtor's assets may largely be items such as marketable securities for which (assuming they do not constitute a control block) there is no extra value in keeping them together. Or the debtor may be liquidating and seeking to dispose of its assets on a piece-by-piece basis. In such cases it may be preferable to respect the actual rights of the secured creditors once the situation becomes clear.[1] Respecting the rights themselves is the most accurate way of respecting the underlying value, and in certain cases doing so will impose no loss on the unsecured creditors.

Finally, the justifications for the automatic stay are the most short-lived in cases of its application to a bailor of property that the debtor has in possession at the moment a bankruptcy case commences. Unless the bailment involves an executory contract, the justification for the automatic stay is simply to preserve the status quo for as long as it takes to sort out whether a true bailment exists. Once that is determined, the bailor should be able to recover its property. Thus, when the debtor is a dry cleaner, its prebankruptcy patrons should not be required to wait any length of time for the return of their clothes (as long as they pay for any cleaning done).

Along with the automatic stay, however, another principle should apply to debtors that are in bankruptcy. Because it exists to solve a common pool problem created by diverse prebankruptcy owners and their individual collection rights, bankruptcy should not be used to give debtors any special consideration concerning future operations. A debtor may be in the business of producing silicon chips. Its assets may be worth $2 million doing that—in the sense that a buyer would pay $2 million for the assets freed of prebankruptcy liabilities. The buyer who buys the assets at a certain price, however, calculates that price given the existence both of the need to buy supplies and hire workers and of a set of legal rules, regulations, and restrictions. A governmental rule may require,

---

1. This will not always be the case. If the property is worth more than the debt to the secured creditor, the secured creditor may have insufficient incentive to sell the property for the optimal amount, as any surplus must be returned to the debtor under Uniform Commercial Code §9-504 (1978). In those cases the best solution may be to have the debtor sell the property and pay the secured creditor in full.

for example, as a condition of operation for anyone producing silicon chips, the installation of environmental equipment at a cost of $500,000. If the assets could be used to produce silicon chips *without* complying with this regulation (and assuming that there would be no feasible tort suits by pollution victims), the assets would then be worth $2.5 million to a buyer. That fact, however, is completely irrelevant outside of bankruptcy because it describes a mode of operation that, like using the assets to manufacture LSD, is illegal.

It should be irrelevant in bankruptcy as well. Resorting to a set of procedures designed to ameliorate a common pool problem is not an occasion to allow the creditors (who now, like a new buyer, "own" the assets) any relaxation of the restrictions governing the use of the assets. This principle, moreover, applies to more than governmental regulations. It applies to inducing others to deal with the debtor—inducing suppliers to supply goods, labor, and credit, and inducing buyers to buy the debtor's output. Because bankruptcy judges cannot (and in any event should not) order a supplier to deliver needed materials to the debtor, the debtor in bankruptcy, like others, must negotiate with suppliers in order to operate.

Thus, the rule permitting postbankruptcy suppliers to get paid before general creditors makes sense. If prebankruptcy creditors decide to use the assets to continue to operate the business, they, like any buyer, need to persuade others to deal with the debtor. This requires payment or reasonable assurance of payment. Thus, the creditors must use the assets to pay for these supplies.[2] Bankruptcy law should not impede prebankruptcy creditors in their quest for the optimal use of the assets, but to avoid skewing the deployment decision that would be made outside of bankruptcy, it should not free them from nonbankruptcy constraints either.

This rationale for administrative expense priority derives from the realities of getting suppliers (and others) to deal with an insolvent enterprise. It also provides a basis for testing the status of postbankruptcy tort claims, an issue addressed by the Supreme Court in *Reading Co. v. Brown*.[3] In that case Justice Harlan, for the Court, concluded that the tort victims of a fire resulting from the negligence of a debtor during its bankruptcy proceedings had rights to the assets superior to those of the prebankruptcy unsecured creditors of the debtor. He reasoned: "In considering whether those injured by the operation of the business dur-

2. We will explore the operation of this principle more systematically later in this chapter.
3. 391 U.S. 471 (1968).

ing an arrangement should share equally with, or recover ahead of, those for whose benefit the business is carried on, the latter seems more natural and just. Existing creditors are, to be sure, in a dilemma not of their own making, but there is no obvious reason why they should be allowed to attempt to escape that dilemma at the risk of imposing it on others equally innocent."[4] Chief Justice Warren, however, dissenting with Justice Douglas, maintained that this result upset the bankruptcy policy of pro rata distribution. In his view the result of the Court's decision was that "the status of a tort claimant depends entirely upon whether he is fortunate enough to have been injured after rather than before" bankruptcy.[5]

It is fruitful to recharacterize the underlying dispute in *Reading Co. v. Brown* as essentially one of whether the transfer of ownership of the corporation to its creditors should be deemed to occur at the moment bankruptcy is filed or at the moment the process is over.[6] Consider, first, the case of a liquidating corporation. Such a corporation, if it were to dissolve outside bankruptcy, would parcel out its assets as the final step in the dissolution process. Tort claims that accrued after the decision to dissolve but before the actual dissolution would presumably share pro rata with the other general creditors in the distribution. No postdissolution torts would be committed by the corporation because by definition the corporation would no longer exist.

This analogy supports the dissenting view of Chief Justice Warren. The bankruptcy process may be part of a *decision* to dissolve, but its commencement is not tantamount to a dissolution. Justice Harlan's view is supported by a slightly different analogy whereby the decision to invoke bankruptcy is itself a triggering event that transfers ownership of the corporation to its creditors. The general creditors are treated as the new equity owners of the corporation.[7] The corporation in bankruptcy is then like a corporation held by shareholders. Any debts that

4. Id., at 482-83.

5. Id., at 486.

6. In the case of debtors that are individuals this question would seem not to arise. The commencement of the bankruptcy case itself divides the debts into those that arose prepetition, presumptively are discharged, and share in prepetition assets and those that arise postpetition and are not discharged but have claims against the individual's human capital and other postpetition assets. In those cases Justice Harlan's line at the point of filing seems to mirror that sharp division. (One might want to return, at this point, to the discussion of asbestos claims in Chapter 2.)

7. They are treated as shareholders in the sense that tort claimants, as creditors, have the right to be paid in full before shareholders receive anything. In bankruptcy this is the consequence of administrative expense status that allows such holders to be paid in full before unsecured creditors receive anything. See §§507, 726.

the corporation incurs during the bankruptcy proceeding have priority over prepetition unsecured claims because debts take priority over equity claims. Upon completion of the bankruptcy process and dissolution of the corporation the tort claims that arose during the bankruptcy proceeding would have priority over the prepetition claims of the general creditors, which are viewed, for purposes of bankruptcy law, as equity owners.

Similarly, consider the case of a continuing corporation that has been sold either to a third party or to the creditors themselves in a bankruptcy proceeding. Again, to resort to the closest nonbankruptcy analogy—that of a sale of the corporation—claims that accrued during the negotiation process preceding the sale would be treated as general unsecured claims. At the time of consummation of the sale, the buyer would impose a new capital structure on the firm, and postsale tort claims would share depending on the capital structure imposed. Again, this view seems to support Chief Justice Warren's vision of the process. The analogy in support of Justice Harlan's vision is slightly different. It again would view the commencement of a bankruptcy case as the operative event— as tantamount to a sale of the business to the creditors. During the bankruptcy process, while the general creditors qua owners are deciding on what to do with the assets and whether there should be a new capital structure placed on the business, the corporation is treated as having an all common-stock structure insofar as the claims of prepetition general creditors are concerned.[8] So viewed, torts that accrue during the bankruptcy process have priority over prepetition unsecured claimants. Upon consummation of a plan of reorganization (or a sale to a third party) a new capital structure will be placed on the corporation, and how postconfirmation tort claimants fare will depend on the details of that capital structure.

The selection between these competing scenarios should be based on minimizing the costs of a transition to the collective regime. The closest nonbankruptcy analogy in the case of business entities seems to be that in which the commencement of bankruptcy is viewed as the beginning of the process of dissolution or negotiation over the change of ownership, not its end. This conclusion would avoid the possibility that creditors would reject the collective procedure because they would fare worse than they would if they remained outside of bankruptcy. If, when creditors avoid using bankruptcy in converting ownership of the assets to themselves, tort claims that accrue during the transitional process share

8. Secured creditors come ahead of administrative expense priorities. See §§725, 726.

pro rata, use of bankruptcy to occasion that conversion should have no different attributes.

This argument for pro rata treatment, however, only applies—as does Chief Justice Warren's dissent—to nonconsensual claims. The costs of bankruptcy procedures themselves are properly charged against the creditors. Those costs are like the brokerage costs associated with selling a house or the investment banker costs associated with making a stock offering. They are properly charged against the group for whose benefit the proceeding is being run. Consensual creditors, moreover, also need administrative expense priority, although for a somewhat different reason. The advent of a bankruptcy proceeding inevitably communicates negative information about the financial solvency of the debtor. Should the creditors want to keep the debtor operating, they will have to provide incentives for people to deal with it. These incentives, in the case of a debtor that presumptively is insolvent, can be developed only by providing consensual claimants with a greater level of priority than sharing pro rata with the prepetition general unsecured creditors. The same result would occur where the creditors avoided using bankruptcy if the information about the debtor's financial health were available to supliers.

Thus, although there is much to be said for Justice Harlan's analogy to a business with an all common capital stock structure—and hence for his conclusion that postpetition tort claimants are entitled to administrative expense priority—the analogy ultimately seems the less persuasive one. In a world in which the owners of a business are free to impose on it a capital structure that affects the payment prospects of tort claimants, the proper bankruptcy mirror would seem to be that of holding the existing capital structure as fixed until the conclusion of the bankruptcy proceeding. To be sure, this conclusion means that the incentives to take precautions against the torts are not fully internalized, but this result is a consequence not of bankruptcy law but of nonbankruptcy law. Insolvent businesses that dissolve or are sold outside of bankruptcy treat claimants that arise during the dissolution or sale process as indistinguishable from claimants that arose before such processes were commenced. The best bankruptcy mirror would seem to be one that treats the end of the bankruptcy process, not its commencement, as the equivalent to the dissolution or sale.

The Automatic Stay and Postbankruptcy Deals with Prebankruptcy Creditors

Two operating principles should thus govern the period after a bankruptcy case is commenced. The first manifests itself in an automatic stay designed to preserve relative values and to prevent strategic jockeying by one creditor (or group of creditors) during the bankruptcy process. The second is the notion that nonbankruptcy rules concerning operations should not be relaxed for the benefit of prebankruptcy creditors.

Many of the sharpest debates in bankruptcy law involve one or both of these principles. The debates themselves are interesting as a normative matter because they call for a sensitive understanding of the relationship of these principles to what happens in bankruptcy. They also provide a useful focus for examining, as a positive matter, what appear to be some of bankruptcy law's most complex issues.

Consider, for example, the question of whether and how the automatic stay should apply to postbankruptcy refusals to deal by an entity that is also a prebankruptcy creditor. Implementation of the concept of relative values requires that the use of baseline creditor remedies—those rights that *all* creditors have outside of bankruptcy—be halted in bankruptcy. Thus, bankruptcy law must supplant creditor remedies such as obtaining execution liens or security interests (or indeed cash). In addition, other informal remedies available to all creditors, such as (to the extent legal) cajoling and harassment, should also cease.

The concept of relative value, however, also means that bankruptcy law should respect the value of priority rights given to creditors outside of bankruptcy. Thus, although a secured creditor or prebankruptcy lienholder cannot exercise its default rights in bankruptcy, the priority value of those rights should be respected. But at this point an apparent tension is created by the fact that debtors in bankruptcy should receive no special treatment with respect to their ongoing operations. Bankruptcy provides relief from the common pool problems of prebankruptcy creditors, but once those creditors become owners of the business in bankruptcy, they should make their way in the world like other owners.

What, however, is the position of a claimant that wears both hats—is both a prebankruptcy claimant and a postbankruptcy supplier? This issue can arise in a number of contexts. A supplier who is owed money for prebankruptcy shipments may refuse to deliver additional supplies, even on a COD basis. An insurance company with unpaid premiums may refuse to renew the fire insurance of a debtor in bankruptcy or may attempt to cancel an insurance policy (pursuant to a general cancellation term) upon learning that a debtor is in bankruptcy.

Seen as an issue simply of postbankruptcy refusals to deal, these cases seem easily resolved by means of an application of the second principle. Just as Continental Airlines cannot (and should not) require me to fly on it because it is in bankruptcy and needs my business to survive as a going concern, so, too, a supplier or insurance company cannot (and should not) be forced to deal with a business simply because it is in bankruptcy and needs supplies or insurance. But if the supplier is also a prepetition creditor or the insurance company's premium has not yet been paid, the postbankruptcy refusals to deal may be seen as bald attempts to collect on a prepetition debt. Does such activity violate the automatic stay, and if so, how do we resolve the apparent conflict between the notion that prepetition creditors must cease their collection efforts and the notion that debtors must make their way unaided with respect to future operations?

The first consideration is that this characterization may misstate the real question. Is it truly a conflict? The answer, I believe, is no, because instead the focus should be on an application of the concept of relative values. The difficult question is not one of a conflict of principles but rather one of ensuring that the residual class—the unsecured creditors—make the decision whether acquiescence in the demand is in their interest or not.

Suppose that Debtor is a shoestore and Supplier has been, for many years, Debtor's source of fancy men's shoes.[9] When Debtor files for bankruptcy, it owes Supplier $40,000 for some prebankruptcy deliveries. Unless Supplier has taken a security interest in its shoes or in other assets of Debtor, this $40,000 debt would be classified as an unsecured obligation of Debtor for purposes of bankruptcy. Supplier then refuses to deliver any more shoes to Debtor unless Debtor pays (or promises to pay) the $40,000 debt in full. Assume, too, that this action taken by Supplier can be shown to be simply for the purpose of collecting on its prepetition debt instead of languishing in the class of unsecured creditors.

Should Supplier's refusal to deliver be subject to bankruptcy's automatic stay? One's first response may be that this action, like all similar attempts to collect on prepetition debts by unsecured creditors, should

---

9. This is based on the facts of *In re* Ike Kemper & Bros., Inc., 4 Bankr. 31 (Bankr. E.D. Ark. 1980).

be interdicted.[10] But that response may be an oversimplification. We first need to assess the relative standing of Supplier vis-à-vis other creditors. This problem is thus one of relative values. Supplier may have a valuable property right—the right to refuse to deliver more shoes—that it could use outside of bankruptcy to ensure payment. Because this right would be effective against lien creditors outside of bankruptcy (who could not require Supplier to deliver shoes),[11] its relative value should be respected in bankruptcy.

In many cases the relative value of Supplier's nonbankruptcy right to refuse to deliver more shoes (without having it constitute a breach) will be close to zero. This would be true, for example, when Supplier is a source of a fungible item like wheat. If Supplier refuses to deliver any more wheat unless its prepetition claims are paid in full, Debtor can and should find another source. If the costs of locating another source are trivial (and since the new source is entitled to be paid in full for its deliveries because of the principle of no special advantages for debtors in bankruptcy), Supplier's threat carries no weight. Because they could easily switch to another source, the creditors as a group would not acquiesce in Supplier's demand to be paid in full on its prepetition debt as a price for continuing to deliver more wheat, and Supplier's right is without special value.

The situation is of more interest when Supplier's nonbankruptcy right to refuse to deliver more shoes except on its own terms has some substantial value. Supplier's shoes may not be entirely fungible with other brands. Debtor, for example, may be known as a source of Selby, not Florsheim, shoes. Moreover, Debtor may have only an incomplete stock of sizes of a particular line of shoes and would need to replenish its missing sizes before advertising could usefully be undertaken. Even if Debtor could eventually switch to suppliers of other brands of shoes, it would be difficult for it to make the transition immediately without loss of value. Because of these circumstances, which have resulted from Supplier's past dealings with Debtor, Supplier has acquired some leverage.[12]

10. Section 362(a)(6), for example, stays "any act to collect, assess, or recover a claim against the debtor that arose before commencement of the case under this title."

11. If Supplier had promised Debtor to deliver shoes, there would be an executory contract. In that event Supplier's cancellation would be a breach, entitling Debtor to sue for damages. (The case is unlikely to be a candidate for specific performance.)

12. See O. Williamson, *Markets and Hierarchies* 34–35 (1975); Demsetz, "When Does the Rule of Liability Matter?" 1 *J. Legal Studies* 13, 23–25 (1972); Kronman, "Specific Performance," 45 *U. Chi. L. Rev.* 351, 367 (1978). Prepetition creditors may have other levers. For example, a creditor may have a guarantee of its loan by an officer or principal share-

It is attempting to draw on the value of that leverage by requiring payment in full on its prepetition claims.

Supplier's method should not obscure the consequence of its act: Supplier is, in essence, making the price of future deliveries higher than in a world where it continued to deliver shoes (at the standard price) and waited in line as an unsecured claimant on its prepetition debts. It may nonetheless be in the interest of the creditors as a group to acquiesce to this request: although they would lose if they must pay Supplier's prepetition claims in full, they may lose more if Supplier in fact refused to deliver any more shoes. If Supplier has the right to impose this demand, self-interest may lead the creditors to accept it.

Is this, however, the kind of right whose relative value should be respected in bankruptcy? Consider a nonbankruptcy analogue. If the business was sold outside of bankruptcy, Supplier would have the right to insist—and it very well might—that the new owners pay for the debts of the prior owners as a condition of the delivery of more shoes. This suggests that Supplier may well have an asset (the right to withhold needed goods until paid for previous deliveries) that has value outside of bankruptcy. Supplier's action would run afoul of the goals of the bankruptcy process only if it reflects an attempt to opt out of one class into another. But if the underlying attributes of Supplier's rights are taken into account, it may be wrong to see this as opt-out activity by one of a group of unsecured creditors with equal priority. Supplier's rights have a *greater* relative value than the rights of unsecured creditors whose future supplies or services are not needed by Debtor. Because its relative value is greater outside of bankruptcy (where it could make the same demand of *anyone* who owned Debtor or its assets as a condition of future shipments), it should be respected in bankruptcy as well. Supplier's rights are, in that respect, similar to the rights of a secured creditor. Here, the asset is the right to have Supplier deliver shoes in the future.

Supplier's insistence, to be sure, may lead to a decision to liquidate if the general creditors would lose more from paying Supplier in full than

---

holder of the debtor. This case would be analyzed the same way as the one in text. The creditors, as new owners, can decide whether to pay the claim or let the guarantor suffer the consequences. What, then, about a creditor who is an especially effective "badmouther" of entities that do not repay loans? Does this creditor likewise hold something of relative value that should be respected in bankruptcy? Here the answer would seem to be no. There is no effective way to test the assertion that this creditor's badmouthing ability is superior without letting every creditor make the same assertion. The difficulties of resolving the resulting factual issues may warrant a flat rule prohibiting badmouthing. This is distinct from an ability to withhold goods or services, the effectiveness of which *can* be tested by marketplace equivalents.

they would by liquidating the assets.[13] But this does not mean that Supplier's action violates the collectivization norm. These decisions are the kinds of decisions creditors have to make all the time in the face of nonbankruptcy costs of continuing in business. It is wrong, accordingly, to think of Supplier as wearing only a prepetition hat. It is also a post-

13. This case requires some consideration. It raises the following problem: how does bankruptcy law respect the relative value of entitlements when the relative values themselves are defined by what happens to the assets? Consider the nearest nonbankruptcy analogy. Supplier is owed $50,000 on a prepetition debt. Supplier insists on being paid in full as a condition of fulfilling future orders, Supplier's goods are needed in order for Debtor to continue in business, and no substitute is available. If Debtor continues, its assets are worth $200,000; if it liquidates, its assets are worth $180,000. (The $200,000 figure is derived by netting out the costs of the future deliveries of Supplier (just as all future costs of doing business are netted out).) Debtor has $300,000 in other prepetition claimants.

In order for the business to continue, $50,000 of the $200,000 must flow to Supplier, which would leave $150,000 for the other $300,000 in claimants. Supplier gets paid in full; the other claimants get fifty cents on the dollar. If Debtor liquidates, however, it does not need to buy goods from Supplier; Supplier's threat has no value, and Supplier would be treated as an ordinary unsecured creditor. The result would be that everyone gets somewhat more than fifty cents on the dollar ($180,000 would be split among $350,000 in claims). Thus, the general creditors other than Supplier do slightly better; the group, of course, does worse.

What then should happen in bankruptcy? An issue exists because the relative rankings of creditors are different in a piecemeal liquidation than in a continuation of the business: in a continuation Supplier in effect has the status of a secured creditor; in a liquidation Supplier is nothing more than a general creditor. Resolution is achieved by treating the creditors as the owners of the business with the power to decide what to do with the assets. In this case they would opt for piecemeal liquidation unless they could negotiate a deal with Supplier.

This outcome mirrors the result that would be reached outside of bankruptcy. The case could be recast as follows with no substantive difference: Debtor has 350,000 shares of stock outstanding and no debt. Supplier owns 50,000 shares. Supplier decides to raise the price of the goods it sells to Debtor in the future by $50,000. If Debtor agrees to this and pays the money, then Supplier gets $50,000 more, and $150,000 is left for the other shareholders. The amount is $150,000, not $200,000, because the $50,000 is now considered a cost of continuing in business in the future, which it was not in the prior example; the effect on the residual class, however, is identical. If Debtor does not agree to this, it must liquidate piecemeal (since it cannot get needed goods), and the shareholders as a group (including Supplier) get a total of $180,000, the liquidation value of the assets.

It is the same result, but in this case bankruptcy policy would be irrelevant. In bankruptcy one should think of the creditors as the new residual owners of the assets—so one should think of them as the shareholders in analyzing the problem. One might object to this last illustration on the ground that Supplier's action might not be permitted as a matter of nonbankruptcy law because, for example, of antitrust prohibitions. But that should not matter. If raising the price is not permitted as a matter of nonbankruptcy law, it is difficult to see why doing it in a roundabout way (by demanding payment in full on a prepetition debt) should be any more permissible as a matter of that nonbankruptcy law. The point, however, is that limitations on Supplier's rights should come from nonbankruptcy law, not bankruptcy policy.

petition supplier of goods, and whether the assets are worth more together than broken apart depends in part on what postpetition suppliers charge.[14] Moreover, the issue is more likely to be distributional. Supplier gains nothing if its insistence on payment in full leads the creditors to decide that their best course is liquidation (where Supplier shares as an unsecured creditor in whatever the assets fetch). Supplier's threat is more likely to be made when the best course of action for the creditors as a group is one of continuing the business whether or not Supplier's demand is met.[15] In those cases, which are likely to be far more common, the issue is not that of asset deployment but the quintessential nonbankruptcy issue of asset distribution.

To say that Supplier has this power, moreover, does not mean that Supplier will necessarily exercise it. Supplier has this power outside of bankruptcy as well, even against a solvent debtor. Because of the position it acquired through its past dealings and the fact that its shoes are not perfectly fungible with another brand, Supplier could refuse, outside of bankruptcy, to deliver more shoes to Debtor unless Debtor agreed to pay it a higher-than-usual price for (say) the next six months' worth of shipments, and Debtor might be required to acquiesce. Notwithstanding that power, reputational and repeat-dealing concerns are likely to deter Supplier from using that sort of leverage.[16] Supplier may not be much more likely to do so in bankruptcy because, even though Debtor's cred-

14. Another way to approach this is to refer to the example in the prior note where Supplier had a $50,000 prepetition claim. Instead of demanding payment of the prepetition debt in full, Supplier could achieve an identical result by raising the price of its future deliveries by $50,000, which would reduce the going-concern value of the assets to $150,000. Then it would appear that liquidation would be the wiser course because $180,000 would be available for the claimants. In some respects this exercise is equivalent to playing with mirrors: it makes it difficult to ascertain which view (going-concern greater than liquidation or liquidation greater than going-concern) is correct because the answer depends on which way Supplier formulates its demand.

15. Sometimes a contracting party threatens nonperformance when it is not in its interest in order to gain a reputation as a "tough" negotiator. See Posner, "Gratuitous Promises in Economics and Law," 6 *J. Legal Studies* 411 (1977). But there is little to be gained from such a course here. Whether the creditor should be able to withhold services during the bankruptcy process raises a slightly distinct concern—that of getting the creditors as a group to agree on which course of action to pursue. As such, this reflects a variant on the problem discussed in connection with *Texlon* and *EDC Holding Co.* later in this chapter.

16. See generally Goetz & Scott, "Principles of Relational Contracts," 67 *Va. L. Rev.* 1089 (1981); Williamson, "Transaction-Cost Economics: The Governance of Contractual Relations," 22 *J. L. & Econ.* 233 (1979); Macneil, "Contracts: Adjustment of Long-Term Economic Relations under Classical, Neoclassical and Relational Contract Law," 72 *Nw. U. L. Rev.* 854 (1978). Applications of certain statutes, such as the Robinson-Patman Act, may call into question some of these tactics. If so, this is another nonbankruptcy rule that should apply to similar tactics in bankruptcy.

itors may have to agree to such a payment requirement in the short run, they, too, can begin to search for an alternative source of shoes to replace Supplier. Moreover, if Supplier becomes known for making such demands on companies in bankruptcy, shoe retailers may become more reluctant to start using Supplier in the first place.[17] Thus, to say that this power exists and should be respected in bankruptcy is not to say that it will be exercised frequently. Indeed, the number of cases that have addressed this issue is astoundingly small,[18] and it is a smallness that cannot be explained by the clarity of the legal answer on this point.

There are other reasons to conclude that the relative values of this sort of power should be respected. Had Debtor negotiated a long-term supply contract with Supplier, the price Debtor would have to pay to keep that supply contract in force, under section 365, would be payment of prebankruptcy debts on that contract in full.[19] If no such long-term supply contract has been negotiated, Debtor should not be able to gain such a contract by judicial fiat in bankruptcy without paying the costs that section 365 would have imposed.[20]

What is unique, then, about this kind of harassment by Supplier for payment is that it reflects a power that is not shared by all claimants. It has a relative value that ordinary rights of execution lien or harassment by prebankruptcy claimants that are not postbankruptcy suppliers (or at least not postbankruptcy suppliers of nonfungible goods) do not give.

The underlying issue is no different in the case of insurance contract cancellation; what *is* different is the likelihood that acquiescence in the (implicit or explicit) underlying demand to pay prepetition claims is much smaller because of the probability that insurance is largely fungible. Consider, for example, the facts of *Cahokia Downs*.[21] Cahokia Downs,

---

17. The retailer may not care sufficiently about the reputation of Supplier in bankruptcy, because the effects will be felt by the retailer's creditors, not the shareholders. But if the *creditors* are aware that the retailer is using Supplier (as they are likely to be), and if they are aware of Supplier's reputation (which may be somewhat more dubious), the creditors will be less likely to deal with the retailer, inducing it to "care" more about Supplier's reputation in bankruptcy.

18. In addition to *Ike Kempner*, see *In re* Sportfame of Ohio, 40 Bankr. 47 (Bankr. N.D. Ohio 1984); *In re* Blackwelder Furniture Co., 7 Bankr. 328 (Bankr. W.D.N.C. 1980).

19. §365(b). We explored the justification for this in Chapter 5.

20. Otherwise, Debtor has no incentive to follow §365(b).

21. 5 Bankr. 529 (Bankr. S.D. Ill. 1980). The discussion in text simplifies somewhat the actual facts, where there was also an underwriter and an agent. Nothing, however, turns on the change in facts. (The agent had prepaid the premium but had not been repaid by Cahokia Downs. The effect of the cancellation, then, was to improve the agent's position, by the rebate of premiums.) Refusals to renew were discussed in *In re* Garnas, 38 Bankr. 226 (Bankr. D.N.D. 1984) (holding the refusal tantamount to a violation of §365(e)(1)),

Inc., operated a race track in Illinois. Holland America Insurance Co. had issued it a fire insurance policy for the period from July 26, 1979, to July 26, 1980. In October 1979 the Illinois Racing Commission denied racing dates to Cahokia Downs for the 1980 spring and summer racing seasons. On April 2, 1980, Cahokia Downs was pushed into bankruptcy. On April 11 Holland America, pursuant to a clause in its insurance contract permitting it to cancel at any time on thirty days' notice, cancelled the policy.

Does the cancellation violate the automatic stay? On the one hand, the action may be entirely unrelated to a prepetition debt. Bankruptcy may signal to an insurance company a greater fire risk, because the managers may care less what happens to the premises, since the creditors will get them anyway. The point of a clause permitting cancellation at any time, moreover, would seem to be one of allowing insurance companies to cancel without needing elaborate proof. On the other hand, the fact that the premium had not been paid may have motivated the cancellation. The effect of cancellation was to improve Holland America's status in bankruptcy (from the holder of an unsecured claim for twelve months' premiums to the holder of an unsecured claim for ten months' premiums).

The fact that a prepetition debt may have been involved, however, does not distinguish this case from Supplier's refusal to deliver new shoes. Instead, one has to analyze what *kind* of prepetition debt is at issue.[22] Holland America had this right as a matter of nonbankruptcy

---

and *In re* Heaven Sent, Ltd., 37 Bankr. 597 (Bankr. E.D. Pa. 1984) (stating that nothing in the Bankruptcy Code authorizes a court to direct renewal). Neither of those cases, however, clearly involved a prepetition claimant.

22. The court failed to do that. It held that the cancellation violated the automatic stay, *In re* Cahokia Downs, 5 Bankr. 529, 531 (Bankr. S.D. Ill. 1980): "In the instant case, there is no question but that a policy of insurance, especially one in which the premium has been paid, is a valid and binding contract between the insurance company and the insured and would constitute an asset of the bankruptcy estate. Furthermore, fire insurance is a necessary protection for both the debtor and its creditors. The cancellation of the insurance would certainly come within the provisions of the automatic stay under §362(a)(3). It is also property which could, within the meaning of §363, be used by the Trustee, and certainly paragraph (l) of §363 would be applicable to the cancellation provision in spite of the fact that the provision does not refer to insolvency or the financial condition of the debtor. This is especially true when, as in the instant case, it is quite obvious that the prime reason for the attempted cancellation of the insurance was the bankruptcy."

Section 363(l) provides another bar to the effectiveness of ipso facto clauses, this time stating that the trustee may use, sell, or lease property under §363 notwithstanding such a clause. *Cahokia Downs*'s reliance on it, however, misperceives the role of the automatic stay (as well as the role of bans on ipso facto clauses). A clause permitting cancellation for

law (defined in a way that was applicable generally, not just to situations in bankruptcy), and it was a right that is effective against lien creditors outside of bankruptcy. Its exercise in bankruptcy, accordingly, should not be barred.[23] There is no need even to engage in an inquiry into whether the cancellation was due to a change in fire risk or to an attempt to require payment of the prebankruptcy debt, or perhaps to a mixture of both reasons, unless applicable nonbankruptcy law would give the insured a right to contest the cancellation by insisting on proof of a change in fire risk.[24]

To the extent that Holland America was, by threatening cancellation, seeking payment of the entire prepetition debt to it, it is unlikely that its cancellation (or threat thereof) would be effective. Insurance is largely fungible, with dozens or hundreds of sources of insurance. If Holland America will not supply insurance except upon payment of the prepetition debt for the ten months of insurance already provided, almost certainly similar insurance can be obtained from another source. Thus, *if* the cancellation was designed to coerce payment of a prepetition debt and unless there had been a general shift upward in insurance rates (making a replacement policy at the same risk level more expensive), there is no reason to think the threat would be successful. Why, then, did Cahokia Downs resist the cancellation?[25] One suspects that a replacement policy (from Holland America or another company) would in fact have been more expensive, probably because of an increased worry of greater risk. But this simply restates the consequence of the principle

---

any reason, even if *used* to cancel upon bankruptcy, is vastly different from a clause permitting cancellation only upon bankruptcy.

23. Consideration of the executory contract provisions change nothing. Had Cahokia Downs wanted to assume the policy, it would have had to pay Holland America the full insurance premium, see §365(b). Moreover, apart from that point, the contract that would be assumed would come with its nonbankruptcy attributes, including the power of cancellation at any time on thirty days' notice.

24. This is the error of *In re* Garnas, 38 Bankr. 221 (Bankr. D.N.D. 1984), which held that because policies were "usually" renewed, there was an executory contract, the nonrenewal of which violated §365(e)(1) because it "would have [been] automatically renewed had it not been for the fact that they filed for relief under the Bankruptcy Code" and "[n]onrenewal would seriously impair the reorganization . . ." The proper inquiry would have been whether nonrenewal was actionable under nonbankruptcy law in analogous cases.

25. The obvious reason may be that Cahokia Downs hoped to get several more months of insurance by paying only a fraction (to the holder of a prepetition claim). Viewing the insurance policy as an executory contract, however, would dramatically change that conclusion. See supra note 23.

that a debtor in bankruptcy should be given no special advantage concerning future operations. Cahokia Downs' "asset"—the Holland America policy—came in with its prebankruptcy attributes, including cancellation at any time on thirty days' notice. Bankruptcy law should provide Cahokia Downs with no special rights in connection with its desire for insurance while it is in bankruptcy.

To be sure, the filing of bankruptcy may have been the cause of Holland America's cancellation, even if the insurance company was not seeking to coerce payment of the prepetition debt. The filing of bankruptcy is an event that carries with it certain information. Here the relevant information may have been an increased likelihood of fire. Had the bankruptcy petition never been filed, Holland America may never have discovered that information on its own. Moreover, if Holland America was cancelling because it was trying to coerce payment of the prepetition debt, the filing of bankruptcy may, too, have been the cause of the cancellation in the sense that it carried information about Cahokia Downs' solvency that Holland America may not otherwise have discovered until too late. But to say that there are consequences associated with the filing of bankruptcy because it conveys information is not to say that this is a bad thing. Generally, increases in information are considered to be good. Problems of this kind that arise from the filing of bankruptcy petitions are the subject of the next chapter, but it does not seem that any qualification on the discussion of whether the automatic stay should apply to such actions is indicated.

In both cases, then—Supplier's demand regarding future deliveries of shoes and the insurance company's demand for prebankruptcy premium payments as a condition of continuing or renewing insurance—it is incorrect to see a conflict between the policy of the automatic stay and the policy of no special advantages. The relevant issue is that some parties have superior relative values and that bankruptcy law respects them.[26]

---

26. Similarly, this appears to be the issue raised in a case such as Donovan v. TMC Industries, Inc., 20 Bankr. 997 (N.D. Ga. 1982). Workers with claims for unpaid wages persuaded the Secretary of Labor to bring a suit to enjoin the shipping of the debtor's inventory as "hot goods" in violation of the Fair Labor Standards Act (FLSA). The court viewed the case as one of balancing FLSA policies against bankruptcy policies. The proper view of the case, however, is one of relative values. If the FLSA were construed to prohibit the sale of the "tainted" goods by anyone, including a liquidator of the debtor or a subsequent secured party, until the workers' minimum wage claims had been paid, then the workers' claims are tantamount to secured claims, and their value as such should be respected. This case is discussed in greater detail in Jackson, "Translating Assets and Liabilities to the Bankruptcy Forum," 14 *J. Legal Studies* 73 (1985).

There is, however, another problem associated with these cases. Supplier or insurance company makes its demand. Who should decide whether the demand should be met? It is important that the proper group of claimants makes the decision as to whether acquiescence in connection with the demand of Supplier or insurance company is in the interests of the estate as a whole. This is not a decision that should be made by the representatives of the shareholders. Instead, it is a decision that should be left in the hands of the residual class—the class that derives the benefits of the choice and pays the costs. That class presumptively is the class of unsecured creditors.

This is an application of the problem of diverse ownership. In the analysis of preference law in the previous chapter this problem manifested itself in the fact that the shareholders or managers of an insolvent debtor may be indifferent as to who gets the assets. Once it becomes clear that there will not be enough to pay the creditors in full, continuing the decision-making authority in the hands of shareholders and their agents effectively separates the decision maker from the group that stands to gain or lose as a consequence of the decision. We saw that this problem called for a transitional response in the immediate prebankruptcy period. The problem can similarly replicate itself in the post-bankruptcy period. Because of the concept of the "debtor in possession," the decision-making authority remains lodged in the prepetition managers and shareholders.[27]

Consider, for example, a scenario that has become known as the *Texlon* problem.[28] Lender is a prepetition creditor of Debtor that has loaned Debtor $1 million on an unsecured basis. When Debtor goes into bankruptcy, it requires additional operating funds. Lender agrees to supply another $1 million, but as a condition of making the loan it insists on a security interest in all of Debtor's assets and asks that this security interest secure Debtor's entire debt to Lender, not just the postpetition loan. This is a form of a "cross-collateralization" clause: a security interest taken in connection with one loan that is used to secure other loans as well.

Should the terms of this loan be approved? The answer to that question is "it depends." The problem posed by *Texlon* is that of ensuring that the right group makes the call. In *Texlon* itself the deal was approved on an *ex parte* application of Lender and Debtor to the bankruptcy court. Here, moreover, who the Debtor is is important: the Debtor for this

27. This is not necessarily bad. Use of existing managers may have substantial advantages over shifting to a disinterested trustee who is unfamiliar with the business.

28. Because of *In re* Texlon Corp., 596 F.2d 1092 (2d Cir. 1979).

purpose is the old management, operating the business as debtor in possession.

The representatives of shareholders, however, are presumptively the wrong group to make this call in most bankruptcy cases. The cross-collateralization clause is a part of the price of obtaining new credit. Whether it is a good deal or not depends on whether it was necessary to borrow money and whether giving the cross-collateralization clause would save more in interest charges than it would cost other creditors as a result of improving the status of a prebankruptcy unsecured claim.[29] The costs of the clause may far exceed the interest rate advantages (if any) associated with the loan.[30] The only way that decision can be made without bias is for it to be made by the group that will reap the benefits of a successful decision and pay the costs of an unsuccessful decision. That group consists of the residual claimants, who in the case of an insolvent company are almost always the unsecured creditors. It is they that should determine whether a loan is worthwhile and whether its terms are the best they can get.

The problem in *Texlon* was the decision maker; as Judge Friendly noted, "[t]he debtor in possession is hardly neutral."[31] Outside of bankruptcy, this may also be the case (the interests of the shareholders may conflict with the interests of the creditors). There, however, countervailing constraints exist: creditors may have covenants or an ability to

29. See, e.g., *In re* General Oil Distributors, Inc., 20 Bankr. 873 (Bankr. S.D.N.Y. 1982). In that case Bank had a perfected security interest in General Oil's accounts receivable and was, at the time of the bankruptcy petition, fully secured. It agreed to advance further funds to the debtor on the condition that it be granted a security interest in all of the debtor's unencumbered property to secure all loans. The cross-collateralization clause did not improve Bank's position if its prepetition loan was in fact already fully secured. Moreover, given that Bank already had a security interest in General Oil's accounts, General Oil would be forced by §363 to provide it with adequate protection before General Oil could use any of the cash acquired when account debtors paid their bills. The cross-collateralization clause gave Bank only rights that it could have insisted on in any event, and the clause may not have placed any general creditors in a worse position than if the loan had not been made.

30. For example, consider the following. Assume there were $3 million of unsecured claims, including Bank's $1 million claim, and $2 million of assets. Before Bank's deal all the creditors were going to receive sixty-seven cents on the dollar. After Bank's deal (forgetting the new loan, which is presumably offset by new assets) Bank will get $1 million instead of $667,000 on account of its prepetition loan. The remaining creditors will have $1 million left to satisfy their $2 million of claims, leaving them with fifty cents on the dollar. The effect of the cross-collateralization clause, then, is a transfer of $333,000 from the unsecured creditors as a group to Bank. That seems to be a staggering cost for the new loan.

31. 596 F.2d, at 1098.

call in their loans if they do not like what Debtor is doing. The constraints are weakened in bankruptcy because the automatic stay restricts exercise of these rights. Therefore, these monitoring mechanisms are needed. Because the show in bankruptcy is usually being run for the creditors, they should be consulted.

The procedural rule announced in *Texlon* serves an an appropriate response to the problem. Cross-collateralization clauses in new loans on an *ex parte* order were prohibited and instead a hearing at which the creditors could appear was required. The court noted that "[a] hearing might determine that other sources of financing are available; that other creditors would like to share in the financing if similarly favorable terms are accorded them; or that the creditors do not want the business continued at the price of preferring a particular lender."[32] This solution, as Judge Friendly noted, was not perfect. If the loan was needed quickly, it might be hard to decide who the creditors were that needed to be consulted. But it seems better than the alternatives. Indeed, there is no reason in principle to limit this solution to cross-collateralization clauses. In cases where there is likely to be substantial fungibility of sources of new capital, *all* postpetition deals with prepetition lenders should be scrutinized with care.

Because of the presence of a market alternative, the procedural solution of *Texlon* seems well suited to the problem underlying postpetition deals with prepetition claimants—that of identifying whether the costs are worth it for the residual class. In other cases solutions will be harder, however, because more is involved than whether the deal is a good one for the estate. Where the question of *who pays for* the deal is not clear (in *Texlon* the appropriate group was clearly the unsecured creditors), simply consulting the relevant classes is not enough.

Consider the following problem, derived (loosely) from *EDC Holding Company*.[33] Bank has loaned Debtor $10 million, secured by a security interest in cheese. At the time bankruptcy is filed, the cheese, if it is sold within the next sixty days, will be worth $10 million. If not sold by then, the cheese will spoil, and its value will quickly fall to zero. At the time of bankruptcy Debtor also owes workers $4 million for pension contributions and various trade creditors $20 million. Debtor is insolvent, and its assets (including the cheese, if used within sixty days) are worth $20 million.

If the situation was permitted to run its course in bankruptcy with no

32. Id., at 1098–99.
33. 676 F.2d 945 (7th Cir. 1982).

postbankruptcy moves by any of the players, the cheese would be sold, and Bank, out of the proceeds of that sale, would be repaid in full. The remaining $10 million of assets would be split among $24 million of unsecured liabilities;[34] unsecured claimants would get approximately forty cents for each dollar of claim.

This conclusion assumes no postbankruptcy action on the part of any claimants. In fact, however, the relative value of the claimants' rights may have been misdescribed. Under applicable labor law doctrines workers have a right to strike and picket,[35] and these rights are effective against lien creditors outside of bankruptcy. Thus, they have relative values inside of bankruptcy greater than those of an unsecured creditor. Because of a requirement of labor law that courts are not to issue injunctions in labor law disputes, moreover, it has been construed that the *rights* of strike and picketing, not just their relative values, are to be respected in bankruptcy.[36]

Whether one sees this as a question of respecting the rights themselves or just their relative values, however, two distinct issues must be resolved. The first issue is whether it is in the interests of the claimants as a group to pay the workers their $4 million prepetition claim if the workers set up a picket line and demand such payment. In the example we are considering, the answer would be yes. If the workers are paid off and the cheese sold, the remaining assets for the residual claimants are $16 million. If the workers are not paid off and their picket line is effective, the cheese will spoil, leaving only $10 million of assets for all the claimants as a group (and even less for the nonworker claimants, once the workers' pro rata share is paid).

Thus, the answer to the first question is that it is in the interests of the claimants as a group to acquiesce in this demand. But there is now

34. Ignoring, for present purposes, the possible priority for some of the workers' claims under §507(a)(3) and (4).

35. Section 4 of the Norris–La Guardia Act, 29 U.S.C. §104, withdraws jurisdiction from all courts of the United States to issue injunctions against strikes "in any case involving or growing out of a labor dispute." Section 13(c) of that Act, 29 U.S.C. §113(c), defines "labor dispute" as "[a]ny controversy concerning terms or conditions of employment."

36. See Briggs Transportation Co. v. International Brotherhood of Teamsters, 739 F.2d 341 (8th Cir. 1984); *In re* Crowe & Associates, 713 F.2d 211 (6th Cir. 1983); *In re* Petrusch, 667 F.2d 297 (2d Cir.), *cert. denied*, 456 U.S. 974 (1981); but see *In re* Tom Powell & Son, Inc., 22 Bankr. 657 (Bankr. W.D. Mo. 1982) (Norris–La Guardia Act prohibition does not apply to statutory injunctions); Note, "The Automatic Stay of the 1978 Bankruptcy Code Versus the Norris–La Guardia Act: A Bankruptcy Court Dilemma," 61 *Tex. L. Rev.* 321 (1982) (arguing that an injunction would be appropriate). The union may not have the legal right to keep others from crossing the picket line, but if other unions respect the picket line, the situation described in text would exist.

a second question: who pays for it (and also who decides how much to pay)? This is akin to the problem of allocating gains from synergistic mergers, where it seems that no simple "correct" allocation rule can be formulated.[37] But an operating principle exists: we want to ensure that disputes about the distributional question do not adversely affect the deployment question—in our example, by letting the cheese spoil.

This point suggests the unattractiveness of several solutions. Permitting one group or the other to negotiate a deal seems unpromising. Giving Bank, for example, the power of negotiation may lead Bank to pay the full $4 million to workers (instead of negotiating for a lesser sum), because the general creditors, not Bank, pay for that result.[38] Giving the general creditors the power of negotiation may be little better, because they may prolong the negotiations beyond what is best for Bank and the general creditors considered as a group on the ground that Bank, who stands to lose more if a deal is not struck, may be forced to reach a side deal with the workers in which Bank makes a payment out of its own money.

The most promising solution would be to try to separate the two questions and decide the distributional question in a way that would generate the incentives to negotiate the correct deployment result. For example, one could allow Bank to negotiate but require that any deal it struck would have to leave the general creditors in the position they would have been in had there been no buy-out of the workers and no picketing. Bank would then have the incentive to ensure that the workers were given the same terms they would have received if Bank's interests and the interests of the general creditors were consolidated.

This kind of rule, to be sure, ensures a proper incentive in the distributional issue at stake between Bank and the general creditors on the one hand and the workers on the other only by dictating the outcome of the distributional question as between Bank and the general creditors. The rule, moreover, would have to be refined where the harm from picketing would fall, in the first instance, on *both* Bank and the unsecured creditors, as would be the case if the cheese was worth $15 million instead of $10 million. In that case the costs of the deal struck might have to be

---

37. Compare Brudney & Chirelstein, "Fair Shares in Corporate Mergers and Take-overs," 88 *Harv. L. Rev.* 297 (1974), with Lorne, "A Reappraisal of Fair Shares in Controlled Mergers," 126 *U. Pa. L. Rev.* 955 (1978); Toms, "Compensating Shareholders Frozen Out in Two-Step Mergers," 78 *Colum. L. Rev.* 548 (1978). See also Brudney, "Equal Treatment of Shareholders in Corporate Distributions and Reorganizations," 71 *Cal. L. Rev.* 1072 (1983).

38. The workers stand to lose as well by maintaining their picket line; thus, it is by no means clear that the necessary "buy-out" price is $4 million.

allocated—like gains from synergistic mergers—on the basis of two-thirds to Bank and one-third to the general creditors.

As long as the operating rule minimizes the incentives to reach the wrong deployment result, the fact that bankruptcy law is directing the distributional outcome with respect to Bank and the general creditors does not seem particularly worrisome. In bankruptcy, where the goal is to ensure that individual initiatives do not destroy the collective weal, presumptive distributional rules are the order of the day. The rule that unsecured creditors share pro rata is, for example, a presumptive distributional rule based on relative values. Here, dictating a distributional outcome because it ensures the correct deployment decision seems consistent with what bankruptcy is all about.

The underlying problem is not unique to bankruptcy law, nor one caused by a conflict of bankruptcy policies and nonbankruptcy policies. Rather, it is a problem characteristic of diverse ownership, when benefits (and costs) are spread among different classes. It is a problem that is most acute in bankruptcy, however, because when a debtor is insolvent, more groups are likely to be vitally interested in the outcome.

Distinguishing Actions of Prebankruptcy Claimants from Postbankruptcy Operations

Because of the twin principles we have been examining in this chapter, it is critical to distinguish between prepetition rights of the claimants that the bankruptcy process helps by solving a common pool problem and the postpetition rights of entities that form part of the ongoing world that the debtor (and its prepetition claimants) has to make its way in. On the one hand, allowing the automatic stay to bar suits by postpetition suppliers (and others) would interfere with the principle that the debtor in bankruptcy must continue to do business with the rest of the world as usual. On the other hand, not having the automatic stay apply to a party that is a prepetition claimant runs the risk of assigning its relative priority incorrectly.

Consider the consequences of the Third Circuit's reasoning in *In re M. Frenville Co.*,[39] a case holding that the automatic stay did not apply to a suit for indemnification because it did not "arise" until after the bankruptcy petition was commenced. In that case Bank sued Accounting Firm in 1981, alleging negligence in the preparation of Frenville's fi-

---

39. 744 F.2d 332 (3d Cir. 1984).

nancials for 1978 and 1979 that harmed Bank. Bank, however, did not sue Frenville, presumably because Frenville had filed for bankruptcy in 1980, and any suit by Bank in 1981 for negligence or fraud on account of 1978 or 1979 financials would be barred by the automatic stay, as an action of a prepetition creditor seeking to establish its claim.[40]

Following Bank's suit against Accounting Firm, however, Accounting Firm sued Frenville for contribution and indemnity. The Third Circuit held that this suit was not barred by the automatic stay, reasoning that section 362 applies only to a proceeding that "was or could have been commenced" before the filing of the petition or one based on a prepetition "claim." The Third Circuit concluded neither event was met in the facts before it. According to the court, Accounting Firm's suit for contribution and indemnity could not be filed, as a matter of state law, until Bank filed its suit against Accounting Firm. Since Bank's suit dated from 1981, Accounting Firm's suit against Frenville was a proceeding that "was or could have been commenced" only *after* Frenville filed for bankruptcy. Similarly, the court concluded that Accounting Firm's "claim" was postpetition: Accounting Firm had no "right to payment" from Frenville until, at the earliest, suit was filed by Bank against it.[41]

To be sure, section 101(9) makes the question of when a claim arose decisive (as it should). But the question is one for bankruptcy law to decide, looking to nonbankruptcy law only to see if the putative claim has the proper attributes, which first requires one to have a normative grasp as to what attributes *are* relevant. Just as bankruptcy law is not constrained by nonbankruptcy labels, so too it surely is not (and should not be) bound by nonbankruptcy procedural rules specifying when a claimant may *file* a suit. The relevant attributes, bankruptcy policy suggests, relate to whether the claim is based on a prebankruptcy action of the debtor whose consequences would continue to exist even if the debtor were to go out of business or die the moment that the bankruptcy petition was filed.

We saw in Chapter 2 a similar failure to pay attention to the normative role of when a claim arises in distinguishing between rights derived from prepetition acts of a debtor and rights derived only from the continued postpetition existence of a debtor. *Frenville* illustrates the same underlying failure and the destructive consequences of that failure. Bank could

---

40. §362(a)(1) and (6).

41. 744 F.2d, at 337 ("Since the banks' suit began some fourteen months after the filing of the Frenvilles' involuntary chapter 7 proceedings, A&B's claim, as well as its cause of action, arose post-petition"). The Second Circuit has intimated that it may not agree with this reasoning. See *In re* Baldwin-United Corp., 765 F.2d 343, 348 n.4 (2d Cir. 1985).

not sue Frenville directly, because of the automatic stay. It had to either seek relief from the automatic stay or have its claim decided in the bankruptcy forum. In either event its claim was almost certain to be that of an unsecured prepetition creditor in Frenville's bankruptcy. Accounting Firm's suit for contribution and indemnification, however, is simply a pass-through of liability from Accounting Firm to Frenville. The underlying cause of action is the same. *Frenville,* in deciding that the automatic stay did not apply to the action, held that it was a postpetition claim. Postpetition claims, however, get paid *before* prepetition unsecured claims. Thus, the Third Circuit decided a priority issue along with the automatic stay issue. The resulting priority determination, moreover, is surely wrong. Had Bank sued Frenville directly, it would have sued as the holder of a prepetition claim. But when Bank recovers from Accounting Firm and Accounting Firm gets indemnification or contribution from Frenville because Accounting Firm's claim is deemed postpetition, Frenville will have to pay in full before the prepetition unsecured creditors receive anything. This result shows the dangers of trying to apply the automatic stay section with no understanding of the two principles that are the focus of this chapter.

Such an understanding is crucial for resolving a host of bankruptcy issues. It, for example, illuminates the meaning of the exception in the automatic stay provision for governmental regulatory actions. Section 362(b)(4) exempts from the automatic stay imposed by section 362(a)(1) "the commencement or continuation of an action or proceeding by a governmental unit to enforce such governmental unit's police or regulatory power." The line that should be drawn is clear. On the one hand are attempts by a governmental unit to get paid on account of some prepetition action of the debtor. These attempts to get paid are actions that, like all other actions, should be stopped at the commencement of the case after which the underlying priority issue can be addressed and resolved. If the governmental unit holds an unsecured claim, the automatic stay shoud remain in effect to ensure that the state receives no more than its pro rata share of the assets as an unsecured creditor. If the governmental unit, however, holds a fully secured claim, then the continuation of the stay should be measured by the same standards as any secured claim. Because in that case the governmental unit must be paid in full for the claim eventually, it may be proper to lift the stay and let it collect now. On the other hand are actions by governmental units to require the debtor to play by the ongoing rules of the game with respect to its operations in or after bankruptcy. Since debtors should be required to abide by the rules of the postbankruptcy world, the automatic stay should not apply to those actions.

Consider how this distinction works. Assume that Firm, a manufacturer of silicon chips, owns land in California on which it has dumped toxic wastes in violation of state and federal law. In an action by the California attorney general, a court has ordered Firm to clean up the toxic wastes. This cleanup will cost Firm $200,000. The land, when cleaned up, will be worth $50,000. California has also received a court order enjoining Firm from further production of silicon chips unless it installs environmental equipment at a cost of $300,000. Firm also owes $800,000 to a number of general creditors.

The automatic stay should not apply to the injunction that prohibits Firm from producing any more silicon chips until it installs the environmental equipment. This order is directed at Firm's future operations and relates to a cost of doing business in the future that the owners of Firm would face whether or not it was in bankruptcy. It is not a prepetition claim because it has no value if Firm ceases operations at the moment it goes into bankruptcy. If Firm ceases to exist, the injunction has no meaning because there will be no further pollution by Firm and no future silicon chip manufacturing to enjoin. So when Firm files for bankruptcy, its claimants have to decide whether its assets are worth more in the production of silicon chips, which will require spending $300,000 for the environmental equipment, than they would be if otherwise deployed (such as being broken up piecemeal). The fact that they would be worth the most producing silicon chips *without* spending $300,000 for the environmental equipment is and should be irrelevant from any bankruptcy perspective.

Whichever decision is made, assume that the Firm's assets (including the land on which toxic wastes were spilt) are worth $500,000. What is the correct treatment of the order to clean up the toxic wastes that are already there? This is properly categorized as a prepetition claim because the damage arose from a prepetition action of Firm. Firm's continued existence is irrelevant to the fact that toxic wastes are already spilt, which decisively differentiates the situation from the pollution associated with the future production of silicon chips.[42] Is the cleanup order nonetheless the kind of prepetition action that should not be subject to the automatic stay? Is it, in the language of section 362(b)(4), an "action . . . by a gov-

---

42. The analysis of this point is explored in conjunction with Ohio v. Kovacs, 105 S.Ct. 705 (1985), supra Chapter 2.

ernmental unit to enforce such governmental unit's police or regulatory power"?[43]

The answer derived from the two policies that are the focus of this chapter is that in the applicability of the automatic stay the line should be drawn between pre- and postpetition actions of the debtor. Because this cleanup order is directed at a prepetition action of Firm, California is properly considered a prepetition claimant. The relevant question in this case is the *status* of California's claim, not whether the automatic stay applies in the first place.

To see why this is so, consider first the situation that would exist if Firm decided that its best course of action was to sell its assets and liquidate: the $500,000 it would garner would be more than it would gain by remaining in business (where it would have to spend $300,000 to install environmental equipment). Unlike the order requiring installation of environmental equipment as a condition of further operations—an order that has zero value in a liquidation—California's cleanup

---

43. Toxic waste cleanup cases can be complicated by the fact that a cleanup order may have some attributes in common with both a prepetition and a postpetition claim. For example, if the toxic waste site emits harmful fumes at a constant rate each day, there may be "future" harms (in the sense of potential future tort claims). These would be characterized as postpetition claims because they arose only because the site was not cleaned up. (In the case of firms, as analyzed supra notes 6–8, tort claims accruing during the bankruptcy process should be treated equivalently with prepetition tort claims. This view, however, was rejected by the majority in Reading Co. v. Brown, 391 U.S. 471 [1968].) The state, however, may believe that the victims will not sue (for one reason or another). If the state were to force internalization of this sort of cost by a daily fine until the site was cleaned up, such a fine would seem to be postpetition until the time the debtor actually dissolved under state law because the fine is a surrogate for postpetition tort claims. And, accepting *Reading Co. v. Brown,* such claims would be entitled to at least administrative expense priority. See *In re* Charlesbank Laundry, Inc., 755 F.2d 200 (1st Cir. 1985); but see previous textual discussion questioning normative desirability of *Reading Co. v. Brown.* But what if the state decides that determining the amount of the future harms caused by continuation of the toxic wastes at the site is so difficult that it wants simply to *prohibit* the harm by way of a mandatory injunction ordering cleanup of the site? Such an order has elements in common with a postpetition claim of the sort just discussed. Whether the creditors should pay for the cleanup in such a case, however, still depends on nonbankruptcy attributes. If the debtor could avoid the effect of that injunction by dissolving under state law (the question explored in text), the state's injunction still may have a nonbankruptcy relative value no greater than that of an unsecured claim. The best bankruptcy analogue may then be to stay enforcement of this injunction until the creditors decide whether to liquidate or not. That, of course, underdeters them from deciding quickly. But it may be a consequence of a state proceeding by injunction instead of by fines that accumulate over time. The state could still show the harms that were being incurred and perhaps argue for a portion of the injunction cost being converted into a postpetition claim over time, as a surrogate for those costs. In this respect it is similar to the conversion of a specific performance claim into a damage claim. See supra Chapter 2.

order has value (because it is prepetition) whether Firm liquidates or continues. The question is one of relative priority, and the answer to that should come from nonbankruptcy law.

The relevant comparison would be what would happen in a state-law dissolution of Firm. Many outcomes are possible. It is worth briefly considering three of the most probable ones. First, consider the case where the obligation to clean up the toxic waste site would be treated as an unsecured obligation in a state-law dissolution (and one that would not travel with the site property or any of Firm's other assets following a sale). In that case, if Firm were to dissolve, its assets would be sold for $500,000, and each of its claimants, including California, would receive fifty cents on the dollar. At the conclusion of this process, there would be no remaining assets and Debtor would dissolve.

Nothing really changes—or should change—if Firm were to file a chapter 7 proceeding in bankruptcy.[44] The state-law relative values of the various claims should be maintained; all the claimants (including California) should be treated as unsecured and would thereby receive fifty cents on the dollar. Although Firm does not receive a discharge,[45] this is not a substantive change, for Firm, following bankruptcy, has no assets and is free to dissolve under state law. When it does, its debts will be effectively discharged because, again, there would be no debtor to sue and no assets to claim.

The problem with concluding that section 362(b)(4) of the automatic stay exempts California's action to get Firm to clean up the toxic waste site becomes clear. That conclusion, because it would mean that California could require Firm to expend the $200,000 necessary to clean up the site and thereby satisfy California's claim in full, is the resolution of a priority question—and an incorrect resolution under our current assumptions.

This mistake was made in *Penn Terra,* where the court concluded that the automatic stay did not apply to state cleanup orders.[46] Although the Third Circuit correctly focused on the important distinction in connection with the automatic stay as to whether the action in question was one directed at the past or the future, it incorrectly concluded that the cleanup order was postpetition because it was an "equitable action to prevent

---

44. See Southern Ry. Co. v. Johnson Bronze Co., 758 F.2d 137 (3d Cir. 1985).

45. §727(a)(1).

46. Penn Terra Ltd. v. Department of Envtl. Resources, 733 F.2d 267 (3d Cir. 1984). See also Note, "Cleaning Up in Bankruptcy: Curbing Abuse of the Federal Bankruptcy Code by Industrial Polluters," 85 *Colum. L. Rev.* 870 (1985); Note, "Belly Up Down in the Dumps: Bankruptcy and Hazardous Waste Cleanup," 38 *Vand. L. Rev.* 1037 (1985).

future harm."[47] The key attribute relates not to when the harm is realized but to when the *action* from which the harm is derived takes place. In holding that the automatic stay did not bar the action, the Third Circuit was deciding a priority issue without even facing it.

To be sure, to say that the automatic stay applies to cleanup orders does not mean that a state must stand in line as an unsecured creditor. The two issues are distinct. There are many ways in which a particular claimant can have rights greater than those of an unsecured creditor. To continue with our example, it seems quite likely that California would have at least the equivalent of a statutory lien on the toxic waste site. This would stem from its power to require *any* owner of the site to clean up the toxic waste spill there.[48] Given that restriction and the fact that the site, cleaned up, is worth only $50,000, the site has no value to any purchaser. Whether or not the site reverts to the state or not, the state could easily end up gaining the $50,000 value in the site by offering to clean the site up in exchange for ownership of the site. Any owner would gladly agree to that exchange. In that case California would spend $200,000 and have an asset worth $50,000. Its remaining $150,000 "claim" could then go against the remaining $450,000 of Firm's assets—again, absent something else, as an unsecured creditor, sharing pro rata with the other $800,000 of unsecured claimants.

Finally, it is possible that California might have a priority on *all* of Firm's assets, as would seem to be the case, for example, under a recently enacted New Jersey statute.[49] In that event California would have the right to collect the entire $200,000 from the assets of Firm before other claimants received anything.

In all events the relevant question is a priority one. Resolution of the automatic stay issue should not decide a priority issue that would be decided differently by nonbankruptcy law. Here, as always, the issue is one of nonbankruptcy attributes. The Bankruptcy Code should be construed to create as few dislocations as possible in the value of nonbankruptcy entitlements.

This, then, would suggest that the line to be drawn by section 362(b)(4) is one between regulatory actions directed at future operations (such as a requirement that silicon chips be manufactured only after installing

47. Id., at 278.

48. Assuming, as seems almost certain, that such a power exists.

49. See chapter 11 of the 1985 Laws (Senate No. 1423) (lien filed by the Administrator of the New Jersey Spill Compensation Fund against the property of a discharger that is subject to a cleanup order will have priority over all other claims or liens that are or have been filed against the property).

environmental controls) and regulatory actions designed to "fix" something the debtor did in the past. The former derives from the notion that no special advantages regarding future operations should be given to debtors in bankruptcy; the latter reflects the fact that at issue is a claim by one of the prebankruptcy group for whom the bankruptcy proceeding is being run.

Note that nothing in this conclusion suggests that the toxic wastes should not be cleaned up and as promptly as possible. Nothing in the application of the automatic stay should prevent the site from being cleaned up and the continuing harms thereby avoided. The issue is one of who pays for the cleanup. If the state has the equivalent of a statutory lien or security interest on all of the assets of the debtor, then there may be few reasons not to lift the stay and require that those assets be used to clean up the site. But whether that is the proper distributional outcome, the state can always spend its own money to clean up the site and then file its claim in bankruptcy. Whether it gets its claim paid in full or not will depend on applicable nonbankruptcy rules governing relative priority, not on anything stemming from bankruptcy law itself.

To this point we have been assuming that Firm was liquidating and discussing the nonbankruptcy question of relative priorities of claims. Does anything change if we conclude that Firm decides to continue in business? Firm might, for example, decide that it is worth $500,000 as a going concern, even after spending $300,000 to install environmental equipment, and that $500,000 is more than it could achieve from shifting to another business or liquidating. In this event an examination of applicable nonbankruptcy law may show that, as we have seen before, relative priorities of prepetition claims *are* different from what they were in the case of liquidation. For example, a state might have a requirement that it will renew annual operating permits of manufacturing companies only upon certification that all environmental orders have been complied with. If California were to enact such a statute, even if the cleanup order were otherwise tantamount to an unsecured claim, a cost of Firm's continuing in business would be the requirement that it clean up the toxic waste site. Without a cleanup of the site, California could withhold the operating permit.

This does not mean that the automatic stay should not apply. The relevant inquiry is one of relative values. Like a liquor license that can be renewed or transferred only on payment of state taxes,[50] a conse-

---

50. *In re* Anchorage International Inn, Inc., 718 F.2d 1446 (9th Cir. 1983), discussed supra Chapter 3.

quence of the operating permit requirement is that California has a right to be paid first out of Firm's assets as a condition of obtaining the permit's renewal. Firm's claimants, then, are put to another choice. If they want to continue in the business of manufacturing silicon chips, they need an operating permit. Because of the toxic wastes spill, this will cost $200,000. But this is a cost of doing business, like the $300,000 charge for installing environmental equipment. It is one of the factors that Firm's claimants have to consider in deciding whether to continue in business (in which case they will have to pay that charge) or liquidate (in which case California's claim will be treated as an unsecured claim). Putting them to that choice simply continues to reflect relative values and respects the fact that, because of nonbankruptcy attributes, the relative value of California's claim may be greater in a continuing business than in a liquidating business.

What, then, about the applicability of the automatic stay? Because the cleanup order derives from a prepetition act of Firm, the automatic stay should apply in the first instance. Should Firm decide to continue in business, however, the relative value of California's right is tantamount to a secured claim, and it is entitled to be paid in full. Since bankruptcy law is principally concerned with relative values, it would be proper to order the issuance of the operating permit upon receipt of "adequate assurance" that the $200,000 claim would be paid in full.[51] It might also be proper to lift the stay and let the right itself be respected, not just its value. It then becomes an issue like that of continuing the stay against any other secured creditor, a topic that we consider in the next subsection.

Before turning to that, however, it is useful to look at a 1986 opinion of the Supreme Court that is amenable to the same analysis. In *Midlantic National Bank v. New Jersey Department of Environmental Protection,*[52] similar issues were involved in the context of the propriety of abandonment of a toxic waste site under section 554, which permits abandonment of property "that is burdensome to the estate or that is of inconsequential value and benefit to the estate." The Supreme Court held that "a trustee may not abandon property in contravention of a state statute or regu-

51. §362(d), discussed next. This may pay state in full, with Firm later deciding to liquidate. But this is a consequence of needing an operating permit during a period of uncertainty about what to do with Firm's assets. Exactly the same problem would exist outside of bankruptcy. See also supra note 13.

52. 106 S. Ct. 755 (1986). The opinion has been widely interpreted as assigning priority to the cleanup order. See, e.g., id., at 767 (Rehnquist, J., dissenting); *N.Y. Times,* Jan. 28, 1986, p. 32. The opinion, however, noted twice that it did not involve the underlying priority issue. See 106 S. Ct., at 758 n.2 and 759 n.4.

lation that is reasonably designed to protect the public health or safety from identified hazards." It also noted, however, that the state's claim for administrative expense priority for its cleanup expenditures, was not before the Court. This distinction is correct, at least as long as the prohibition on abandonment does not resolve the priority issue in a de facto manner—by, as the dissent warned, "requir[ing] the trustee to expend all of [the debtor's] available assets to clean up the sites." Just as the trustee's power to use or sell property (cocaine, for example) under section 363 is surely limited by nonbankruptcy laws substantively regulating use and sale, so, too, should the power to abandon property under section 554 be so limited. To say that, however, does not mean that cleanup orders come ahead of other claims. To resolve that question, one must look to the proper nonbankruptcy analogy. In *Midlantic National Bank,* the debtor was liquidating, and the proper nonbankruptcy analogy would be that of a state-law liquidation. As such, the underlying priority issue is identical to that just discussed in connection with toxic waste cleanup orders and the automatic stay.

Relief from the Automatic Stay and the Costs of Delay in Bankruptcy

Application of the automatic stay to fully secured creditors makes sense in the first instance. To permit a secured creditor the full exercise of its rights may hinder efforts to preserve the value of the debtor's assets.[53] It may be in the interests of the owners as a group to stay the repossession rights of a secured creditor and to substitute a requirement that the secured creditor instead accept the asset's liquidation value.[54] Because of the costs repossession and subsequent repurchase may bring, it is consistent with the collectivization norm to substitute for a secured creditor's actual substantive rights under nonbankruptcy law a requirement that the secured creditor accept the equivalent value of those rights. Thus, application of the automatic stay to the secured creditor, with a

53. See supra Chapter 2.

54. This distinction is reflected in the House and Senate Reports to the bills that became the Bankruptcy Code. See S. Rep. No. 898, 95th Cong., 2d Sess. 53 (1978) ("There may be situations in bankruptcy where giving a secured creditor an absolute right to his bargain may be impossible or seriously detrimental to the policy of bankruptcy laws. Though the creditor might not receive his bargain in kind, the purpose of the section is to insure that the secured creditor receives in value essentially what he bargained for"); H. Rep. No. 595, 95th Cong., 1st Sess, 339 (1977) (same quote).

substitution of the relative value of rights in place of the rights themselves, is consistent with bankruptcy's role as a collective debt-collection device.

Under what circumstances, however, should the stay be kept in existence? If there are few or no costs to recognizing application of actual rights themselves, doing so is preferable even to respecting their value, because the fewest dislocations are achieved when the substantive right itself is respected.[55] In certain cases permitting the secured creditor to repossess and sell its collateral is probably the preferred course of action. These cases would seem to exist when two factors coexisted. The first factor would be that the amount owed to the secured party is equal to or in excess of the collateral in question. In that case the secured party has every incentive to sell the collateral, following repossession, for as much as possible.[56] In cases in which the collateral is worth more than the amount owed to the debtor, there is no similar assurance that the secured party will expend the effort to sell the collateral for more than the amount owed it. Accordingly, in cases in which the collateral is worth more than the debt, continuation of the automatic stay would be proper, because it permits debtor's unsecured creditors, who have more appropriate incentives, to sell the collateral. There is a second factor, however: even if the amount owed the secured party is in excess of the value of the collateral, it is possible that the assets of the debtor kept together are worth more than the value of the assets separated. In that event continuation of the stay would still be proper.

Thus, the cases in which lifting the stay would be proper—allowing the secured creditor to actually exercise its rights of repossession and sale—would seem to be those in which (a) no surplus value accrues to the assets in the possession of the debtor, and (b) the collateral in question is worth no more than the amount of the secured party's claim. This is essentially the test for relief from the stay represented by section 362(d)(2), which requires relief from the stay "of an act against property" if "(A) the debtor does not have an equity in such property; and (B) such property is not necessary to an effective reorganization."

This analysis aids in considering how terms such as *effective reorganization* should be interpreted. In *Koopmans*,[57] for example, the court con-

---

55. See supra Chapter 2.

56. See Schwartz, "The Enforceability of Security Interests in Consumer Goods," 26 *J. L. & Econ.* 117 (1983).

57. *In re* Koopmans, 22 Bankr. 395 (Bankr. D. Utah 1982); but see *In re* Jug End in the Berkshires, Inc., 46 Bankr. 892 (Bankr. D. Mass. 1985).

cluded that this section applied both to reorganizations under chapter 11 and to liquidations under chapter 7:

> Property in which the debtor has no equity is necessary to an effective reorganization whenever it is necessary, either in the operation of the business or in a plan, to further the interests of the estate through rehabilitation or liquidation . . . The property may be important to the liquidation of other property, as for example a warehouse or refrigerator which, although overencumbered, may be needed to store inventory or groceries pending sale. The property standing alone may have no equity, but when sold as a package, may bring a better price for other assets, as for example, workings for watches yet to be assembled, or contiguous parcels of real property.

This approach is sound: if the asset is worth more in the hands of the debtor than it would be in the hands of a third party, the stay should not be lifted, even if the debtor has no equity in the property.

To say that the stay should not be lifted implies only that the rights themselves of secured creditors should be stayed. It does not preclude preserving the relative value of those rights. It remains the case that, notwithstanding the automatic stay, the value of the rights of repossession and sale that existed at the time of the filing of the bankruptcy petition should be preserved in full. The normative answer to the question of what constitutes "adequate protection" of a secured creditor in bankruptcy thus becomes clear: absent reinstatement under section 1124, it is whatever gives the secured creditor the same value as the rights of repossession and sale would have given it.

Because this is one of the most frequently misunderstood points in bankruptcy law,[58] it is worth detailed examination to show that nothing in bankruptcy policy calls for its compromise.[59] Preserving the full value of a secured creditor's rights is simply an application of the notion that bankruptcy law concerns itself with deployment questions and should not change distributional entitlements because to do so in bankruptcy

58. See *In re* Bermec Corp., 445 F.2d 367 (2d Cir. 1971); *In re* South Village, Inc., 25 Bankr. 987 (Bankr. D. Utah 1982); *In re* Briggs Transportation Co., 780 F.2d 1339 (8th Cir. 1985); O'Toole, "Adequate Protection and Postpetition Interest in Chapter 11 Proceedings," 56 *Am. Bankr. L.J.* 251 (1982).

59. Nor is there anything in the Bankruptcy Code as enacted. See *In re* Martin, 761 F.2d 472 (8th Cir. 1985); Grundy Nat'l Bank v. Tandem Mining Corp., 754 F.2d 1436 (3d Cir. 1985); *In re* American Mariner Industries, Inc., 734 F.2d 426 (9th Cir. 1984); Note, "Compensation for Time Value as Part of Adequate Protection During the Automatic Stay in Bankruptcy," 50 *U. Chi. L. Rev.* 305 (1983).

would interfere with bankruptcy's attempt to solve the common pool problem.

The best way to keep the asset deployment question separate from the distributional question is to ensure that the parties who decide how to deploy assets enjoy all the benefits and incur all the costs of their decision.[60] Bankruptcy rules that enable classes of investors to gain from any upswing in the debtor's fortunes while avoiding the full costs of an attempt to keep the assets together create an incentive for those investors to make such an attempt, even if it is detrimental to the investors as a group. That is to say, they will attempt to keep the assets together even when an individual who had complete ownership of the assets would liquidate them immediately. Imposing on the residual class the risks of keeping a firm intact removes this incentive. Adequate protection of secured creditors in bankruptcy is an application of that principle in response to the fact that bankruptcy proceedings are not instantaneous.

The question of whether a debtor should be kept together as a unit is usually answered by estimating the income stream the assets would generate if they were kept together, discounting that stream to present value, and comparing it to the amount the assets would realize if they were sold off in separate pieces.[61] According to this view, a debtor should be kept intact only if it has more value as a going concern than liquidated, because the assets will generate more.[62]

Consider the following example. Investor lends firm $10,000. Firm promises to repay Investor in one year. Even if Firm were certain to repay the $10,000 at the end of one year, Investor would insist on some form of interest; receiving $10,000 one year from now is not the same as having $10,000 in hand today.[63]

Firm, of course, is not certain to repay the $10,000 in full and on time. There is a risk that Firm will either hide its assets[64] or become

60. This point is made in a different context in Easterbrook & Fischel, "Corporate Control Transactions," 91 *Yale L.J.* 698, 698 (1982).

61. See, e.g., J. VanHorne, *Financial Management and Policy* 105-41 (5th ed. 1980).

62. Again, as the text makes clear, although I generally refer to *economic* value, it is not necessary to be concerned solely with economic effects. See supra Chapter 2, note 4.

63. See R. Brealey & S. Myers, *Principles of Corporate Finance* 10–22 (2d ed. 1984). The problem will be analyzed without considering the effects of inflation. Consideration of inflation, of course, makes the point about the time value of money more vivid.

64. Such an action would doubtless constitute a fraudulent conveyance. See Uniform Fraudulent Conveyance Act §4 (1919); cf. Clark, "The Duties of the Corporate Debtor to Its Creditors," 90 *Harv. L. Rev.* 505, 517–33 (1977). But a fraudulent conveyance action against a debtor will provide little solace when, as is usually the case, the debtor is insolvent and the assets either cannot be traced or are in the hands of a bona fide purchaser for value. See Uniform Fraudulent Conveyance Act §9(1) (1919).

insolvent. Above and beyond the inherent time value of money, the risk of nonrepayment increases the cost of lending $10,000 to Firm, and Investor, if the transaction is voluntary, will insist on receiving compensation for taking that risk. If Investor takes a security interest in Firm's drill press, which is worth $10,000, Investor may be able to reduce the risk substantially, but it will not be able to eliminate it entirely. There is, first of all, a risk that the drill press will decline in value either because of fluctuations in its market value or because it wears out as it is used and thus depreciates in value. There is also a risk that Firm will not allow Investor to have the drill press upon default, and Investor will then be forced to resort to a lengthy court proceeding to obtain the asset. Such a delay imposes costs of two sorts on Investor. First, Investor continues to bear the risk of depreciation and value fluctuation. Second, even if the collateral does not depreciate and is stable in value, Investor bears the time value cost of delay. It is not enough to say that Investor has a right to the collateral in priority to other creditors; one has to establish *when* Investor has a right to the collateral.[65] A secured creditor with a right to take possession of a $10,000 machine in January of a given year and sell it is better off than a secured creditor with a right to take possession of a $10,000 machine in July of that year.

For this reason one cannot ask simply *how much* a secured creditor would receive under state law; one must also ask *when* the secured creditor would receive it. Under state law the filing of a bankruptcy petition usually identifies the "when." At least if Firm is liquidating, Investor's right to seize its collateral and to sell it to satisfy the debt presumptively ripens with the filing of the bankruptcy petition.[66] Outside of bankruptcy, foreclosure and sale may take time, particularly if Firm is recalcitrant,[67] but the nonbankruptcy processes could presumptively be set in motion at the time of the filing of the bankruptcy petition. If Investor is not given the liquidation value of the asset at the time it would have obtained money through a sale of the asset if a default occurred and a bankruptcy petition has not been filed, the value of its nonbankruptcy rights are not being protected. The intrinsic value of Investor's security interest, therefore, is the right it gives Investor to sell the drill press and thereby to

65. See James & Kirkland, "Adequate Protection through Augmented Interests in Reorganization Plans," 58 *Am. Bankr. L.J.* 69 (1984).

66. See supra Chapter 2. A different answer would be given, as analysis later in this chapter shows, if the firm were reorganizing *and* the debtor was willing to reinstate the entire contract, §1124.

67. If Investor cannot repossess the collateral "without breach of the peace," it must seek the assistance of a court. See Uniform Commercial Code §9-503 (1978).

obtain its liquidation value before the rights of other creditors at a particular time.

Providing a secured creditor with this right will not result in liquidation when the assets are worth more as a going concern. The rights of a creditor who has a security interest in a drill press are fixed by the amount the drill press would bring if it were sold to a third party on the open market.[68] If the firm is in fact worth more as a going concern than sold piecemeal, then there necessarily must be enough to pay a secured creditor the full liquidation value of the machine. One follows from the other. To say that a firm has a going-concern surplus is simply to say that the sum of the liquidation values of its assets if sold one by one is less than the going-concern value of those assets kept together.[69]

The firm, moreover, can pay the secured creditor out of cash reserves, or it can borrow the money on a secured, unsecured, or equity basis from a new investor. The secured creditor does not need to be given cash at the time of the petition in order to be given the full value of its nonbankruptcy rights.[70] As long as the package of rights the secured creditor is given is worth the liquidation value of the collateral—can be sold by the secured creditor for that amount at the time of the petition— it has received the value of its rights under nonbankruptcy law.

In principle, then, any firm that is worth more as a going concern than sold piecemeal will be able to give the secured creditor the value of its state-law rights. To be sure, doing so may mean that the other owners, such as general creditors or shareholders, will receive less or perhaps nothing of what is owed to them, but how rights to the assets are divided among the investors is distinct from the question of how the assets are deployed. Only the latter is a question related to collectivizing debt-collection procedures. Giving the secured creditor the benefit of its

68. Some secured creditors have argued that their rights should be judged by the collateral's going-concern value, not by its liquidation value. Absent reinstatement under §1124, a going-concern valuation would overcompensate them, however, because such a valuation is not a right that they have under state law. See *In re* American Mariner Industries, Inc., 734 F.2d 426 (9th Cir. 1984). The differences between the two valuations, however, are probably not as great as bankruptcy judges often make them seem, at least when a secondary market for the collateral is well developed. A liquidation value is not the same as the price the collateral would fetch in a fire sale. Liquidation value also should include the value that a third party would enjoy by virtue of having the opportunity to sell it back to the debtor.

69. Both going-concern and liquidation values represent future income streams discounted to present value, and the concept of a going-concern surplus means that the stream represented by the going-concern value is larger than the stream represented by the liquidation value.

70. See James & Kirkland, supra note 65, at 83–84.

bargain should not prevent a firm from staying together when a sole owner would keep it together. Indeed, a failure to recognize the secured creditor's rights in full will *undercut* the bankruptcy goal of ensuring that the assets are used to advance the interests of everyone. If those who stand to benefit from delay do not bear its costs (including the costs that secured creditors face), they will have an incentive to keep firms together even when a sole owner would not.

The discussion to this point, however, is incomplete. Adequate protection based on a creditor's rights of repossession and resale assumes a default. In applying it, one needs to remain sensitive to the relevant nonbankruptcy analogy. In a liquidation case, such as we have been dealing with, bankruptcy is treated as an event of default. Such is not necessarily the case where the debtor is continuing—is in bankruptcy to reorganize. The appropriate analogy is a change of stock ownership, an event that does not, as a matter of nonbankruptcy law, trigger automatic defaults. Assuming a decision has been made to reinstate the loan pursuant to section 1124, then, it is inappropriate to look to a default-based adequate protection analysis. Following reinstatement, the secured creditor's rights are set by its nondefault contract rights. This is the result provided in the postbankruptcy period by sections 1124 and 1129 (a)(8). Viewing the automatic stay, and hence adequate protection, as a vehicle for neutralizing the fact that bankruptcy proceedings take time, therefore, means that this outcome should be replicated during the pendency of the bankruptcy proceeding. This means looking to the terms of the reinstated contract, not to default-based adequate protection.

To this point the discussion has ignored the fact that the optimal course of action is not always clear at the start of a bankruptcy case. Nothing, however, hinges on that. To be sure, reorganizations (and other bankruptcy proceedings) take time (indeed, that fact is the focus of the discussion in this chapter). In the real world, moreover, valuations are hard to establish. It may not be clear whether a firm is worth keeping intact, and determining the optimal capital structure of a reorganized firm takes time. But it does not follow that protecting the relative value of the secured creditor's nonbankruptcy law rights promotes liquidations when the appropriate course is patience. Again, the appropriate normative focus is one that takes benefits and costs into account.

Waiting for changed conditions or for more information imposes a cost. If a debtor's assets would fetch $10,000 on liquidation today, an investor who owned the debtor's assets outright would have to weigh the value of obtaining $10,000 immediately against the more uncertain value that waiting would bring. The analysis should be exactly the same if the firm's ownership is dispersed. If the secured creditor receives the time value of its claim and junior creditors remain the ones who decide whether to try to reorganize, no incentives are introduced that would lead to a decision different from the one a sole owner would reach. That is the goal of bankruptcy law.

Assume, for example, that Debtor consists of assets that can be sold piecemeal for $10,000 today.[71] Assume further that Debtor has an 80 percent chance of being worth (discounted to current dollars) $12,000 in one year's time if an effort is made to keep the business running. There is, however, a 20 percent chance that the effort will fail and the assets will have to be sold on the open market at the end of the year. Such a sale will realize only $8,000 in current dollars. (The $2,000 difference between liquidation today and liquidation in a year's time arises from the time value of money and perhaps also from the depreciation that the assets will suffer in the intervening year.) In this case the attempt to keep the business running ought to be made. If the assets are kept together for another year, the best guess of their worth in present dollars is $11,200.[72] A third party would pay $11,200 today for the assets as a unit, while various third parties would pay only $10,000 for the assets on a piecemeal basis. A sole owner, therefore, would keep the assets together, either in its own hands or sold to a third party.

Giving the secured creditor the value of its nonbankruptcy rights in the face of uncertainty does not impair the effort to keep the assets together. If the assets are kept together and sold for $11,200 to a third party, the secured creditor can receive $10,000 from the proceeds. If the firm is reorganized (in effect a sale to the existing owners who pay for the assets),[73] nothing changes except the nature of the compensation. The secured creditor can be given a share in the reorganized company— approximately 89.3 percent of it[74]—worth $10,000 today, and the next class of owners, be they general creditors or shareholders, can divide among themselves a 10.7 percent share in the reorganized company worth $1,200.

There is, of course, a 20 percent chance that the reorganized Debtor will fail and be sold piecemeal for $8,000 (in present dollars) in a year's

---

71. All numbers in this example will be discounted to current dollars.

72. This is the case because $.8(\$12,000) + .2(\$8,000) = \$11,200$.

73. We examine in Chapter 9 the desirability of a separate reorganization chapter and explore in detail this way of viewing the reorganization process.

74. The expected value of the firm today is $11,200. If the secured creditor is given a little less than 89.3 percent of the stock in the firm (assuming no other form of ownership claim is used), its stock will have a present value of $10,000.

time, in which event a secured creditor who did not resell its shares would eventually receive less than full payment (approximately $7,140),[75] and the other owners would receive a small amount (approximately $860) for their 10.7 percent share. But if the secured creditor is compensated for the risk of failure, it is not injured. In other words, it is fully compensated if it is given enough stock so that, in the event of success, the secured creditor's share in the reorganized company will be worth, in today's dollars, approximately $10,715. The extra $715 of present value in the event of success compensates the secured creditor for the one chance in five that it will suffer a $2,860 loss in the event of failure.

Unlike a sole owner, dispersed investors, because their relative rights differ, have an incentive to make the wrong decision if unchecked: the secured creditors will rush to liquidate, and the general creditors and shareholders (who often have more to gain than to lose from delay) may tend to be excessively optimistic and opt for a reorganization when it is unwarranted. It is a mistake to assume that a junior class (or any other class) will make the correct decision about the deployment of the assets from the perspective of the owners as a group without a legal rule that forces it to take account of costs as well as benefits. A rule that forces general creditors and shareholders to give secured creditors the full value of their claims (including compensation for the time value of money) imposes the cost of a decision to reorganize the firm entirely on the junior classes, who already stand to benefit if the firm succeeds. As a consequence, they have incentives that approximate those of a sole owner, and their decision about how to deploy the debtor's assets will not be distorted by self-interest.[76]

75. Again, to lay things out explicitly, .893($8,000) equals approximately $7,140.

76. Addressing a related issue, Raymond Nimmer has suggested that the argument behind compensating time value through adequate protection not only fails to account for the costs it imposes in "effectively preclud[ing] reorganization in many cases" but also rests on "an assumption of economically rational actors acting to optimize benefits." Nimmer, "Secured Creditors and the Automatic Stay: Variable Bargain Models of Fairness," 68 *Minn. L. Rev.* 1, 13–14 (1983). He proposes a model of adequate protection that is derived from the type of result that should follow from different behavioral assumptions and a focus on "overall reorganization goals." Id., at 51.

I disagree with this approach, largely because I do not think that recognizing the value of the nonbankruptcy rights of secured creditors has the effect of discouraging reorganizations that the owners as a group would desire (which, rather than some absolute number of reorganizations, is the proper focus). In making this argument, moreover, I do not assume that the actors in a bankruptcy proceeding are rational profit-maximizers. Rather, I make the more modest assumption that they are sensitive in some measure to the economic costs and benefits of their actions, and that legal rules should ensure that the

We have seen, however, that liquidation-based adequate protection analysis is inappropriate in the absence of a default, such as exists in a reorganization where the loan is reinstated. What does one do, then, with the fact that, during the bankruptcy process, the decision might not yet be made whether to continue or liquidate—to reinstate or not? In structuring a bankruptcy rule, the important point would seem to continue to attempt to formulate a rule that created no incentives for delay in cases where a sole owner would not seek delay. This requires an "either/or" form of protection until the decision is made whether to continue the debtor *and* to reinstate the loan pursuant to section 1124. In the case of reinstatement, the protection is provided by the process of reinstatement itself. Section 1124 provides that if the debtor is unable to pay over the accrued payments (with, it would seem to follow, interest at the market rate), then the loan cannot be reinstated and must be treated as in default. As for the other contingency, where the decision is ultimately made either to liquidate the debtor or to continue the debtor but not reinstate the loan, liquidation-based adequate protection should be provided in the interim. This requires either protecting the liquidation value of the collateral and accruing (in a protected way) market rate interest on that value, or making periodic cash payments designed to reach the same result (payments that would have to be returned should the loan ultimately be reinstated and to the extent that they exceeded the payments due in the interim under the reinstated loan).

A Postscript: Operating after Bankruptcy Is Over

When a corporation is involved, bankruptcy policy is concerned with ensuring that distributional conflicts do not result in poor deployment decisions. To the extent that this means that bankruptcy can be used to ensure that common pool problems do not result in the untimely dismemberment of assets and the liquidation of debtors that are more profitable to their owners as going concerns, one can state that an *effect* of bankruptcy policy is sometimes to keep firms alive. This, however, is

---

decisions of those involved are not, as a result of this sensitivity, systematically biased in favor of either liquidation or reorganization. Making certain that the residual claimants enjoy the same benefits and incur the same costs as a sole owner does not depend on deep assumptions about economic rationality. Whatever the basis for a decision, it should not be distorted because the benefits fall on one party and the costs on another. Whether residual claimants act in a way that is economically rational when their incentives are not skewed is entirely up to them.

very different from saying that bankruptcy law embodies a distinct substantive fresh-start policy for corporations.

Liquidating corporations do not need the bankruptcy process in order to gain a discharge of debts because they can accomplish that end through dissolution under state law. Indeed, the current Bankruptcy Code provides no discharge for liquidating corporations,[77] underscoring the point that discharge of corporations is not an intrinsic bankruptcy policy. Corporations that reorganize under chapter 11 do, to be sure, receive a discharge.[78] Even there, however, it is wrong to conclude that the reasons for such discharge are derived from a financial fresh-start policy. Unlike individuals, corporations are not entitled to shield any assets from prepetition claimants, whether liquidating or reorganizing. Instead, from the perspective of bankruptcy law as a collective debt-collection device, the reasoning behind a discharge for reorganizing corporations would be that, in order to allow a firm's owners to make an unbiased decision as to whether to continue or liquidate, they have to be able to obtain— as a sole owner would—the same results under either path. In the case of a reorganization, the prebankruptcy claimants have had their claims converted into new ownership interests, and it is in their interest as a group to treat this as final payment.

It is important not to forget the policy that a debtor in (or through) bankruptcy should receive no special advantages in its future business. In a number of cases various prepetition claimants may continue to hold rights that give their prebankruptcy claims greater relative value than those of other unsecured creditors. Members of the Chicago Board of Trade[79] may have the right to stop a sale of Debtor's membership but not the right to force a sale. Because of that, if Debtor kept its membership through bankruptcy, the debts to members might have been treated as unsecured claims, given that there was no occasion for the members to assert their special rights. But if, following bankruptcy, Debtor then attempts to sell its membership in the Board of Trade, there is no reason why the members should not be able to assert their rights at that time. Whether the relative values arise from rights that can be exercised in bankruptcy or after should make no difference.

Seen this way, bankruptcy's treatment of such rights would be akin to the doctrine of lien pass-through, which permits secured creditors that have not had their claims satisfied in full in bankruptcy to pursue

---

77. §727(a)(1).

78. §1141(a), (c), (d).

79. Recall *Chicago Board of Trade v. Johnson*, 264 U.S. 1 (1924), discussed supra Chapter 4.

their collateral, if still in the hands of the debtor, after bankruptcy, notwithstanding discharge.[80] In the case of the membership in the Board of Trade, the member's rights are akin to a lien on an asset of Debtor— the membership—that passes through bankruptcy along with the membership.

Because of this point—which is a conflux of the fact that bankruptcy law should respect relative values of claims whether it does so in or after bankruptcy and the fact that it is wrong to speak of a financial fresh start for a corporate debtor—the sections of the Bankruptcy Code dealing with the effect of discharge[81] should be viewed with care when dealing with a corporate debtor that has received a discharge in a chapter 11 proceeding. Section 524 should be construed, just as section 362 should, to bar the assertion of rights held by all prebankruptcy unsecured claimants, but *not* to bar the assertion of rights—such as those of members of the Board of Trade whose prebankruptcy claims have not been paid in full—that give a particular prebankruptcy claimant greater relative value. Similarly, section 525 should not be construed, as it sometimes has been,[82] to prohibit, say, a state from enforcing its restrictions on transfers of liquor licenses without payment of prepetition state taxes in full, as long as the value of that restriction on transfer would have been recognized in bankruptcy as well. Seeing these sections as implementing a fresh-start policy when the debtor is a corporation mixes apples and oranges. Instead, they represent a playing out of the notion of relative values already embodied in the bankruptcy statute.

80. This doctrine was announced in Long v. Bullard, 117 U.S. 617 (1888) and has been codified in §524(a)(2). See also *In re* Tarnow, 749 F.2d 464 (7th Cir. 1984); United States v. Marlow, 48 Bankr. 261 (D. Kan. 1984); H. Rep. No. 595, 95th Cong., 1st Sess. 361 (1977) ("The bankruptcy discharge will not prevent enforcement of valid liens").

81. §§524, 525.

82. *In re* Aegean Fare, Inc., 35 Bankr. 923 (Bankr. D. Mass. 1983) (state statute requiring a licensee to pay prepetition taxes as a condition for renewal of liquor license violated the supremacy clause, because of §§362 and 525).

8

Timing the Bankruptcy Proceeding:
The Problems of Proper Commencement

ENSURING THAT bankruptcy cases are initiated only when they are needed, and then neither too early nor too late, is a difficult task. We examine in this chapter some of the problems with commencement of a collective proceeding and some of the possible legal responses. It is analytically useful to separate the two issues. We shall first consider the problem of inappropriate uses of the bankruptcy process and then focus on the timing of the advent of the bankruptcy proceeding.

The "Good Faith" of Bankruptcy Petitions: Strategic Misuses vs. Common Pool Problems

As emphasized throughout this book, whenever bankruptcy law changes the relative value of nonbankruptcy rights, incentives are created for inappropriate uses of the bankruptcy process. This can be seen in countless cases in practice. Consider the case of Tinti Construction Company,[1] a corporation wholly owned by two brothers in the business of constructing single-family homes. In mid-1980 Tinti (as a member of a construction association) entered into a two-year collective bargaining agreement with the local carpenters' union. Tinti began to suffer large losses in 1981, in part as a result of a construction slump and in part because it had lost a number of bids to non-union companies. According to the court, if Tinti could not be released from its union contract, it "will almost certainly fail, and its 8 to 12 employees will be out of a job."

---

1. These facts come from *In re* Tinti Construction Co., 29 Bankr. 971 (Bankr. E.D. Wisc. 1983).

Tinti, however, did not have a common pool problem. Tinti bought most supplies on a cash basis and had never borrowed extensively, except in the form of equity infusions from its shareholders. At the time it tried to use bankruptcy, Tinti had "no outstanding claims other than those of the Union for contributions to employee benefit plans and unpaid wage differentials." Thus, Tinti was a one-creditor case. Tinti nonetheless filed for bankruptcy.

The reasons for this filing quite certainly had nothing to do with ameliorating the destructive effects of individual creditor remedies. Although Tinti might have been insolvent, it had only one creditor. To be sure, it also had equity owners, and that explained the filing. Tinti's management wanted to be free of its collective bargaining agreement and thereby possibly save something for equity.[2] Outside of bankruptcy, collective bargaining agreements cannot be unilaterally avoided; instead, the employer must bargain with the union for changes in the terms and conditions of employment. In bankruptcy, however, it has been held that collective bargaining agreements are executory contracts that can be rejected, a solution codified in section 1113. This represents a substantive rule change in bankruptcy that is unrelated to a common pool problem. Predictably, it creates incentives to use the bankruptcy process simply to gain access to that rule change. There was no debt-collection-related reason for bankruptcy in *Tinti*, no race to the assets to ameliorate. In that case the bankruptcy process was being misused, which the court saw.[3] It is easy to see that such a case represents misuse of bankruptcy as a debt-collection device because of the absence of the necessary condition of a common pool problem.[4]

In a number of other cases the commencement of a bankruptcy case stems from a transparent attempt to delay a secured creditor from exercising its foreclosure rights. This is clearest in the cases where a debtor forms a new corporation on the eve of bankruptcy, the secured assets of the debtor are placed in that new corporation, and the corporation

2. Whether that strategy would have been successful is a separate question and depends, in part, on the form of the union's resulting damage claim.

3. The issue arose in the context of rejection; the court's opinion, however, would equally apply to a decision to dismiss the petition under section 305 for not being filed in "good faith." Not all judges agree that one-creditor bankruptcy cases are necessarily inappropriate. See, e.g., *In re* Waldron, 36 Bankr. 633 (Bankr. S.D. Fla. 1984) (proper to use bankruptcy solely to avoid an option to purchase real property granted by debtors).

4. Of course, the existence of a common pool problem would not *justify* a rule change (rejection of collective bargaining agreements is proper) that was not justified in the one-creditor case.

then files for bankruptcy.[5] These cases, too, are clearly not common pool cases. Instead, they reflect the consequences of a shift in relative values. Although I have discussed how "adequate protection" should be interpreted, many bankruptcy judges do not agree.[6] In many cases, moreover, it is assumed that bankruptcy judges, even when applying the correct legal standard, will nonetheless undervalue in practice the compensation necessary to protect a secured creditor in full.[7] When the effect of using bankruptcy is to undercompensate secured creditors, delay works to the interest of the debtor or unsecured creditors because some of the costs of the delay are borne by the secured creditors. Such undercompensation, therefore, reflects another change in relative values that induces bankruptcy filings for purposes other than solving common pool problems. Again, the test for establishing the propriety of a bankruptcy petition in such cases is that of "good faith."

Widespread reliance on a good faith test, however, may be symptomatic of a deeper problem. The use of the good faith test to deny access to bankruptcy when the reasons are blatantly to gain a rule change suggests that, when starkly presented with the problem, bankruptcy law generally is perceived as a collective debt-collection device and should not be used as a vehicle for policies such as rejecting collective bargaining agreements or undercompensating secured creditors. But if it is perceived to be an incorrect use of bankruptcy when done baldly, it should not be a *correct* use of bankruptcy when combined with insolvency and diverse creditors. Many inquiries into good faith could be avoided if bankruptcy law adhered faithfully to the notion of preserving relative values. If bankruptcy law did not serve as the occasion for changing relative values, many of the common strategic uses of bankruptcy would be avoided.[8]

5. These cases are legion. Most but not all courts view such actions as abuses of bankruptcy. Compare *In re* Spenard Ventures, Inc., 18 Bankr. 164 (Bankr. D. Alaska 1982) with *In re* 2218 Bluebird Ltd. Partnership, 41 Bankr. 540 (Bankr. S.D. Cal. 1984); *In re* Thirtieth Place, Inc., 30 Bankr. 503 (9th Cir. Bankr. App. 1983); *In re* Dutch Flat Investment Co., 6 Bankr. 1134 (Bankr. N.D. Cal. 1980).
6. See supra Chapter 7.
7. See Blum, "The Law and Language of Corporate Reorganizations," 17 *U. Chi. L. Rev.* 565, 577–78 & n.18 (1950); Festerson, "Equitable Powers in Bankruptcy Rehabilitation: Protection of the Debtor and the Doomsday Principle," 46 *Am. Bankr. L.J.* 311, 329 (1972). Much of this may simply be the result of the unwitting use of heuristics, which leads judges to be overoptimistic. I discuss these cognitive biases in Chapter 10.
8. See, e.g., Comment, "Good Faith Inquiries under the Bankruptcy Code: Treating the Symptom, Not the Cause," 52 *U. Chi. L. Rev.* 795 (1985). Much finance literature on bankruptcy, in fact, treats the bankruptcy decision as one whereby a "coalition of claimants

Following through on the implications of using bankruptcy as a collective debt-collection device designed to ameliorate common pool problems would vastly reduce the need to rely on a good faith inquiry. In general, such a reduction would be desirable. A good faith inquiry is inevitably fact-specific and costly. In addition, it cannot respond adequately to the "mixed motive" cases—cases where there are multiple creditors *and* a selfish strategic goal. Good faith is simply a label for those cases in which a bankruptcy proceeding is appropriate. One can flesh out its meaning only if one understands the goals and limits of bankruptcy law.[9]

All this, however, is not to say that if bankruptcy law limited itself to collectivizing debt-collection procedures, it could do away with a good faith inquiry entirely. Because bankruptcy's procedures are different from nonbankruptcy procedures, it is virtually impossible to eliminate the problem of strategic uses of bankruptcy. For example, we previously examined rules that permitted the bankruptcy court to estimate claims instead of adhering to nonbankruptcy judicial trial procedures.[10] We justified them as a sensible cost savings device in cases where the debtor was insolvent and hence in the interests of the claimants as a group. But the debtor may not be insolvent. Or, notwithstanding these advantages, the claimants as a group may be better off avoiding bankruptcy because of certain costs associated with its use. Although such estimation procedures may make sense in the context where bankruptcy is otherwise desirable, because they inevitably change the costs of establishing claims outside of bankruptcy (as is their goal), these estimation procedures may provide an incentive for a litigating party to favor (or oppose) the use of the bankruptcy forum precisely *because* of the change in costs, whether or not bankruptcy is otherwise necessary.[11]

One, then, cannot avoid the fact that bankruptcy law, precisely because it has specialized procedures to respond to a common pool problem,

---

with negotiating power can gain from immediate liquidation," Bulow & Shoven, "The Bankruptcy Decision," 9 *Bell J. Econ.* 437, 454 (1978); see also White, "Public Policy Toward Bankruptcy: Me-First and Other Priority Rules," 11 *Bell J. Econ.* 550 (1980); Ang & Chua, "Coalitions, the Me-First Rule, and the Liquidation Decision," 11 *Bell J. Econ.* 355 (1980).

9. For example, one may need to inquire if the debtor was insolvent at a time when it had multiple creditors. For a possible example of such a case, see *In re* Win Sum Sports, Inc., 14 Bankr. 389 (Bankr. D. Conn. 1981).

10. See supra Chapter 2.

11. For a possible example of such a case, see *In re* Tarletz, 27 Bankr. 787 (Bankr. D. Colo. 1983). Cf. *In re* Cordova, 34 Bankr. 70 (Bankr. D.N.M. 1983) (single-creditor involuntary bankruptcy proper because bankruptcy process could sell ongoing business better and sheriff ill-equipped to do so).

inevitably will create strategic incentives unassociated with solving that problem. Consequently, it is probably necessary to formulate some rules to define when the bankruptcy process can be used.

The problem is one of defining rules that accommodate what bankruptcy is trying to do. As we have seen, bankruptcy appropriately responds when multiple claimants are likely to exercise individual creditor remedies and the debtor does not have enough assets to satisfy them. This is a condition of insolvency or, as often called, "insolvency in the bankruptcy sense." It is a status where, whether or not the debtor has enough liquid assets to pay current bills, it is not expected to be able to generate enough to pay all of its obligations over time. The Bankruptcy Code seems to define this properly, at least for a first cut, as the status that exists when assets at fair valuation are not expected to be able to meet liabilities at fair valuation.[12]

Further reflection, however, indicates that in a world in which information is not perfect even the theoretical answer is not so simple. We do not usually know, for certain, the value of assets at any point in the future. One effect of this is that the common pool problem created by individual creditor grab remedies can exist even when this definition of insolvency is not met. The value of assets depends on their value in use, which in a world of imperfect information is itself a "best guess" about the likelihood of future courses of action. As a consequence, saying that a debtor's assets are worth more than the debtor's liabilities at fair valuation is a numerical answer that assimilates a probability distribution about the value of assets. In a number of these cases the statement that the debtor's assets at fair valuation exceed its liabilities is consistent with the statement that there is a substantial probability that the assets will *not* be worth enough to pay off the debts in full.[13] In that case, although the debtor is technically solvent, the creditors may grab for assets anyway, because they would be the group to feel the effects of the downside possibilities, while the benefits of the upside possibilities would flow to other groups, such as shareholders.[14]

For example, consider a firm that has $100,000 of claims and one

12. §101(29).

13. In fact, it is true in every case that there is a statistical chance that a company will become insolvent—even a company such as IBM. But there is unlikely to be a common pool problem whose redress would require bankruptcy until that chance of insolvency looms large. In the case of IBM, for example, there are unlikely to be events of default triggering a creditor rush to the assets. And if one creditor withdraws, it is no problem to find a replacement.

14. See, e.g., Baird & Jackson, "Fraudulent Conveyance Law and Its Proper Domain," 38 *Vand. L. Rev.* 829 (1985).

kind of asset, one hundred lottery tickets that it just purchased for $1,200 each. Each ticket will pay $2,400 upon the occurrence of the same event— that a flip of a coin will land as "heads"—and return nothing if the coin shows "tails." (The firm, for unknown reasons, did not diversify its holdings.) These tickets could be sold for an aggregate of $120,000.[15] Thus, at fair valuation this firm is solvent, because its assets exceed its liabilities. But the creditors will note what will happen if they wait. If the lottery tickets are winners, there will be $240,000, of which $100,000 will go to the creditors and $140,000 to the shareholders. Thus, the creditors are limited on the upside to $100,000. But if the lottery tickets are losers, there will be nothing, and the creditors will not receive a cent. It is clearly in the interest of each particular creditor to seek to exercise its individual rights against these tickets, attempt to levy on them, and sell them for cash. Thus, there will be a scramble for assets, notwithstanding that the firm is technically solvent.[16] If a common pool problem existed (as it might well), a collective bankruptcy proceeding would be appropriate in this case as well.[17]

There is often thought to be a different kind of case in which a bankruptcy proceeding is appropriate—the circumstance where the debtor faces what is euphemistically called a *liquidity crisis* because it is unable to pay its debts as they mature, even though the value of its assets exceeds its liabilities. It is often referred to as "insolvency in the equity (or cash flow) sense." It is perhaps, however, more useful to think of this less as a distinct category of cases as another way in which insolvency in the bankruptcy sense is the basic issue. In many cases these kinds of cash flow problems tend to be symptomatic of an underlying problem of not enough assets to pay liabilities, because with a "temporary" liquidity crisis it should be possible to borrow against the remaining assets to regain liquidity. Thus, when a cash flow crisis is announced, it is likely that the company is in fact insolvent in the bankruptcy sense, or at least enough uncertainty will exist as to its status that it will be unable to borrow the money necessary to pay its current debts. In either event the creditors

15. Their sale, presumably, would be to someone who, unlike firm, holds a diversified portfolio.

16. Again, it would be necessary to find an event of default. In this case such a gamble might trigger application of fraudulent conveyance rules. See Baird & Jackson, supra note 14.

17. In this example there would be no going-concern surplus to keeping the assets together. The benefits, if any, from a bankruptcy proceeding would accordingly have to come from other sources. See supra Chapter 1. But the point is clear, and in a number of cases there may be a going-concern surplus as well.

as a group would be understandably nervous, and this nervousness would lead them to use individual creditor remedies.

In each of these cases, then, a collective bankruptcy proceeding might be an appropriate outcome. What does this suggest for tests of appropriate access to the bankruptcy process? The problem is clear: one wants to demark the cases where there is likely to be a common pool problem and to exclude those cases that are likely to be fueled simply by a selfish claimant seeking a strategic advantage.

As a first approximation in accomplishing these goals, it seems that bankruptcy law could do no better than to formulate a test that requires those advocating a bankruptcy proceeding to show that there is a reasonable likelihood that the debtor is or might become in the future insolvent in the sense of not having enough assets to pay off its creditors in full. Because of the likelihood that a debtor with cash flow problems meets that test, a demonstration that the debtor is in such a position would be one way of satisfying the requirement of showing a reasonable likelihood of insolvency.

This test itself may not always be sufficient. There may be cases, for example, where the creditors, either explicitly or implicitly, have agreed among themselves not to use bankruptcy at the present time.[18] Consider, for example, the case of a start-up company attempting to develop a new technology. While the technology is under development, those who infused capital into the company in the form of debt may have implicitly agreed not to take over the stock in the company, which they might be able to do if they resorted to bankruptcy (because the possibility of failure is sufficient to characterize the company as insolvent under fair valuation tests). But until circumstances change or time passes, upsetting that deal by using bankruptcy would be inappropriate, because, although there is insolvency, there is as yet no common pool problem.

That insolvency tests may not be sufficient does not mean that resort to an open-ended good faith inquiry is necessary to pick up these unusual cases. Such an inquiry might be appropriate, but the gains from such an approach (more accurate determinations of when bankruptcy is needed)

---

18. For an example of an explicit agreement, see *In re* Old Colonial Ford, Inc., 24 Bankr. 1014 (Bankr. D. Utah 1982). There is no reason why creditors, or debtors other than human beings, should not be able to waive their right to resort to bankruptcy. Although courts frown on such agreements, see United States v. Royal Business Funds Corp., 724 F.2d 12 (2d Cir. 1983), much of this is a result of an unthinking application of the nonwaivability of the right of discharge for *individuals*. That a corporate debtor agrees not to use bankruptcy would not stop its creditors from using it.

may not be worth its costs (case-by-case inquiries). The problem, however, may not be severe. If bankruptcy's rules have been appropriately designed, most cases can be handled reasonably well by creating a rebuttable presumption of appropriateness upon showing that there are multiple creditors and a reasonable prospect of insolvency. In a start-up company, for example, it is unlikely that the creditors will advance their interests by seeking to take over the entire firm, upside and all. It is likely that much of the upside potential resides in the skill and know-how of those working in the company, who may be the very shareholders who would be squeezed out. Indeed, their agreements may be written in a way that leaves the debtor without defaults. In those cases, where there is no immediate common pool problem, the creditors should be refused access to the bankruptcy process.[19]

This analysis of the role of insolvency tests permits us to make two observations about the current status of the Bankruptcy Code. First, the test in section 303(h)(1) of showing that the debtor is "generally not paying debts as they become due" is, as a matter of theory, insufficient by itself.[20] A debtor might be insolvent in the sense of not having enough assets to satisfy all of those with claims against it and still be able to meet current debts as they become due. And even though these two tests may tend to collapse as creditors accelerate their loans, they will not always. At the time Manville filed its petition, for example, it seemed to be insolvent in the sense of not having enough assets to pay all its claimants in full, but because of the fact that the unmanifested asbestosis claimants could not yet demand payment from Manville, it was possible that Manville could have met its debts as they became due for years to come. And yet Manville may well have been an appropriate candidate for bankruptcy because of a resulting common pool problem. To say this, however, is not to say that the justification for using section 303(h)(1) exclusively rests easily on the ground that it functions as an easy-to-apply rule and one that will pick up most cases where bankruptcy is needed. It is by no means clear that the test is that easy to apply[21] or that adding an alternative insolvency test would make *all* inquiries too fact-specific.

Second, there is no particular reason why these tests should not apply to petitions filed by the debtor (except when the debtor is a human being

19. Even the "reasonable likelihood of insolvency" test may, therefore, be considered a surrogate for a more fundamental showing: there is a good likelihood that creditors will begin to grab for assets in an uncontrolled race.

20. The development of the inability-to-pay test is traced in McCoid, "The Occasion for Involuntary Bankruptcy" (draft 1985).

21. *In re* B.D. International Discount Corp., 701 F.2d 1071 (2d Cir. 1983).

who might file for bankruptcy in order to get a fresh start). The decision of shareholders or management of a debtor should be subject to the same scrutiny as petitions by creditors. They are all actions to commence bankruptcy by various species of owners, and when no independent social policy is being served by bankruptcy (as there is in the case of individuals seeking the right to a fresh start), there is no reason to draw a sharp line between the tests for commencement of voluntary and involuntary petitions—a line that, in practice, is not that clear in any case.[22]

This discussion suggests that a series of tests designed to determine if there is, or is likely to be perceived to be, insolvency and a resulting scramble for assets is appropriate for deciding whether a bankruptcy case should proceed. These tests must be admittedly crude, because so much is uncertain at the commencement of a case. Other possible solutions, however, do not seem promising. At one level it might seem preferable to resolve bankruptcy commencement issues by vote of the general creditors as to whether they think bankruptcy is needed.[23] Not only would this be the inappropriate group to vote in cases where the debtor is clearly solvent,[24] however, but it is also not clear that the correct group could be identified at the commencement of a case. Much of the bankruptcy process is spent determining who are the unsecured creditors and the amount of their claims. There is no easy way, therefore, to establish appropriate voting procedures designed to correctly decide an issue that must be resolved at the beginning of the case.

For this reason tests that are incapable of precise application (such as insolvency tests) may be the best compromise. Once obvious rule changes in bankruptcy are avoided, moreover, it would be possible to implement this test by a series of presumptions: presume that bankruptcy is proper unless it can be shown that the petitioning entities (or others connected to them) were using bankruptcy in the service of some self-interested end that would be destructive of the common weal.

The current Bankruptcy Code has another route into bankruptcy. Involuntary petitions are permitted if "within 120 days before the date of the filing of the petition, a custodian, other than a trustee, receiver, or agent appointed or authorized to take charge of less than substantially all of the property of the debtor for the purpose of enforcing a lien

22. Many corporations "agree" to file a voluntary petition following the threat of a creditor to file an involuntary petition.

23. Such votes occur, for example, with the election of the trustee, §702, although even here Congress has had to try to limit the ability to manipulate the vote. See id.

24. When the creditors will get paid in full, they may be indifferent. In that case the shareholders would be the appropriate group, if any would be.

against such property, was appointed or took possession."[25] At one level this alternative approach is sensible. The best way to ensure that non-bankruptcy collective proceedings play by the same baseline rules as bankruptcy law is to permit any claimant who thinks it is getting less outside of bankruptcy than it would inside to force the switch.[26] On another level, however, it is unclear that this path should be an *alternative* to insolvency tests. A nonbankruptcy collective proceeding might be commenced for suspicious reasons as well. Instead of having bankruptcy follow suit, it would be better to dismiss *both* kinds of proceedings.[27] Perhaps the appropriate way to accomplish that is to have the proceeding transferred to the bankruptcy forum and then have it dismissed, on application of the insolvency tests—which suggests that the propriety of this path into bankruptcy should not be resolved without resort to bankruptcy's insolvency tests as well.[28]

Finally, what about the additional requirements of section 303(b)?[29] A bankruptcy proceeding should be a response to a genuine common pool problem. In light of that, requiring bankruptcy petitions to be filed by more than one creditor and requiring the creditors to be unsecured (so presumptively they may have something to gain from bankruptcy) makes theoretical sense. The problem, however, is a practical one. It is uncertain that such requirements can provide more than formalistic protection, given the ability of a creditor to "buy" the cooperation of other creditors in filing a petition.[30]

25. §303(h)(2).

26. Jackson, "Bankruptcy, Non-Bankruptcy Entitlements, and the Creditors' Bargain," 91 *Yale L.J.* 857, 867 (1982).

27. Such a dismissal would not be proper where the nonbankruptcy collective proceeding was perceived to be part of the original entitlements, irrespective of whether it followed bankruptcy rules. In that case the case also should not be moved to the bankruptcy forum. Again, application of the insolvency tests would accomplish this result.

28. If the question of insolvency was decided in the nonbankruptcy law collective forum, its decision could be applied in bankruptcy as well as long as the attributes on which the decision were based were the same that bankruptcy law would apply. Cf. Brown v. Felsen, 442 U.S. 127 (1979).

29. Section 303(b) requires involuntary petitions to be filed "(1) by three or more entities, each of which is either a holder of a claim against such person that is not contingent as to liability or the subject on [sic] a bona fide dispute, or an indenture trustee representing such a holder, if such claims aggregate at least $5,000 more than the value of any lien on property of the debtor securing such claims held by the holder of such claims; (2) if there are fewer than 12 such holders, excluding any employee or insider of such person and any transferee of a transfer that is voidable under section 544, 545, 547, 548, 549, or 724(a) of this title, by one or more of such holders that hold in the aggregate at least $5,000 of such claims."

30. See, e.g., *In re* Win Sum Sports, Inc., 14 Bankr. 389 (Bankr. D. Conn. 1981); see also Bankruptcy Rule 1003(c).

More problematic are the exclusions from petitioning creditor status for holders of "contingent" claims or those that are the subject of a "bona fide dispute." Presumably, these exclusions are designed to keep categories of claimants that are likely to seek bankruptcy for selfish goals from filing petitions.[31] But it is not clear at all that this sort of game is worth the price (in terms both of legitimate filings and inquiry costs) in cases in which the threshhold insolvency requirements can be met.

Rules for Optimal Timing Incentives

To this point, we have looked at tests that try to decide whether a bankruptcy proceeding is appropriate at all. We now need to consider timing rules. A bankruptcy proceeding can commence too early in that even though a common pool problem exists, consensual negotiations outside of bankruptcy would be preferable from the perspective of the group of creditors. A bankruptcy proceeding can also commence too late, in that individual creditor remedies have already had harmful results.[32]

The problem of uncertain information, moreover, exacerbates both problems. One of the greatest costs of using the bankruptcy process in a number of cases comes from the informational content of a filing. A firm's financial problems may be vaguely known or vaguely focused on. The filing of a bankruptcy petition, however, operates as a fairly clear signal to the world that the firm is in financial trouble. It is a reasonable inference, from the filing of a bankruptcy petition, that a firm is not likely to be in operation in the future. This informational content to a filing can be particularly harmful to a firm.[33] The debtor may have trouble finding buyers for its products because potential buyers may fear

31. These selfish reasons might be using bankruptcy's rules for resolving disputes or to put pressure on a debtor to resolve a dispute.

32. See Report of the Commission on the Bankruptcy Laws of the United States, Part I, at 14–15 (1973). It is commonplace to cite statistics about the number of firms that fail notwithstanding bankruptcy, see LoPucki, "The Debtor in Full Control—Systems Failure under Chapter 11 of the Bankruptcy Code? (pt. 1)," 57 *Am. Bankr. L.J.* 99, 100–01 (1983), as evidence that bankruptcy petitions are filed too late. I agree that most petitions are probably filed too late, but a statistic about failures tells us only that most businesses that use bankruptcy are better off liquidating than continuing. That, itself, tells us nothing about timing.

33. It may, ironically, be beneficial to society. Generally, more information is preferable to less. If, on balance, the informational content of a bankruptcy filing is accurate across a range of cases, it is conceivable that buyers (and others) are *better* off. But to the extent the information would be in the control of a sole owner (or a unanimous group of diverse owners) who could avoid the use of bankruptcy, it nevertheless represents a cost of using bankruptcy to the relevant group—the owners.

that the debtor will not be in a position to honor its warranties (a problem a durable goods manufacturer, such as an automobile manufacturer, might find more vexing than a restaurant chain or a manufacturer of consumables). Managers or entrepreneurs may be less willing to join the business and learn firm-specific skills. The debtor may also find it harder to collect money it is owed. Its debtors may simply fail to pay or impose bogus defenses, thinking that repeat dealings with the debtor are no longer important and that their reputations will suffer little if they fail to pay a firm in bankruptcy.[34]

Bankruptcy rules themselves do not directly cause these harms. A business may experience financial trouble and suffer similar losses without using the bankruptcy process. But the filing of a bankruptcy petition conveys information to customers, suppliers, and others in a way that other mechanisms may not.[35] Especially where the firm is *not* worth more dead than alive but is simply suffering from the problem of too much fixed debt, it may be inordinately hard to convey that message in a satisfactory and timely fashion to the appropriate entities who (rationally) assume the worst when they hear of the bankruptcy filing.

As a practical matter, therefore, the filing of a bankruptcy petition itself may hurt the debtor and all its creditors by reducing the value of the debtor's business.[36] In many cases those informational costs may create strategic incentives to use or avoid using the bankruptcy process. Normally, one might think that this would lead bankruptcy proceedings to commence too late, as the debtor and its creditors try to avoid the sending of this informational signal, but such is not necessarily the case. A creditor of a debtor who is also a competitor or who is angry with the debtor for other reasons may favor commencement of the bankruptcy case precisely because this informational signal will unjustly (from the perspective of others) impose a cost on the debtor.[37]

Other informational problems are likely to exist. The financial decline of a firm is likely to be recognized first by the firm's managers and

---

34. It is a widespread phenomenon that the value of outstanding accounts receivable falls sharply for a firm in bankruptcy. See, e.g., "The Business in Trouble—A Workout without Bankruptcy," 39 *Bus. Lawyer* 1041 (1984); *In re* Lackow Brothers, Inc., 16 Bankr. 566 (Bankr. S.D. Fla. 1981), aff'd, 22 Bankr. 1018 (S.D. Fla. 1982).

35. It is a form of financial signal. On signaling theory in general, see A. Spence, *Market Signaling: Informational Transfer in Hiring and Related Screening Processes* 1–4 (1974).

36. Query, however, whether, in aggregate, this is a bad result. Generally, more information is preferable to less. If the signal is accurate on balance, it may be better to have others draw the inference than not. This, of course, does not speak to any particular case.

37. Or the creditor may simply attempt a form of blackmail and use bankruptcy to make the future threat more credible. See Posner, "Gratuitous Promises in Economics and Law," 6 *J. Legal Studies* 411 (1977) (analyzing a similar problem in contract modification).

principal shareholders. One response to this is an extended preference period for "insiders." But the problem is larger: because of the problem of diverse ownership, the interests of shareholders and creditors do not correspond. When the shareholders of a firm discover that it is likely that the firm is insolvent, they will realize that the advent of a bankruptcy proceeding will come as a "day of reckoning" for them in which they are entitled to get nothing. Their incentives, then, are to delay the advent of this day as long as possible and instead "gamble" with the remaining assets of the firm. They have nothing to lose by this course of action, and they may have something to gain.[38] When a firm is insolvent and has $100,000 in debts and only $80,000 in assets, it is unlikely that it would be in the interests of the creditors to have that $80,000 placed on number 20 at a roulette wheel in Atlantic City, but it clearly would be in the interests of the shareholders to do so.

Once one eliminates obviously improper tactical uses of bankruptcy (such as to reject collective bargaining agreements), shareholders of a firm, therefore, are likely to delay too long in filing a bankruptcy petition. Even where they can use bankruptcy for delay, their optimal strategy when dealing with an insolvent debtor will be to delay first outside of bankruptcy and then delay again inside of bankruptcy.[39] One may think that the creditors have the opposite set of incentives—to commence bankruptcy too soon. But this is probably wrong. As a group they have no incentive to commence a bankruptcy case too early (in the sense that the debtor is still solvent) or where nonbankruptcy negotiations would leave a larger pool. By doing so, although they get paid in full, they get no extra value from the shareholders. There are, moreover, reasons to think that the incentives of any individual creditor to start a collective proceeding (as opposed to pursuing its own remedies) also will lead creditors to delay. When the information about the debtor's insolvency begins to spread to the creditors, for example, the response of each individual creditor may be to try to collect first instead of starting the collective proceeding and hope that the preference period passes before someone else commences the bankruptcy proceeding.

This is not uniformly true. Consider a supplier of meat to a restaurant

---

38. See Baird & Jackson, "Corporate Reorganizations and the Treatment of Diverse Ownership Interests: A Comment on Adequate Protection of Secured Creditors in Bankruptcy," 51 *U. Chi. L. Rev.* 97 (1984); R. Brealey & S. Myers, *Principles of Corporate Finance* 392 (1981). In addition, psychological factors may lead the manager to be too optimistic about the firm's future chances. See R. Nisbett & L. Ross., *Human Inference* (1981).

39. This seems to be the case, for example, in *In re* Old Colonial Ford, 24 Bankr. 1014 (Bankr. D. Utah 1982). Nor is this "solved" by giving shareholders some mechanisms, as current chapter 11 does, for negotiating back some of the firm's value. They hold that power even if they first delayed using bankruptcy.

chain. Since postpetition deliveries are entitled to administrative expense priority, one might think that the supplier would want to see the debtor pushed into bankruptcy where it would be sure to be paid in full for future deliveries. Concerns such as these have sometimes created legal responses designed to induce suppliers *not* to push for bankruptcy. The six-months' rule giving priority to supplies to a railroad delivered within six months of a bankruptcy proceeding is perhaps an example of this.[40]

It is not, however, clear either that such a bankruptcy incentive exists on the part of suppliers or that such incentives, if they exist, would necessarily be bad. As for the first point, suppliers that are not completely fungible should be able to insist on payment for prepetition deliveries as a price for continuing postpetition deliveries. Moreover, the response of a supplier who fears a collective proceeding might be to insist on dealing on a COD basis instead of commencing a bankruptcy case.[41] As for the latter point, the supplier might seek administrative expense priority precisely because it fears the debtor is insolvent. In such cases, where there is a reasonable likelihood that the debtor is insolvent, it is not clear that supplier's action in filing a petition is detrimental to the creditors as a group.

In view of all these reasons—and particularly when one also notes the small number of bankruptcy cases commenced by creditors[42]—it is likely that a bankruptcy case typically will be commenced too late rather than too early. There will, to be sure, be exceptions, when bankruptcy is being used to the strategic advantage of a particular party. However, once most relative changes in the value of entitlements in bankruptcy are avoided, it seems fair to predict that the largest problem remaining will be that of bankruptcy cases that are commenced too late rather than too early.

Fashioning a solution to this problem, however, may not be easy. The most promising route might be to try to provide an incentive to the

40. This principle was first recognized in Fosdick v. Schell, 99 U.S. 235 (1879). See generally FitzGibbons, "The Present Status of the Six Months' Rule," 34 *Colum. L. Rev.* 230 (1934). It continues to be applied to railroad reorganizations, *In re* Boston & Maine Corp., 634 F.2d 1359 (1st Cir. 1980), although not to other debtors, *In re* B & W Enterprises, 713 F.2d 534 (9th Cir. 1983).

41. The supplier may then not jeopardize its chance of getting paid in full on outstanding debts.

42. Statistical Analysis Division, U.S. Bankruptcy Courts, table F-2A (1984) (1804 of 349,232—about one-half of one percent—of bankruptcy cases filed in 1983 were involuntary). This statistic is somewhat misleading, because most bankruptcy cases are filed by individuals to discharge debts, and one would expect those cases to be voluntary. Even as a subset of business bankruptcies—of which there were 58,986 in 1983—the number of involuntary cases is small. Id.

group that is most likely to learn first about debtor's insolvency to commence a bankruptcy case instead of to delay. That group would be the shareholders, through their agents, the managers. The problem with bankruptcy law from the perspective of shareholders is that there is nothing in it for them when a firm is insolvent. Their incentives, then, are to gamble with the assets instead of to commence the bankruptcy case. Perhaps one should consider devising a counterbalancing incentive—a sort of "bounty"—to encourage shareholders to file a bankruptcy petition at the appropriate time.[43]

The difficulty with this suggestion, of course, is that of fashioning the proper bounty.[44] One approach would be to calculate, in rough fashion, the net increased value of the assets owing to the use of the bankruptcy process and give the shareholders a portion of that difference in value. Thus, for example, someone—a court-appointed expert or the like—would calculate what the assets would have fetched if they had been broken apart piecemeal in an individual remedies grab race and what the assets actually fetched in the bankruptcy proceeding and allocate, say, 25 percent of the difference to the shareholders.[45] This could be given whether the debtor liquidated, was sold as a unit, or reorganized.[46]

No such solution will work perfectly. Any bounty fixed by a legal rule is likely to be either overgenerous or undergenerous. Moreover, it may be imprecise in its calculation, particularly where it requires the calculation of a fictional number—what the assets *would* have fetched had

43. For a discussion of bounties, see Landes & Posner, "Private Enforcement of Law," 4 *J. Legal Studies* 1 (1975); Becker & Stigler, "Law Enforcement, Malfeasance, and Compensation of Enforcers," 3 *J. Legal Studies* 1 (1974). The text discusses providing a bounty to shareholders. A system of bounties for creditors could also conceivably be designed, although it would be harder to do so. Any bounty that would give them more than payment in full might make a creditor too eager to commence a bankruptcy case (and would have to be counterbalanced by a system of penalties). Any bounty that gave less than that might not induce the creditor to file. (Instead of bounties, it would also be possible to fashion a system of penalties for delayed filings.)

44. In addition, one has to deal with agency problems: if the managers have the inside information, perhaps a portion of the bounty would have to be directed at them. See Easterbrook & Fischel, "Corporate Control Transactions," 91 *Yale L.J.* 698 (1982); Fama & Jensen, "Separation of Ownership and Control," 26 *J. L. & Econ.* 301 (1983).

45. One properly should net out costs. It may be simpler, however, to presume that the costs of bankruptcy for the parties (other than would be reflected in the value of the debtor's assets) match the nonbankruptcy costs for those parties.

46. The justification for this split of the going-concern surplus is vastly different from the usual justification for the split of that surplus in a chapter 11 reorganization. Here, it is used to encourage optimal use of the bankruptcy process; in the context of chapter 11 reorganizations the justification for a split in the context of §1129 is quite dubious. See Chapter 9.

there been no collective proceeding. Notwithstanding these caveats, it is worth considering whether it might be preferable to a system, such as the present, where there is no bounty at all and decisive factors leading to tardy commencements of bankruptcy cases. A bounty would function like the preference section: a rule-based solution to an incentive problem that it would be too costly to solve by means of a standard.[47] Although insolvency and the need for bankruptcy do not go hand in hand, a bounty based on the extra value gained by resorting to the bankruptcy proceeding states the correct incentive: no bounty when there is no benefit.[48]

47. It also implements a policy first embodied in the Statute of 4 Anne, ch. 17 (1705). In that statute merchant debtors were given an incentive to cooperate in locating their assets. A cooperative debtor could keep (in addition to his life) 5 percent of his assets and receive a discharge.

48. One may want to consider whether penalties for wrongful filings by debtors would also be appropriate, akin to those now imposed on creditors by §303(i) and (j). In the case of solvent firms the penalty could be imposed on the firm itself. But if the firm was insolvent and bankruptcy thought inappropriate nonetheless (because, for example, it was a one-creditor case), the penalty would have to be imposed on the shareholders or officers and directors. Otherwise, it would just be taking from the creditors to give to the creditors.

9

Reconsidering Reorganizations

THE REORGANIZATION provisions of the Bankruptcy Code constitute a stage in the historical evolution of creditors' remedies against business debtors, from common law receiverships to the formal process governing corporate reorganizations now embodied in chapter 11 of the Bankruptcy Code.[1] Because of this long history, much conventional wisdom has been generated and reflexively accepted about the usefulness of the corporate reorganization process. As a result, here, perhaps more than elsewhere in the provisions of the Bankruptcy Code dealing with rights among claimants, it is necessary to return to first principles to ascertain what a reorganization process should be doing and how it should go about doing it.

As we have seen—although it probably cannot be said too many times—there is a distinction between business failure and the problems bankruptcy law is designed to solve. A firm can fail—in the sense that its assets are better used elsewhere—whether it is owned by thousands of creditors and shareholders or whether it is owned by one person. The problems of business failure themselves are not bankruptcy problems. The resolution of them should not be thought of as bankruptcy-specific.

Bankruptcy law does have a role when there are numerous creditors and a potential common pool problem. But just as business failures can occur when there is no common pool problem, so, too, can a common pool problem exist in the absence of a business failure. The fact that a business may have liabilities in excess of assets itself says nothing about whether the assets should be doing what they are doing or something

1. This process is traced briefly in Clark, "The Interdisciplinary Study of Legal Evolution," 90 *Yale L.J.* 1238, 1250–54 (1981).

else. In the case of Manville, for example, it is entirely possible that the current use of its assets (as a construction supply company) is the best use of those assets, and that it would be worth assembling them for that purpose if Manville did not already exist. It is not inconsistent with that observation to further note that Manville may in fact be insolvent because of torts committed in its past.

There is, in other words, no correlation between whether firms should stay in business and solving a common pool problem.[2] If it is important for firms to stay in business because of the jobs they save or because of their importance to their communities, that policy should be implemented as a matter of general law. It should not turn on whether ownership of the business is diverse, as it will if the policy is located in bankruptcy law. It is wrong to think that there should be an independent substantive policy of reorganization law to give firms breathing space or to reorganize them to preserve jobs. These policies should not be bankruptcy policies. If a sole owner or unanimous group of owners could ignore these policies by avoiding bankruptcy, the fact that a common pool problem exists is no reason to import them into bankruptcy, where they will interfere with bankruptcy's core role as a collective debt-collection device. Instead, nonbankruptcy law decides who has rights to a firm's assets. The only question of relevance for bankruptcy is the most appropriate deployment for the group of the firm's assets given the initial entitlements.

Thus, chapter 11's reorganization provisions should be tested against the standard of whether they facilitate achieving the asset deployment of greatest benefit to the claimants as a group. A focus on the common pool problem indicates that this question is the proper one for bankruptcy law. The justification for chapter 11, in other words—and the measure against which its provisions should be examined—is whether the reorganized firm is better for its owners as a group than alternative uses of the assets.

Reorganizations as a Form of Asset Sale

From this perspective it is possible to set out a conceptual understanding of what a reorganization is. At least as a start, a reorganization may be viewed as one *form* of the kind of decision relating to asset deployment

---

2. This, however, is a common mistake. See, e.g., *In re* South Village, Inc., 25 Bankr. 987 (Bankr. D. Utah 1982).

that is made in any bankruptcy proceeding.[3] In a prototypical liquidation proceeding, for example, the firm's assets are sold to third parties for cash or securities. They may be sold piecemeal, in blocks, or as a unit. In all cases the decision maker in a liquidation proceeding should decide on the course of action that provides the most for the claimants.

The key conceptual difference between a reorganization and a liquidation is that in a reorganization the firm's assets (or most of them) are sold to the creditors themselves rather than to third parties. The principal distinction is *not* that the assets are kept together in a reorganization; they can be kept together in a chapter 7 liquidation proceeding as well if they are sold as a unit to a third-party buyer. Indeed, the policies of bankruptcy law—to gain the most for the claimants as possible—would demand that such a going-concern sale be made in a chapter 7 proceeding if doing so would bring more for the firm's assets than would another course. The key distinction between a reorganization and a liquidation is who are the new owners of the assets: third parties or the former claimants.[4]

Reorganization proceedings, then, are basically a method by which the sale of a firm as a going concern may be made to the claimants themselves. This process, like any liquidation procedure, involves two steps: first, the assets of the firm are sold; second, the claims against the debtor are paid out of the proceeds of this sale.[5]

What differs in the situation in which the firm is sold to its own claimants in a reorganization is that the valuation of the proceeds out of which the claims against the debtor are to be paid is more difficult. In a straight piecemeal liquidation either the assets are distributed in kind to secured claimants (thus mimicking their nonbankruptcy rights) or the assets are sold (usually for cash) and the cash is distributed to the parties, principally in the order of their relative nonbankruptcy entitlements. In a going-concern liquidation the business is sold to a third party, usually for cash and/or marketable securities. In either of these cases the valuation procedures are far from intractable.[6] The claims are measured, their relative priority is determined, and the proceeds, which because they are cash or marketable securities are easily valued, are

3. See Clark, supra note 1.
4. In a given reorganization, of course, there may be a mixture of both systems. Some of the firm's assets may be sold for cash. Shares in the reorganized firm may, moreover, be sold to a new investor.
5. I first proposed this as a way of viewing corporate reorganizations in Note, "Giving Substance to the Bonus Rule in Corporate Reorganizations: The Investment Value Doctrine Analogy," 84 *Yale L.J.* 932, 943–46 (1975).
6. See Clark, supra note 1, at 1252.

distributed to the claimholders in the order of their relative nonbankruptcy entitlements. In a reorganization, however, the proceeds from the "sale" out of which claims against the debtor will be paid will consist principally of new claims against the same firm. This makes the valuation of the payment to the claimants substantially more difficult because the value of the reorganized firm's securities will depend on its value as a going concern.[7] Determining these values without using a market pricing mechanism is one of the hallmarks of a bankruptcy reorganization proceeding.[8] It is principally these valuation issues that lie at the core of the reorganization chapter's provisions.[9]

The critical question to be asked in examining the reorganization provisions, then, is whether there is a net gain to the common pool from proceeding with a reorganization instead of a liquidation. The difficulties associated with a reorganization proceeding are in the valuation of the proceeds received—the reorganized firm's securities—upon the fictional sale of the firm back to its prebankruptcy claimants. Whether the process is a piecemeal liquidation, a going-concern liquidation, or a reorganization, nothing in the form of the process itself seems to call for a different standard of *allocation among claims* (the second step) in one type of proceeding than in another.[10] Because distributional questions should not affect the deployment of assets, this suggests that the relevant inquiry in choosing a chapter 7 liquidation (piecemeal or going concern) or a chapter 11 reorganization should be made at the first step when the decision is made as to which of these three routes should be taken. This decision should be made on the basis of which path provides the greatest

7. When the consideration consists of claims against the firm, valuing the consideration necessarily involves valuing the firm. See Blum, "Corporate Reorganization Doctrine as Recently Applied to the Securities and Exchange Commission," 40 *U. Chi. L. Rev.* 96, 110 (1972).

8. See Blum, "The Law and Language of Corporate Reorganizations," 17 *U. Chi. L. Rev.* 565, 569 (1950).

9. §§1111(b), 1121–29; *In re* Barrington Oaks General Partnership, 15 Bankr. 952 (Bankr. D. Utah 1981). These provisions state the basis for determining who formulates a "plan" and what sorts of constraints exist on the terms of a plan, and they provide a set of procedures for approving the plan. These provisions also demonstrate that the universe of potential arrangements (e.g., whether bondholders get debentures or common stock) is expanded greatly when the consideration used to pay off claims is other than cash or market-tested equivalents. Their absence in chapter 7 reflects the substantially easier valuation and payment questions that confront a sale of assets for cash or market equivalents.

The change in relative values (this time in favor of secured creditors) implemented through §1111(b) is cogently criticized in Eisenberg, "The Undersecured Creditor in Reorganizations and the Nature of Security," 38 *Vand. L. Rev.* 931 (1985).

10. See Brudney, "The Investment Value Doctrine and Corporate Readjustments," 72 *Harv. L. Rev.* 645, 677 (1959).

aggregate dollar-equivalent return from the assets—a determination that should be made without considering the claims outstanding against those assets (this consideration becomes relevant at the payout but not at the sale stage).

The rationale behind the original absolute priority rule can be seen in light of this reasoning. That rule, as announced by Justice Douglas in *Case v. Los Angeles Lumber Products Co.,*[11] seems designed to mimic relative nonbankruptcy entitlements. Under the absolute priority rule as articulated in *Case,* claimants were entitled to have their relative values respected in full, according exactly to their nonbankruptcy entitlements. The fact that there was a going-concern surplus to the assets as a whole was irrelevant.[12] This represented part of the value of the debtor's assets that the creditors had a right to over shareholders outside of bankruptcy, and the absolute priority rule respected that right inside of bankruptcy. Because the rigors of the absolute priority rule in practice turn on the accuracy with which valuations are made, the absolute priority rule was frequently circumvented in practice.[13] But the theory was one of respecting the value of nonbankruptcy entitlements.

Negotiations and Valuations in the Reorganization Process

The question remained, however, whether that expression of the absolute priority rule accurately captured the value of the nonbankruptcy entitlements of *junior* classes. In *Case* itself, Justice Douglas refused to consider "intangible" factors in applying the absolute priority rule.[14]

11. 308 U.S. 106 (1939). *Case* derived the doctrine from earlier equity receivership cases, such as Northern Pacific Ry. Co. v. Boyd, 228 U.S. 482 (1906), and declared that this "fixed principle" was inherent in the statutory language "fair and equitable."

12. 308 U.S., at 123 ("The fact that bondholders might fare worse as a result of foreclosure and liquidation than they would by taking a debtor's plan [of reorganization] can have no relevant bearing on whether a proposed plan is 'fair and equitable' under that section").

13. Blum, supra note 8; Friendly & Tondel, "The Relative Treatment of Securities in Railroad Reorganizations under Section 77," 7 *Law & Contemp. Prob.* 420, 423 (1940).

14. 308 U.S., at 122–23: "[Lower court findings that stockholder participation] will be beneficial to the bondholders because those stockholders have 'financial standing and influence in the community' and can provide 'continuity of management' constitute no legal justification for the issuance of new stock to them. Such items are illustrative of a host of intangibles which, if recognized as adequate consideration for issuance of stock to the valueless junior interests, would serve as easy evasions of the principle of full or absolute priority . . . Such items, in fact present here, are not adequate consideration for issuance of the stock in question. On the facts of this case they cannot possibly be translated into

Arguments of the shareholders that the firm was worth more with them than without them—and that this was an asset that the creditors did not have a right to outside of bankruptcy—were characterized by Justice Douglas as representative of a host of intangibles that would work to undermine the absolute priority rule. Yet in those arguments were the seeds of the present version of the absolute priority rule, embodied in section 1129 of the Bankruptcy Code. It provides a two-part test. First, individual creditors have a right, waivable only by their own individual consent, to receive as much as they would have in a liquidation under chapter 7 (the "best interests of creditors" test).[15] Second, a class of creditors has a right to insist on payment in full before any junior class can receive anything on account of its claims or interests (the original absolute priority rule), but this right can be waived by a vote of the members of the class that hold 50 percent in number and two-thirds in amount of the claims in the class.[16]

The justification for permitting waiver of the absolute priority rule by class vote is that, notwithstanding nonbankruptcy entitlements, the allocation of the going-concern surplus is properly the subject of negotiations among classes of creditors.[17] This kind of reasoning, however, should be examined with care. Exactly *what* is being negotiated and *why* is it a proper subject for negotiations in the bankruptcy framework?

The underlying justification for a reorganization process, seen in terms of bankruptcy as a collective debt-collection device, must be that the assets are worth more to the claimants themselves than they would be to third parties. Robert Clark has suggested that the reorganization process "made economic sense whenever there were no or few potential outside buyers with accurate and timely information about the true state of affairs and future prospects of the business or when the process of searching for and educating outside buyers would itself be very expensive."[18] We will examine shortly the circumstances under which this justification might hold true. Suppose, for the moment, that it holds true some of the time. This justification suggests that the extra value attributable to selling the business back to the prebankruptcy claimants is the

money's worth reasonably equivalent to the participation accorded the old stockholders. They have no place in the asset column of the balance sheet of the new company. They reflect merely vague hopes or possibilities."

15. §1129(a)(7). There is an exception for loans whose maturities have been reinstated pursuant to §1124. See Chapter 2.

16. §§1126, 1129(a)(8), 1129(b).

17. See J. Trost, G. Treister, L. Forman, K. Klee, & R. Levin, *Resource Materials: The New Federal Bankruptcy Code* 335–39 (1979).

18. Clark, supra note 1, at 1252.

difference in the value of the firm owned by them and what a third party would be willing to pay for it. This means that the baseline protection for an individual claimant should be what the assets could be sold for in a liquidation, assuming they were sold for their highest and best use. It is improper, even accepting this rationale for the reorganization process, to establish the baseline protection for an individual claimant as that of a piecemeal liquidation standard.

Thus, it is likely that the proper subject for negotiation, even accepting the premise that reorganizations are justified, is smaller than commonly recognized.[19] One should be negotiating only over the difference in value of the assets, put to their highest and best use, in the hands of a third party and the value of those assets in the hands of the prebankruptcy claimants. There is, however, a more troublesome question associated with this justification for the reorganization process. This justification for chapter 11's negotiation rules ultimately rests on the ground that having it permits the claimants as a group to enjoy a larger asset pie than otherwise. Any other justification simply masks an inquiry into the wisdom of initial entitlements and is not an expression of bankruptcy policy.

When one focuses on this, however, one realizes that negotiations for their own sake are not desirable. The question is whether the benefits of negotiating how to split the surplus obtained by selling the assets back to the claimants instead of to third parties is worth the cost of those negotiations. This requires making some assessment of both the costs and benefits expected from the negotiation.[20]

Many of the costs of negotiation are clear. In any process that avoids marketplace pricing mechanisms, there will be innumerable disputes about the value of the assets, and the value of the claims against those assets.[21] There will also be disputes about the relative values that the various classes are adding to the future well-being of the enterprise.[22] In addition, because the process of voting over the surplus is determined

---

19. Generally, the "best interests of creditors" test of §1129(a)(7) is treated as if it is a piecemeal liquidation standard. Nothing in that section or its policy, however, suggests that is the proper interpretation. See Jackson, "Bankruptcy, Non-Bankruptcy Entitlements, and the Creditors' Bargain," 91 *Yale L.J.* 857, 893 & n.168 (1982).

20. A detailed and persuasive examination of this question, also concluding that chapter 11's rules have not been shown to be justified, is contained in Baird, "The Uneasy Case for Corporate Reorganizations," 15 *J. Legal Studies* 127 (1986).

21. See, e.g., *In re* Atlas Pipeline Corp., 39 F.Supp. 846 (D. La. 1941); *In re* Merrimack Valley Oil Co., 32 Bankr. 485 (Bankr. D. Mass. 1983); *In re* Landmark at Plaza Park, 7 Bankr. 653 (Bankr. D.N.J. 1980).

22. This point is made in Baird, supra note 20, at 142.

by class-wide vote, it becomes important to structure the classes properly; but there may be no absolute answer to the question of "proper" classification.[23] (Should, for example, a creditor that is contractually subordinated to another be placed in the same or a separate class? I have seen no answer to this that, under various valuation assumptions, would not invite strategic placement.) Thus, new procedural rules must be formed—such as classification rules[24]—and these new procedural rules inevitably bring costs when compared with a world (sale of assets to third parties) where similar rules would not be necessary.[25] The groups, moreover, are negotiating distributional issues in a bilateral monopoly context, and any time this is done there is some danger that the distributional conflicts will interfere with the optimal deployment result.

There is another, less obvious, cost. For firms that are insolvent, diverse ownership creates vastly different incentives for different groups of owners. Specifically, it is in the interests of shareholders to delay. Any event that fixes values today, such as a sale of assets or even a consummation of a plan of reorganization, leaves them with nothing as their baseline entitlement. When a group has nothing to lose by delay, that group will in fact favor delay. Much of the law of bankruptcy must concern itself with that incentive. It drives, for example, the notion of adequate protection for secured creditors, so as to require a group that might benefit from delay to pay for it. No similar device, however, exists (or can be readily devised[26]) to require shareholders to compensate unsecured creditors for the costs of delay. Accordingly, if things turn out worse, the creditors pay for it. If things turn out better, the unsecured creditors may get some of those benefits, but they do not get them all.[27]

---

23. Some of the problems with manipulations of the classification system are explored in D. Baird & T. Jackson, *Cases, Problems, and Materials on Bankruptcy* 665–72 (1985); see also *In re* Pine Lake Village Apartments Co., 19 Bankr. 819 (Bankr. S.D.N.Y. 1982).

24. §§1122, 1123.

25. Sometimes it may be necessary to classify, if it became crucial to resolve a dispute over whether steps to sell assets were cost-justified. Most of the time, however, this would not appear to be a significant problem.

26. Shareholders are protected by the doctrine of limited liability. Nor should it necessarily be abrogated here, for many shareholders may have little say over what a few shareholders (or management) do. Perhaps penalties could be attached to managers or large shareholders, but it is not clear that these devices would work particularly well, especially where the harm from delay reached millions of dollars.

27. See generally Baird & Jackson, "Corporate Reorganizations and the Treatment of Diverse Ownership Interests: A Comment on Adequate Protection of Secured Creditors in Bankruptcy," 51 *U. Chi. L. Rev.* 97 (1984). This is the root problem of a case such as *In re* Lionel Corp., 722 F.2d 1063 (2d Circ. 1983). The creditors wanted to sell a profitable operating subdivision of Lionel for cash; the shareholders predictably resisted. The Second

Thus, the *process* of negotiation itself can be used to implement delay.

Outside of bankruptcy, the event of insolvency permits general creditors to withdraw their contributions to the firm and stop the delay. It is a right to freeze the value of assets at a particular time and take away from the shareholders the possibility of future gain.[28] Bankruptcy law should respect the relative values of these rights, just as it respects the relative values of innumerable other rights. When bankruptcy procedures are used to delay this cash-out, absent a corrective cost imposed on the group that benefits from the delay, these procedures skew non-bankruptcy relative values and interfere with the common pool solution bankruptcy offers.

To minimize these costs, Mark Roe has suggested, in an astute analysis that is sensitive to the types of concerns expressed here, that firms in a chapter 11 reorganization be required to make a stock issuance to the public of 10 percent of the total stock the firm will ultimately issue.[29] In this way a value of the enterprise as a whole can be obtained. Roe then would require the remainder of the claims against the enterprise to be issued as common stock and distributed (along with the proceeds from the 10 percent sale to the public) to the prebankruptcy claimants in accordance with their relative entitlements. In short, Roe's proposal would solve many of the costs associated with chapter 11 negotiations by reliance on market pricing mechanisms and avoidance of the negotiations themselves.

This proposal, however, although promising, would seem to be responsive to no particular normative view about what chapter 11 should be doing. It solves the negotiation problems, to be sure, but only by doing away with the negotiation process. To justify eliminating negotiations, one must assume that there was nothing warranting negotiation. It solves the valuation process by having the marketplace do the valuations. The justifications for a chapter 11 process, however, assume

---

Circuit ruled that the rights of the shareholders to control the reorganization process and promulgate a plan of reorganization overrode the creditors' rights to sell assets under §363. This reading, as a positive matter, rests on the not implausible assumption that Congress intended to give shareholders procedural rights of value in the reorganization process. The normative question of whether this can be justified as in the interests of the claimants as a group is, of course, another matter.

28. As such, it can be viewed as an option. See Black & Scholes, "The Pricing of Options and Corporate Liabilities," 81 *J. Pol. Econ.* 637 (1973). These are often the result of covenants or default clauses. See Smith & Warner, "On Financial Contracting: An Analysis of Bond Covenants," 7 *J. Fin. Econ.* 117 (1979).

29. See Roe, "Bankruptcy and Debt: A New Model for Corporate Reorganization," 83 *Colum. L. Rev.* 527 (1983).

that it is valuable either because its claimants have better knowledge about the value of the firm or because valuable contributions are being made to the future well-being of the firm by the various claimants. Roe's solution "solves" the negotiation and valuation problems currently existing in chapter 11 by assuming that neither of these justifications holds any force. But, as we shall see, if one reaches that conclusion, there is no longer any need for a Chapter 11 process.

Why Not Eliminate Chapter 11?

It is to that—the $64,000 question in the field of corporate reorganizations—that we now turn: why have a separate reorganization process at all?[30] Consider, first, the justifications for negotiating based on dividing the surplus gained by using chapter 11 instead of chapter 7. This assumes there is such a surplus. One argument supporting that assumption is that buyers will not pay as much as the assets are worth because they lack information that the current owners have as to the real value of the assets.[31] This argument, however, seems suspect. The question must be: "Better valuations compared to what?" To say that the market might undervalue because it lacks access to adequate information might be true in the abstract.[32] But if market pricing mechanisms are not used, the alternative seems to be not the claimants themselves but the bankruptcy judge. To be sure, if the claimants can reach unanimous agreement among themselves, they can decide valuation issues. In those cases, however, they may not have needed bankruptcy's reorganization procedures at all. Moreover, it is one thing to say that insiders have superior information but another to assume that all owners asked to negotiate or approve a plan have such information. Owners include trade creditors, taxing authorities, and tort victims. They vote on plans of reorganization. In order to vote sensibly, they need to be given the information of the insiders as to *why* the business is worth more than the market thinks. If they can be given the information necessary to vote intelligently, how-

30. Again, for an interesting extended treatment of this question, see Baird, supra note 20.

31. Clark, supra note 1, at 1252.

32. Although the relevant information may sometimes lead the market to overvalue, reorganizations are not concerned with such cases because there it is in the interests of the parties to sell the assets to unsuspecting third parties. This informational point, moreover, has little empirical support. See Altman, "Bankrupt Firms' Equity Securities as an Investment Alternative," *Fin. Analysts J.* 129 (July–Aug. 1969) (finding no evidence of market undervaluations).

ever, one must then face the difficult question of why the market could not be given the information as well.

Thus it involves a nonsequitur to say that negotiations are appropriate because of superior information held by insiders; such a statement makes sense only when *all* share that information. Moreover, a second problem exists: unanimous agreement is unlikely. In that case claimants do not ultimately decide valuation issues. The claimants may negotiate among themselves to split the surplus, but the bankruptcy judge must assess value for two purposes. First, the bankruptcy judge has to determine what third parties would pay for the assets in order to ensure the baseline protection for any particular dissenting creditor in applying the "best interests of creditors" test of section 1129(a)(7). Second, in any case where the creditors are getting paid not in cash but in new pieces of paper against the reorganized enterprise, the bankruptcy judge must also value those pieces of paper to see whether they are adequate under the standard of section 1129(a)(7) to protect the dissenting claimant.[33] But one cannot determine the value of this paper in the abstract or by focusing on its nominal (or face) value. Instead, the value of these pieces of paper depends on the value of the firm itself.

There is no escaping the fact, then, that the bankruptcy judge must ascertain the value of the firm both in the hands of third parties and in the hands of its former claimants. This, however, suggests that the justification for chapter 11 based on undervaluations by third parties is suspect, at least in a society such as our current one with well-developed capital markets.[34] In order to make these valuations, the bankruptcy judge must be provided information about the operations of the firm in the hands of its prebankruptcy claimants. If the bankruptcy judge can be given such information in order to enable him to make an intelligent valuation determination, however, the question again is starkly posed. why cannot this information be given to marketplace buyers?

There seems to be no easy "because" answer. It may be more costly

33. It is thus unclear why in principle full valuation hearings are avoided if the absolute priority rule of §1129(b) is not called into play. See J. Trost, et al., supra note 17, at 337; cf. H. Rep. No. 595, 95th Cong., 1st Sess. 414 (1977) ("While section 1129(a) does not contemplate a valuation of the debtor's business, such valuation will almost always be required under section 1129(b) to determine the valuation of the consideration to be distributed").

34. Roe agrees, supra note 29, at 564–66. Indeed, the one study on the issue concluded that the securities of firms in bankruptcy were (because of high risk) *overvalued*. See Altman, supra note 32. To say that is not to say that markets worked comparably well in the nineteenth century. Clark's historical explanation, Clark, supra note 1, at 1250–54, may be correct; what may have changed is the presence of "better" markets.

to provide information to the world or more time-consuming to find buyers and have them put together deals.[35] But it is by no means certain, even putting aside the costs of consensual negotiations among claimants, that providing suitable information (for purposes of voting) to claimants without special inside information and then litigating disputed valuation questions before a bankruptcy judge (who also has to be provided with that information) would be *less* costly than finding suitable third-party buyers.

Moreover, there is likely to be a cost to valuations by a bankruptcy judge that is not present in marketplace valuations. Substantial evidence suggests that valuations by bankruptcy judges are systematically too high.[36] Most firms that reorganize fail shortly thereafter,[37] notwithstanding the fact that a bankruptcy judge has made a finding of "feasibility." There is no reason to believe that bankruptcy judges are particularly good valuators. And there are, moreover, some reasons to think that even good-intentioned bankruptcy judges may be overly optimistic about a firm's chances of success—and hence its value.[38] Cognitive processing

---

35. Investment bankers, for example, are not inexpensive in mergers or public offerings and are likely to be expensive in bankruptcy proceedings as well. Yet they *are* used in consensual deals; the question is their cost relative to the costs of the current bankruptcy process.

36. See, e.g., *In re* Nite Lite Inns, 17 Bankr. 367, 373 (Bankr. S.D. Cal. 1982); Blum, supra note 8, at 577–78 & n.18; see also Trost, "Corporate Bankruptcy Reorganizations: For the Benefit of Creditors or Stockholders?," 21 *UCLA L. Rev.* 540, 548–49 (1973); Brudney, supra note 10, at 679.

37. See LoPucki, "The Debtor in Full Control—Systems Failure under Chapter 11 of the Bankruptcy Code? (pt. 1)," 57 *Am. Bankr. L. J.* 99, 100–01 (1983). A high failure rate itself does not necessarily show that firms are being reorganized that should not be. Even if most firms fail, it may be correct to reorganize many firms. For this to be true, however, two conditions would have to be met: (1) it must be very difficult to distinguish firms with a high probability of succeeding from those with a low probability; and (2) the costs of failure must be low (in the sense that the liquidation value of the firm is not significantly less if an effort is made to reorganize and fails than if it is never tried at all). It is clear, however, that reorganizations are not justified on these grounds; instead, the judge generally makes a finding of "feasibility" without such qualifications.

38. There are, in addition, some reasons to think that the *methods* used are wrong. It has been a long-standing notion that the new securities of the reorganized enterprise need not sell immediately for what the bankruptcy judge says they are worth. See, e.g., *In re* Atlas Pipeline Corp., 39 F.Supp. 846, 848 (D. La. 1941) (describing the contrary view as "cold blooded"); Blum, supra note 8, at 578. See also Citibank, N.A. v. Baer, 651 F.2d 1341, 1347–48 (10th Cir. 1980) (argues, following "throes of bankruptcy," that "the actual market value of a share of stock may be considerably less than the pro rata portion of the going concern value of the company represented by that stock"). This evolved into using a prediction of what the securities would be worth in a couple of years. See Coogan, "Confirmation of a Plan Under the Bankruptcy Code," 32 *Case W. Res. L. Rev.* 301 (1982): "The valuation was not necessarily a statement of the entity's present earnings or present

errors may lead judges, like most individuals, to underestimate risks and to overestimate chances of success.[39] Few corrective constraints on such cognitive biases exist. Whereas market participants lose money when they make an incorrect decision, no similar consequence befalls a bankruptcy judge. Nor are there likely to be effective constraints analogous to the discipline a market imposes on buyers who make systematic errors.[40]

For all these reasons it is unlikely that an argument based on market undervaluations provides a strong justification for having negotiations among both informed and uninformed claimants followed by valuation decisions by bankruptcy judges. If so, undervaluation arguments also fail as a justification for the existence of the special reorganization rules of chapter 11.

The remaining justification for these special procedures is not one that depends on more accurate valuation mechanisms. It, instead, echoes the point first raised, and rejected, before Justice Douglas in *Case v. Los Angeles Lumber Co.*[41]—that the firm is actually more valuable in the hands of its current claimants than it would be in the hands of third parties. The existing shareholders, for example, might be thought to have special knowledge or expertise, and without their participation the firm would be worth less. This knowledge and expertise, moreover, is *not* an asset that the prebankruptcy creditors are entitled to (because they have no way of requiring shareholders to remain in the enterprise). Since as a result of this fact prebankruptcy shareholders also have a relative value,

---

market value, but rather, what its earnings and values would be should it recover from the trauma of reorganization, perhaps two or three years hence." This assumes, probably incorrectly, that markets cannot accurately value firms that have been through the "trauma" of bankruptcy or that one should only look at the upside of what the firm would earn *if* "it recover[s] from the trauma of reorganization." See Altman, supra note 32; Langbein & Posner, "Market Funds and Trust Investment Law," 1976 *Am. Bar. Found. Research J.* 1; Gilson & Kraakman, "The Mechanisms of Market Efficiency," 70 *Va. L. Rev.* 549 (1984). The effect is predictable, for "[j]acking up value is an obvious device for circumventing the absolute priority rule," Gardner, "The S.E.C. and Valuation under Chapter X," 71 *U. Pa. L. Rev.* 440, 456–57 (1943); see also Blum, "Full Priority and Full Compensation in Corporate Reorganization—A Reappraisal," 25 *U. Chi. L. Rev.* 417, 444 (1958).

39. See Tversky & Kahneman, "Judgment under Uncertainty: Heuristics and Biases," 185 *Science* 1124, 1129 (1974); see also R. Nisbett & L. Ross, *Human Inference* 17–192 (1980); Tversky & Kahneman, "Extensional Versus Intuitive Reasoning: The Conjunction Fallacy in Probability Judgment," 40 *Psychological Rev.* 293 (1983).

40. See Schoemaker, "The Expected Utility Model: Its Variants, Purposes, Evidence and Limitation," 20 *J. Econ. Literature* 529, 541 (1982); Schwartz & Wilde, "Intervening in Markets on the Basis of Imperfect Information: A Legal and Economic Analysis," 127 *U. Pa. L. Rev.* 630, 662–66 (1979).

41. See supra note 14.

this justification would suggest that it, too, should be respected in a way that the absolute priority rule fails to. The way to respect it is to permit the parties to negotiate with respect to how much these assets being contributed by the shareholders are worth to the firm's future operations. Thus, in order to maximize the value of the firm, this justification would suggest, it is necessary to keep the shareholders in place, which requires that the creditors reach a consensual deal with these shareholders as to how much of the value of the firm they are entitled to keep.

This justification, however, rests on dubious assumptions. In many firms there is substantial separation of ownership and control.[42] The people who work at the firm and its officers and directors are often likely to be insignificant shareholders of the enterprise. Usually, when the issue is the future value associated with having existing people stay on board, the individuals in question are employees and officers, not shareholders. Any group that takes over the business, be it a third party or the existing claimants, will have to deal with these people (if they do not have existing employment contracts) in order to have them continue with the firm. These negotiations are as necessary in bankruptcy as they are outside of bankruptcy, but they do not justify the current structure of chapter 11 where the negotiations relate to what portion of the going-concern surplus should be passed on to the *shareholders*. In publicly held companies it is odd to justify compensating the shareholders because the *managers* have firm-specific skills that give it greater value.

The ultimate issue is one of negotiations to acquire valuable post-bankruptcy assets for a firm. There is nothing unique about these negotiations to bankruptcy, and they would not seem to justify the existence of chapter 11's special negotiation rules. These rules may seem to have some value where the firm is closely held, in the sense of having a substantial overlap between its shareholders and its managers. In those cases, whoever acquires the assets, if it wishes to keep them as a going concern, may have to reach negotiations with the current managers/shareholders. Given that these bargains will have to take place in any case, it may seem appropriate to negotiate them in the context of a chapter 11 proceeding.

---

42. This point was first made in a seminal book by A. Berle & G. Means, *The Modern Corporation and Private Property* (1932). Many of the issues of corporate law must deal with the problems that arise because the interests of managers are not entirely congruent with the interests of shareholders. See Kraakman, "Corporate Liability Strategies and the Costs of Legal Controls," 93 *Yale L. J.* 857 (1984); Easterbrook & Fischel, "Corporate Control Transactions," 91 *Yale L. J.* 698 (1982); Fama & Jensen, "Separation of Ownership and Control," 26 *J. L. & Econ.* 301 (1983).

This, however, is not an independent justification for the chapter 11 process. The assets could still be sold in a chapter 7 proceeding to third parties who, in deciding how much to pay for the assets, would have to reach (or factor in the costs of) a deal with the existing managers/shareholders to turn over a certain percentage of the firm to them. Those negotiations may be difficult, but they are not constrained by the artificiality of the setting of a chapter 11 reorganization process. In the latter case the parties on both sides of the table are fixed, and there is an aspect of a bilateral monopoly. In the case of bargaining in the chapter 7 context, however, the buyer is not constrained; it is free to walk away from the negotiations, and other potential buyers can enter them (including, if they so desire, a coalition of existing claimants).

For these reasons the premises for negotiation in a chapter 11 process seem unproven and unpromising. Roe is probably correct in suggesting that they should be eliminated.[43] Once that point is reached, however, there seems to be no remaining justification for chapter 11 at all. Roe envisions a solution of an all common capital stock structure and a 10 percent float. But once the justifications for negotiation have been dismissed and one decides to rely on market pricing mechanisms, there is no particular reason to think that these artificial constraints on capital structures are necessary or appropriate.[44] There is no reason why chapter 7 could not be used as the vehicle to sell the firm as a going concern in the same way that companies go public. The assets of the firm could be transferred to a new corporation. This new corporation could have a capital structure placed on it. A public offering of the shares in the various classes of that corporation could then be made. Such a solution avoids the interclass conflicts about distribution that pervade chapter 11 (because it is in the interest of no class to oppose selling the assets for

43. Roe, supra note 29. He limits that suggestion to publicly traded companies. Id., at 563 n.126. As I suggest in text, however, there is no particular reason to require existing creditors (who, like trade suppliers and tort claimants, are not necessarily insiders) to remain owners simply because the prebankruptcy stock was closely held or there is a strong overlap between those shareholders and managers.

44. Roe relies on the Modigliani and Miller "irrelevance proposition" that if capital markets are perfect, information is perfect, all actors have homogeneous expectations, bankruptcy costs are zero, and no taxes exist, a firm cannot increase its value by altering its capital structure. See Modigliani & Miller, "The Costs of Capital, Corporation Finance and Theory of Investment," 48 *Am. Econ. Rev.* 261 (1958). But even though we may not know quite *why* the irrelevance proposition fails, in fact it does not describe the world as it is—a world with stratified capital structures. It thus is by no means clear that imposing an all common capital structure on a firm—even if it is subsequently recapitalized—has no costs. In any event, since creditors could adopt that rule in a chapter 7 liquidation if they desired, there seems to be no good reason to impose it on them in chapter 11.

more rather than less)[45] and avoids the artificiality of an imposed capital structure designed to solve that problem within the current confines of chapter 11.

To be sure, this solution would require changes in other legal rules. The powers of the trustee as well as the rules concerning the continuation of the business by the debtor in possession would have to be modified so as to permit what occurs in the operation of the business in chapter 11 to occur with equal ease in chapter 7.[46] It would also be necessary to eliminate existing laws that give investors different rights if a firm is liquidating rather than reorganizing because these are bankruptcy-specific rules that impede the asset deployment question. The trustee should be able to transfer to a third-party buyer not merely all the tangible assets of the firm but also the intangible ones, including such things as the lawsuits the firm has against others.[47] Some tax rules provide additional examples. Under existing law a tax-loss carryforward disappears when a firm is sold for cash, but it survives a sale of the firm for securities (even if they can be readily converted into cash), and it survives when a firm is reorganized under chapter 11.[48] The rule governing tax-loss carryforwards should be independent of what kind of bankruptcy proceeding is involved.

None of this, however, should obscure the underlying point. It would be letting the tail wag the dog to suggest that chapter 11 should be preserved (with or without its special bargaining rules) because existing rules permit certain assets—such as tax attributes—to survive only in the case of a reorganization. The preferable inquiry is to ascertain if anything in chapter 11's *procedures* provides claimants with a better opportunity to achieve a correct distributional result. If not, then there is no reason to preserve rules, in or out of chapter 11, that force its use.

45. There sometimes would be problems of deciding which class was the residual class on which to impose the power to make the decisions as to what kinds of efforts should be made to sell the assets and whether and when an offer to buy should be accepted. See Baird, supra note 20. Some costs (such as the decision to hire an investment banker) are far from trivial. But we commonly observe such deals outside of bankruptcy, which suggests that their net costs are perceived to be lower than other ways of selling securities.

46. At present, only in chapter 11 does the debtor presumptively remain in possession, see §§701–04; only in chapter 11 does the business presumptively continue to operate, compare §721 with §1108; and only in chapter 11 are sales in the ordinary course of business permitted without first obtaining court consent, §363(c)(1).

47. The sale, as we saw in Chapter 2, should be free of liabilities. See also Roe, "Bankruptcy and Mass Tort," 84 *Colum. L. Rev.* 846 (1984).

48. Internal Revenue Code §§381, 382.

10

The Fresh-Start Policy in Bankruptcy Law

Thus far the discussion has focused on the notion of bankruptcy as a collection device for claimants of an insolvent debtor, whether the debtor be a corporation, a partnership, or an individual. Another key policy in bankruptcy law applies only to debtors that are individuals. That policy, commonly seen as one of discharge, has nothing to do with the rights of claimants inter se or with the notion that bankruptcy exists to solve a common pool problem. It, instead, measures the rights of those claimants against those of a debtor who is an individual and ascertains what assets the individual should be able to keep out of the hands of his creditors. Discharge thus represents a substantive bankruptcy policy designed to upset nonbankruptcy entitlements. At least some of the time the rights of creditors outside of bankruptcy are irrelevant; that nonbankruptcy situation and its relative value are ignored in this context.

Discharge, moreover, is far from a trivial policy. Indeed, the principal advantage bankruptcy offers a debtor that is an individual lies in the benefits associated with discharge. Unless he has violated some norm of behavior specified in the bankruptcy laws, an individual who resorts to bankruptcy can obtain a discharge from most of his existing debts in exchange for surrendering either his existing nonexempt assets or, more recently, a portion of his future earnings.[1] Discharge not only releases the debtor from past financial obligations but also protects him from some of the adverse consequences that might otherwise result from that release.[2] For these reasons discharge is viewed as granting the debtor a financial fresh start.

1. The content of the debtor's half of the exchange depends largely on whether he uses chapter 7 or chapter 13. The differences between these two forms of bankruptcy are explored briefly infra Chapter 11.

2. The protections are described in §§524 and 525. See also Fair Credit Reporting Act,

The availability of discharge raises a series of questions that the notion of bankruptcy as a response to a common pool problem will not answer. For example, why does the "honest but unfortunate debtor"[3] enjoy a right of discharge at all? Why cannot an individual, confident in his knowledge of his own best interests, expressly waive the right when he seeks to obtain credit? Why does discharge, while allowing an individual to keep human capital and its proceeds as well as certain other assets, generally require him to surrender other forms of his wealth? Why, if we assume the appropriateness of a financial fresh start, is an individual freed of only some and not all adverse consequences of exercising his right to discharge? Why, finally, is discharge denied to an individual who had defrauded his creditors, but not to others, such as murderers or arsonists, who are morally reprehensible in other ways? This chapter will attempt to provide a framework for the analysis of these and related questions. The next chapter will apply that framework to aspects of discharge policy and exempt property.

The Fresh-Start Policy in Perspective

Because discharge policy historically has been embodied in bankruptcy law, we sometimes lose sight of the distinction between the law of discharge and the law relating to the creditor-oriented collection function of bankruptcy. As the first nine chapters have emphasized, most of bankruptcy law is concerned not with defining a debtor's right of discharge but with providing a compulsory and collective forum for satisfying the claims of creditors.[4] Discharge, which is available only to

---

15 U.S.C. §1681c(a)(1) (1982) (credit bureaus may keep and disseminate bankruptcy records for only ten years).

3. This phrase—which has passed into bankruptcy lore—comes from Local Loan Co. v. Hunt, 292 U.S. 234, 244 (1934) (bankruptcy "gives to the honest but unfortunate debtor who surrenders for distribution the property which he owns *at the time of bankruptcy*, a new opportunity in life and a clear field for future effort, unhampered by the pressure and discouragement of preexisting debt").

4. Indeed, from a historical perspective discharge is a relatively recent addition to bankruptcy law. The first English statute governing bankruptcy, passed in 1542 and called "An Act Against Such Persons As Do Make Bankrupt," provided for a collective proceeding but not for discharge. See 34 & 35 Henry 8, ch. 4, §6 (1542). A statute passed in 1705 allowed merchants to be discharged from their debts, see 4 Anne, ch. 17, §7 (1705), but the discharge was conceived more as a means to encourage merchant-debtors to disclose their assets to creditors (and thus to facilitate collection) than as a way to give individuals a fresh start. (Indeed, noncooperative debtors could be sentenced to death.) See Jones, "The Foundations of English Bankruptcy: Statutes and Commissions in the Early Modern Pe-

individuals,[5] could be granted without a collective proceeding,[6] just as a collective proceeding for parceling out existing assets could be provided without discharge. The fresh-start policy is thus substantively unrelated to the creditor-oriented distributional rules that give bankruptcy law its general shape and complexity.

Nonetheless, the link between the two in bankruptcy law is not surprising. If an individual were allowed to demand discharge as long as he agreed to surrender certain assets, he would be likely to avail himself of that right only when his liabilities exceeded the value of those assets. In those instances, collection rules based on a principle of first-come, first-served would function poorly. The creditors, faced with a common pool problem, presumably would want to coordinate their actions to ensure not only that all would share in the assets but also that their efforts to collect would not decrease the aggregate value of those assets. Because bankruptcy's collective process achieves such a coordinated sharing, it serves an appropriate function once the decision to discharge debts has been made.[7] Nevertheless, the justifications for discharge do not relate to the concerns of the creditors. Even though it makes sense to locate an individual's financial fresh start in a statute largely concerned with collection procedures, the social and economic concerns that lie behind the fresh-start policy are distinct.

It is important to recognize that the present contours of the fresh-start policy are not immutable. Our bankruptcy statutes have always taken discharge to mean, essentially, that an individual's human capital (as manifested in future earnings) as well as his future inheritances and gifts are freed of liabilities he incurred in the past. Yet a financial fresh start could be conceived in other ways.[8] It is not self-evident that bank-

---

riod," 69 *Transactions Am. Phil. Soc'y* pt. 3 (1979). The comparative newness of the fresh-start policy in bankruptcy law was noted in *United States v. Kras*, 409 U.S. 414, 446–47 (1973).

5. See §727(a)(1) ("The court shall grant the debtor a discharge, unless (1) the debtor is not an individual . . ."). Corporations must reorganize before they can obtain a discharge. The policy underlying this requirement has little to do with the rationale for the fresh-start policy.

6. For example, the law might grant discharge through a system of public notice whereby certain assets (such as future wages) would be freed from the claims of existing creditors. The mechanism of public notice would inform creditors of the debtor's election.

7. This conclusion might suggest that an individual should have the right to refuse discharge when the bankruptcy process has been forced upon him through an involuntary petition. One problem of implementing such a right lies in the difficulties in distinguishing voluntary refusals from those coerced by creditors. Even so, perhaps debtors generally should be given such an option (subject to a cooling-off period to ensure that they were not acting impulsively).

8. Many cases focus on whether a certain outcome provides a head start rather than a

ruptcy discharge should primarily protect an individual's human capital instead of his other assets. Like a corporation, whose going-concern value can be determined by capitalizing the return on its assets, so too can an individual's present economic value be roughly calculated by extrapolating from his expected use of existing forms of wealth, the most valuable of which is often his human capital. The line between an individual's present and future assets (or between tangible or financial assets on the one hand and human capital on the other) is therefore by no means clear.

Human capital and exempt property[9] have traditionally been protected by different legal regimes, making the reach of bankruptcy's fresh-start policy even more ambiguous. Although human capital and exempt property share an important attribute—creditors cannot force a debtor to work, nor can they reach his exempt property without his consent—bankruptcy law approaches the two species of assets differently. Bankruptcy law itself puts human capital, as it manifests itself in earnings, beyond the reach of creditors.[10] Yet it generally leaves to nonbankruptcy law the protection of other kinds of assets as exempt property,[11] which means that *bankruptcy's* fresh-start policy is largely limited to the protection of human capital. Our analysis should continue, then, by justifying bankruptcy's discharge policy and playing out the consequences of the fact that it is largely limited to human capital.

The Normative Underpinnings of a Fresh-Start Policy

Two Partial Justifications for the Nonwaivable Right of Discharge: Risk Allocation and Social Safety Nets

In considering why society would deem it desirable to allow individuals to discharge virtually all their debts in exchange for surrendering a

---

fresh start. See, e.g., Lines v. Frederick, 400 U.S. 18, 21 (1970) (Harlan, J., dissenting) (arguing that the Court's order "not only permitted [the debtor] a *fresh* start, it gave him a *head* start"); *In re* Cerny, 17 Bankr. 221, 224 (Bankr. N.D. Ohio 1982) ("Any other result would appear to go beyond the fresh start policy . . . and would effectively give a debtor a head start"). But this question, by itself, is empty. One must always ask fresh start or head start *relative to what?* A system that gave creditors access to *any* of the debtor's assets would detract from some absolute sense of a fresh start. One first needs a normative theory of what a fresh-start policy should be doing in order to evaluate what should and what should not be encompassed within it.

9. Within the term *exempt property* I am including property that is not usually referred to as exempt but on which creditors cannot levy, such as Keogh accounts. See infra Chapter 11.

10. See Local Loan Co. v. Hunt, 292 U.S. 234 (1934).

11. §522(b)(2).

portion of their total wealth, recent scholarly treatments of discharge law have focused on whether the debtor or the creditor is the superior risk bearer and whether discharge should be presumptively available. For example, in one of the first serious efforts to consider the extent to which discharge should be available, Theodore Eisenberg offers an explanation that, although not presented in these terms, would support a general presumption of *non*dischargeability.[12] He suggests that risk bearing is the main issue underlying the right of discharge: "A discharge system provides a technique for allocating the risk of financial distress between a debtor and his creditors."[13] That suggestion, in turn, draws on recent theoretical work on risk allocation in cases of contractual impossibility. That work has suggested that when the contract is silent, risk should be placed on the party best able to bear it. A party's ability to bear risk, in turn, depends both on its capacity to avoid deleterious events and on its ability to insure efficiently against those events.[14] Although he concludes that the superior insurer cannot be determined a priori, Eisenberg suggests that the debtor should be presumed to be the superior risk bearer because he is in "greater control of [his] financial activities than any particular lender" and thus better able to judge when he is taking on too much credit.[15]

Yet the conclusion that the debtor is likely to be the superior risk bearer is by no means beyond question. Discharge may be viewed as a form of limited liability for individuals—a legal construct that stems from the same desires and serves the same purposes as does limited liability for corporations. Richard Posner identifies two reasons why limiting the liability of corporations is sensible.[16] First, creditors of an enterprise are in a better position to appraise the risks of extending credit to an enterprise than are its shareholders and hence are superior risk bearers. Second, limited liability may be advantageous—at least in the case of publicly held corporations with widely dispersed ownership—because

12. See Eisenberg, "Bankruptcy Law in Perspective," 28 *UCLA L. Rev.* 953, 976–91 (1981); see also Weistart, "The Costs of Bankruptcy," *Law & Contemp. Probs.*, Autumn 1977, at 107 (discussing by analogy to contract impossibility whether discharge is desirable).

13. Eisenberg, supra note 12, at 981.

14. See Posner & Rosenfield, "Impossibility and Related Doctrines in Contract Law and in Economic Analysis," 6 *J. Legal Stud.* 83, 89, 92 (1977); see also Weistart, supra note 12, at 111–12 (suggesting the analogy between the contract law doctrine of impossibility and discharge policy).

15. Eisenberg, supra note 12, at 982.

16. See Posner, "The Rights of Creditors of Affiliated Corporations," 43 *U. Chi. L. Rev.* 499, 507–09 (1976). See generally Halpern, Trebilcock, & Turnbull, "An Economic Analysis of Limited Liability in Corporation Law," 30 *U. Toronto L.J.* 117 (1980) (discussing justifications for the limited liability of corporations); R. Clark, *Corporate Law* ch. 1 (1986) (same).

the shareholders are likely to be more risk averse than the creditors and thus willing to pay to have the creditors bear a greater share of the risk.

Both of these reasons could also support limited liability for individuals. As to the first, the creditors of an individual, having gained experience through dealing with many debtors, may be more adept than the individual at monitoring his borrowing. This argument contradicts Eisenberg's analysis. Moreover, Posner's second justification for limited liability may be especially powerful with respect to individuals. To the extent that individuals can invest their capital in securities and various other income-producing assets, they can further their desire to avoid risk by diversifying their holdings. Yet an individual's capital may consist largely of *human* capital—especially in the case of a young person—and this particular form of property cannot readily be diversified by investing in assets with different risk characteristics.[17] Thus, like business associations that find the corporate form and its accompanying limited liability worth the increase in the cost of credit, individuals may also derive a net benefit from the limited liability that discharge affords them.

Even if we could determine whether the debtor or his creditor is more likely to be the superior risk bearer in any particular situation, risk-allocation analysis of this sort yields no more than a presumption. Such an analysis cannot explain why the presumption should be frozen into a nonwaivable right of discharge. Indeed, businesses commonly contract out of the presumption that creditors are better risk bearers than the shareholders. The corporate form is merely an alternative to other forms of conducting business—such as sole proprietorships and partnerships—in which the liability of the equity owners is not limited by statute. Guarantees and similar arrangements, moreover, permit circumvention of limited liability by contract even when the corporate form is used. Risk-allocation analysis by itself suggests no reason why this elective feature should not apply as well to the limited liability of individuals.[18]

If contract law does not provide a pertinent analogy, another area of law might. The nonwaivability of the right of discharge might be justified—although only partially—by the existence of various social insurance programs, such as unemployment insurance, Medicare, and Social Security. By this, I do not mean to imply that discharge is justified simply because it resembles other paternalistic social programs that have gained general acceptance. Instead, I mean only that against the background

17. See, e.g., A. Alchian & W. Allen, *Exchange and Production: Competition, Coordination, and Control* 162–64 (2d ed. 1977) (discussing attributes of human capital).

18. Individuals might well seek such limited liability by contract were it not provided by discharge. See Rea, "Arm-Breaking, Consumer Credit, and Personal Bankruptcy," 22 *Econ. Inquiry* 188, 191 (1984).

of general social programs bankruptcy's fresh-start policy may be justified in part because it reduces the "moral hazard" that those social programs create.[19] The existence of social welfare programs leads individuals to undervalue the costs of engaging in risky activities today because they can depend on society to bear a portion of the costs that may arise tomorrow. A person who breaks his legs while mountain climbing may be entitled to unemployment benefits, food stamps, health care, and the like. The knowledge that such assistance is available invites the individual to discount (although not to anything like zero) the costs of possible future injury when deciding whether to climb.[20] Accordingly, such programs can be viewed as a form of social insurance, paid for in the form of general taxes. Because the "rate" that any individual pays for the insurance is not geared to the probability that he will engage in a risky activity, such insurance creates what is commonly referred to as a *moral hazard:* a situation in which individuals systematically—and rationally—underestimate the real costs of engaging in a risky activity because some of those costs are borne by someone else.

If there were no right of discharge, an individual who lost his assets to creditors might rely instead on social welfare programs. The existence of those programs might induce him to underestimate the true costs of his decisions to borrow. In contrast, discharge imposes much of the risk of ill-advised credit decisions not on social insurance programs but on creditors. The availability of a limited nonwaivable right of discharge in bankruptcy therefore encourages creditors to police extensions of credit and thus minimizes the moral hazard created by safety-net programs. Because creditors can monitor debtors and are free to grant or withhold credit, the discharge system contains a built-in checking mechanism.[21]

The function of creditors as monitors and the role of discharge in

19. For a discussion of moral hazard, see A. Polinsky, *An Introduction to Law and Economics* 54–55 (1983).

20. See J. Elster, *Ulysses and the Sirens: Studies in Rationality and Irrationality* 85–86 (1979) (noting that "it is crucial that there is some correlation between the extent to which individuals engage in risky activities and their contribution to social welfare funds; otherwise their refusal to bind themselves would not be an expression of spontaneity, but an attempt to operate as free riders"); T. Schelling, *Choice and Consequence* 7 (1984) ("There is no getting away from it. Almost any compensatory program directed toward a condition over which people have any kind of control, even remote and probabilistic control, reduces the incentive to stay out of that condition and detracts from the urgency of getting out of it").

21. See Rea, supra note 18, at 192 (creditors who loan to consumers are "specialists in monitoring the consumer's asset position" and record of repayment and are in a position to withhold future credit). Rules are designed to take advantage of monitoring capabilities in many fields, see Kraakman, "Corporate Liability Strategies and the Costs of Legal Controls," 93 *Yale L.J.* 857, 888–96 (1984) (discussing the advantages of rules that place the risk of corporate misbehavior on corporate "gatekeepers").

providing incentives for such monitoring have important policy implications for social insurance. Consider, for example, John Weistart's suggestion that the federal government leave debts undischarged by guaranteeing that no one, regardless of his debts, be permitted to fall below a certain standard of living—the government would provide food, clothing, and shelter for debtors and help to minimize creditors' losses as well.[22] This proposal has at least two apparent virtues: debtors and those who depend on them for support would be assured the necessities of life, and creditors would retain the hope of eventually being paid in full. As Weistart notes, the proposed system has another feature that would arguably represent an improvement on the current system: it would extend protection only to people who need a discharge to keep them from falling below a certain standard of living. The difficulty with a solution whereby the government "use[s] its revenues to make grants to reduce the losses that creditors sustain,"[23] however, is that it aggravates the problem of moral hazard. An individual would "buy" insurance simply by paying his taxes. He would then have an incentive to incur large debts or undertake risky activities, because he would know that he could never fall below the minimum standard of living guaranteed by the government.

The importance of encouraging creditor monitoring in a society that provides other safety nets may help explain why the right of discharge is nonwaivable, but this explanation has its limits. If the reason for making bankruptcy's discharge nonwaivable is to lighten the burden on the public fisc by reducing reliance on safety-net programs, there are alternative means to achieve this goal that would restrict individual autonomy less than the existing discharge rules do. If discharge law were concerned only with furthering this narrow goal, it could simply allow the debtor, after bankruptcy, to shield from garnishment a sum equal to the average weekly value of the safety-net benefits he would otherwise be entitled to.[24] Bankruptcy's fresh-start policy, however, provides substantially broader protection to debtors. The question remains whether more satisfying explanations for that protection can be demonstrated.

Volitional and Cognitive Justifications

Perhaps the most general question raised by bankruptcy discharge is whether the nonwaivability of the right of discharge, although it inhibits

22. See Weistart, supra note 12, at 119–21.

23. Id.

24. The essence of such a rule exists outside bankruptcy. See Consumer Credit Protection Act §303, 15 U.S.C. §1673(a) (1982) (restricting wage garnishment).

a borrower's individual autonomy, does not in fact faithfully protect his interests and those of noncontracting parties. To my mind, the answer is a qualified yes. I will argue in this section that a key to bankruptcy discharge policy has to do with inherent biases—uncorrected by marketplace constraints—in the ways most individuals make decisions that lead them to overconsume and undersave. This view, in turn, is based on available evidence that suggests that many people systematically fail to pursue their own long-term interests when making decisions about whether to spend today or save for tomorrow. It is important to be precise about the problem I am identifying. The problem cannot be simply that people come to regret some of their actions because they or their circumstances have changed over time. Rather, in order to justify nonwaivability, it must be shown that individuals *systematically* misjudge (or ignore) their own interests and that this bias consistently leads them in one direction—to consume too much and save too little.[25]

Several theories suggest that our decisions about how to allocate wealth over our lifetimes are biased in favor of present consumption. Recent philosophical work has focused on the fact that people's personalities change substantially over time—that individuals in effect become different people. Over time, the argument runs, changes in the way an individual evaluates his opportunities, desires, and risks lead him to experience regret.[26] In order to shield the individual from such regret and from the unfortunate consequences of these regretted decisions, society is justified in imposing "paternalistic" restrictions on the individual's freedom of contract, among them, the nonwaivability of discharge.[27]

25. In the next section it will be argued that societal intervention in the decisions of individuals to consume credit may be justified by the negative effects that those decisions may have on third parties.

26. See Parfit, "Later Selves and Moral Principles," in *Philosophy and Personal Relations* 137, 144–46 (A. Montefiore ed. 1973) (discussing the effects of changing personality on the validity of earlier promises); Note, "The Limits of State Intervention: Personal Identity and Ultra-Risky Actions," 85 *Yale L.J.* 826, 834 (1976) (arguing that identity changes create, in effect, "other persons" who must be protected by the state against the actions of the present self); Sen, "Rational Fools: A Critique of the Behavioral Foundations of Economic Theory," 6 *Phil. & Pub. Aff.* 317, 322 n.9 (1977); Dworkin, "Paternalism," in *Morality and the Law* 107 (R. Wasserstrom ed. 1971).

27. See Kronman, "Paternalism and the Law of Contracts," 92 *Yale L.J.* 763 (1983). Kronman distinguishes between disappointment and regret in that he uses *regret* to describe a situation in which "a person's goals have changed significantly, [so that] his earlier decisions may now appear irrational," id., at 780. *Disappointment* describes merely defeated expectations regarding the result of a particular decision. He suggests that "the idea of regret . . . does help explain . . . the inalienability of the debtor's right to a discharge." Id., at 785. Kronman adds: "One reason for giving the debtor a fresh start is to counteract the self-hatred he may feel, having mortgaged his entire future in a series of past decisions

For three reasons, however, this theory, by itself, seems inadequate as an explanatory tool. First, many of the short-term shifts in judgment that produce regret are not functions of fundamental shifts in personality.[28] Second, the theory of regret does not satisfactorily explain why individuals, in making decisions about the future, cannot adequately take into account the possibility that their ideas and values will change. It should not defy anticipation, for example, that the student radical of twenty may become a business leader—or a born-again Christian—by forty. Such about-faces, although by no means the rule, do occur with frequency and can be anticipated. Individuals have the luxury of observing how parents, grandparents, and others have changed with time. Third, the notion of personality shifts does not itself provide a basis for determining *which* of the individual's successive personalities should be recognized as his "true" personality, the one that expresses his real preferences.

Impulse Control: A Volitional Justification. The theory of regret, then, does not by itself explain why society should honor the preference of the future self at the expense of the present one. The concept of *impulse* provides at least a partial answer. When presented with a choice, individuals tend to choose current over postponed gratification, even if it is known that the latter holds in store a greater measure of benefits. Although, by itself, this behavior might be explained by a rational tendency to discount the value of deferred benefits, such an explanation does not account for this further observation: the same individuals will never-

---

he now regrets. Whatever its macroeconomic function, the bankruptcy discharge has a moral purpose as well—to restore to the debtor some measure of confidence in his capacity to arrange his future as he wishes, free from the dead hand of the past. Without such confidence, the debtor may lose even that minimum of self-respect that is a condition for his taking an interest in himself and his own life." Id., at 785–86.

28. Regret may arise from short-swing fluctuations in an individual's likes and dislikes rather than profound and permanent shifts from one personality to another. As Thomas Schelling has observed: "[The] phenomenon of rational strategic interaction among alternating preferences is a significant part of most people's decisions and welfare and cannot be left out of our account of the consumer. We ignore too many important purposive behaviors if we insist on treating the consumer as having only values and preferences that are uniform over time, even short periods of time." Schelling, "Self-Command in Practice, in Policy, and in a Theory of Rational Choice," 74 *Am. Econ. Rev.* 1, 5 (1984); see also J. Elster, supra note 20, at 41–42, 109–11 (discussing notion of multiple concurrent "selves"); T. Schelling, supra note 20, at 93–94 (arguing that deciding how to prefer one of several personalities becomes a problem akin to problems of social choice). In addition, some restrictions on planning cannot be attributed to protecting the decision maker's future self. The rule against perpetuities, for example, prevents a testator from exerting long-term control over assets after his death—when, presumably, he will no longer be experiencing personality shifts.

theless sometimes favor a rule that avoids the choice and requires them to defer gratification.[29] The famous literary example is that of Ulysses being tied to his ship's mast so that he could see the Sirens without losing self-control. A more modern example is the practice at gambling houses that permits an individual, at the start, to set a limit on the extent of his gambling, which is enforced by the house notwithstanding his subsequent protestations. More commonly, smokers give their cigarettes to a friend with instructions not to let them have one for a certain period. In all these cases people are consciously restricting their ability to act impulsively in the future.

This tendency of individuals to impose external restraints on their impulses provides a basis for deciding which of an individual's personalities to favor. One personality is the rational planner; it carefully assesses the relative merits of current versus future consumption. The impulse personality, in contrast, approaches life like an addict, unable to consider or plan for the future. The impulse personality does not authentically choose because it does not rationally ponder how a given decision will affect the individual's long-term interests. The rational self, to the contrary, suppresses the temptation to act impulsevely, resolving instead to act in accordance with the individual's entire set of wants and desires.[30]

The control of impulsive behavior, then, may provide a key insight on the road to justifying discharge policy. If unrestrained individuals would generally choose to consume today rather than save for tomorrow, and if this tendency stems in part from impulse, they may, given the chance, opt for a way of removing or at least restricting that choice in advance. If individuals cannot control the impulse themselves, they may want the assistance of a socially imposed rule, one that will simply enforce the hypothesized decisions of their fully rational selves.

The question remains what form such a rule should take. In some

---

29. See, e.g., J. Elster, supra note 20, at 36–111; Schelling, supra note 28, at 1 (describing impulse control as "anticipatory self-command"). A nice summary of experimental research on impulse control may be found in Rachlin & Green, "Commitment, Choice, and Self-Control," 17 *J. Experimental Analysis Behavior* 15 (1972): "When offered a choice between small immediate reward and a large delayed reward, pigeons invariably chose the small immediate reward. However, if pigeons are offered the choice now to restrict their future choices so that they can only select the large delayed reward, they will do so. In other words, they will choose now to eliminate the small immediate reward from their future opportunity sets."

30. See T. Schelling, supra note 20, at 94. This behavior has been analyzed in terms of agency cost theory (where it is viewed as an internal conflict of interest) by Thaler & Shefrin, "An Economic Theory of Self-Control," 89 *J. Pol. Econ.* 392 (1981).

circumstances the solution can be cast in the form of a cooling-off period—an interval during which an individual is permitted to undo the consequences of his impulsive behavior. Yet whereas particular kinds of credit transactions may profitably be subjected to a cooling-off rule,[31] it would be almost impossible to apply such a rule to all credit transactions without substantially undercutting the certainty of expectations essential to the functioning of a credit economy.[32] Consequently, it would be preferable to deal with impulsive credit acquisition by restricting an individual's ability to act impulsively in the first place.

More specifically, a legal rule discouraging the extension of credit might be the best means to assist individuals in controlling impulsive credit decisions. A nonwaivable right of discharge controls impulsive credit decisions by encouraging creditors to monitor borrowing. Other less intrusive rules would not be nearly as effective in controlling an individual's urge to buy or borrow on credit. Consider, for example, a rule that allowed an individual to decide for himself whether to be subject to a legally enforceable right of discharge. For such a rule to work, the individual's decision would have to be irrevocable—either it would have to be enforceable by some form of specific performance or the individual would have to face some nontrivial penalty for reneging on his initial choice. Otherwise, an individual in the grip of an impulse could revoke his decision to embrace or forego the right of discharge, just as a smoker can revoke his New Year's resolution not to smoke whenever he is seized with the urge to light up. Moreover, even if the decision were made irrevocable, problems would remain in setting limits on *when* the decision would have to be made. We are all relatively constant consumers of credit. As a result, the choice might be deferred beyond the time a nonimpulsive individual would choose. Conversely, the election itself might be made impulsively.

Thus, although the law might respond to the problem of impulsive credit behavior by letting individuals choose whether or not to waive the right of discharge, the problem may better be handled by means of a legal rule that uniformly disallows waiver. This kind of rule is justified by the kind of hypothesized Rawlsian original position touched on in looking at bankruptcy's compulsory collective system of debt-collection rules in Chapter 1: if the members of society had gathered together before the fact and had anticipated the human tendency toward im-

31. See 16 C.F.R. §429.1 (1984) (FTC regulation giving purchasers of goods sold door-to-door a three-day cooling-off period in which to void the sale).
32. See Kronman, supra note 27, at 796.

pulsive behavior, they would have devised a rule that denied them the opportunity to behave impulsively in the future.[33]

Incomplete Heuristics: A Cognitive Justification. Whereas impulsive behavior is volitional, there is a closely related cognitive feature of decision making that makes the need for a legal rule perhaps more evident. Individuals appear to make choices by processing information in a way that consistently underestimates future risks. This problem—which I shall call the problem of *incomplete heuristics*—provides a powerful argument that most individuals, *whether or not* they are prone to impulsive behavior or have undergone personality shifts, would favor a legal rule making discharge nonwaivable. Like impulsiveness, incomplete heuristics may lead the individual to favor present consumption in a way that does not give due regard to his long-term desires and goals. Likewise, incomplete heuristics would justify the decision to adopt a universal nonwaivable right of discharge on a Rawlsian ground: if individuals in the "original position" had recognized that they would face informational constraints when making credit decisions, they would probably have chosen a system that would make some of the consequences of their borrowing avoidable.

As used here, the term *heuristics* refers to tools that individuals employ in processing and assessing information. These tools aid us in digesting immense quantities of information by breaking it down into familiar groupings. Robert Nisbett and Lee Ross suggest that "the use of such simple tools may be an inevitable feature of the cognitive apparatus of any organism that must make as many judgments, inferences, and decisions as humans have to do."[34] Although reliance on these heuristic rules of thumb enables us to make decisions quickly, evidence suggests that it also causes us to make systematic cognitive errors such as "anchoring," "presence," and "representativeness." *Anchoring* occurs when a decision maker processes new information in a way that leaves him too close to the conclusion he would have reached in the absence of that information.[35] For example, proponents and opponents of the death

33. See J. Rawls, *A Theory of Justice* 136–42 (1971) (discussing the concept of the "veil of ignorance").

34. R. Nisbett & L. Ross, *Human Inference* 18 (1980).

35. See Slovic, Fischhoff, & Lichtenstein, "Cognitive Processes and Societal Risk Taking," in *Cognition and Social Behavior* 165, 172 (J. Carroll & J. Payne eds. 1976). A good example of anchoring and of the conservatism it engenders is found in the following: "[L]et us try an experiment with you as subject. This bookbag contains 1000 poker chips. I started out with two such bags, one containing 700 red and 300 blue chips, the other containing 300 red and 700 blue. I flipped a fair coin to determine which one to use. Thus, if your

penalty will tend to read new studies on the efficacy of the death penalty in a way that reinforces their original views.[36] *Presence* occurs when a decision maker gives undue emphasis to the factors most readily visible to him.[37] The enactment of much safety legislation, for example, can be attributed to presence. Such legislation often is passed after a spectacular accident, even though the probability that similar accidents will happen in the future is unchanged. *Representativeness* occurs when a person weighs normal (or typical) characteristics too heavily in his decision making.[38] If people are given a stereotyped character description, for example, and are asked to assess the likelihood that the person is a member of the stereotyped class or some other group, the responses generally underweigh the frequency in which the stereotyped class appears in the population as a whole.[39]

Much evidence indicates that the errors associated with incomplete heuristics, especially anchoring, lead decision makers systematically to

---

opinions are like mine, your probability at the moment that this is the predominately red bookbag is 0.5. Now, you sample, randomly, with replacement after each chip. In 12 samples, you get 8 reds and 4 blues. Now, on the basis of everything you know, what is the probability that this is the predominately red bag?

"If you are like a typical subject, your estimate fell in the range from 0.7 to 0.8 . . . If we went through the appropriate calculation, though, the answer would be 0.97. Very seldom indeed does a person not previously exposed to the conservatism finding come up with an estimate that high, even if he is relatively familiar with Bayes's theorem." Edwards, "Conservatism in Human Information Processing," in *Formal Representation of Human Judgment* 19, 20–21 (B. Kleinmuntz ed. 1968). Anchoring affects the speed with which people will change beliefs in the face of new evidence—an observation Francis Bacon made in somewhat different terms back in 1620. See F. Bacon, "The New Organon," in *The New Organon and Related Writings* 50 (F. Anderson ed. 1960).

36. Lord, Lepper, Ross, "Biased Assimilation and Attitude Polarization: The Effects of Prior Theories on Subsequently Considered Evidence," 37 *J. Personality & Social Psychology* 2098 (1979).

37. See R. Nisbett & L. Ross, supra note 34, at 43, 62, 122–27; T. Schelling, supra note 20, at 336; see also Slovic, Fischhoff, & Lichtenstein, supra note 35, at 170–72 (suggesting that people overestimate dramatic or publicized dangers and underestimate unpublicized dangers). Similarly, in considering whether to pass a "jobs tax" or similar bill, a legislator is likely to focus on the defined beneficiary class, ignoring (or understating) the job *losses* that may be caused by such a tax, because the victims are hard to identify at the time the bill is passed. Or a bankruptcy judge may decide that a firm should be kept in business because of the jobs it saves without considering the employment effects of a shift of the debtor's assets to other sectors.

38. See R. Nisbett & L. Ross, supra note 34, at 24–28, 115–22, 141–50; Kahneman & Tversky, "Subjective Probability: A Judgment of Representativeness," in *Judgment under Uncertainty: Heuristics and Biases* 32, 33 (D. Kahneman, P. Slovic, & A. Tversky eds. 1982); Nisbett, Krantz, Jepson, & Kunda, "The Use of Statistical Heuristics in Everyday Inductive Reasoning," 90 *Psychological Rev.* 339 (1983).

39. R. Nisbett & L. Ross, supra note 34, at 25–26.

overestimate chances of success and to underestimate the corresponding risks.[40] I have already suggested that this tendency leads bankruptcy judges to be relatively poor evaluators of firms in the context of corporate reorganizations. But it seems to apply to discharge policy as well. Such a tendency suggests that the methods people adopt for planning in the face of uncertainty do not accurately reflect their own subjective preferences for consumption versus savings. In particular, these heuristics apparently tend to lead individuals in one direction: toward *underestimating* the risks that their current consumption imposes on their future well-being. A debtor might think: "I will be able to repay the loan as long as I keep my job, my salary increases as it has in the past, I have no accident, the economy remains stable, etc." Underestimation of the risk of each of these events will tend to compound itself.

The existence of such biases, even if true, is, to be sure, not conclusive. We might, for example, attempt to adjust our ways of making decisions in order to compensate for the apparent bias produced by incomplete heuristics. The phenomenon of risk averseness, for example, may to some extent represent a countervailing reaction to that bias.[41] Never-

40. Consider the following analysis by Amos Tversky and Daniel Kahneman: "Studies of choice among gambles and of judgments of probability indicate that people tend to overestimate the probability of conjunctive events and to underestimate the probability of disjunctive events. These biases are readily explained as effects of anchoring . . . Note that the overall probability of a conjunctive event is lower than the probability of each elementary event, whereas the overall probability of a disjunctive event is higher than the probability of each elementary event. As a consequence of anchoring, the overall probability will be overestimated in conjunctive problems and underestimated in disjunctive problems.

"Biases in the evaluation of compound events are particularly significant in the context of planning. The successful completion of an undertaking, such as the development of a new product, typically has a conjunctive character: for the undertaking to succeed, each of a series of events must occur. Even when each of these events is very likely, the overall probability of success can be quite low if the number of events is large. The general tendency to overestimate the probability of conjunctive events leads to unwarranted optimism in the evaluation of the likelihood that a plan will succeed or that a project will be completed on time. Conversely, disjunctive structures are typically encountered in the evaluation of risk." Tversky & Kahneman, "Judgment under Uncertainty: Heuristics and Biases," 185 *Science* 1124, 1129 (1974). Much of the empirical work supporting the hypothesis of overoptimistic risk assessment is drawn together and discussed in R. Nisbett & L. Ross, supra note 34, at 17–192. Although none of this work directly addresses the risks of nonpayment in credit decisions, these hypotheses suggest that individuals will underestimate the risks inherent in repayment. Nonetheless, it would be useful to have this theory tested empirically by examining the effect of heuristic biases on credit decisions. Alan Schwartz and Louis Wilde think that the existing data provide no firm basis for deciding whether consumers underestimate the likelihood that they will default on their obligations. See Schwartz & Wilde, "Imperfect Information in Markets for Contract Terms: The Examples of Warranties and Security Interests," 69 *Va. L. Rev.* 1387, 1442–46 (1983).

41. Building on a related idea, Robert Scott has questioned the relevance of the literature

theless, the existence of the bias seems a salient fact. Adjusting our thinking to overcome the bias would be difficult, not only because the heuristic tools are too convenient to be readily abandoned but also because the nature of the bias can be hard to recognize.[42] Perhaps some of the adverse consequences of incomplete heuristics could be minimized by providing the individual with more information before he makes his decision or by allowing him to reverse his decision when more information becomes available. But because of the frequency of investment decisions and the strong preference for autonomy in our society, general solutions of this nature are probably too costly. Moreover, the amount of information needed to overcome the heuristic biases might well prove too difficult to acquire or retain.

If these solutions are not promising and if individuals are not likely

---

on incomplete heuristics to legal decision making. Scott, "Error and Rationality in Individual Decision-Making: An Essay on the Relationship between Cognitive Illusions and the Management of Choices" (draft). Relying to some extent on impulse control strategies, he "illustrate[s] how a self-imposed constraint on free choice will necessarily affect the process of judgment or decision-making. Suppose, for example, that an individual faced with a choice between alternatives A, B and C, voluntarily limits her choices to A and B. This behavior might be characterized as an "erroneous" judgment when measured against the theoretical ideal of the rational utility-maximizer, but it also may be characterized as the 'correct' response to a wholly rational strategy of self-control." Id., at 3. This line of analysis provides crucial insights into legal responses to human decision making. I do not believe, however, that Scott's important qualification has much impact on the question of long-term temporal consumption choices in the face of incomplete heuristics. Cognitive errors that lead individuals to underestimate risks in making consumption versus savings choices seem difficult to justify as a "rational strategy of self-control." To be sure, it warrants examination whether other strategies of behavior impose a form of self-control on individual decision making. We might, for example, sign up for pension plans as a form of self-control and then be reluctant to cancel them. But there is an underlying problem with this form of anlysis. If we truly do not understand our cognitive shortcomings, then there is no reason to believe that we will exercise sufficient self-control to correct for them. In setting up a pension plan, if I underestimate risks, presumably the plan I would set up would be too small measured against what I would do if fully aware of my use of incomplete heuristics.

42. See Kahneman & Tversky, supra note 38, at 32 ("[P]eople do not follow the principles of probability theory in judging the likelihood of uncertain events . . . [T]he deviations of subjective from objective probability seem reliable, systematic, and difficult to eliminate"); Schoemaker, "The Expected Utility Model: Its Variants, Purposes, Evidence and Limitations," 20 *J. Econ. Literature* 529, 545 (1982) (suggesting "that people are intendedly rational, but lack the mental capacity to abide by [expected utility] theory" and that "[t]his limited information processing capacity compels people to simplify even simple problems, and forces them to focus more on certain problem aspects than others"). Lee Ross and Craig Anderson suggest that these biases "can fairly be regarded as 'domain specific' failings of inferential strategies and tactics that are at least cost efficient (and probably generally quite accurate as well) in the organism's overall experience," Ross & Anderson, "Shortcomings in the Attribution Process: On the Origin and Maintenance of Erroneous Social Assessments," in *Judgment under Uncertainty*, supra note 38, 129, at 135.

to develop corrective devices on their own, the underlying problem remains: how do we free the individual from the adverse effects of incomplete heuristics and ensure that his decisions adequately reflect both his present and future wants and needs? The problem is not one of "pure" irrationality but one of incomplete information—whose incompleteness is unknown to the individual. Framing the problem this way allows us to see how a system premised on individual autonomy can accommodate certain socially imposed restrictions on activity that are commonly deemed paternalistic.[43] In light of evidence that the phenomenon of incomplete heuristics makes individuals overly optimistic about the future, the need to redress this problem offers a second normative justification for a nonwaivable right of discharge, one that complements the need for impulse control.

The Justification for a Socially Mandated Rule. The preceding discussion suggests that what seems initially to be a paternalistic justification for discharge may in fact be consistent with society's preference for individual autonomy. If people in the "original position" were aware of the problems of incomplete heuristics and impulsive behavior and about the difficulty of adjusting for these problems in making credit decisions, they presumably would opt for a legal rule designed to avert those problems in advance. The self-protective course is similar to the one that individuals follow when they take steps to remove their ability to act on later impulses.

A nonwaivable right of discharge may be desirable even if some individuals do not need its protection, as long as (1) a substantial number of people are likely to experience unanticipated regret as a result of impulsive behavior or unwitting reliance on incomplete heuristics and (2) it is either impossible or extremely expensive to distinguish those who will experience such regret from those who will not. To justify a nonwaivable general rule, one need not show that all people require its protection; it is enough to show that the rule promises to be less intrusive or less costly than one that attempts to discriminate between people who are likely to experience regret because of impulsive behavior or the use of incomplete heuristics and those who are not.

Development of more discriminating rules does not appear promising.

---

43. Restrictions that an individual would like to impose on himself are paternalistic only in a special sense. See J. Elster, supra note 20, at 85 ("To the extent that bans on cigarette advertisements stem from the actual or potential consumers themselves, who want to protect themselves against the Sirens of publicity, one should not talk about paternalism"); Calabresi & Melamed, "Property Rules, Liability Rules, and Inalienability," 85 *Harv. L. Rev.* 1089, 1113–14 (1972) (distinguishing between "self paternalism" and "true paternalism" and noting that the former "is not in any real sense paternalism").

If impulsiveness were the only problem, the necessary sorting might be accomplished by means of a rule providing for a cooling-off period or one that offered each individual an irrevocable choice of whether to embrace the right of discharge. But because the situation is further complicated by the problem of incomplete heuristics, it is much harder to fashion an accurate sorting device. The interval between the time one makes a decision on the basis of incomplete heuristics and the time one comes to regret that decision is likely to be substantially longer than the corresponding interval when regret follows an impulsive decision. The time lapse in the former case not only makes it more difficult to restore the status quo but also makes it harder to determine whether the regret is a product of incomplete heuristics or simply a response to a calculated gamble that one lost.

Our general belief that individuals should be able to set their own priorities suggests a larger problem with sorting devices. We cannot determine whether an individual makes rational credit decisions on his own behalf unless we know how he perceives his present and future wants and needs. When society attempts to distinguish individuals who act impulsively or who rely on incomplete heuristics from those who do not, it runs the grave risk of substituting an external social judgment for the subjective wants and needs of the individual.[44] Consider, for instance, the broad prophylactic rules by which the Bankruptcy Code regulates reaffirmation agreements.[45] The cases applying these rules contain little evidence that judges do anything other than impose their own view of what is in the individual's best interest in deciding which reaffirmations to permit.[46] Similarly, a case-by-case attempt to single out

44. See Kronman, supra note 27, at 796 ("[D]istorting passions may be at work even in the most mundane commercial transactions, but there is no way of distinguishing these cases from those in which the parties' judgment is unclouded without an intrusive and probably futile inquiry into their feelings and motives").

45. See §524(c)-(d). A reaffirmation agreement is an agreement by a debtor at or after bankruptcy to "reaffirm" an obligation notwithstanding discharge. Contract law has long permitted such waivers, despite the apparent lack of consideration. See Restatement (Second) of Contracts §83 (1981). The Bankruptcy Code, however, allows reaffirmation agreements only if made prior to discharge and subjects those that are made to a cooling-off period lasting the greater of sixty days or until the time of discharge. If the debtor is an individual, the court must advise him of the consequences of his actions. Moreover, in the case of consumer debts the court must approve the substance of the reaffirmation agreement unless the debtor was represented by an attorney during the negotiation.

46. See, e.g., In re Bryant, 43 Bankr. 189 (Bankr. E.D. Mich. 1984) (disapproving reaffirmation of debt on luxury automobile on ground that reaffirmation was not in debtor's best interests); In re Avis, 3 Bankr, 205 (Bankr. S.D. Ohio 1980) (disapproving reaffirmation agreement aimed at relieving the debtor's friend from liability as a co-signor of the loan on ground that approval "would weaken the 'fresh start' for the bankrupt").

individuals who need the protection of a right of discharge may result not in the identification of individuals whose choices do not accurately reflect their personal desires but rather in the identification of individuals whose choices strike judges as somehow odd or aberrant.

Rational Behavior and the Notion of Externalities

The above justifications for societal intervention in individuals' credit decisions rest on the claims that most people suffer distortions in making those decisions caused by defects in their volitional and cognitive processes, that they would agree in advance to protect against them, and that creating a nonwaivable right of discharge is a fairly effective way to achieve that protection. Another justification for a uniform, nonwaivable discharge rule, however, derives from the possibility that waiver of the right of discharge will generate externalities. The cost to the debtor of waiving that right might not reflect the costs to third parties of such a decision. To avoid these externalities, which individuals might systematically ignore if permitted to do so, it might be appropriate to impose a nonwaivable discharge rule. Such a rule helps curtail the costs otherwise imposed on a wide range of people—from family and friends, to business associates, to society in general.

Family members and perhaps even close friends who depend on another individual for support may need discharge to safeguard their own financial or psychological well-being. Yet the claim that society must protect such dependents through a nonwaivable right of discharge presumes that an individual will not sufficiently take his dependents' interests into account when making credit decisions. This assumption may appear improbable: aside from himself, these would seem to be the people the individual is most likely to consider when making his decisions. In that sense the interests of these third parties may simply be a part of his calculus and not external at all.[47] Moreover, these are the people perhaps best able both to negotiate with the individual to protect their interests and to monitor him to ensure that he does not ignore their interests when making credit decisions.[48] Nonetheless, the existence

---

47. See R. Axelrod, *The Evolution of Cooperation* 134–36 (1984) (demonstrating how teaching people to care about each other ameliorates the prisoner's dilemma, as each individual's preferences begin to incorporate those of others); Kronman, "Contract Law and the State of Nature," 1 *J. Law, Econ., & Organization* 5 (1985) (arguing that the notion of "union" between parties—such as husband and wife—can serve as a way of minimizing problems of enforcing contracts).

48. These negotiations may not eliminate the problem. Children, for example, may not

of informational barriers suggests that some externalities will inevitably be imposed on dependents. For example, dependents may have different risk or time preferences than the individual does, and it may be too difficult—or too costly—to inform him of these differences. The methods-by which people communicate their preferences to others may also cloud the accuracy of any information that *is* transmitted.[49]

In addition, an individual who is overburdened by undischarged debts may generate more general externalities. John Weistart has suggested that "excessive debt, with its attendant pressure on family and emotional stability and job security . . . [might] so inhibit productivity that there would be a net social gain from terminating costly collection actions, excusing the debts, and giving the poorer-but-wiser debtor a second chance."[50] Terminating collection actions would lead to a net social gain, however, only if continued collection efforts would yield a negative social externality. No such externality would result if the social costs of collection efforts—in the form of lower productivity on the debtor's part—were internalized by the debtor in the form of lower wages.[51]

Requiring debts to be paid out of future income may lead an indebted individual to devote more of his energies and resources to leisure, a consumption item that his creditors cannot reach.[52] By doing less work and enjoying more leisure, the individual undoubtedly decreases his

---

be able to negotiate effectively with an impulsive parent. Although a spouse may sometimes be able to intercede on the children's behalf, the use of an intermediary multiplies the risk of problems in the exchange of information.

49. When people are asked what they prefer, they sometimes exaggerate—taking a lesson from street-market haggling. For example, a debtor's friend may be much more risk averse (or preferring) than the debtor. If the friend believes that the debtor may make a different decision than he would, the friend may exaggerate his own risk averseness (or preference) in order to bring the debtor's ultimate decision more in line with his own inclinations.

50. Weistart, supra note 12, at 111.

51. Costs that are internalized are not externalities. See J. Dukeminier & J. Krier, *Property* 56 (1981).

52. Until the point of insolvency, the obligation to repay debts may lead an individual to work harder because such increased work levels will support higher net future consumption levels. If an individual is faced with no realistic prospect of an ability to pay his existing debts, however, this phenomenon is likely to reverse itself. This is a part of a question of the strength of income effects relative to substitution effects (i.e., the shift from work to leisure). In the wage area most economists view the substitution effect as dominant. See J. Hirshleifer, *Price Theory and Its Applications* 447–53 (2d ed. 1980). Once an individual makes the substitution, it may take some time for his wages to adjust downward (a form of wage "stickiness"). During that time society will suffer a net loss that is external to the individual.

productive contributions to society. As long as the productive value of those contributions is accurately measured by his wage rate, no externality results. But even if we assume that wages will accurately reflect a debtor's falling productivity, collection actions will still produce negative externalities if the individual's wages prior to his substitution of leisure systematically *underestimated* the marginal value of his productive efforts.[53]

Thus, there may be several reasons to believe that a negative externality exists. First, in an extreme case an individual may shift from work to leisure at no personal cost at all. Assume that Debtor owes Creditor $1 million and has an expected annual income of $50,000 if he continues in his current occupation. If the interest rate on the debt is more than 5 percent, Debtor will never be able to repay the debt even if all his income is devoted to repayment. Faced with a world in which he can either work—only to have Creditor garnish his wages—or enjoy leisure, Debtor's choice seems clear: because Creditor, not Debtor, bears the cost of the substitution of leisure for work, Debtor will make the substitution. In such a case the social cost of lost productivity exceeds Debtor's personal loss in shifting to leisure. The substitution creates an externality unless Debtor internalized the risk of that excess social cost by paying more for credit in the first place—a matter over which there is some debate.[54]

This example obviously poses an extreme case and ignores such factors

53. According to economic theory, wage rates are set at the margin—where the labor supply and demand curves cross. See A. Alchian & W. Allen, supra note 17, at 386; J. Hirshleifer, supra note 52, at 462. Across industries as a whole employers enjoy a consumers' surplus by paying this wage for people not at the margin (just as an employee who is not at the margin enjoys an economic rent—a producer's surplus). Id., at 189–225, 446–483. Thus, collection efforts may entail greater costs to society than those reflected by the individual's wage rate. Nonetheless, because the individual must forfeit *his* producer's surplus as well, there is no way of assessing whether the aggregate externality is positive or negative. Id., at 212, 478. For a number of reasons, such as monopsony, monopoly, shifts in labor markets, and "job stickiness," a worker's marginal productivity to society will sometimes not be reflected in his wage rate. But this fact does not suggest the existence of a systematic externality, either positive or negative. Cf. Frank, "Are Workers Paid Their Marginal Products?" 74 *Am. Econ. Rev.* 549 (1984).

54. Compare Meckling, "Financial Markets, Default, and Bankruptcy: The Role of the State," *Law & Contemp. Probs.*, Autumn 1977, at 13, 19–21 (arguing that the supply of credit is fully elastic and that the costs of discharge are therefore borne by debtors as a group, although they may be partially shifted from high-risk to low-risk debtors), with Weston, "Some Economic Fundamentals for an Analysis of Bankruptcy," *Law & Contemp. Probs.*, Autumn 1977, at 47, 48–51 (questioning the elasticity of the supply of credit and, accordingly, the extent to which costs of discharge are borne by debtors as a group).

as the ability of Creditor and Debtor to agree to have only a portion of Debtor's wages garnished.[55] Nonetheless, it illustrates the elements of an externality that may exist in less extreme cases. Creditor may bear at least some of the costs of Debtor's decision to substitute leisure for wages. Moreover, because of prohibitions on slavery and the like, Creditor has no effective way, at the time it extends credit, to negotiate with Debtor to prevent the substitution.[56] To be sure, Creditor will pass at least some of the additional costs back to Debtor in the form of higher interest charges; to the extent that Creditor does so, Debtor will internalize the costs and there will be no externality. The internalization, however, may not be complete,[57] in which case some measure of externality will persist.

There are other reasons to believe that externalities may exist in connection with credit decisions by individuals. Consider, for example, the nonconsensual extension of credit that occurs whenever a tort is committed. There is no contractual mechanism such as raising the initial price of credit that the tort victim (creditor) may use to force the tortfeasor (debtor) to internalize the full social costs of the latter's decision to engage in the tortious activity. The existence of an obligation to compensate the victim may lead the tortfeasor to substitute leisure for work without accounting for the costs of the switch.[58]

Moreover, in many professions an individual's wages systematically underrepresent the marginal social value of his labor. Many jobs have a social utility that wage rates do not fully reflect; the costs to the worker in such a job of substituting leisure for work are less than the costs to society. Consider the case of a law professor. Assume that all law professors are suited equally to either teaching or practice and that prevailing wage rates are set at a level that will attract the necessary number of law professors. Under these assumptions law professors pass up the prospect of significantly higher wages in order to remain law professors. They may prefer academia for the lower proportion of work to leisure—

55. It is in both Debtor's and Creditor's interest to negotiate such a result. Creditor will receive at least partial repayment and Debtor will continue to collect wages. In addition, statutory limits on garnishments are imposed under 15 U.S.C. §§1671–1677 (1982).

56. An obvious additional problem for any creditor would be the difficulty of monitoring the debtor to prevent shirking and other subtle forms of substitution. See generally Jensen & Meckling, "Theory of the Firm: Managerial Behavior, Agency Costs and Ownership Structure," 3 *J. Fin. Econ.* 305, 312–15 (1976).

57. See supra note 54.

58. An example is given in Jackson, "The Fresh-Start Policy in Bankruptcy Law," 98 *Harv. L. Rev.* 1393, 1422 n.95 (1985).

as economists use the term *leisure*[59]—or they may simply find the academic working environment more appealing. Even if they spend as many hours on the job, law professors enjoy more freedom in their work habits than is generally available to practicing lawyers.[60] In either case law professors must regard those nonpecuniary benefits as worth the wage differential, because they remain academics. Assuming the prevailing salary of law professors to be $75,000 a year and that of practicing lawyers to be $150,000, the law professor at the margin will be enjoying $75,000 of nonpecuniary benefits from his job. Because of the assumption of full substitutability of law professors for lawyers, the social benefit of the two jobs will be equal, notwithstanding the wage differential. But because wages can be reached by creditors whereas the other job benefit cannot, a law professor faced with a lifetime of wage garnishment might switch to a job with a lower wage level but similar amounts of leisure and nonpecuniary benefits. Even though the lower absolute level of entitlements (wages plus leisure and nonpecuniary benefits) reflects a socially less productive job, the switch would be less costly to the law professor than it would be to society.[61]

The fact that negative externalities may follow from certain behavior does not automatically justify a societal prohibition of such behavior. Society does not require us to become lawyers rather than law professors or janitors just because externalities may result. In this context the benefits of allowing us to choose for ourselves may simply outweigh the costs of our decision not to be as productive as we could be. But when the preference for leisure stems from an overconsumption of credit, a nonwaivable right to discharge might be justified in spite of the constraints it imposes on an individual's freedom to choose his own course.

At bottom, this line of analysis suggests that the right of discharge and the institution of credit itself have distinctive features that warrant special treatment. To give concrete meaning to this perceived need for special treatment, it is necessary to balance the social costs of allowing

59. Leisure is defined by economists as time spent on activities other than paying work. See A. Alchian & W. Allen, supra note 17, at 448; J. Hirshleifer, supra note 52, at 448 n.1.

60. I do not mean to imply from this observation that teaching is necessarily the more desirable vocation. Many individuals enjoy dealing with clients, engaging in the "sport" of litigation, or experiencing the excitement of a "done deal," and find practice far preferable to anything a law professor does. My point is that the differences between such jobs are not fully measured either by salary or by leisure (as traditionally defined), and that leisure is probably a closer substitute for nonpecuniary benefits than it is for wages.

61. Again, for an example, see Jackson, supra note 58, at 1423 n.98.

borrowing—that is, the risks of overindulgence due to impulsiveness, incomplete heuristics, and the failure to account for externalities—against the need for credit in our economic system.

The Advantage of a Creditor-enforced Limitation and the Costs of Discharge

Society allows individuals freedom in many areas that, on the basis of the rationales explored above, it might seem justified in restricting. We remain free to undertake numerous risky activities—such as climbing mountains, smoking, or skiing—even though impulsive behavior, incomplete heuristics, and disregard for externalities may lead us systematically to underestimate the personal and social costs of those activities. The crucial question relating to risky activities is not whether individuals should be altogether barred from engaging in them[62] but rather which such activities should be permitted and which should not.[63] In each case society decides—or should decide—at what point the expected costs of a given activity outweigh the prospective benefits to the individual and society.

Borrowing, however, cannot be regulated by means of the rough general rules employed in certain other contexts. Murder and prostitution, for instance, are subject to blanket prohibitions, which are enforced through the mechanisms of the law. But we may assume that society is not willing to prohibit extensions of credit altogether. Liquor and cigarettes, although not actually prohibited, are taxed: one possible reason (although by no means the only one) is that the government is trying to deter people from participating in the activity by making it more costly.[64] But what may work tolerably well for liquor does not necessarily work well for credit. Discharge aside, society cannot easily regulate the extent to which an individual may obtain credit unless the

62. In their clearest form prohibited activities are those that either violate a property right held by another, see Calabresi & Melamed, supra note 43, at 1124–27, or are prohibited by state fiat, most obviously in the form of a criminal rule. The extent to which society successfully discourages the activity, of course, may vary with the associated penalty as well as with the chance of detection.

63. All activities that we engage in, from sitting on the front porch to parachuting, involve lesser or greater degrees of risk. Risk is not all negative. Many arguably risky activities may also *increase* life expectancy, health, wealth, or whatever. But that does not change the point: it is still risk.

64. The rationale behind taxes on liquor and cigarettes is clearly complicated: subsidies for growing tobacco exist at the same time that cigarettes are taxed.

law imposes arbitrary limits on borrowing.[65] Besides being insensitive to an individual's particular circumstances,[66] such arbitrary rules would entail obvious administrative costs that would make them unattractive as a solution to the problem of regulating credit. Another shortcoming of such rules would be their inability to deal effectively with nonconsensual extensions of credit.

Discharge policy provides an alternative: it leaves the determination of whether to extend credit to *creditors,* who presumably are better trained in credit policy than are legislators, and who are better able, by observing individual debtors or by employing specific contractual covenants, to monitor individuals' consumption of credit.[67] To be sure, creditors would engage in some degree of monitoring even if the right to discharge were unavailable; they would still have an incentive to prevent an individual from falling so heavily into debt that he would lose the ability to repay. Discharge, however, heightens creditors' incentives to monitor: by providing for a right of discharge, society enlists creditors in the effort to oversee the individual's credit decisions even when the individual has not fully mortgaged his future. The availability of the right of discharge induces creditors to restrict the individual's credit intake and thus to assist in ensuring that he does not seriously underestimate his future needs. The nonwaivability of the right forces the individual—and hence his creditors—to leave uncommitted a portion of his future wealth. Moreover, a nonwaivable discharge rule does what other laws regulating credit cannot do as effectively: it allows individuals to present their particular needs and desires to creditors, thereby permitting creditors to tailor their responses to individual circumstances.

To exercise the right to a financial fresh start, the individual must pay a price. That price has two principal components. First, the individual may not obtain a discharge until he surrenders to his creditors a portion of his wealth—all of those assets that fit within certain defined categories. When particular noncash assets are worth more to the individual than

65. Rules prohibiting individuals from borrowing more than $10,000 and proscribing extensions of credit to individuals in excess of their average annual income for a five-year period are two examples of such limits. Individual credit institutions are free to adopt such rules, but in a competitive market it is unlikely that *all* will use the same rules.

66. Attempts to raise costs to individuals—to make them their own monitors—by devices such as taxing credit likewise seem unpromising, since they are no more discriminating vis-à-vis individual circumstances than the rules considered in the previous note. In addition, such devices may be unable to distinguish between credit to individuals and credit to businesses.

67. This is a form of what Renier Kraakman calls, in another context, a "gatekeeper" response. See Kraakman, supra note 21, at 888–98.

to his creditors, the debtor bears an additional cost, because he pays more to obtain the discharge than his creditors acquire. I shall call this cost the *asset-loss cost*. Second, by using bankruptcy in order to obtain a discharge, the individual puts others on notice that he might resort to it again. By exercising his right of discharge, then, the individual sends out a signal that may decrease his access to credit in the future.[68] Because these two costs deter people from seeking discharge, it is useful to consider whether discharge should cost the debtor anything at all.

The reasons for these disincentives to the exercise of the discharge right are in fact easily identified. To be sure, the extent to which an individual should be made to pay for the right of discharge is an open question, one whose answer depends on such uncertain factors as the importance of having access to credit and the actual degree of distortion introduced by volitional and cognitive factors. That the exercise of the right of discharge should come at *some* cost, however, is not—or at least should not be—an open question. Because of the nature of credit, free access to discharge would be disastrous for a credit-based economy.

Decreasing the costs associated with the *exercise* of the discharge right would simply increase the costs occasioned by the *availability* of the right. The availability of discharge represents a cost as well as a benefit to the individual debtor. The more readily available the benefit, the higher the cost of credit. If exercise of the right of discharge were costless, in the sense that individuals could wipe out their debts without surrendering any assets and without any future consequences, resort to discharge would be limited only by individuals' ethical sensibilities. There would be, in other words, an inevitable and substantial moral hazard problem.[69] In this situation, however, creditors would no doubt protect themselves by sharply curtailing the availability of credit. Exercise of the right of discharge, therefore, must entail some cost, unless society believes that the problems of impulsive behavior, incomplete heuristics, and externalities are so pervasive that the best way to deal with them is to abolish the institution of credit altogether.

For an illustration of this, consider the case of student loans. As a general rule, college and graduate students have few current assets but

68. By using discharge, the individual not only demonstrates that he is morally willing to use discharge but may also signal that he is impulsive or suffers from the use of incomplete heuristics. The duration of these reputational consequences, however, is limited by the Fair Credit Reporting Act, 15 U.S.C. §1681c(a)(1) (1982), which permits credit bureaus to keep and disseminate bankruptcy records for a maximum of ten years.

69. This point is made in a different context by Kaplow, "An Economic Analysis of Legal Transitions," 99 *Harv. L. Rev.* 509 (1986).

large future income streams. Using bankruptcy is relatively painless to them, as they have few assets to lose,[70] and obtaining a discharge offers a substantial benefit, as it frees up their future income stream from the substantial obligation of repaying a student loan. As a result it is not surprising that many students enthusiastically discharged student loans[71] before Congress dampened the practice by making student loans non-dischargeable.

Had the private market been providing funds, student loans would have become substantially more expensive than many other kinds of loans. To be sure, creditors might have resorted to other ameliorative devices, such as parent guarantees, which find a deeper pocket and perhaps increase policing. But this solution assumes that the individual *has* solvent guarantors, whereas at least a part of the idea behind educational loans is to make education available for people who do not already have access to existing forms of wealth to finance education. If students had been provided with the opportunity to opt out of their discharge right with respect to such loans in return for a significantly lower cost, undoubtedly many would have elected such an option. (In fact, any other choice would probably have made credit overly expensive.[72]) By doing so, the individual would effectively have mortgaged a portion of his future. Yet neither notions of impulse, incomplete heuristics, nor externalities suggests that the decision to *acquire* human capital is something that society should attempt to restrict by legal rule, because such decisions in fact evidence a desire to favor the future over the present.[73]

Excluding student loans from discharge in bankruptcy provides an

70. There may be a cost in that the use of bankruptcy may make it harder for them to obtain credit in the future. Even here, however, the six-year bar on a new discharge, §727(a)(8)–(9), and the fact that these people are unlikely to use bankruptcy again may reduce even that deterrence.

71. See Report of the Commission on the Bankruptcy Laws of the United States, H. Doc. No. 137, 93rd Cong., 1st Sess. pt. 2 140 (1973) (noting the "rising incidence of consumer bankruptcies of former students motivated primarily to avoid payment of educational loan debts" and predicting an increase in the trend).

72. See, e.g., Stiglitz & Weiss, "Credit Rationing in Markets with Imperfect Information," 71 *Am. Econ. Rev.* 393, 393–95 (1981) (discussing phenomenon of "adverse selection").

73. Another solution to the problem of widespread defaults on student loans would be to require individuals who invoke discharge to use chapter 13 and to pay out a substantial portion of their future wages in satisfaction of these claims. The 1984 amendments moved somewhat in that direction—although by no means limited to student loan cases—by permitting dismissal of a chapter 7 case that involves a debtor whose debts are primarily consumer debts, on the ground that its use would be a substantial abuse of the bankruptcy process and by requiring in such cases a pay-out in chapter 13 measured by what the individual is able to pay. See §§707(b), 1325(b).

example of how particular problems of credit availability may be solved by deviating selectively from the general guarantee of the right of discharge. As the statute currently is drafted, the beneficiary of the exclusion is the federal government, whose effective subsidy is lower. If the federal government, however, decides to curtail its student loan program, Congress could consider exempting *privately* funded student loans from discharge as a means of encouraging private sources to provide more educational credit to students. In fact, there is no obvious reason why such an extension has not already been made.

11

The Scope of Discharge and Exempt Property

BANKRUPTCY's financial fresh-start policy, because it represents an independent substantive goal of bankruptcy law designed to override nonbankruptcy entitlements, creates a conflict that does not arise in the analysis of bankruptcy as a collective debt-collection vehicle used to solve a common pool problem. There the basic role of bankruptcy law is to translate relative values of nonbankruptcy entitlements into bankruptcy's collective forum with as few dislocations as possible. Bankruptcy law's few substantive refusals to recognize the value of nonbankruptcy entitlements (such as with preferences or ipso facto clauses) relate to ensuring that the transition from an individual to a collective debt-collection regime is not the occasion of strategic advantage-taking.

Discharge law is quite another matter. If bankruptcy law intends to free a debtor's human capital from prebankruptcy claims, not only must the value of prebankruptcy claimants to pursue manifestations of that in the future be overridden but so too must prebankruptcy garnishments and the like.[1] Preserving relative values among creditors is no longer the focus, and when the focus has shifted, so too may respect for the rights of a lien creditor or the like relative to unsecured claimants.

This distinction, however, does not mean that the analysis in the first nine chapters no longer plays any role. Indeed, I believe that the opposite is true. To understand discharge law, we must precisely identify nonbankruptcy attributes and then relate them to bankruptcy's fresh-start policy. When that is done, we will see that bankruptcy's fresh-start policy— at least as currently embodied in the Bankruptcy Code—may have less

1. See Local Loan Co. v. Hunt, 292 U.S. 234 (1934).

to say about continued recognition of the value of those attributes than is commonly assumed.

The Scope of Bankruptcy Law's Fresh-Start Policy

First, however, we need to focus precisely on what is meant by bankruptcy law's fresh-start policy. Bankruptcy law has never been the sole source for protecting a debtor's wealth. It is, accordingly, incorrect to think of the subject of a financial fresh start as embodied entirely in bankruptcy law's discharge policy. Although bankruptcy's discharge policy withholds certain assets from the reach of prepetition creditors, some other assets of individuals never become subject to the claims of creditors in the first place. Recognition of this fact is an important first step toward examining the shape and structure of the Bankruptcy Code as it relates to an individual's financial fresh start. It makes our inquiry correspondingly more difficult, as the positive implications of the line bankruptcy law has drawn should be kept separate from the normative question of where the line should be drawn.

A relatively constant line has been maintained in bankruptcy law during this century: discharge, as defined by federal bankruptcy law, basically has focused on freeing an individual's future income from the claims of prebankruptcy creditors. Bankruptcy law has generally extended no similar protection to most of the individual's other assets.[2] But to say that they have not been protected by bankruptcy law is not to say they have not been protected at all. Nonbankruptcy law historically has placed certain existing property beyond the reach of creditors. The decision whether to make certain assets exempt has traditionally been left to the states, and the states' decisions have been incorporated into bankruptcy law, which has had simply the effect of nationalizing the scope of those exemptions.[3]

This distinction is important in examining bankruptcy law, yet it raises troubling normative questions of its own. As it stands, nonbankruptcy law (which applies across the board) defines certain assets that creditors cannot look to in pursuit of involuntary creditor remedies, but at least a portion of human capital *can* generally be reached by creditors, except when a bankruptcy proceeding is commenced. From the perspective of

2. See §541(a)(6). There is an exception for certain trusts in §541(c)(2) and for future inheritances and gifts by negative inference of §541(a)(5).

3. See Hanover Nat'l Bank v. Moyses, 186 U.S. 181, 188–90 (1902); *In re* Sullivan, 680 F.2d 1131, 1133–36 (7th Cir.), *cert. denied*, 459 U.S. 992 (1982).

the previous chapters, a "bankruptcy only" rule may appear troubling. Moreover, the accommodation currently embodied in the Bankruptcy Code is by no means ineluctable. Because the distinction between existing and future assets is not always clear,[4] a discharge system that focuses on protecting human capital but not existing tangible assets is but one possible solution. Nor is there an obvious reason why bankruptcy law has chosen to protect human capital yet has largely delegated the choice of exemptions to state (and nonbankruptcy federal) law.

For example, to relate the question to the policy persistently addressed in the first nine chapters: instead of making discharge policy a part of bankruptcy law, why not incorporate whatever protections nonbankruptcy law chooses to extend to the debtor? The reasons, I believe, have to do with the distinct role bankruptcy law serves in this context and the fragile tie that discharge bears to credit availability. In considering how to distribute assets among claimants in the first nine chapters, we were dealing with problems creditors caused to themselves through individual debt-collection efforts. In that respect the resulting common pool problem could be addressed most precisely by adhering to the value of the underlying nonbankruptcy attributes. Discharge policy, however, differs in a subtle way. Consider the case of human capital. A state law rule that said human capital would *never* be available to creditors would substantially reduce credit availability, especially for younger people (with few other assets) seeking to smooth out their lifetime consumption patterns. Thus, if human capital is to be protected, it needs to be protected on some trigger—at some cost.

The question is not, then, really one of bankruptcy law versus nonbankruptcy law—at least as we have defined that distinction in the first nine chapters. It is state versus federal. If there is a reason for federalizing protection of human capital, then there is a reason for placing that protection in a bankruptcy statute. The occasion for a debtor to trigger the protections that discharge gives to human capital is also likely to be the occasion for a collectivized collection system for creditors.

Thus the question really is: why is the special trigger rule applicable to human capital a federal rule? That question is less a bankruptcy law issue than it is an issue of general federal versus state regulation. Perhaps the answer in federalizing fresh-start law as it relates to human capital has to do with a belief that impulsive behavior, incomplete heuristics, and externalities generate a standard problem with respect to human

---

4. Many, if not most, of an individual's future assets are, at least in a predictive sense, in existence today.

capital that is amenable to a uniform, nationwide rule. Moreover, although no clear conceptual line separates one form of wealth from another, it is not surprising that federal bankruptcy law has traditionally afforded distinctive protection to human capital. Of the various forms of wealth, human capital not only is the least diversifiable but also has the most direct bearing on the future well-being of the individual and the people who depend on him. Yet even though human capital may be especially deserving of protection through bankruptcy law, it does not follow that such special protection is equally justifiable in all cases. If an individual holds large amounts of wealth in the form of human capital but has few other existing assets, he may justly be required to have the proceeds of his human capital subject to at least certain debts—in particular, debts such as student loans, which the individual incurred in order to acquire human capital.[5] In contrast, younger people can make perhaps the most persuasive claim to having their human capital stringently protected, since they are at an age when they are more likely to make decisions that will later induce regret. Whatever the cause of regretted decisions—be it impulsiveness, incomplete heuristics, or something else—someone who is fifty-five years old is less likely to experience such regret than someone who is twenty. Hence, discharge policy, in theory at least, should treat younger debtors more generously than older ones.

How does this observation translate into policy? It seems to call for a scheme that would protect a decreasing portion of one's wealth as one grows older. A focus on protecting human capital arguably reflects that policy. As one advances in age, the portion of one's wealth that consists of human capital is likely to decrease, while the value of one's other assets is likely to increase. Accordingly, limiting discharge to the freeing of human capital may in fact achieve the goal of protecting youth from later regret.

Concern for externalities may supply another reason why the protection of human capital is at the core of bankruptcy's discharge policy. Consider human capital in relation to durable forms of wealth. Like durable goods, human capital is consumed over time. These assets differ, however, in other respects. A durable good can be seized and its consumption halted abruptly: if an individual is deprived of his automobile, its future consumption value for him falls to zero and he will have to

---

5. We analyzed this in the last chapter as a consequence of making discharge too freely available. It might also be possible to view student loans as akin to purchase money interests on human capital. See Girardier v. Webster College, 563 F.2d 1267, 1277–78 (8th Cir. 1977) (Bright, J., concurring).

spend a certain amount of money to reacquire it or obtain a replacement. By contrast, in a world in which slavery is prohibited, human capital can be seized only by seizing its proceeds—that is, by garnishing wages if and when they are earned. Yet an individual has considerable control over the amount of future earnings derived from his existing human capital. If discharge did not protect human capital, many individuals would counter attempts at garnishment by substituting leisure, which creditors cannot reach, for wages. As suggested in the previous chapter, the debtor may not internalize the full cost of this substitution. By largely exempting human capital from the bankruptcy estate, society avoids this undesirable externality.

More subtle but equally important are the problems of measuring the present value of human capital. These problems probably cannot be solved with any degree of precision.[6] Although human capital is in some sense an existing asset, an individual can augment it by replacing leisure, which is something an individual can enjoy but his creditors cannot reach, with labor (including further education). Treating an individual's lifetime income stream as an existing form of wealth fails to account for this substitutability. Thus, to say that human capital is in existence at the time of bankruptcy does not mean that creditors are entitled to claim all of the debtor's measurable future income as an existing asset because some of that income will depend on future efforts by the debtor to acquire human capital—efforts over which the creditors have no control and that society does not require.

6. This may be illustrated by the following example. Assume that an individual was a salesman prior to his bankruptcy. Assume further that his creditors have a claim on all his human capital "existing" prior to bankruptcy, but no claim on his "future" human capital. Following bankruptcy, the individual goes to medical school and becomes a doctor. What portion of his wages as a doctor is a consequence of human capital in existence at the time of his bankruptcy? The question cannot easily be answered, because there is no simple measure of what portion of his human capital was acquired after bankruptcy, other than the *cost* of attending medical school. Yet that cost is unreliable as a determinant of value, in part because the cost itself (including tuition, lost wages, lost leisure, and "pain and suffering") is hard to calculate and in part because the degree of consumer surplus attributable to education is hard to measure. These problems arise in other contexts. For example, in community property (and perhaps other) states, courts must resolve to what extent a spouse can lay claim to his partner's income stream as a doctor because he was married to her while she attended medical school. See *In re* Marriage of Sullivan, 37 Cal.3d 762, 691 P.2d 1020, 209 Cal.Rptr. 354 (1984); Mahoney v. Mahoney, 91 N.J. 488, 453 A.2d 527 (1982); Krauskopf, "Recompense for Financing Spouse's Education: Legal Protection for the Marital Investor in Human Capital," 28 *U. Kan. L. Rev.* 379 (1980). Moreover, the problem exists even if the individual does not change fields of work: one's growth in a profession over time cannot sensibly be treated entirely as an asset in existence at the beginning of one's career.

Many reasons for safeguarding human capital—such as the avoidance of regret and the prevention of externalities—may apply as well to other kinds of assets. Accordingly, such assets may justifiably be protected under a fresh-start policy. But here, in contrast to the situation with human capital, bankruptcy law is generally not the source of protection. Two examples of such protection in current nonbankruptcy law are the exemptions of wage substitutes and certain durable goods from creditor attachment and hence ultimately from the bankruptcy estate.[7] The rationale for protecting wage substitutes—such as pension funds and retirement income—may be that they, like human capital itself, are among the least diversifiable assets.[8] The rationale for protecting durable goods may be that they constitute a form of savings, in the sense that their value is consumed over time. Because the main problem caused by impulsive behavior, incomplete heuristics, and externalities is the tendency to overconsume today and undersave for tomorrow, the decision of exemption law to protect savings for future consumption follows reasonably closely from the core notion of the fresh-start policy itself. Individuals may underestimate the extent to which they jeopardize their future consumption of existing durable goods when they borrow. This tendency can prove especially costly when the assets have substantially greater value to the individual than to any third party, since the defaulting debtor may have to pay off his debts in assets that are worth more to him than the repayment of the loan.[9]

Because the fresh-start policy could not protect all existing assets without sharply curtailing the availability of credit, the law needs some mechanism for choosing which assets to shelter. One solution would be to allow individuals to protect all those durable assets that they felt were essential to their future well-being or that, if turned over to creditors, would result in a substantial asset-loss cost. In practice, though, it would be necessary to impose some limit on the list of protected assets to prevent the debtor seeking discharge from asserting that all his property is essential. To solve this problem, society could formulate a relatively short list of assets considered vital to the typical individual's well-being. Property-exemption systems arguably serve that purpose. Another option

7. Exempt property becomes property of the estate under §541 but can then be removed from the assets the creditors may claim, §522.

8. See §522(d)(10)–(11).

9. If an asset—say an antique sofa that has been in the individual's family for one hundred years—is worth $1,000 to a creditor (its market value) but $2,000 to the individual (because of its sentimental value), the individual's loss when the asset is taken will exceed the creditor's gain.

may better reflect the individual's subjective belief about his needs for various assets in the future: society could allow the debtor to exempt a specific amount (say $25,000 worth) of existing assets (over and above human capital and, perhaps, wage substitutes) and leave the individual to decide which of his existing assets to exempt.[10]

Thinking About Kinds of Assets Protected from Creditors

How should one approach the question of which assets should be kept from creditors in a bankruptcy proceeding? Determining what assets are available for claimants depends, in all cases, on a sensitive analysis of the impact of nonbankruptcy rules on the scope and extent of assets. For corporations and other firms, this inquiry involves a question of determining the relative value of the entitlements vested in particular claimants that, in turn, determines the scope of the debtor's assets available to the general pool of unsecured claimants. Those questions, however troublesome, can be resolved without taking into account one further complexity found when individuals become debtors in bankruptcy, where the fresh-start policy of the law—whether bankruptcy law or nonbankruptcy law—dictates that certain assets are available only for the debtor (and perhaps his future creditors) but not for his prebankruptcy claimants. With debtors other than individuals, the problem cannot arise. To be sure, it is possible to envision certain assets that would not survive bankruptcy (such as letter of credit draws that had to be made by "Jones, as president" of the debtor when a trustee has taken over management of the debtor). It is, however, almost without meaning to think that a corporation as debtor could have an asset that is not available to its claimants—one that the corporation could keep following a bankruptcy proceeding but that the corporation's creditors could not reach or derive value from.

In contrast, the fresh-start policy introduces these difficulties into all individual bankruptcy cases. Thus with individual debtors, it is necessary to determine whether certain assets are exempt and hence unavailable to creditors[11] and to draw a distinction between present and future assets

10. Vern Countryman has argued for such a system. See Countryman, "For a New Exemption Policy in Bankruptcy," 14 *Rutgers L. Rev.* 678, 746–47 (1960). By adding a $4,150 "wild-card" exemption to the Bankruptcy Code in §522(d)(1), (5), Congress has taken a first tentative step toward providing debtors greater freedom to choose which assets shall be shielded from creditors. Some states have similar statutes. See, e.g., Ill. Rev. Stat. ch. 110, §12-1001(b) (1983).

11. §522.

of the estate.[12] These inquiries, however, can be aided substantially by focusing on the *attributes* of assets protected by the fresh-start policy. We can in fact return to a comforting theme of the first nine chapters and consider in this context the derivative nature of bankruptcy rules from nonbankruptcy entitlements.

Exemption law, historically, might have reflected the policies of a fresh start, but it did not reflect *bankruptcy* law's fresh-start policy because exemption law, until recently, was distinct from federal bankruptcy law.[13] Thus, when one focuses on bankruptcy law's fresh-start policy as embodied in the notion of a discharge, one focuses on the ability of a debtor to gain future income (and related future assets) and apply it to future creditors.[14] This division is impossible to achieve exactly, as debtors never enter the postbankruptcy period completely free of assets from their prior existence. As we have seen, for example, it is possible to characterize human capital as an existing asset for certain purposes.

Nonetheless, a fruitful line can be drawn that seems to capture the essence of what bankruptcy law is attempting to achieve, as a positive matter, in its discharge policy. Consider, for a moment, bankruptcy as a form of financial "death" for the individual in question. If a debtor, knowing he was to die tomorrow, attempted to gather together his assets, we would find three rough categories. The first category would consist of assets that are reachable today by creditors of the debtor, such as his computer, automobile, and books. The second category would consist of assets that are reachable today neither by his creditors nor by the debtor—assets that have value to the debtor if he lives but whose value would disappear if the debtor (and others) knew that he would die tomorrow. Human capital is in this category, as are its particular manifestations, such as law or medical degrees. Also in this category are special forms of nonbankruptcy property rights, such as spendthrift trusts and future inheritances. Finally, the third category would consist of assets that can be reached by the debtor today but are unavailable to his creditors unless the debtor first "cashes in" on them. In this category are traditional exempt property as well as certain types of rights such as Keogh retirement plans and a variety of miscellaneous rights such as a spouse's right of election against a will.

The first category of property is protected neither by nonbankruptcy

12. See §541(a)(6).

13. There is a bankruptcy set of exemptions in §522(d). However, a substantial majority of states have used the power granted to them under §522(b) to disallow their residents from using the exemptions specified in §522(d).

14. See §§727; 524; see also Local Loan Co. v. Hunt, 292 U.S. 234 (1934).

law nor by bankruptcy law's fresh-start policy. It, therefore, forms the property of the estate that the claimants share and for which bankruptcy's collective proceeding serves their interest. The second category of property, generally speaking, includes the types of property protected by bankruptcy law's fresh-start policy—assets that, like human capital, are available to the debtor only if he lives and that his creditors can likewise receive only if he continues to live. The core of bankruptcy law's fresh-start policy seems to dictate that these assets should belong to the debtor and the debtor's future creditors as and when they "mature" under nonbankruptcy law. As such, they are future assets that should not be considered to be property of the estate.[15]

The third category of property is perhaps more difficult to assess but gains in clarity by focusing on attributes. This is a form of property that, as a matter of nonbankruptcy law, the creditors cannot reach by their own actions, but the debtor can reach it, and once reached, it can often then be reached by the creditors.[16] The relevant attribute of such property—that it is not reachable by creditors until *after* the debtor reaches it—is shared by a form of property that creditors cannot get in bankruptcy: property that is exempt under applicable nonbankruptcy law.[17] Indeed, the *only* common attribute of property generally labeled "exempt" by state law is its freedom from involuntary creditor execution. But it should not matter what state law calls the property in question. The relevant question is whether it shares the essential attribute of exempt property—its unavailability for involuntary creditor execution.

This approach explains a case such as *McCourt*.[18] McCourt's wife had

15. The reasons for protecting human capital are explored earlier in this chapter. The reasons for "protecting" inheritances and gifts have to do with the fact that, even in the absence of such protections, creditors would be unlikely to enjoy them (because they would not be made if the sole beneficiaries were creditors). See Segal v. Rochelle, 382 U.S. 374 (1966).

16. Unless called exempt, this was property under old Bankruptcy Act §70a. See Countryman, "The Use of State Law in Bankruptcy Cases (pt. 1)," 47 *N.Y.U.L. Rev.* 407, 439–33 (1972). That policy arguably is continued by §541(c)(1), although the impact of that section is debatable in light of Congress's last-minute compromise on exempt property. Eisenberg, "Bankruptcy Law in Perspective," 28 *UCLA L. Rev.* 953, 972 n.60 (1981), discusses this point as follows: "The statements in the House and Senate Reports about the all inclusive scope intended for §541 were made at a time when the House version of the bankruptcy reform bill contained a system of federal exemptions that was available in bankruptcy regardless of state law. A system of federal exemptions that could not be stripped away by the states may have been viewed as fair compensation to debtors for the all inclusive nature of §541. Once §522 was recast on the eve of passage . . . the trade-off between federal exemptions and a broad view of §541 arguably should no longer govern."

17. See, e.g., N.Y. C.P.L.R. §5205.

18. 12 Bankr. 587 (Bankr. S.D.N.Y. 1981).

died, leaving all of her property to her father. Under applicable state law McCourt had a "right of election" against his spouse's will[19]: he could elect to receive, in lieu of what he was provided in the will (in this case, nothing), one-third of his spouse's estate. McCourt filed for bankruptcy after his wife's death but before the time for making the election had expired.

The consequences of making the election are clear. Upon making the election, McCourt would receive one-third of his spouse's net estate, and that would constitute property that his prepetition creditors could draw on to satisfy their claims. If McCourt did not make the election, the property would pass to the people named in the will, and McCourt (and his creditors) would get nothing.

Is the right of election something that passes to the trustee for the benefit of the prepetition creditors? The court analyzed the problem as one of state labels and concluded that "the interest in question is solely of a personal nature and not a property right."[20] But one should be suspicious of an analysis that looks to state law for labels instead of attributes. In this case, without even delving into the estate-planning features of nonexercise of a right of election that might suggest its waiver was more than an attempt to keep assets from claimants, the attribute is clear. A state court had previously held that a right of election "cannot be exercised in his behalf by a party acting in hostility to the spouse, nor may he be compelled to exercise it for the benefit of creditors."[21] Thus an examination of attributes reveals the right of election to be, from the perspective of creditors, exempt property, unavailable to creditors unless the debtor exercises it first. As such, at least for a debtor electing his nonbankruptcy exemptions, it should be considered exempt property within the purview of section 522(b).[22]

Focusing on attributes, and recognizing the key attribute of exempt property, is both proper and relatively easy. Consider, for example, a fairly common case—that of money in a Keogh retirement account. Many courts have considered whether these assets are shielded from creditors in bankruptcy either as a "spendthrift trust" under section

19. N.Y. Estate Powers and Trust Law §5–1.1.

20. 12 Bankr., at 589.

21. Dalisa v. Dumoff, 286 App. Div. 856, 141 N.Y.S.2d 700, appeal denied, 286 App. Div. 967, 146 N.Y.S.2d 477 (1955).

22. Had the debtor elected his bankruptcy exemptions, in §522(d), this approach would not work. Under the analysis in text and assuming (as is almost certainly the case) that the right of election would not be protected by §541(c)(2), one would conclude that the right of election passed to the trustee. One may doubt that this is what Congress intended, but it is still not clear that the solution is to manipulate the definition of *property*.

541(c)(2) or as exempt property under section 522(b). The overwhelming consensus is that they are not shielded under either section.[23] Although that conclusion is probably correct under section 541(c)(2),[24] it seems senseless as an interpretation of secton 522(b). Keogh Plans are self-employment retirement trusts established pursuant to congressional authority. As a condition of receiving tax deferral, the plans must exclude alienation or assignment of benefits. It is, however, possible for the plan beneficiary to withdraw the funds by forfeiting tax benefits and paying a tax penalty. This right of withdrawal, together with the fact that the legislative history of the Bankruptcy Code does not *list* Keogh Plans as property exempted by nonbankruptcy federal law, has led courts to conclude that this property is not exempt within section 522(b)(2).[25]

Consider as a matter of attributes, however, this result is wrong. The notion of exempt property in section 522(b) should be construed as referring to property having certain nonbankruptcy attributes, not to property that nonbankruptcy law labels "exempt."[26] Exempt property would then be categorized by looking at property that shares the relevant attribute of not being reachable by creditors as a class in priority to the debtor. All property sharing that attribute would be excluded from the reach of creditors in bankruptcy as well. Keogh Plans in fact share the one key attribute with mine-run exempt property. Because of the restrictions on alienation in a qualified Keogh Plan, assets are not avail-

23. See, e.g., *In re* Goff, 706 F.2d 574 (5th Cir. 1983); *In re* Graham, 726 F.2d 1268 (8th Cir. 1984); *In re* Johnson, 724 F.2d 1138 (5th Cir. 1984).

24. Spendthrift trusts, as distinct from exempt property, have *two* principal attributes: they (like exempt property) are not subject to creditor execution and they (unlike exempt property) are not reachable by the debtor. Keogh Plans fail this second test. See *In re* Lichstrahl, 750 F.2d 1486 (11th Cir. 1985); see also SSA Baltimore Fed. Credit Union v. Bizon, 42 Bankr. 338 (D. Md. 1984); *In re* Kwaak, 42 Bankr. 599 (Bankr. D. Maine 1984) (particular ERISA trust met spendthrift trust tests); but see Note, "Corporate Pension Plans as Property of the Bankruptcy Estate," 69 *Minn. L. Rev.* 1113 (1985); Note, "*Contra Goff:* Of Retirement Trusts and Bankruptcy Code §541(c)(2)," 32 *UCLA L. Rev.* 1266 (1985).

25. See *In re* Graham, 726 F.2d 1268 (8th Cir. 1984).

26. In many states property is exempt *either* because it is on a list of exempt property *or* because it is deemed inalienable. For example, in New York the assignment or transfer of a claim for personal injury is prohibited, N.Y. Gen. Obligation Law § 13-101, and under C.P.L.R. §5201(b), a "money judgment may be enforced against any property which could be assigned or transferred . . . unless it is exempt from application to the satisfaction of the judgment." Courts have had no problem in seeing claims for personal injury in New York as exempt under §522(b). See *In re* Mucelli, 21 Bankr. 601 (Bankr. S.D.N.Y. 1982). Under this analysis Individual Retirement Accounts (IRAs) should be treated differently from Keogh accounts, because IRAs are not "qualified" plans under §401 of the Internal Revenue Code. As such, they are not subject to the antialienation provisions of §401(a)(13) and are subject to creditor garnishment. See CCH Pension Plan Guide ¶2533.65.

able for involuntary creditor execution unless the debtor first withdraws the funds. Given that assets in a Keogh Plan are functionally exempt outside of bankruptcy, they should be exempt in bankruptcy as well.

The Effect of Discharge and Attributes of Exempt Property

To this point we have been treating bankruptcy law's discharge policy as fundamentally concerned with human capital and tracing out the consequences of bankruptcy law's incorporation of nonbankruptcy law rules on other forms of exempt property. But the current Bankruptcy Code, even in relation to nonbankruptcy exemption law and not the set of bankruptcy exemptions specified in section 522(d), does in fact affect nonbankruptcy exemption law in several ways. It is worth focusing on these provisions through the normative lens of discharge policy.

In section 522(f) nonconsensual liens and nonpossessory, non–purchase money security interests in certain categories of exempt property are avoided. In part, this section is necessary because of the bankruptcy exemptions of section 522(d). These kinds of property are protected by bankruptcy law itself and may have picked up liens or security interests outside of bankruptcy, where they may not have been considered exempt. But the lien avoidance provisions of section 522(f) apply as well to nonbankruptcy exemption systems, and it is that focus that concerns us now.

Consider, first, the ability to avoid certain consensual security interests on exempt property. In a regime that leaves the question of what property is exempt to nonbankruptcy law, is there a justification for this provision in bankruptcy? The question whether a debtor should be able to waive his right to exempt certain assets, as he in effect does by granting a security interest in those assets, is generally considered by nonbankruptcy law to be part of the broader question of consensual alienation of exempt property.[27] Society does not require the individual to buy particular types of exempt property in the first place; nor does it demand that he keep any such property he might acquire. Like the decision to invest in human capital (for instance, by attending college), the decision whether to defer consumption by using durable goods—perhaps the

27. The current practice of allowing security interests in exempt property is generally defended on the ground that the greater power to alienate exempt property by sale or gift includes the lesser power to encumber that property. See, e.g., State v. Avco Fin. Serv., 50 N.Y.2d 383, 388, 406 N.Y.S.2d 181, 183–84 (1980).

prototype of exempt property—over time is generally left to the individual's discretion.

Notwithstanding the individual's general freedom to alienate exempt property, bankruptcy law may still forbid him to subject such property to general (that is, non–purchase money)[28] security interests enforceable in bankruptcy. Federalizing fresh-start law as it relates to human capital can be justified, as we have seen, on the ground that a nationwide problem is involved that is amenable to a uniform rule. In contrast, the decision to leave exemption law to the states is perhaps justified on the view that the categories of property appropriate for exemption vary among states and that states are best able to tailor those categories to their citizens' particular needs. But even if states are better able to define general categories of exempt property, a federal rule barring creditors from enforcing certain security interests on such property may nonetheless be justified on the ground that the pervasiveness of impulsiveness, incomplete heuristics, and externalities arguably makes waiver of those exemptions a proper subject for uniform national legislation. When an individual *sells* an asset, he trades it for cash. In contrast, an individual who grants a general security interest in an asset retains possession and use of the asset but pledges to relinquish it upon the occurrence of a contingency—default—the probability of which he may underestimate because of incomplete heuristics. It is this latter aspect that makes the problem of security interests in exempt property distinct from the problem of sale and suggests why one may not simply be a lesser-included case of the other.

To say this, however, does not indicate why a ban on the enforceability of security interests on exempt property is a restriction enforceable in bankruptcy only instead of a federal rule applying across the board. The reason may be similar to the reason why human capital and its proceeds are exempt only in bankruptcy: a desire not to inhibit the ability of creditors and debtors to work out consensual deals outside of bankruptcy, to cover the wide range of cases where bankruptcy is not likely to occur.

Although a ban on the granting of fully enforceable *general* security interests in exempt property can thus be justified in light of the normative underpinnings of the fresh-start policy, purchase money security inter-

---

28. A purchase money security interest is a security interest retained by a seller selling on credit or taken by a lender whose loan is directly used to finance the debtor's acquisition. See Uniform Commercial Code §9-107 (1978). A general security interest binds specified assets (which may include existing assets) as security on a loan, whether or not the loan enabled the acquisition of those assets.

ests arguably should be treated differently. Unlike general security interests, purchase money interests are secured by the same asset that the extension of credit helped the debtor to obtain. Because the debtor's ability to acquire—and hence to consume—the asset in the first place derives from his waiver of the property's exempt status vis-à-vis the purchase money loan, purchase money security interests should be excepted from any general rule barring secured creditors from reaching exempt assets in bankruptcy.[29]

These justifications, however, only relate to consensual alienation, in the form of borrowing for current consumption by pledging an asset that the individual otherwise would want to keep. Involuntary creditor execution is a different story. In a case where involuntary creditor execution is the norm, the property will not be exempt under applicable nonbankruptcy law (because freedom from execution is the key attribute of exempt property), and there will be no occasion to use section 522(f). There may be occasions, however, where property is generally not subject to involuntary creditor execution outside of bankruptcy but where nonbankruptcy rules give special rights to particular kinds of creditors, such as tax claimants or tort victims.[30] In these cases the property's exempt status has been granted vis-à-vis general creditors only, not vis-à-vis special categories of creditors. In a regime where nonbankruptcy law determines what is exempt and when the special categories are nonconsensual instead of consensual, there is little reason for bankruptcy law to override that state balance. Even viewing bankruptcy law as drawing a distinction between present and future assets provides no basis for reassessing the state's limitation on this form of exempt property.

This point is related to a recurrent issue. Section 525 of the Bankruptcy Code prohibits governmental units from, inter alia, denying, revoking, or refusing to renew a license, permit, or similar grant based on a debtor using bankruptcy or based on a debt that was discharged in bankruptcy. This doctrine derives from *Perez v. Campbell*,[31] which, under the supremacy clause, struck down a state action that had refused, after bankruptcy, to renew debtor's driver's license because of nonpayment of an automobile tort judgment that had been discharged in bankruptcy.

How does a refusal to renew a driver's license if there are unpaid tort

---

29. This would be an alternative justification for treating student loans as nondischargeable. See discussion supra Chapter 10.

30. See, e.g., Calif. Code Civ. Proc. §704.140(c) (exception from exemption for causes of action for personal injury, claims of health-care provider for services related to the injury); N.Y. C.P.L.R. §5206(a) (homestead exemption does not apply to tax claims).

31. 402 U.S. 637 (1971).

judgments from vehicle operation interfere with a debtor's fresh start? In order to drive, the debtor must pay off the tort victim in full. This payment is likely to come from the debtor's future income and thus will infringe on his human capital to some extent. But this is true whenever a debtor wants to keep an asset that has passed through bankruptcy with an unavoided lien.[32] In all these cases the debtor is faced with a choice of paying the claimant from other sources of funds or losing the asset.

Analytically, the issue is no different from the following. If the state had provided the tort victim with a lien on a particular asset of the debtor, then the lien would pass through bankruptcy unless the debt had been paid in full or the asset was exempt property subject to the debtor's avoiding powers under section 522(f). The outcome should be the same whether the nonbankruptcy label for the tort victim's right is a lien on the debtor's assets or a cancellation right. The asset in question is a driver's license, but there is no reason to think that should make a difference. A driver's license undoubtedly is important, but that does not necessarily mean that it should be protected by bankruptcy law's fresh-start policy, particularly given the fact that, apart from human capital, bankruptcy law leaves to nonbankruptcy law the question of what is exempt property.

Even viewing bankruptcy law's fresh-start policy as drawing a distinction between existing and future assets would not seem to change anything. If Henderson is a member of the Chicago Board of Trade at the time of bankruptcy, for example, his membership is an asset of the estate. The fact that retention or renewal of it is subject to certain conditions (such as paying prepetition claimants who are also Board members) should not change the fact that one has defined an existing property right. This would be in contrast to the status of a membership that Henderson may acquire in the future. The possibility of acquiring an asset may be an expectancy, but it is not an existing asset.

The fact that the asset in question comes from the state would seem to change nothing. A person who has a driver's license but can lose it under certain conditions (such as nonpayment of a debt) would seem to have an existing property interest. Similarly, a person who has a liquor license or an environmental operating permit has an asset of value at the time of bankruptcy. The fact that he can lose the asset *after* bankruptcy for nonpayment of debts that would have occasioned its loss *during* bankruptcy (had the event of renewal come up during bankruptcy) should

---

32. See §524. See also Long v. Bullard, 117 U.S. 617 (1886); *In re* Tarnow, 749 F.2d 464 (7th Cir. 1984); United States v. Marlow, 48 Bankr. 261 (D. Kan. 1984).

make no difference with respect to the relative priority of the claimants.

The error made in section 525, then, consists in analyzing the two situations differently. The effect of the section is to make *all* forms of government entitlements in the hands of individuals equivalent to exempt property. Whether or not that is how bankruptcy's fresh-start policy *should* be cast, it is certain that the issue has never been analyzed in those terms because the attributes have been obscured by labels. In a world in which nonbankruptcy law is the source of exempt property, the proper reach of section 525 seems narrower. Bankruptcy law seems concerned with protecting future assets—assets that the debtor would not have if he were to die at the time of bankruptcy. Existing drivers' licenses, liquor licenses, and environmental operating permits would be deemed existing assets under this view, but many forms of governmental entitlements would not be. For example, a person who applies for a government job or a governmental benefit after bankruptcy and is refused on the ground that he has been through bankruptcy arguably has been the victim of interference with bankruptcy law's fresh-start policy, in the sense that he has been deprived of future assets because of a discharge in bankruptcy. As with human capital itself, the fresh-start policy may decide that this is a future asset that is not availale for prepetition creditors.

Similarly, retaliation by an employer in denial of jobs may appropriately fit in section 525. The core of bankruptcy's fresh-start policy is protection of human capital and its future manifestations. An employer who fires a debtor either because he used bankruptcy or because he discharged a debt owed to the employer or another is in effect attempting to treat the job as another asset over which the employer has leverage. As such, it seems analytically very similar to the power a creditor gains through garnishment on wages, and disregarding such garnishments is at the center of bankruptcy's fresh-start policy.

In all these cases analysis of the proper normative role of section 525 is aided by focusing specifically on what bankruptcy law's fresh-start policy protects—human capital and various other future assets—and on what role nonbankruptcy law plays in defining what property from his past a debtor may keep. A similar issue arises in the context of section 524. Assume that Insurance Company had provided Debtor with health and life insurance. As a result of Debtor's using bankruptcy, unpaid premiums on the policy are treated as prepetition claims and paid pro rata with other unsecured creditors. Debtor then receives a discharge. Subsequently, Debtor asks Insurance Company for a renewal of its policy. Insurance Company refuses to renew the policy (and assume that this refusal can be shown to be based on its policy of "no payment for outstanding debts, no renewal"). Is this an action by a prepetition claimant to collect on a discharged debt, proscribed by section 524?

At first glance, it may seem to be just that. But as we saw in Chapter 7, there is another characterization: the renewals of Insurance Company can be seen as a form of property right in which Insurance Company has a form of lien. How effective Insurance Company will be at achieving full payment will depend on whether or not Insurance Company has any sort of nonfungible commodity to offer. If its commodity is fungible, its policy will not result in payment because Debtor can go to another insurance company. But if the commodity is not completely fungible, Debtor might decide that it is better to pay the prepetition debt in full in order to secure the property than not. Any time a decision such as this is made, it means that Debtor (and his future creditors) get less of his human capital. But that is not the relevant question. Analytically, this appears to be a case of lien pass-through because it is a right that Insurance Company has that is distinct from the rights of ordinary, prepetition unsecured creditors. As with section 525, there is no reason to construe section 524 any other way in a world in which nonbankruptcy law determines what is exempt property.

These issues involving postdischarge consequences on prepetition creditors suggest another question about postdischarge effects on exempt property. Sometimes exempt property is defined in a way that exempts both the property and its proceeds.[33] Such definitions are akin to an exemption system that permits a debtor to shelter a certain amount of cash through bankruptcy and pose no particular postdischarge problems; such cash is an asset that the debtor (and his future creditors) are entitled to while the prepetition creditors are not. But more frequently exempt property is defined as referring to the property itself; proceeds received on the sale of the property are *not* exempt.[34]

In that case should a bankruptcy discharge protect not only the exempt property but also the proceeds of that property when under nonbankruptcy law the proceeds would not be exempt? Property that passes through bankruptcy as exempt under applicable nonbankruptcy law will remain exempt from the claims of postpetition creditors as well until its sale. At that time the debtor may have to share the proceeds with his

33. See, e.g., Calif. Code Civ. Proc. §704.010(a), (b) (exempting motor vehicles and, for a period of ninety days, proceeds); id., §704.100(a), (c) (life insurance policies and proceeds); id., §704.110(d) (proceeds from public retirement benefits); N.Y. C.P.L.R. §5205(b) (proceeds, for one year, from causes of action for taking exempt property).

34. See, e.g., N.Y. C.P.L.R. §5205(a), (c).

postpetition creditors. The question is whether the prepetition creditors are entitled to treat the proceeds as assets that they can pursue as well. Again, section 524 might seem to answer this question "no." But from the perspective of a fresh-start policy that resorts to nonbankruptcy law to define exempt property, it is not clear whether this answer is right— at least with respect to all kinds of exempt property.[35] Again, it may be analytically more useful to try to distinguish cases where the proceeds are another form of an *existing* asset from cases where they can be viewed as capturing the attributes of future assets protected by bankruptcy's fresh-start policy.

Consider, first, ordinary forms of exempt property, such as automobiles, books, or tools of the trade. States have defined particular assets such as these as exempt. The reason must be that the states wanted to protect the assets, not their cash-equivalent value. Those states never said that a debtor could shield cash, but only the defined kinds of property. When such an asset is sold, its proceeds are, as a matter of non-bankruptcy law, no longer exempt. Given that, once the debtor sells the asset, there is no reason, from a normative view of bankruptcy law, why these proceeds should be shielded from prepetition claimant, when non-bankruptcy law does not protect them.

To say this, however, is not necessarily to say that there are no practical reasons not to treat bankruptcy as the end of the road for the general claimants (without rights in particular assets). Administratively, a system that allowed prepetition claimants to pursue the proceeds of exempt property might replicate the grab race that existed outside of bankruptcy. To solve that by, for example, having a rule that the trustee could pursue the proceeds for pro rata division among the prepetition claimants would generate a problem of allocating the right to those proceeds between the prepetition and postpetition claimants. Requiring the trustee to be notified upon the sale of exempt property, for example, would probably give the trustee too much relative to the postpetition claimants and the debtor. A rule that permitted the trustee to participate in a grab race with postpetition creditors and the debtor might provide too little incentive to the trustee to do anything at all. For these reasons a rule shielding both exempt property and its proceeds from prepetition claimants may be justified, but the justification is one of administrative convenience, not of playing out bankruptcy's fresh-start policy.

35. For a case raising a related issue (in which each judge on the panel saw the case fundamentally differently), see *In re* Weiman, 22 Bankr. 49 (9th Cir. Bankr. App. 1982) (dealing with statute where liens could be obtained on homestead but not enforced until sale; question was whether trustee had such a lien for benefit of prepetition creditors).

Keeping in mind the distinct attributes of the kinds of assets protected by bankruptcy's fresh-start policy and those protected by nonbankruptcy exemption systems allows us to look at assets that seem to have attributes of both. Consider the case of retirement accounts. These, like Keogh Plans, generally are free from involuntary creditor attachment. But occasionally they are not, as is the case with Army retirement funds.[36] Although subject to garnishment, they are not payable in advance: the creditor must wait for the debtor to become entitled to these payments in the ordinary course of his life.[37] These funds are the product of past efforts and to that extent are considered an existing asset. Many forms of exemption law, moreover, treat them as exempt.

How should bankruptcy law, then, treat Army retirement funds? Because of creditor garnishment, these are funds that creditors can reach in priority to the debtor. Yet in certain respects such retirement funds share attributes in common with human capital where, but for bankruptcy law, a creditor's garnishment takes priority over a debtor's right to receive wages. Although nondischargeability will not cause substitution problems (as it would for wages) because the asset is already "earned" in that sense, the point of such assets is to serve as a *replacement* for wages in the future, and like human capital they are relatively nondiversifiable. For these reasons the policy that protects human capital as it manifests itself in wages may also reach retirement funds as they become payable to the debtor. Because of the close kinship this asset bears to property at the core of bankruptcy's fresh-start policy as it is currently framed, that fresh-start policy could be seen as overriding the fact that nonbankruptcy law does not treat the right to payment as exempt from garnishment. Indeed, even where retirement funds *are* exempt from garnishment, generally the proceeds after payment to the debtor are not. Here, too, because these proceeds reflect substantial attributes in common with wages, it would be an easy step to see them as protected by bankruptcy law's fresh-start policy, even though the proceeds of other forms of exempt property are not so protected.[38] In the case of ordinary

36. See *In re* Haynes, 679 F.2d 718 (7th Cir. 1982) (army retirement funds not property of the estate because they are "really" future wages in compensation for reduced services during retirement); *In re* Harter, 10 Bankr. 272 (Bankr. N.D. Ind. 1981) (same result, because their "qualities liken the payments to wages" and because the debtor can only receive the payments by living).

37. *In re* Harter, 10 Bankr. 272, 275 (Bankr. N.D. Ind. 1981).

38. In the case of human capital, when the debtor dies, so does the value. Retirement funds, however, sometimes are different. There may be a residuary beneficiary. If, as a matter of nonbankruptcy law, creditors could reach the retirement funds in priority to the residuary beneficiary, there is no reason stemming from bankruptcy's fresh-start policy

forms of exempt property, what is being protected is the asset itself for its own sake. Retirement accounts are protected, however, not for their own sake but rather for the sake of the future income stream they will generate.

Other Ways to Formulate Bankruptcy's Fresh-Start Policy and the Relationship of Chapter 13 to Chapter 7

To this point we have been playing out the consequences of viewing the fresh-start policy as embodied in bankruptcy law as one of protecting human capital and related future assets, while leaving to nonbankruptcy law the protection of other forms of wealth. The justification for this was that protecting human capital represented a nationwide problem amenable to a uniform rule, whereas other forms of wealth were perhaps best left to the states, so that they could tailor their categories of exempt property to their citizens' particular needs. But there is nothing absolute about this particular balance. If it were thought that certain forms of wealth other than human capital shared particular attributes with it— such as nondiversifiability or representing a form of savings for the future—they, too, might be considered amenable to a nationwide solution.

Nor does focusing the fresh-start policy on human capital necessarily mean that individuals should not be able to choose the mix of human and other capital that will constitute their fresh start. None of the three reasons I have offered for making discharge nonwaivable—impulsive behavior, incomplete heuristics, and the disregard of externalities—argues against allowing individuals to decide which of their assets should be protected by discharge, assuming that the amount available to creditors is held constant. For two reasons individuals are unlikely to make systematic errors of judgment in choosing whether to protect human capital or other forms of wealth: first, the measure of what must be handed over to creditors is in either case the market value of the debtor's existing tangible assets; second, human capital and durable goods both represent future consumption items. Although an individual may overestimate the degree to which he will be able to fund payments out of future income, the risk of error seems slight because the debtor's plan will be subject to judicial oversight and his creditors will retain the right

---

to exclude prepetition claimants of debtor from participating in that asset under such circumstances.

to seize tangible assets if the debtor's future income proves inadequate.

There is, moreover, a strong reason for allowing debtors to choose which forms of their wealth to protect. Only an individual can accurately measure the difference between the value he places on an asset and the market price.[39] Giving the individual the choice exploits his knowledge of his own subjective preferences. Bankruptcy law's increasing tendency to let the individual choose between protecting human capital and protecting other forms of wealth, therefore, seems sound.

The election that many debtors face between seeking protection under chapter 7 or chapter 13 may be seen as an example of this choice: whereas chapter 7 protects human capital at the expense of other assets, chapter 13 protects existing assets at the expense of some human capital.[40] Nothing in the nature of the trade-off between chapters 7 and 13 suggests, however, that the choice of which assets to protect should change the *extent* of the discharge. Chapter 13, however, does affect the extent of the discharge by permitting discharge without the limitations of section 727 and by treating as dischargeable (upon completion of payments under a chapter 13 plan) all categories of debt (other than alimony) considered nondischargeable under section 523. This change in the scope of discharge is puzzling in terms of the fresh-start policy.

Limits on the Right of Discharge Itself: Denying Access to Discharge in Order to Enforce Social Norms

Discharge is principally a device for freeing up a debtor's human capital; its grant or denial is generally of no concern when the subject is that of a debtor's exempt property, for that property remains exempt because of nonbankruptcy law, not the grant of a discharge in bankruptcy. We must ask when discharge should be granted or withheld in the context of human capital. Most explanations of bankruptcy law insist that discharge should be available only to the "honest but unfortunate" debtor. But if notions of impulsive behavior, incomplete heuristics, or externalities justify the right of an individual to free up his future income stream in the first place, why should an individual be denied discharge because of mistakes of whatever sort he made in the past? To what extent

---

39. Cf. Schwartz, "The Case for Specific Performance," 89 *Yale L.J.* 271, 275–78 (1979) (arguing that one justification for specific performance is the difficulty of placing a value on certain contractual agreements).

40. Compare §§524, 727 with §§1306, 1325(a)(4), (b)(1)(B).

should an individual's commission of certain acts deprive him of a fresh start, either in toto or with respect to a particular debt?

One commonly asserted reason for denying discharge to those who have engaged in certain undesirable activities is that denial will help deter such conduct. The activities listed in section 727 of the Bankruptcy Code—like those listed in analogous provisions of bankruptcy statutes for the past one hundred years or so—have one attribute in common: they all concern fraud or similar misbehavior against creditors.[41] Unlike prohibitions on the contractual waiver of discharge rights, the prohibitions on fraud and similar conduct may be viewed as designed to deter various activities regardless of whether they are products of impulsiveness, incomplete heuristics, or the disregard of externalities.

The question is therefore whether denying a debtor the right of discharge is an appropriate means of preventing fraudulent conduct. Section 727 does not deny discharge to debtors who commit arson or murder, although these acts are usually thought of as more egregious than fraud. And many criminal sanctions—such as short prison terms or probation—inflict a less severe financial penalty on the individual than does section 727. Moreover, denying debtors discharge is not the exclusive way to deter their misbehavior toward creditors. Fines, prison terms, and other criminal or quasi-criminal sanctions are alternatives sometimes used in conjunction with denial of discharge and that could be used in lieu of it. Thus, it is not necessarily the case that the appropriate legal response to defrauding creditors must be tied to discharge.

Nonetheless, bankruptcy discharge does seem like a natural starting place for lawmakers designing penalties for certain fraudulent activities

41. A debtor will be denied discharge if he (a) intentionally makes fraudulent transfers, §727(a)(2); (b) destroys without justification pertinent business records, §727(a)(3); (c) lies or makes bribes in connection with the bankruptcy case, §727(a)(4); (d) fails to explain satisfactorily any deficiency of assets, §727(a)(5); or (e) refuses to obey a lawful court order, §727(a)(6). In addition, such activities in conjunction with another bankruptcy case involving an insider will result in a similar penalty, §727(a)(7).

The justifications for subsections (a)(8) and (a)(9) of section 727 are distinct from the rest of the section. Those subsections provide, with several qualifications, for a six-year bar on the reuse of bankruptcy to discharge debts. To my mind, these provisions are quite different from the others in section 727(a) and contrary to the usual view—see Perry v. Commerce Loan Co., 383 U.S. 392, 399 (1966); Note, "Toward a Reform of the Six-Year Bar to Discharge in Bankruptcy," 97 *Harv. L. Rev.* 759, 759–61 (1984)—seem best explained on the ground that they *protect* debtors. Because of these provisions, an individual who has recently been through bankruptcy and has retained few assets may still be able to obtain credit because potential creditors know that their claims cannot be discharged for a six-year period. The impact of this protection, however, is watered down by the fact that neither chapter 11 nor chapter 13 bars the use of those chapters within six years of a chapter 7 case, nor does either chapter bar repetitive use of those chapters within a six-year period.

directed against creditors. The relation between the activities covered by section 727 and creditors' collection efforts may be so close as to justify presumptively denying discharge to a debtor who engages in such activities—in addition to imposing whatever other penalties he might deserve. Section 727 proscribes behavior directed at foiling creditors' collection efforts during the individual debtor's insolvency, behavior that is likely to occur in connection with a bankruptcy proceeding. Unlike murder, the occurrence of which is likely to be unconnected to the advent of a bankruptcy proceeding, such actions may best be deterred by a sanction that substantially eliminates their usefulness.[42]

Even if a socially disfavored activity is so closely linked with bankruptcy or creditor collection efforts that some restriction of the debtor's financial fresh start is justified, a complete denial of discharge is not necessarily an appropriate response. In determining the proper penalty, one must weigh the benefits of the fresh-start policy against the effectiveness of using denial of discharge as a lever to enforce behavioral norms.

Consider, in this light, section 727(a)(2), which provides for denial of discharge if

the debtor, with intent to hinder, delay, or defraud a creditor or an officer of the estate charged with custody of property under this title, has transferred, removed, destroyed, mutilated, or concealed, or has permitted to be transferred, removed, destroyed, mutilated, or concealed

(A) property of the debtor, within one year before the date of the filing of the petition; or (B) property of the estate, after the date of the filing of the petition.

With this provision in mind, consider whether a debtor should be denied discharge for converting his nonexempt assets to exempt ones on the eve of bankruptcy in order to maximize his exemptions in an anticipated bankruptcy proceeding.[43] Despite a legislative statement suggesting that the Bankruptcy Code does not reach acts of this kind,[44] courts frequently

42. A general theory of crime may similarly look at the effectiveness of punishment and focus on ways of keeping it from being discounted for the passage of time. See J. Wilson & R. Herrnstein, *Crime and Human Nature* (1985).

43. This can represent a form of opt-out behavior, see Eisenberg, supra note 16, at 996–98. This type of behavior would largely disappear in a regime in which exemptions were limited by dollar amount instead of by property type. A related form of opt-out behavior, known as "loading up," where an individual goes on a credit binge before bankruptcy, was made a prohibited activity, in the sense that certain of the resulting debts are nondischargeable, in 1984. See §523(a)(2)(C).

44. Both the House and Senate Reports state: "As under current law, the debtor will be permitted to convert nonexempt property into exempt property before filing a bankruptcy petition. The practice is not fraudulent as to creditors, and permits the debtor to make full use of the exemptions to which he is entitled under the law." S. Rep. No. 989,

treat such intentional conversions as falling under the ban of section 727 (a)(2).[45] The court in the principal case reaching that result commented: "It would constitute a perversion of the purposes of the Bankruptcy Code to permit a debtor earning $180,000 a year to convert every one of his major nonexempt assets into sheltered property on the eve of bankruptcy with actual intent to defraud his creditors and then emerge washed clean of future obligation by carefully concocted immersion in bankruptcy waters."[46] To analyze the desirability of the court's result, one must carefully balance a number of factors, not the least of which are the reasons for treating certain assets—and only certain assets—as exempt and the relationship between federal discharge policy and state exemption law.

Generally, exemption systems protect specific assets and not a sum of money. There presumably is some reason to prefer protection of particular assets: because the individual may underestimate the likelihood that his credit decisions will cause him to lose certain assets or because the assets are more valuable to the debtor than they are to his creditors. Goods acquired solely for the purpose of sheltering greater wealth through bankruptcy do not raise the same concerns. A person why buys $100,000 of exempt property on the eve of bankruptcy is, from a normative standpoint, in the same position as a person who hides $100,000 in cash in order to keep it from his creditors. Neither of the problems that asset-specific exemption law is designed to ameliorate is involved when the property is acquired solely to shelter wealth.[47]

This analysis, however, is incomplete. One cannot actually address the

---

95th Cong., 2d Sess. 76 (1978); H. Rep. No. 595, 95th Cong., 1st Sess. 361 (1977). The interpretive relevance of the statements is a matter of doubt because both were made before Congress reached the compromise allowing states to opt out of the federal exemption system. See Mickelson v. Anderson, 31 Bankr. 635, 637–38 (Bankr. D. Minn. 1982) (asserting that the legislative comment "lacks authority").

45. See, e.g., *In re* Reed, 700 F.2d 986, 991 (5th Cir. 1983); *In re* Collins, 19 Bankr. 874 (Bankr. M.D. Fla. 1982); *In re* Mehrer, 2 Bankr. 309 (Bankr. E.D. Wash. 1980); but see *In re* Blum, 41 Bankr. 816 (Bankr. S.D. Fla. 1984).

46. *In re* Reed, 700 F.2d, at 992. The court reached this result notwithstanding its conclusion that under Texas law the property was entitled to remain exempt.

47. If the function of exemptions is to protect a particular type of durable good on the ground that such assets are usually worth more to the debtor than to his creditors, then it indeed matters whether the debtor has acquired the asset on the eve of bankruptcy. Steven Harris has argued to the contrary, see Harris, "A Reply to Theodore Eisenberg's *Bankruptcy Law in Perspective*," 30 *UCLA L. Rev.* 327, 341–42 (1982), but his position is persuasive only with regard to state laws that offer exemption of either a specific durable good or the cash necessary to purchase that good. Most states do not follow that route: a creditor is not given a choice between protecting a specific asset or an equal amount of cash. Permitting eve-of-bankruptcy conversions may, however, amount to the same thing, as we examine in text.

issue posed by eve-of-bankruptcy conversions without recognizing that its two components—the propriety of the exemption and the desirability of denying discharge—are integrally related, notwithstanding that nominally the first is a nonbankruptcy issue and the second a bankruptcy issue.

In cases involving nonbankruptcy exemption systems the question of what is exempt property is controlled not by the Bankruptcy Code but by nonbankruptcy law. A state could decide to have an exemption system that allowed an individual to shelter a specific amount of money, say $100,000, and that decision would be respected in bankruptcy. A state that uses a system permitting eve-of-bankruptcy conversions, in the sense of exempting converted assets, may in effect be simply permitting an individual to shelter cash. To the extent that a state allows its residents to keep (as exempt) property acquired on the eve of bankruptcy, denial of discharge may be inappropriate. For although the question of denial of discharge goes principally to protecting human capital and hence is at the core of federal bankruptcy policy, the question of what "hinder[s], delay[s], or defraud[s] a creditor"[48] still gets its attributes from nonbankruptcy law.[49] It may therefore be difficult to conclude from section 727(a)(2) that a midnight conversion hinders, delays, or defrauds creditors of a debtor living in a state that would extend exempt status to the resulting property.[50] In a state that treats eleventh-hour conversions as forfeiting the exemption, however, the question of discharge under section 727(a)(2) would remain a question of federal law because the question of the debtor's *intent* to hinder, delay, or defraud is unaddressed by the state's position on exempt status. A judge in a bankruptcy proceeding would not be compelled to conclude, simply because the state court denied exemption, that the debtor intended the conversion to impede his creditors.

Assuming that intent to impede creditors can be demonstrated, how severe should the penalty be? Several considerations suggest that the penalty should be more severe than the mere recapture of assets.[51] Re-

---

48. §727(a)(2).

49. The question of what hinders, delays, or defrauds creditors is thus similar to the question of what is "property of the estate" under §541. Although that is a federal question, its attributes come from state law. See Chicago Board of Trade v. Johnson, 264 U.S. 1 (1924), discussed in Chapter 4.

50. This reasoning suggests that *In re* Reed, 700 F.2d 986 (5th Cir. 1983), and similar cases may have been wrongly decided. If the state permits the asset to remain exempt, it then seems to be part of state exemption policy. Under such circumstances denial of discharge on the ground of a fraudulent transfer appears to override that state policy.

51. The point that recapture is not a sufficient deterrent is, of course, a general one for remedies of all kinds involving fraud or other undesirable activities (such as antitrust

capture is, after all, a relatively mild penalty for fraud. Because fraud often escapes detection, recapture will almost surely be an insufficient deterrent. Faced only with the threat of recapture, many debtors would deem it worthwhile to engage in fraudulent activity in the hope that it might go undiscovered. Additional punishment may be called for in order to make misbehavior a riskier—and thus less desirable—alternative.[52] Denial of discharge serves this function. Admittedly, denying an errant debtor discharge may not always be appropriate; indeed, as a response to many types of behavior, it may be excessive. One must in each case weigh the benefits of the fresh-start policy against the harm deterred by the denial of discharge.

Similarly, questions of the nondischargeability of particular debts should be analyzed against what bankruptcy law is trying to do through its fresh-start policy.[53] Consider, for example, tort claims. Unlike the situation

---

violations, sanctioned by treble damages). The penalty for preferences, by contrast, is recapture alone. This scheme may be more appropriate when the activity in question is not per se undesirable. See Eisenberg, supra note 16, at 996–98; see also discussion in Chapter 6.

52. See, e.g., Clark "The Interdisciplinary Study of Legal Evolution," 90 *Yale L.J.* 1238, 1249–50 (1981) (arguing that the underdetection of misbehavior is a rationale for the doctrine of equitable subordination, which reaches beyond those activities actually shown to harm creditors). One should be careful not to blur the issue of denying discharge with the issue of leaving the states responsible for exemption law.

53. Other questions arise in considering nondischargeable debts under §523. "[W]illful and malicious injury . . . to another," §523(a)(6), for example, is a prohibited activity that denying discharge of the associated debt deters. The general difference between the categories of activities covered by section 523 and those dealt with in section 727 has to do with the extent of harm the activities engender. In the case of activities covered by section 727 the harm is generalized: it is not directed at any particular claimant. In the case of activities listed in section 523 the harm, in the first instance, seems more directed at discrete claimants.

This line, however, is not clear in practice. Consider *In re* McCloud, 7 Bankr. 819 (Bankr. M.D. Tenn. 1980). In that case the court treated the unauthorized sale of a secured creditor's collateral as an occasion to invoke section 523(a)(6), consequently treating the creditor's claim as nondischargeable. But the activity arguably harmed other creditors as well. Assume a debtor has a drill press worth $10,000 that secured Bank's $10,000 loan, other assets worth $20,000, and other claims of $40,000. Unless the drill press is converted, Bank would receive the full $10,000 in a bankruptcy proceeding while the other creditors would receive $20,000 for their $40,000 of claims, or fifty cents on the dollar. After a conversion and assuming proceeds cannot be traced, all creditors, including Bank, share equally in $20,000 to $30,000 of assets. (The actual amount depends on whether the debtor has dissipated the proceeds in a way that did not increase the value of his existing assets.) Bank is clearly hurt. If the assets remaining after the conversion are less than $25,000, the other creditors are harmed as well. Section 523 solves this allocation problem by treating Bank's claim as nondischargeable. This easy-to-apply rule may be an appropriate solution but is not justified on the ground that Bank was the only one harmed by

with consensual credit, overextensions due to torts may seem less deserving of discharge. Because of the social policy that calls for tortfeasors to internalize the costs of these torts, impulse and incomplete heuristics perhaps should not provide excuses from such internalization. For these reasons torts present a much less appealing case for discharge than do consensually created debts.

That is hardly the end of the matter, however. As a matter of legal rules, torts are dischargeable by corporations in the sense that the shareholders are protected by the doctrine of limited liability. Consequently, corporations will not necessarily internalize fully the costs of their torts. In a world where the owners of corporations can discharge torts, it would not seem appropriate to deny discharge of tort claims to individuals in bankruptcy. For with individuals there is the additional problem of what a failure to discharge would mean in terms of future productive effects. Thus one should be cautious—here as elsewhere in bankruptcy law— of making changes in a vacuum. To truly grasp bankruptcy policy, we must examine it in the context of the larger legal universe. It is precisely *that* feature of bankruptcy law that makes it continually challenging and exciting, even after one becomes sensitive to the lessons of collective action and discharge policies.

---

the conversion.

Some courts appear to have been influenced in their choice of a category under section 523 instead of section 727 out of a belief that the penalty of section 727 is harsher than the activity deserves. See *In re* McCloud, 7 Bankr. 819 (Bankr. M.D. Tenn. 1980).

Index to Bankruptcy Code Sections

General Index

Lightning Source UK Ltd.
Milton Keynes UK
UKHW04f1918160918
329016UK00001B/137/P